GLAMOUR, GLITZ, & GOSSIP
AT HISTORIC MAGNOLIA HOUSE

FROM THE SILVER SCREENS OF HOLLYWOOD
TO THE LIGHTS OF BROADWAY,
CELEBRITY SECRETS EXPOSED WITHIN THE WALLS OF
THIS OLD HOUSE

DARWIN PORTER & DANFORTH PRINCE

Built in stages between 1830 and 1870, Magnolia House
is a historic landmark on Staten Island, the least-visited Outer Borough of New York City.

Set within a 10-minute walk from the (free) Staten Island ferry that accesses Manhattan at intervals of every thirty minutes or less, it's the headquarters of the widely distributed independent press, BLOOD MOON PRODUCTIONS, a feisty wordsmith noted for celebrity biographies that have been reviewed in THE DAILY MAIL, the New York DAILY NEWS, show-biz news reports, and literary journals across the country.

Some visitors liken Magnolia House to a *grande dame* with a centuries-old knack for nourishing high-functioning eccentrics. Many of them have lived or been entertained here since New York's State Senator Howard Bayne, a transplanted Southerner, moved in with his wife, the daughter of the Surgeon General of the Confederate States of America, in the aftermath of that bloodiest of wars on North American soil, the War Between the American States.

Since then, many dozens of celebrities—some of them notorious—have whispered their secrets and rehearsed their ambitions within its walls. They've included movie vamps from the silent screen, MIDNIGHT COWBOYS, dancers from the dance, BUTTERFLIES IN HEAT, a heavyweight boxing champ, writers from every hue, faded film goddesses, playwrights who crafted blockbusters for both Marilyn (Monroe) and Elizabeth (Taylor), *ultra-avant-garde* diarists, every known variety of *prima donna* and *diva,* including some from the world of opera, and a world-class Olympic athlete.

They've also included Darwin Porter and Danforth Prince, who spent decades here renovating it and producing a stream of FROMMER TRAVEL GUIDES and award-winning celebrity biographies.

Thanks to the transformation of about a quarter of its floor space into a reasonably priced AirBnb *(for more on this click on **www.AirBnb.com/h/Magnolia-House**)* they've made an attempt, at least, to adapt it to the 21st Century's changing circumstances and values.

This book illuminates Magnolia House's contribution to the American Century, when dozens of individual movers and shakers—some of them sane and emotionally stable, others not—visited Magnolia House.

We'll explore what they did and what they revealed.

Blood Moon Productions is located within Magnolia House. What is Blood Moon Productions?

"Blood Moon, in case you don't know, is a small publishing house on Staten Island that cranks out Hollywood gossip books, about two or three a year, usually of five-, six-, or 700-page length, chocked with stories and pictures about people who used to consume the imaginations of the American public, back when we actually had a public imagination. That is, when people were really interested in each other, rather than in Apple 'devices.' In other words, back when we had vices, not devices."

— The Huffington Post

Biographies that Focus on the Ironies of Fame
www.BloodMoonProductions.com

Award-Winning Entertainment About
How America Interprets Its Celebrities

Who and What Are Some of the People and Things We're Gonna Talk About In This Book?

(See Illustrations that follow.)

Glamour, Glitz, and Gossip

at Historic Magnolia House

Volume Two of Blood Moon's Magnolia House Series
by Darwin Porter and Danforth Prince

Copyright 2019, Blood Moon Productions, Ltd.
All Rights Reserved
www.BloodMoonProductions.com
Manufactured in the United States of America

ISBN 978-1-936003-73-0

Conception, Covers, & Book Design by Danforth Prince
Distributed worldwide through Internet vendors that include Amazon.com

OTHER RECENT TITLES FROM BLOOD MOON PRODUCTIONS

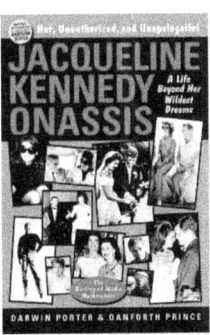

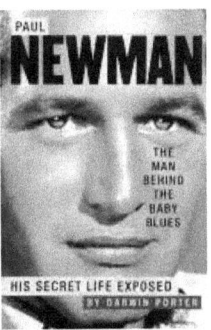
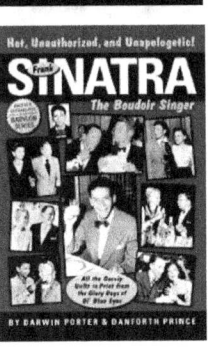

THIS BOOK IS DEDICATED

to peepers, prowlers, pederasts, poon stalkers, panty sniffers, prostitutes (male and female), potheads, and pimps—and also to those who made it big, only to discover that Tinseltown is, indeed, the Boulevard of Broken Dreams

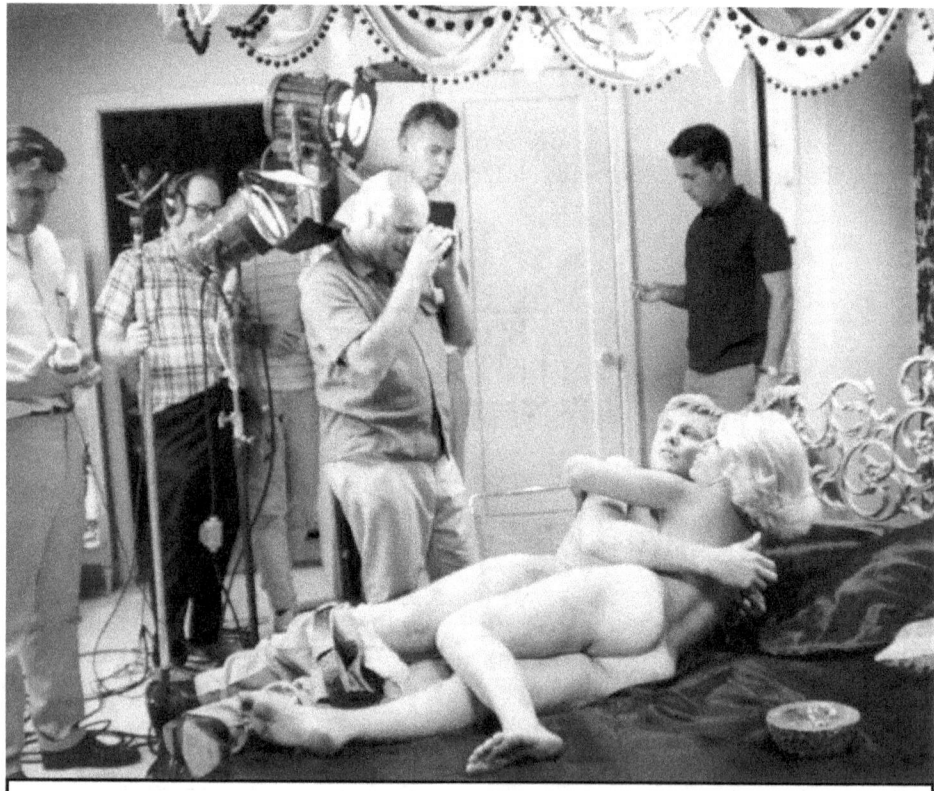

That's Show Biz!
(AKA "YA DO WHAT YA GOTTA DO TO MAKE A LIVING AS AN ENTERTAINER.")

Jon Voight, playing a prostitute, embraces **Sylvia Miles**, also playing a prostitute, under the glare of cameras, kleig lights, and the judgmental gaze of an armada of technicians—including director John Schlesinger— on the set of **Midnight Cowboy** (1969), the first X-rated movie to ever win an Oscar.

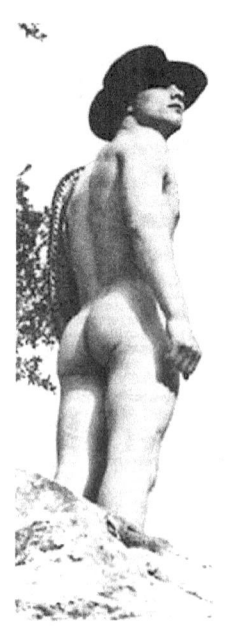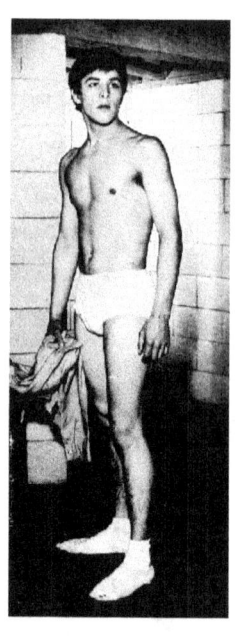

Previous Works by Darwin Porter
Produced In Collaboration with Blood Moon

Biographies

Burt Reynolds
Put the Pedal to the Metal

Kirk Douglas
More Is Never Enough

Playboy's Hugh Hefner
Empire of Skin

Carrie Fisher & Debbie Reynolds
Princess Leia & Unsinkable Tammy in Hell

Rock Hudson Erotic Fire

Lana Turner, Hearts & Diamonds Take All

Donald Trump, The Man Who Would Be King

James Dean, Tomorrow Never Comes

Bill and Hillary, So This Is That Thing Called Love

Peter O'Toole, Hellraiser, Sexual Outlaw, Irish Rebel

Love Triangle, Ronald Reagan, Jane Wyman, & Nancy Davis

Jacqueline Kennedy Onassis, A Life Beyond Her Wildest Dreams

Pink Triangle, The Feuds and Private Lives of Tennessee Williams, Gore Vidal, Truman Capote, and Famous Members of their Entourages.

Those Glamorous Gabors, Bombshells from Budapest

Inside Linda Lovelace's Deep Throat, Degradation, Porno Chic, and the Rise of Feminism

Elizabeth Taylor, There is Nothing Like a Dame

Marilyn at Rainbow's End, Sex, Lies, Murder, and the Great Cover-up

J. Edgar Hoover and Clyde Tolson
Investigating the Sexual Secrets of America's Most Famous Men and Women

Frank Sinatra, The Boudoir Singer. All the Gossip Unfit to Print

The Kennedys, All the Gossip Unfit to Print

Humphrey Bogart, The Making of a Legend (2010), and
The Secret Life of Humphrey Bogart (2003)

Howard Hughes, Hell's Angel

Steve McQueen, King of Cool, Tales of a Lurid Life

Paul Newman, The Man Behind the Baby Blues

Merv Griffin, A Life in the Closet

Brando Unzipped

Katharine the Great, Hepburn, Secrets of a Lifetime Revealed

Jacko, His Rise and Fall, The Social and Sexual History of Michael Jackson

Damn You, Scarlett O'Hara
The Private Lives of Vivien Leigh and Laurence Olivier

Celebrity & The Ironies of Fame

FILM CRITICISM
Blood Moon's 2005 Guide to the Glitter Awards
Blood Moon's 2006 Guide to Film
Blood Moon's 2007 Guide to Film, and
50 Years of Queer Cinema, 500 of the Best GLBTQ Films Ever Made

NON-FICTION
Hollywood Babylon, It's Back! and *Hollywood Babylon Strikes Again!*

NOVELS
Blood Moon,
Hollywood's Silent Closet,
Rhinestone Country,
Razzle Dazzle
Midnight in Savannah

OTHER PUBLICATIONS BY DARWIN PORTER NOT DIRECTLY ASSOCIATED WITH BLOOD MOON

NOVELS

The Delinquent Heart
The Taste of Steak Tartare
Butterflies in Heat
Marika (*a roman à clef based on the life of Marlene Dietrich*)
Venus (*a roman à clef based on the life of Anaïs Nin*)
Bitter Orange
Sister Rose

TRAVEL GUIDES

Many Editions and Many Variations of *The Frommer Guides*, *The American Express Guides*, *and/or* **TWA Guides**, *et alia* to:

Andalusia, Andorra, Anguilla, Aruba, Atlanta, Austria, the Azores, The Bahamas, Barbados, the Bavarian Alps, Berlin, Bermuda, Bonaire and Curaçao, Boston, the British Virgin Islands, Budapest, Bulgaria, California, the Canary Islands, the Caribbean and its "Ports of Call," the Cayman Islands, Ceuta, the Channel Islands (UK), Charleston (SC), Corsica, Costa del Sol (Spain), Denmark, Dominica, the Dominican Republic, Edinburgh, England, Estonia, Europe, "Europe by Rail," the Faroe Islands, Finland, Florence, France, Frankfurt, the French Riviera, Geneva, Georgia (USA), Germany, Gibraltar, Glasgow, Granada (Spain), Great Britain, Greenland, Grenada (West Indies), Haiti, Hungary, Iceland, Ireland, Isle of Man, Italy, Jamaica, Key West & the Florida Keys, Las Vegas, Liechtenstein, Lisbon, London, Los Angeles, Madrid, Maine, Malta, Martinique & Guadeloupe, Massachusetts, Melilla, Morocco, Munich, New England, New Orleans, North Carolina, Norway, Paris, Poland, Portugal, Provence, Puerto Rico, Romania, Rome, Salzburg, San Diego, San Francisco, San Marino, Sardinia, Savannah, Scandinavia, Scotland, Seville, the Shetland Islands, Sicily, St. Martin & Sint Maarten, St. Vincent & the Grenadines, South Carolina, Spain, St. Kitts & Nevis, Sweden, Switzerland, the Turks & Caicos, the U.S.A., the U.S. Virgin Islands, Venice, Vienna and the Danube, Wales, and Zurich.

BIOGRAPHIES

From Diaghilev to Balanchine, The Saga of Ballerina Tamara Geva

Lucille Lortel, The Queen of Off-Broadway

Greta Keller, Germany's Other Lili Marlene

Sophie Tucker, The Last of the Red Hot Mamas

Anne Bancroft, Where Have You Gone, Mrs. Robinson?
(co-authored with Stanley Mills Haggart)

Veronica Lake, The Peek-a-Boo Girl

Running Wild in Babylon, Confessions of a Hollywood Press Agent

HISTORIES

Thurlow Weed, Whig Kingpin

Chester A. Arthur, Gilded Age Coxcomb in the White House

Discover Old America, What's Left of It

CUISINE

Food For Love, Hussar Recipes from the Austro-Hungarian Empire,
with collaboration from the cabaret chanteuse, Greta Keller

AND COMING NEXT FROM BLOOD MOON
Judy Garland & Liza Minnelli
Too Many Damn Rainbows

CONTENTS

PROLOGUE
LITERARY OUTLAWS OF THE POSTWAR AMERICAN CENTURY   PAGE 1
   Tennessee Williams, Gore Vidal, and Truman Capote ("The Pink Triangle') were *Enfants Terribles* from the Golden Age of American Literature. Their biographer and archivist, Darwin Porter, describes their thwarted ambitions and ferocious infighting.

CHAPTER ONE   PAGE 5
   Portrait of the Artist (Tennessee Williams) as a young man. His feuds with the Über-divas of Hollywood: Tallulah Bankhead, Joan Crawford, and Miriam Hopkins.

CHAPTER TWO   PAGE 33
   Broadway Remembers Audrey Wood, the most Influential literary and showbiz agent in the history of the American Theater. How Darwin hosted a black tie mega-party in her honor at Magnolia House.

CHAPTER THREE   PAGE 63
   Joan Blondell: Portrait of a movie star and a Magnolia House "regular." How she seduced Errol Flynn and Clark Gable, transitioned from Pre-Code Hollywood to TV sitcoms, and how she married "double trouble' Dick Powell and Mike Todd.

CHAPTER FOUR   PAGE 95
   MURDER AHOY with Bette Davis: Did she kill her second husband?

CHAPTER FIVE   PAGE 101
   When prostitutes were named after flowers: How Truman Capote's avant-garde, all-black cast danced the Mambo all the way to Broadway.

CHAPTER SIX   PAGE 115
   Myra Breckinridge: Gender-fluid, pink, and crafted by Gore Vidal, he/she became America's foremost literary transsexual.

CHAPTER SEVEN   PAGE 129
   Crazy October: Tricking, treating, arguing, and on the road with Tallulah Bankhead, Joan Blondell, & Estelle Winwood.

CHAPTER EIGHT   PAGE 135
   Midnight Cowboy: The first X-rated movie to win an Oscar, and its link, through its author, to Magnolia House.

Chapter Nine — PAGE 151
When Divas Clash: The real-life fight for Robert Taylor, starring Tamara Geva (the ex-wife of George Balanchine) and how she was assaulted, backstage, by Barbara Stanwyck. PLUS the tormented sexual intervention of the billionaire film producer, Howard Hughes.

Chapter Ten — PAGE 175
Rudolf Nureyev: from Russia with Love (*Tales of Tatar Tail*). His links to Gore Vidal & America's literary *avant-garde*.

Chapter Eleven — PAGE 181
More about Rudolf Nureyev: Seducing his way through the Kennedy clan.

Chapter Twelve — PAGE 191
Nureyev's homage to Rudolph Valentino. How an insanely popular icon from the 1970s reinterpreted the doomed life of a legend from the 1920s.

Chapter Thirteen — PAGE 203
How the Opera Diva, Eleanor Steber generated headlines at a "black tie, black towel gala" at a gay bathhouse in Manhattan, and how she dished the music world's juiciest dirt, including how Adolf Hitler molested boys in Bayreuth.

Chapter Fourteen — PAGE 217
Greta Keller: Hitler's favorite cabaret singer (Europe's "other" Lili Marlene), and her long-term residency at Magnolia House.

Chapter Fifteen — PAGE 233
Edward Albee at Magnolia House: *Who's Afraid of Virginia Wolff?*.

Chapter Sixteen — PAGE 239
Grace Kelly: Beauty, good manners, lucky breaks, & the triumph of myth over reality.

Chapter Seventeen — PAGE 267
Hedy Lamarr: The bizarre story of the political loyalties and censorship problems whirling around the most beautiful woman in the world.

Chapter Eighteen — PAGE 279
Jack Dempsey: The world's heavyweight boxing champ, his widely publicized romp with Mae West, and his links to Magnolia House.

Chapter Nineteen — PAGE 289
Bombshells from Budapest: The Gabors, their formidable mother, Jolie, and her links to Magnolia House

Postscript From the Edge: Boomer Times & Media Buzz — PAGE 299

Scribes & Messengers (Authors' Bios) — PAGE 321

Magnolia House is a proud, architecturally protected landmark within the St. George, Staten Island, Historic District in NYC.

For more information about reasonably priced "celebrity centric" overnight stays at a "grande dame" with astonishing cultural antecedents, click on

www.MagnoliaHouseSaintGeorge.com   or AirBnB.com/h/Magnolia-House

Prologue

ENFANTS TERRIBLES
OF THE GOLDEN AGE OF
POSTWAR AMERICAN LITERATURE:
TENNESSEE WILLIAMS, GORE VIDAL,
& TRUMAN CAPOTE,

& THEIR AWARD-WINNING CONTEMPORARY,
ARCHIVIST & HISTORIAN

DARWIN PORTER

"**The Unholy Trio**," (left to right) **Gore Vidal, Truman Capote**, and **Tennessee Williams**, came together for the first time in the late 1940s.

Everything was peaceful in the beginning, but their relationships, especially between Vidal and Capote, devolved into a series of bitchfests, lawsuits, and libelous exposés. Each of them became adept at stealing each other's boyfriends.

In 2014, the convoluted dynamics of their ferocious rivalries were explored and explained by another *enfant terrible* of the postwar American literary scene, Darwin Porter, in his award-winning triple biography, *Pink Triangle*.

In the aftermath of World War II, during the latter half of "The American Century," when literacy was higher and where more people discussed contemporary books and theater than they do today, three men, each a homosexual, rose from obscurity to positions of spectacular literary fame. Each of them was a playwright and novelist: Tennessee Williams, Gore Vidal, and Truman Capote, subject of a book written by Darwin Porter and published by Blood Moon Productions in 2014 called Pink Triangle.

Collectively, they changed America's tastes in entertainment, expanded the boundaries of censorship, and redefined "The Golden Age of Postwar American Literature."

They paid a high price for their success. Their ferociously competitive personalities and private lives—frequently referenced in the tabloids, in literary journals, and on TV—eventually became more widely reviewed than their writings.

There were many witnesses to the sometimes bitchy dynamics of this infamous trio. Their habit of pulling other famous people into their slugfests invariably drew explosive media coverage and rivers of gossip among insiders on Broadway, in Hollywood, and among the jaded cognoscenti worldwide.

Darwin Porter, the senior co-author of this anthology, began recording its information when—as the youthful Bureau Chief for The Miami Herald in Tennessee Williams' home town of Key West—he began asking questions, taking notes, and dreaming of the

Frenemies: **Tennessee Williams** on the beach in Key West with **Gore Vidal** in the mid-1950s.

Young Truman: Brilliant, precocious, and aggressively searching for a *persona*, a presentation, and a gig.

day when his overview of the "Lavender Literati" could become public.

With the publication of Pink Triangle, Blood Moon made history's first attempt to compile an overview of this brilliant trio into a coherent whole. The Triangle it illuminates was Pink, its references are literate and sexy, its gossip is captivating, and its meat is raw, juicy, and bloody.

Every time a member of this trio descended on New York, Darwin entertained them (usually separately, since their ongoing competitions and feuds meant gathering them into the same room together something of a trial) over dinner at Magnolia House. Each had gossipy tales to relay, and descriptions of recent adventures.

Some of the chapters that follow are excerpts from the larger context of PINK TRIANGLE, excerpted to make celebrity-watching easier, shorter, and more Magnolia-scented.

The photo above shows a slightly drunken, "off" moment when the *literati* (or wannabe *literati*) of Key West gathered for food, drink, and gossip about whichever member might have been missing from the midst of their clique.

A 20-year-old **Darwin Porter** had recently been appointed Bureau Chief of *The Miami Herald* in Key West. One of his first assignments was to cover a gathering to celebrate the publication of the novel *All Fall Down*, written by **James Leo Herlihy**, seated with his eyes closed in the center.

Pictured left to right are shirtless **Frankie Merlo** (Tennessee's lover), **Darwin, Dick Duane, Danny Stirrup, "Billy," Tennessee, Bill Johnson** (with glasses), and **"Raymond."**

This assignment was one of the first of dozens for Darwin, where he'd interview famous people during their visits to Key West. They ranged from John F. Kennedy to Harry S Truman, from Marlon Brando to Cary Grant shooting *Operation Petticoat* (1959).

Enfants Terribles of the Golden Age of Postwar American Literature

DARWIN PORTER
A Portrait of the Artist and Archivist as a Young Man

His witness to many of the events brought out in this book made everything possible.

Photo by Stanley Haggart.

Chapter One

FROM MAGNOLIA HOUSE, DARWIN PORTER REVIEWED

TENNESSEE WILLIAMS'

FEUDS, FURIES, & FIGHTS WITH

THE ÜBER-DIVAS

TALLULAH BANKHEAD, JOAN CRAWFORD, &
MIRIAM HOPKINS

GOD HAS A TALENT FOR CREATING EXCEPTIONAL WOMEN.

They included this unholy trio (from left to right): **Tallulah Bankhead, Joan Crawford,** and **Miriam Hopkins**. Of course, there are those who might say that God had nothing to do with the birthing of this dynamic trio whose formidable presence came onto the stage (in Tallulah's case) and onto the screen (like Crawford and Hopkins) with hurricane force winds.

Darwin Porter met America's most successful and best-known playwright, Tennessee Williams, and his lover, Frank Merlo, during his early days in Key West when they'd been neighbors, and when Darwin had interviewed him and his celebrity associates for *The Miami Herald*.

Darwin later became friends with Williams' literary agent, Audrey Wood, thanks to their introduction through the temperamental theatrical producer, "The Queen of Off-Broadway," Lucille Lortel.

In 2014, Darwin emerged as one of the country's authorities on Tennessee's life and turbulent career, thanks to the publication of his well-reviewed triple biography of the playwright's private life and principle rivals. Winner of several literary awards, it was entitled *Pink Triangle: The Feuds and Private Lives of Tennessee Williams, Gore Vidal, Truman Capote, and Famous Members of their Entourages.*

The excerpts laid out in this chapter and others derive specifically from dialogues at Magnolia House with Tennessee himself, his literary agent, Audrey Wood, and dozens of his friends and frenemies.

Tennessee Williams, attacked for his "incurable sense of decadence," became as notorious as his plays.

In 2014, from **Darwin Porter**'s base at Magnolia House, the playwright's tumultuous private life was explored as never before in **Pink Triangle**, a portrait that's as poignant and flamboyant as any character Tennessee ever created, including that of Blanche DuBois.

***

"He's got a very odd name. Calls himself Tennessee Williams. He's written some one-act plays that are very different from what's out there."

That was Molly Day Thacher speaking to her husband, the actor and director, Elia Kazan. [*She would later urge him to direct the stage version of Tennessee's* A Streetcar Named Desire *(1947).]*

Thacher was a kind of literary scout, a reader riffling through countless plays, hoping to find properties suitable for the Group Theater in Manhattan. Through producer Harold Clurman, she managed to get Tennessee a special prize of $100 for some of his one-act plays collectively entitled *American Blues*.

She sent a check for the prize money and a note of encouragement to his address in California. At the time, he was working sixty hours a week at Clark's Bootery in Culver City as a clerk and salesman. It paid only $12.50 a week.

Thacher even got the emerging playwright a literary agent, Audrey Wood, who would become "his mother, his older sister, and his guiding light," throughout his heyday on Broadway. Along with her husband, William Liebling, Audrey ran the Liebling-Wood Agency at 30 Rockefeller Center.

Deeply unhappy with the frivolous writing assignments he'd gleaned from Hollywood, Tennessee had wanted to try his chances in New York. Transportation was a problem until Wood advanced him the price of a Greyhound bus ticket as an advance on a piece of his short fiction, "The Field of Blue Children," which she eventually sold to *Story Magazine.*

Tennessee arrived in Manhattan at the Port Authority Bus Terminal. Unshaven and in rumpled clothes, he made his way to the RCA Building

Tennessee Williams became the most famous, richest, and most talked-about living playwright in the world.

Unattributed, undated photo of literary agent **Audrey Wood** with two of her most succcessful (and frequently feuding) clients, **Tennessee Williams and Carson McCullers.**

at Rockefeller Center.

There, he encountered Liebling, who—as a casting director—was auditioning thirty hopeful chorus girls, each showing off her legs. As Tennessee remembered them, they were "chattering like birds high on locoweed."

Then he was introduced to Audrey Wood, "a tiny little thing, with very bright eyes. She was witty, bouncing around the room with a certain exuberance. She had hair so bright red it could only have come from a bottle. In all, she reminds me of a porcelain china doll."

"I will always remember the day Tennessee arrived on my doorstep," Audrey told Darwin one Sunday afternoon. She seemed delighted to share old memories, the good and the painful.

"He spoke with a soft Southern accent, and he was so young. Extremely gifted. Broke and battered. I tried to get him a job, first, selling shoes at Macy's, but that didn't work out. His primary need was for survival."

For shelter, he found lodgings in an apartment hotel way up on West 108th Street. It charged $4.50 a week for mostly out-of-work actors and various artists who arrived daily at the Greyhound Bus Station.

Since he had less than ten dollars in his pocket, Tennessee was rescued when Wood persuaded actor Hume Cronyn into taking an option of $50 a month on nine one-act plays by Tennessee.

In a touch of irony, Cronyn would later marry actress Jessica Tandy, who would eventually star on Broadway as Blanche DuBois in *A Streetcar Named Desire*.

There was almost no off-Broadway in those days, and few, if any, producers wanted to invest time and money on one-act plays by this unknown Southern writer. Some of these producers considered the plays "the work of a degenerate."

Eventually, Cronyn's option expired and Tennessee's money dwindled. He returned to his family's home in a suburb of St. Louis, where he occupied a bed in the attic. There, he began to work on a long play entitled *Something Wild in the Country*.

"I am writing furiously with seven wild-cats under my skin," he claimed in a memoir.

The play focused on the social and sexual decadence of a small

Audrey Wood with her husband and business partner, **William Liebling**, poring over a contract she'd arranged for one of her major-league literary clients. In the words of a fan, "Audrey doesn't just represent a playwright...she advocates."

Southern town. A drifter, Val Xavier, arrives in a snakeskin jacket. Here, he finds employment in the shop of the store's dying owner and his sexually frustrated wife, Myra. In addition, Xavier gets involved with a local seer and a religious fanatic.

"On the day of my worst depression," Tennessee recalled, news arrived from Audrey. The Dramatists Guild had awarded him a grant of $1,000 from the Rockefeller Foundation. More good news was on the way about his long play, which he'd retitled *Battle of Angels*. The Theater Guild had taken an option on it. It stipulated that they'd pay him $100 a month for as long as the contract was in effect.

He was aboard the next Greyhound bus pulling out of St. Louis, arriving in New York in January of 1940 with high hopes.

This time, he lodged on the tenth floor of a dingy and cramped room at the local branch of the YMCA on West 63rd Street. During the day, he worked on *Battle of Angels* on his portable typewriter.

At night, he cruised the Times Square area in search of sailors and G.I.'s. As his brother, Dakin Williams, in Key West told Darwin, "Tennessee admitted to me that he cruised Times Square at night, often for hours at a time. No love was involved, only the thrill of pursuit and temporary pleasures with the momentary object of his desires, meaning those young men who agreed to come back with him to the Y, often because they had been unlucky finding a girl for the night."

Tennessee himself admitted in print to this "deviant satyriasis which was a round-the-calendar thing, as opposed to animals which have seasons for it."

In spite of his support from Audrey, Tennessee felt New York was a lonely place, and he wanted to be back in the Taos desert or in a cottage overlooking the Pacific. As he recorded in his journal: "Most people in New York are involved in their own lives. I need somebody to envelop me, embrace me, pull me by sheer force out of this neurotic shell of fear I've built around myself."

Finding New York too distracting, he left on a Greyhound for Boston, where he took a boat to Provincetown. Once there, he settled in to rewrite and polish *Battle of Angels,* hoping for a Broadway opening in the late autumn of 1940.

He wrote his mother, Edwina Dakin Williams, that "Miriam Hopkins, Tallula *(sic)* Bankhead, and even Katharine Cornell were reading *Battle of Angels*." He expressed his belief that Bankhead "would be damned good as Myra, not a little short on tenderness but imbued with plenty of richness and drama."

After writing that, he received word from Audrey that another internationally famous actress was also intrigued by the role of Myra.

Tennessee Meets "The Gorgeous Hussy," aka "Mildred Pierce," aka
JOAN CRAWFORD

In New York, Joan Crawford heard that a young playwright had written a strong role for a woman of a certain age in a play called *Battle of Angels*. Crawford knew that both Miriam Hopkins and Tallulah Bankhead, two failed candidates (like herself) for the role of Scarlett O'Hara, were also considering making bids for the female lead.

Crawford contacted Audrey, who then arranged for the playwright to return from Provincetown to meet the actress at "21" for lunch the following week.

Slightly nervous and feeling inadequate, Tennessee arrived at the chic restaurant wearing a black suit borrowed from a Baptist preacher from Kansas City who stayed at the YMCA to cruise young men.

He wanted to show Crawford great respect, but he'd read F. Scott Fitzgerald's description of her, and, based on that, he seriously doubted if she could play Myra.

Fitzgerald had written of Crawford's "monolithic fierceness: She can't change her emotions in the middle of a scene without going through a sort of Jekyll and Hyde contortion of the face. Also, you can never give her such a stage direction as 'telling a lie,' because if you did, she would practically give a representation of Benedict Arnold selling West Point to the British."

Joan Crawford, the ultimate movie star and "dame." There was no end to morbid gossip about what she did to get ahead.

Before meeting Crawford, Tennessee had seen virtually every movie she'd ever made, finding her for the most part tough, gutsy, and fiercely competitive on screen. He suspected she was like that in real life, too.

In later years, he claimed, "I'm glad I met Miss Crawford before her adopted daughter turned her image into a chiaroscuro of camp."

[He was referring, of course, to that "lynch biography," *Mommie Dearest*, penned by her ferociously disenchanted adopted daughter, Christina Crawford.]

"I liked Joan Crawford," he later

said, "and feared we shared certain things in common—notably a shady background and a tendency to sleep with one man too many. She had worked her way to the top, and I was on my way there, too. She was a rival of such stars as Garbo and Norma Shearer. All of these stars were fading at the box office, and Joan wanted to test her talent on the Broadway stage. She thought my play might do it for her."

"At 21, Joan knew that her days as a big MGM star were numbered," he later claimed. "Beneath the perfect grooming, the expensive clothing, and the glamourous façade lurked a woman who lived in fear. I mean, she'd been born in 1904, or so I'd heard, and it was already 1940. New crops of the young and beautiful were arriving in Hollywood to fuck her long-time beau, Clark Gable."

"Joan had no trouble with my homosexuality," he said. "In Hollywood, she was known as 'Cranberry' to the gay set, including the likes of William Haines and director Edmund Goulding."

"Our luncheon went well until we actually started to talk about her starring in Battle of Angels," he said. "She wanted me to rewrite the play, turning the main character of Val Xavier into a femme fatale in a snakeskin jacket."

"I can see myself arriving in this nothing town and exciting the local men to mayhem and violence," Crawford said. "My death at the end can come from a posse of jealous women who can't stand the competition of a real woman."

He was prepared to make all sorts of changes to the text of his play, but none this drastic. He had to tell her he couldn't do it.

"There is a pivotal scene where a painting of Val as Jesus Christ is displayed," he told her.

"Oh, hell, boy, get me rewrite," she demanded. By this time in the course of their luncheon, she was tanked up on vodka. "That's easy to change. Fuck Christ. Paint me as the embodiment of Mary Magdalene, which would be more interesting than Christ. He's done to death."

For years after their ill-fated sojourn at "21," he regretted that he could not have revised his play into a suitable vehicle for Crawford because he admired her, fully aware that she was not a great actress. "On screen, Joan personified both the dreams and disappointments of millions of American women."

In spite of her hopes, Crawford never got a chance to play a Tennessee Williams character. She felt she would have been ideal cast as Alexandra del Lago in *Sweet Bird of Youth*.

Crawford said that the closest she came to a Williams character was in her role of Eva Phillips in *Queen Bee* (1955), in which she was cast as an imperious, domineering diva presiding over a dysfunctional family in a Georgia mansion. She told the press, "*Queen Bee* owes so much to Tennessee Williams that we should pay him royalties. I felt like Carte Blanche DuBois."

TALLULAH IS OUTRAGED:
"Me, A Southern Lady, Appearing in Such Filth?"

Tennessee heard that Tallulah was starring in a play in the town of Dennis on Cape Cod. Since he'd written *Battle of Angels* specifically for her to play Myra, the female lead, he sent her his first draft of the play. After two weeks, when he hadn't received any word from her, he decided to bicycle to Dennis, a distance of forty miles from Provincetown.

"*Battle of Angels* was a strong drama, far ahead of its time," Audrey said. "There were explicit sexual scenes and outspoken dialogue. The heroine indulged in extremely free sexual relationships. It was heady stuff for 1940."

There as part of a summer tour, Tallulah was starring in Arthur W. Pinero's *The Second Mrs. Tanqueray*, which had had its premiere in London in 1893. She had been cast as Paula Tanqueray, a woman who'd been the mistress of several men. "Type casting, dah-ling," she had told the press.

Backstage, Tennessee was introduced to Colin Keith-Johnson, a distinguished British actor cast as her long-suffering husband. He was handsome, tall, and blonde, with the physique of an athlete. Only later, Tennessee learned that the married actor was also playing Tallulah's husband off the stage as well as on it.

Tallulah herself was emerging from her own failed marriage to actor John Emery, who was unfairly called "a John Barrymore clone" by harsh critics.

At this point in his young life, Tennessee was not used to visiting actresses in their dressing rooms, especially an actress as uninhibited as Tallulah. He'd later see the vaginas of such stars as Vivien Leigh and Elizabeth Taylor, but at this point, he blushed when he discovered Tallulah sitting nude in front of her dressing room mirror, making emergency repairs to her face. "As you can plainly see, *dah-ling*," she said to him, "my breasts, contrary to rumor, are not altogether fallen. Come in."

"It's an honor to meet the great Tallulah Bankhead," he said. "I'm Tennessee Williams."

"I understand you were born in Mississippi," she said. "As you know, I'm from Alabama. Our Southern culture probably forms a bond between us."

"I hope so," he said. "I wrote the role of Myra hoping you could play her on stage. You'd be devastating in the part."

"You do write with a certain sensitivity," she said. "Perhaps we'll work together some day in one of your future plays. But I consider *Battle of Angels* degenerate filth. You must remember this: I am a lady, although not as chaste as Helen Hayes. There is no escaping the fact, young man, that you have written a dirty play."

He tried to defend himself in front of such a formidable presence. "I had hoped that you'd see my play as a mixture of super religiosity and hysterical sensuality spinning around the central character of the drifter, Val Xavier. My play is dedicated to D.H. Lawrence, who inspired some of the themes, mixing Freudian motifs with Christian symbolism and Dionysian myth."

Tallulah Bankhead in her greatest film role, in Alfred Hitchcock's *Lifeboat* (1944).

"Oh, please, dah-ling, all that symbolism is hard to take before I've had my first bourbon of the afternoon," she said. "If you want to write plays, you must learn that on stage, religion and sex do not mix."

"But as Sadie Thompson in W. Somerset Maugham's *Rain*," he said. "you've already played a prostitute deported to the South Seas, a working girl who's degraded and then punished by a zealous reverend mired in his own lasciviousness."

"Oh, *dah-ling*, it's vulgar to speak of one's past indiscretions," she said.

There was a knock on her door, a voice announcing himself as Leonard Bernstein.

"Just a minute, dah-ling," she called out. Then she whispered to Tennessee, "I will not star in your play. I read yesterday that Miriam Hopkins is considering it. We both lost out on the role of Scarlett O'Hara. Maybe she'll make a comeback as your Myra."

"In the meantime, I don't want you to think your bike ride down here was a total waste. I want you to meet this musician, Mr. Bernstein. I had him last night. Perhaps you'll get lucky tonight." She turned toward the door, "Come in, Leonard."

Tallulah as cover girl (March 1939) of *Life* magazine after her wildly successful sojourn in London as "the Toast of the West End"

It was Tallulah herself who brought the flamboyant soon-to-be musical giant of the 20th century together with the flamboyant playwright who would both shock, delight, and dazzle audiences in the 1940s and 50s.

WHERE ANGELS BATTLED, BOSTON WAS ENRAGED

At long last, and after many a struggle, *Battle of Angels* was set to open in Boston on December 30, 1940 at the Wilbur Theatre, with hopes of taking it to Broadway after a two-week run.

Designated as its director, Margaret Webster, who knew nothing about life in a Southern town, was an unusual choice. "I'd been to Washington, but never crossed into Virginia and points south," she said.

The New York-born actress, producer, and director held a dual citizenship. She was the daughter of two famous actors, Ben Webster and Dame May Whitty.

When Tennessee met Webster, she was involved in a longtime romantic relationship with Eva Le Gallienne, one of the most celebrated actresses of the American theater.

Webster later recalled meeting the playwright: "He was a short, sturdy, young man with crew-cut hair, pebble-thick glasses, and an even thicker Southern accent, dressed in shabby corduroy jacket and muddy riding boots."

Webster introduced him to Miriam Hopkins, who had been assigned to star in the play's leading role of Myra, the character's name later changed to Lady Torrance.

After having great success as a film star in the 1930s, Savannah-born Hopkins had scored a number of triumphs at Paramount, especially during the pre-Code era. Her other successes had included three films with Ernst Lubitsch and *The Old Maid* (1939) with her arch-enemy, Bette Davis.

Based on the outfit he was wearing, Hopkins mistakenly assumed that Tennessee was fresh from riding horseback. He had to assure her, "I will never be Tom Mix. I can't ride a horse."

Although known as a difficult actress to work with, she was imbued with Southern charm and graciousness, and even invited him to a champagne-infused supper later that evening. He knew she was "between husbands," having divorced the famous director Anatole Litvak in 1939.

After having been teamed with Davis once again in *Old Acquaintance* (1943), Hopkins seemed to have bowed out of films. "I didn't desert them," she told Tennessee. "No offers were coming in, and that's why I've turned to the stage."

Arriving at her hotel suite in Boston, he feared that she might be intent on seduction. She told him that her favorite line in his play was when Val Xavier is told that all the women in this southern town were suffering from "sexual malnutrition."

"That line could describe my current state of affairs, or I should say 'lack of affairs,'" Hopkins said flirtatiously.

She amused him with stories of Hollywood in the 1930s. "When I can't sleep, I don't count sheep," she said. "I count lovers. And by the time I reach thirty-eight or thirty-nine, I'm asleep. I usually start with actors—Fredric March, Robert Montgomery, Bing Crosby, Maurice Chevalier (he couldn't get it up), Gary Cooper, Franchot Tone, John Gilbert; or else directors—King Vidor or Ernst Lubitsch."

She expressed how embarrassing it had been for her in Boston: "This year, The Harvard Lampoon picked me as 'the least desirable companion on a desert island.'"

Hopkins was no dumb blonde Hollywood actress. She was sharp and insightful, shocking Tennessee when she surmised that "You are actually Myra. And the character you write about, Val Xavier, is the kind of man who makes you swoon, makes you feel helpless, erotic, in love."

"You've nailed me," he admitted to her.

After champagne was consumed, Hopkins finally got around to revealing the purpose of their late supper. She wanted her part greatly enlarged at the expense of the other performers, notably actress Doris Dudley. She also lobbied for a rewrite. "At the end of the play, when I'm shot, I want the character of Val Xavier to carry me up the stairs. That way, I will remain the center of attention on stage, even though dead."

He would later assert that there was a glittering, hot-tempered ferocity to her that would make her ideal in the role. "She has a great Southern pride, typical of her native Georgia, and a feeling of superiority over others. She is one high-spirited blonde with the subtlety of a wrestler in a to-the-death match."

She did ask him a question which he never answered: "How can a play or a motion picture reflect real life when it is created by people who lead artificial lives?"

Even before he left her suite, he knew he was going to reject all of her ideas for script changes. The problem involved summoning enough courage to tell her the next day.

When he was eventually forced to deliver the bad news to her, she attacked him on a sexual level. "I bet you're a premature ejaculator, a real fast starter and a lousy finisher."

"At lease she didn't call me a fag-

Miriam Hopkins in *The Old Maid* (1939), a chronicle of love, desperation, and hate in the mid-19th Century.

In it, she explosively co-starred with her arch-enemy, Bette Davis.

got," he later said. "But in front of cast and crew, Miriam made me feel like two cents—and two inches."

Hopkins and Tennessee did not nurture a grudge and by the time the play opened, they were defending each other artistically. He said, "Miriam could have been an Amanda to rival even Laurette Taylor in The Glass Menagerie. What I liked about her was her love of literature and her ability to recite by heart the poems of Lord Byron, Rossetti, and William Cullen Bryant's 'Thanatopsis.'"

Opening night was disastrous. Many in the audience of tuxedos and expensive gowns thought they were going to see a play about angels. As part of the scenery, an artist had created a backdrop depicting Val Xavier as Jesus Christ. There was a rumbling across the audience and cries of "blasphemy."

Before the play ended, half of the audience had already walked out. Those who remained for the final curtain were nearly asphyxiated. The script called for a building to catch on fire. Smoke pots had been placed about and lit, but too many were added. Both the cast and the audience went into coughing fits.

The next morning, critics were harsh. The New York critic for *Variety* (who was in Boston for the event), defined *Battle of Angels* as "sordid and amateurish." Tennessee said that the Boston audience "received my play like the outbreak of the Bubonic plague."

The Boston City Council was deluged with phone calls, mostly from people who had not seen the play. There were protests that *Battle of Angels* should be forcibly closed.

Members of Boston's City Council met with Webster and Tennessee, demanding the removal of some of the scenes and lines in the play as a condition for letting its short run continue.

In anger, Hopkins called her own press conference, denouncing the members of Boston's City Council. "I suggest that these blue-nosed city fathers be flung into the Boston Harbor like the tea at the historic Boston Tea Party."

At the play's run, the Theater Guild in New York notified Tennessee that it was dropping its option on *Battle of Angels*. "It cannot be brought to Broadway," he was told. "It is not dramatically successful."

He entered into a months-long depression, and for a time was almost suicidal. "But," as he later recalled, "I did not self-destruct easily." He predicted that he would live to see Battle of Angels open on Broadway.

"Battle of Angels was a great disaster, but it didn't shake my faith in this young Southerner," Audrey said. "He had a touch of greatness about him. My fear was that he might self-destruct before achieving it."

In the years to come, he would brush the dust off *Battle of Angels* and continue to rewrite it, hoping for a "kind of perfection" he never obtained, at least not critically.

BRANDO SAYS NO
But Orpheus Descends on Broadway Anyway

In 1957, Tennessee finally presented *Battle of Angels* on Broadway in the form of a rewritten adaptation, *Orpheus Descending*. He had reworked the play, reshaping the plot, characters, and dialogue.

The play still dealt with passion and repression and was replete with lush, poetic dialogue and imagery. It was a modern retelling of the ancient Greek legend of Orpheus, searching the Underworld in an attempt to resuscitate his lover, Euridice.

In Manhattan, Tennessee went to the apartment of Marlon Brando, urging him to accept the role of Val Xavier on the stage, since the male role had not only been enlarged, but vastly improved. He assured the actor that *Orpheus Descending* would bring him even greater acclaim than his role of Stanley Kowalski in *A Streetcar Named Desire* (1947).

"I like some of the lines," Brando said, "particularly when Val classifies people into three types—'the buyers, the bought, and those who don't belong to no place at all.'"

"But this boy Val never takes a stand," Brando continued. "I don't really know what he's for or against. Well, you can't act in a vacuum."

Eventually, Robert Loggia was assigned the role, but after Loggia was dismissed during the play's previews in Philadelphia, it was taken over by Cliff Robertson.

Tennessee later claimed that he thought Robertson was "too clean cut and American to capture the undeniable animal erotic energy and appeal of Val. Brando could have pulled it off."

Maureen Stapleton, whom Tennessee often described as "my favorite actress," starred in its Broadway version as Lady, although in the play's eventual reworking into a movie, [entitled *The Fugitive Kind*], she'd be reduced to playing the very minor role of Vee Talbot, the wife of the local sheriff. As Stapleton ruefully observed, "Sometimes the

As Stanley Kowalski, **Marlon Brando** was "a walking streak of sex" in Tennessee's *A Streetcar Named Desire*, but he also agreed to star as Val Xavier in the film, *The Fugitive Kind*. In it, he played a wandering bum in a snakeskin jacket.

acceptance of a lesser role, regardless of how humiliating, is the question of a paycheck."

Before the play opened for its very brief run, Tennessee told *The New York Times*, "It is still the tale of a wild-spirited boy who wanders into a conventional community of the South and creates the commotion of a fox in a chicken coop. But beneath the surface it is a play about unanswered questions that haunt the hearts of people, as well as the acceptance of prescribed answers that are not answers at all."

As he left the theater, Tennessee was greeted with catcalls and boos. "I just booed right back," he said.

Critics sharpened their knives for their assault on him. *The New Yorker* ignored the play's poetry, labeling it as "cornpone melodrama." Other reviews weren't much better.

A depressed Tennessee told the press, "I feel I am no longer acceptable to the theater public. Maybe they've had too much of a certain dish, and don't want to eat any more from my plate."

> *"Those critics want a quart of my blood"*
> —Tennessee Williams

It took two decades, but finally, Battle of Angels reached the screen with a new title—*The Fugitive Kind*. At long last, Tennessee got his wish. Marlon Brando signed to appear as Val ("Snakeskin") Xavier, the guitar-playing drifter.

The temperamental Italian stage and film actress, Anna Magnani, was cast as Lady, with Joanne Woodward appearing as the second female lead, that of Carol Cutrere, an alcoholic nymphomaniac.

Sidney Lumet signed on as the film's director, although he would later face critical attacks, the *Chicago Reader* claiming, "He is completely baffled by the Gothic South and doesn't quite know what to do with the overlay of Greek myth either."

Anthony Franciosa, the husband of Shelley Winters, Brando's former girlfriend, had agreed to star as Val for $75,000. But Lumet went after Brando when he heard that his bank account was bare, drained not only by his divorce from Anna Kashfi but from the financial failure of his film studio, Pennebaker.

Lumet showed up on Brando's doorstep with an offer of one million dollars. Without hesitation, Brando said, "Sign me up," although he still felt the character of Val Xavier was "a playwright's failure."

He was also concerned that Anna Magnani, in a stronger role, "will wipe my ass off the screen."

The Fugitive Kind, released at last in 1960, was not shot in the South, but in Milton, New York, a small town eighty miles north of Manhattan.

Both Lumet and Tennessee feared the meeting of Brando with Magnani, Tennessee likening it to "two hydrogen bombs going off at the same time."

They were unaware that a younger and sexier Brando had seduced a younger and sexier Magnani on her home turf in Rome years before.

In a private agreement with Lumet, Tennessee agreed to act as a referee between Brando and Magnani. At first, she was enthusiastic. "When I work with Marlon, it is like working with a strange animal about to pounce. It's a wonderful experience to see him so realistic. So completely all man."

Brando had a different view about her, confiding to Tennessee, "When I encountered *La Lupa* [her nickname], I discovered that she had turned into an Italian Tallulah Bankhead, an older creature and one even more sexually aggressive than before. She is that kind of woman, like Tallulah, who makes me flinch. Nothing but a sexual predator and a caricature of the actress she used to be. She once possessed a certain raw beauty. She has now reached the borderline of old and ugly."

Armed with this information, Tennessee tried to discourage Magnani in any fantasy she might have had about pursuing Brando with the intention of bedding him. At that point, she had not told him about her long-ago adventure with him in Rome.

In his autobiography, Brando confessed what happened when he accepted Magnani's invitation to visit her in her suite during rehearsals for *The Fugitive Kind*.

"She started kissing me with great passion," he wrote. "I tried to be responsive, because I knew she was worried about growing older and losing her beauty. As a matter of kindness, I felt I had to return her kisses. But once she got her arms around me, she wouldn't let go. I started to pull away, but she held me tight and bit my lip, which really hurt."

The Italian diva, **Anna Magnani**, was Brando's co-star in the film version of *The Fugitive Kind*.

"She can't find any man with enough fire to burn her down," he said.

[He also wrote: "With her teeth gnawing at my lower lip, the two of us locked in an embrace, I was reminded of one of those fatal mating rituals of insects that end when the female administers the coup de grace. *We rocked back and forth as she tried to lead me to the bed. My eyes were wide open, and as I looked at her eyeball-to-eyeball, I saw that she was in a frenzy, Attila the Hun in full attack. Finally, the pain got so intense that I grabbed her nose and squeezed it as hard as I could, as*

if I were squeezing a lemon, to push her away. It startled her, and I made my escape."]

After filming wrapped, Tennessee told the press, "Marlon and Anna engaged in a clash of egos never before known in the history of cinema."

When *The Fugitive Kind* officially opened, it played to nearly empty houses across the country. Exhibitors reported that audiences often left in disgust before "THE END" flashed across the screen.

Lumet, Brando, and Tennessee were "burned alive" *[the playwright's words]* by the critics. "They wanted not only to behead me but drink a quart of my tainted blood."

Brando with Magnani in *The Fugitive Kind:*

"When you play with her, you either make sure that the parts are equally volatile or plan to carry a fair-sized rock in your hand when you go on camera with her."

Brando was also attacked. Critic Clancy Sigal wrote: "Watching Brando imitating Judy Holliday's impersonation of him in *Bells Are Ringing* is, at its most serious, like seeing a scratchy old film of Duse or Bernhardt; surely someone is kidding someone."

Time Out claimed that "despite the film's stellar credentials, just about everything is wrong in this adaptation of the Tennessee Williams play. Lumet's direction is either ponderous or pretentious, and he failed to crack the problem of the florid stage dialogue and the dangerously weak role of Brando."

In an angry flash, Brando phoned Tennessee. "I told you the role of Val Xavier was weak. If only you would have listened to me." Then, abruptly, he put down the phone.

In Key West, Tallulah Bankhead had just finished the road tour of a play called *Crazy October*. She was staying in the home of its playwright, James Leo Herlihy. Darwin Porter, then the chief of the Key West bureau of *The Miami Herald*, invited Tallulah and Herlihy to a showing of the film in a dingy movie theater along Duval Street.

To the trio's surprise, they found Tennessee and his longtime lover, Frank Merlo, sitting directly behind them.

Tallulah sat patiently through the film adaptation of a play she'd rejected twenty years before. At the end of the screening, she stood up, and in a bellowing voice loud enough to be heard in the back row, she said, "Tennessee dah-ling, they've made an absolutely dreadful film out of a perfectly awful play."

Regrettably, this final failure marked what Tennessee called his "funeral rites. There went my once fashionable reputation. Never again would I be the darling of the critics. From then on, the mere mention of my name would bring only the most savage of attacks, those that tore at a human heart. I had to be a tough old bird to continue to write plays at this point in my life."

Audrey had secured investors and a producer for Tennessee's play, *The Glass Menagerie,* which was to go into rehearsals in Chicago. Margo Jones had already signed on as associate director.

The new producer, Eddie Dowling, was an actor, screenwriter, playwright, director, songwriter, and composer. When he met Tennessee, he announced, "I am a Renaissance man."

"Perhaps his background prepared him to become a producer," Tennessee said rather facetiously. "He was number 14 in a family of 17 children. He dropped out of school when he was eight years old to become a cabin boy on a Mississippi showboat. Later, he became a music hall singer in Brooklyn. At one time, he owned a small sausage factory in Los Angeles."

Dowling also confided a deep dark secret to Tennessee: His name wasn't Eddie, but "Narcissus."

Audrey had been impressed with Dowling. He had already produced plays by such authors as Philip Barry and a young William Saroyan.

Together, Margo and Dowling as its director and producer, set out to cast *The Glass Menagerie.*

It was Margo who suggested the great actress, Laurette Taylor, who was in retirement. Born in 1883 to Irish parents in New York City, she had once been a major star on the American stage and in films. But in 1944, she was a recluse, mired in alcoholism.

When Tennessee first met her in a Chicago hotel room, he discovered that she was drunk. "Not only that, she was a larger-than-life personality, a woman of mercurial moods and great eccentricities, taking refuge from life and its unbearable realities by escaping into romantic daydreams."

In Hollywood in the 1920s, she'd had a torrid affair with screen heartthrob John Gilbert. Greta Garbo had lured him away. Laurette had distinguished herself in such plays as *Peg O' My Heart* [wherein she emoted as the romantic lead in almost 1300 performances, beginning in 1912, endearing her to millions] and *Outward Bound.*

"I had great sympathy for her," Tennessee said. "Far, far, from that lonely hotel, she knew the squalid life, what it was to be cut off from the world and love during her days of purgatory."

In New York, Dowling had delivered a copy of the script of *The Glass Menagerie* to her apartment. She spent all night reading it, and was in Dowling's office when it opened the next morning. "At last I've found the role of Amanda that I have been waiting for all my life. I can play that nagging, down-at-heel, ex-Southern Belle. I know her to my toenails."

LAURETTE TAYLOR
A Retired, Old-Fashioned Eccentric with a Serious Drinking Problem is
AMAZING AS AMANDA

Even as preparations for the production of the play were underway, Tennessee, in a hotel room, continued to polish the characters of *Menagerie*.

[They include the family's toxic matriarch, Amanda Wingfield, whose husband worked for the telephone company "and fell in love with long distance," leaving her to raise her two children under harsh financial conditions.

Her son, Tom Wingfield, is really an autobiographic version of Tennessee himself. He works at a shoe warehouse but aspires to be a poet. His sister, Laura, has a limp, owing to a childhood illness. She also has an inferiority complex and is isolated from the outside world, preferring her menagerie of glass figurines, a unicorn being her favorite.

The Gentleman Caller is Jim O'Connor. A popular athlete during his school days, he works as a shipping clerk at the same shoe warehouse as Tom. Tom invites Jim home for dinner as a possible beau for Laura, not knowing that he already has a girlfriend.]

From the beginning, Dowling himself had made it clear that he wanted to play the role of Tom.

As Laura, he cast Julie Haydon.

Tennessee was unhappy with the choice of Haydon, who had had an undistinguished film career in the 1930s, ending with *A Family Affair* (1937), the movie that launched the Andy Hardy series that made a big star out of Mickey Rooney.

[In 1944, the drama critic, George Jean Nathan, would review both the play and Haydon's performance in it. In 1955, Haydon married him. Throughout her life, Haydon maintained her link to The Glass Menagerie, in spite of Tennessee's objections. In later revivals, as she aged, she assumed the role of Amanda once in a performance off off-Broadway. She lived to the age of 84, and The New York Times, as she had predicted, headlined her demise as "A STAR IN GLASS MENAGERIE DIES"

The casting of Anthony Ross as the Gentleman Caller pleased Tennessee immensely. This was the first and only important role for Ross, who went on to make some undistinguished films at 20th Century Fox and some appearances in television productions before dying in 1955 at the age of 46 of a heart attack.]

Laurette nicknamed Ross and Tennessee as "Big Bum" and "Little Bum," respectively.

How Tennessee Williams, Accompanied by the "Gentleman Caller" from *The Glass Menagerie*, Cruised the Sidewalks of Chicago for
"FLESH ON THE HOOF"

Wandering the streets of Chicago at night, Tennessee found many lovers enrolled at the time at the University of Chicago. He would pick them up, take then to his hotel room, read Hart Crane to them, and then make love to them for most of the night. "These young men, for the most part, were emotionally petulant, but sexual dynamos," he later said. "They were also very fickle. If you dared fall in love with one of them, it was like a fox's teeth biting into your heart."

"Other nights in Chicago, Tony and I went cruising together for rough trade," Tennessee admitted. "I scored more than he did because he'd get too drunk to pick anyone up. Finally, I felt sorry for him and began to purchase flesh on the hoof for him to enjoy if he were sober enough."

"He always pulled himself together the following day at rehearsals. His performance was extraordinary, considering how tormented he was. Or maybe it was that inner turmoil that made him such a good actor."

"It wasn't a different man for me every night," Tennessee said. "Sometimes, I focused on just one man, however brief the affair. I temporarily fell in love with this young Irish actor who was appearing in Chicago in a play called *Winged Victory*. He was remarkably handsome and perhaps more gifted offstage than on. I stayed at the Hotel Sherman, located within the Loop of Chicago. In my single room, this Irishman made the nightingales sing and sing. When I introduced him to Tony, he was very jealous of my catch."

"Alas, this son of Ireland deserted me for another, but I managed to hook up with another handsome student from the University of Chicago. A tall blonde, he and I used to go swimming in the nude at the Y, where he attracted a lot of envious eyes from the other male bathers. With this blonde, the

Former vaudevillian **Laurette Taylor**. Her reputation had been built with frothy turn-of-the-century romances like *Peg O' My Heart*.

In Tennessee's *The Glass Menagerie*, she brilliantly and intuitively adapted her style into that of a devouring Southern matriarch.

nightingales continued to sing their hearts out. The student would explode with a crescendo, sleep for thirty minutes, and then the music would start all over again."

During the day, Tennessee attended rehearsals, noting, to his dismay, that Dowling and Laurette were not compatible. She denounced his lack of talent as an actor and, as a director, she appraised him as inarticulate. "Talking to him is like wading through molasses," she told Tennessee.

Firing back, he said that Laurette's Southern accent was acquired "years ago from some long ago black domestic."

As Laura, Haydon never impressed Tennessee. He called her "bright-eyed attentiveness a symptom of lunacy."

Tennessee was eventually introduced to the financial backer of the play, a shady Chicago entrepreneur, Louis J. Singer, whose main business involved running seedy hotels catering to prostitutes, drunkards, and drug addicts.

The Glass Menagerie had its Chicago premiere the day after Christmas in 1944. The initial opening was lackluster. The critic, George Jean Nathan, defined it as "less a play than a palette of sub-Chekhovian pastels brushed up into a charming resemblance of one."

Laurette Taylor got the best reviews.

In an act of malice, Nathan sent a bottle of liquor backstage to Taylor, knowing that she was on the wagon as an alcoholic struggling to recover. Tennessee never forgave him for this "wanton cruelty."

During the next two weeks, the play was presented to half-full theaters. But two critics, Claudia Cassidy and Ashton Stevens, championed it, writing about it almost daily. Cassidy called it "a rare evening in the theater." Ticket sales rose, and even the mayor of Chicago urged his citizens to go and see it.

A ham actor desperate for applause, Dowling seemed to resent all the acclaim going to Laurette and Tennessee. At one point, he told the press, "I rescued the young playwright from the bottom of a rain barrel." Tennessee, of course, resented Dowling for taking credit for nearly all of his

Even though Tennessee hated her interpretations, actress **Julie Haydon** (depicted above) made recycling *The Glass Menagerie*, something of a cottage industry.

Anthony Ross: Searching for, and interpreting the role of, a gentleman caller.

success. He especially objected to Dowling's claim, "The poor, wilted manuscript arrived on my doorstep, and I struggled to rescue it from a dark oblivion."

Word reached people in show business, who stopped in to see it during their sojourns in Chicago, and Tennessee found himself greeting Katharine Hepburn, who one day would appear on TV as Amanda; Helen Hayes, who would play Amanda in London; Gregory Peck ["He gave me an erection," Tennessee claimed], and such stellar lights as Maxwell Anderson, playwright Mary Chase, Guthrie McClintic, Ruth Gordon, Raymond Massey, and Luther Adler.

Years after its run as a Broadway play, **The Glass Menagerie** was adapted (less sucessfully) into big-screen Hollywood movie starring **Jane Wyman and Kirk Douglas**.

After the run of The Glass Menagerie in Chicago, Tennessee packed his lone suitcase and headed for the uncertainties of Broadway, where both the critics and the theater-going public, in his estimation, "had fang-like teeth."

HE'S AMERICA'S MOST SUCCESSFUL PLAYWRIGHT, BUT IS HE A NATIONAL SECURITY THREAT, TOO?

J. EDGAR HOOVER WARNS PRESIDENT HARRY S TRUMAN: "TENNESSEE WILLIAMS IS A DEGENERATE"

In Manhattan, on the afternoon before the opening of The Glass Menagerie on Broadway, Laurette Taylor seemed to be coming unglued. She kept excusing herself to go to the toilet to vomit. Tennessee himself was in such a nervous state that he later revealed, "I had to have sex every other hour to steady my nerves."

The play opened in Broadway's Playhouse Theater on March 31, 1945. "Even my nemesis, critic George Jean Nathan, arrived in town to see it again. I expected a blistering attack."

Actually, Nathan wrote that *"The Glass Menagerie* provides by long odds the most imaginative evening that the stage has offered in this season."

Tennessee's most treasured review came from Arthur Miller, who said: "The play in one stroke lifted lyricism to its highest level in our theater's history."

At the end of the play, the audience shouted AUTHOR! AUTHOR! From his fourth-row seat, Tennessee rose to take a bow. He bowed to the actors, "thereby presenting a view of my posterior for the world to see."

Backstage, he congratulated Laurette. The play had opened on the day before Easter Sunday. She told him, "Jesus Christ will rise tomorrow—but I shan't."

The Glass Menagerie was swamped with awards, including the Drama Critics Circle Award for Best Play. But the Pulitzer Prize eluded Tennessee, that coveted award going to Mary Chase for her comedy, *Harvey*.

Before the year ended, the original cast gave a command performance of The Glass Menagerie in Washington. First Lady Bess Truman invited the cast to the White House for tea.

Hearing this, F.B.I Director J. Edgar Hoover telephoned the President, warning him that "Tennessee Williams is a degenerate and should not be honored at the White House."

After he put down the phone, Truman told his aides, "To hell with that. The biggest degenerate in Washington is Hoover himself."

Tennessee's *Cat on a Hot Tin Roof* Generates
OUTRAGE & FURY

Maggie the Cat (later retitled *Cat on a Hot Tin Roof*) got off to a rocky start. Deep in his drug-induced paranoia, Tennessee charged that his loyal and longtime agent, Audrey Wood, "detested my play. She even wrote me asking if I had 'flipped out.' She claimed she didn't understand it."

At Magnolia House, Wood denied these accusations. "I received a large, rather bulky and disorganized manuscript," she said. "Most of it had been typed on hotel stationery from various parts of the world—Key West, Los Angeles, Mexico, Rome. Some pages were even handwritten."

"I stayed up until four in the morning, reading every word of this disjointed material, which had enough dialogue for three or four plays. If presented in its entirety, the play would have opened at four o'clock in the afternoon, with the curtain rung down by midnight or later. But from the beginning, I realized its great potential, and, of course, I understood it, including the theme of latent homosexuality. My God, half of my clients, including Bill Inge, were gay."

"I wrote Tennessee that when a shorter draft emerged, Maggie the Cat would be his best play since *A Streetcar Named Desire*. Not only that, but I told him that with the proper script—one that would appease the Production Code in Hollywood—I could get the best movie deal ever for him, at least half a million dollars, enough for him to retire."

With his revised play, by now officially retitled *Cat on a Hot Tin Roof*, Tennessee and Audrey went first to Cheryl Crawford, who had previously functioned as producer (1950-1951) of the theatrical version of *The Rose Tattoo*. Tennessee was greatly disappointed when she rejected his latest play, claiming "There is not one character the audience can root for."

In January of 1955, Wood won the approval of Playwrights' Company to produce the play on Broadway, knowing that—based on its theme of impotence and repressed homosexuality—that it would be controversial.

The play focused on the interactions of characters rarely assembled together on Broadway, centering around members of a rich family, owners of an important plantation in the Deep South. Featured were Brick, a former athlete and now an alcoholic, and his sexually frustrated wife, Maggie the Cat.

Brick is in mourning in the wake of the suicide of his friend, Skipper. It was obvious to hip and sophisticated playgoers in 1955 at the Morosco Theatre in New York City that Brick was really in love with Skipper but had rejected him. Skipper had slept with Maggie to prove that he was not homosexual, but during their interlude together, he was impotent. This was supposedly a key element that contributed to his suicide.

Brick's parents, Big Daddy and Big Mama, were some of the strongest roles ever written for Broadway. The play opens as Big Daddy returns from the hospital. He thinks he was given a clear bill of health, but his greedy family, including Sister Woman, Brother Man, and their "no neck monster children," are fully aware that he is dying of cancer.

In New York, in January of 1955, Tennessee met with the play's director, Elia Kazan, who had previously helmed *A Streetcar Named Desire*. He was shocked at the massive rewrites Kazan demanded. "I fear my original intention has gone the way of my virginity!" he told Kazan. Nonetheless, he agreed to follow Kazan's advice on the rewrites.

Before the end of February, Tennessee found himself back in New York to approve the casting of the play. Several major stars wanted the role of

Homophobia festered in the American swamps and in the tabloid press.

A closeted homosexual himself, **J. Edgar Hoover**, chief of the FBI, led the attack on gays. He was joined by leading columnists of the day.

Walter Winchell called them "limp-wristers," and Dorothy Kilgallen claimed "It's time for TV to switch from switch-hitters."

Brick, but ultimately, it went to Ben Gazzara, with Barbara Bel Geddes cast as his wife, Maggie the Cat.

Rough, virile, and unconventionally handsome, Gazzara later admitted, "I was a babe magnet, also attracting a lot of interest among the gays."

At around the time Tennessee met Gazzara, he was engaged in affairs with both Eva Gabor and Marlene Dietrich. Audrey Hepburn would later fall in love with him.

Even before the play opened on Broadway, rumors surged through Hollywood that *Cat on a Hot Tin Roof* would eventually reach the screen. Even before any movie star saw the play, many actresses wanted to get their claws into the role of Maggie. Interested parties included Marilyn Monroe. On opening night, March 24, 1955, Marilyn showed up with Lee Strasberg of the Actors Studio.

Ben Gazzara with Barbara Bel Geddes in the stage version of *Cat on a Hot Tin Roof*.

Privately, Tennessee claimed that Gazzara, cast as Brick, "is a homosexual with a heterosexual adjustment, a thing I've long suspected of others, especially Marlon Brando."

After the curtain went down that night to the sound of wild applause and standing ovations, Marilyn arrived backstage, where Gazzara saw her talking to Tennessee for at least fifteen minutes.

Finally, she walked over to congratulate Gazzara. Wearing dangerously elevated high heels, she said to him, "I hear you may play Brick in the movie opposite me," using the purring voice of a cat.

Gazzara wondered if Tennessee had promised her the film role.

Before giving Gazzara a wet-lipped kiss, she slipped him her phone number, informing him that she had to go to a party. "Call me and then drop by my suite after ten o'clock. I'm busy until then. Let's see what our off-screen chemistry is like." Then, she seemed to appraise his body. "From the looks of things, I expect an explosion. Tennessee and I like Italian men."

Cat on a Hot Tin Roof ran for 20 months and earned Tennessee a Pulitzer Prize.

ELVIS PRESLEY VS. PAUL NEWMAN:
WHO'S THE MAN?

"My Boy Elvis Will Not Appear in this Perverted Crap!"

—Col. Parker

Many stars, both male and female, coveted the roles of Brick and Maggie the Cat, each of them a centerpiece in the 1958 film version of Tennessee Williams' play, *Cat on a Hot Tin Roof*. Director Richard Brooks had to make a choice—and it was difficult—about who to cast. The eventual stars would also have to be approved by producer Lawrence Weingarten.

Brooks called Lana Turner, telling her, "It's almost certain that MGM is going to ask you to play Maggie the Cat. We want you to come in for a reading with Paul Newman. He's one of the stars who's up for the role of the male lead."

"I'd be thrilled to play Maggie the Cat," Turner said. "I saw it on Broadway. I can be a hell of a lot more feline that Barbara Bel Geddes, darling. I'd adore playing opposite Paul. Who is his competition? Don't tell me... Ben Gazzara!"

"You're not going to believe this," Brooks said, "but yesterday, I got a call from none other than Elvis Presley. I told him about you. He'd love to play Brick to your Maggie."

"You've got to be kidding!" said Lana. "Lana Turner and Elvis Presley starring together in a raunchy Tennessee Williams drama of the Old South!"

"A distinct possibility," Brooks told her. "But you've got the billing out of order. It would be listed as 'Presley and Turner.'"

When Tennessee landed in Hollywood, he learned that Elvis was in town, having flown in from Las Vegas. He'd heard from the cast of *Cat* on Broadway that Elvis had attended a performance, but that he had not come backstage to greet the cast. At the time, Gazzara was fully aware that Elvis was in the audience, but at no time did it occur to him that Elvis wanted to play Brick, a repressed homosexual.

When Elvis called with an invitation, Tennessee eagerly accepted. But in advance of his meeting with Elvis, he called Weingarten. Tennessee had learned that Elvis wanted to make a serious movie, and Tennessee thought he'd be ideal as Brick.

"The brass is considering casting Elvis as Brick, with Lana Turner as Maggie," Weingarten said. "Their eyeballs are registering dollar signs at the box office."

"Elvis with Lana!" Tennessee said. "That's Hollywood!"

A paid companion drove Tennessee to Elvis' rented home and stayed in the car throughout the course of Tennessee's visit. A member of Elvis' Memphis Mafia let Tennessee in and offered him a drink, telling him that "The Boss" would be down in fifteen minutes when he got off the phone.

A short while later, Elvis bounced down the stairs. Back then, he was still in good physical shape, and Tennessee was impressed with his startling good looks, even better in person than on the screen. He radiated vitality.

"Mr. Playwright," Elvis said to Tennessee. "Welcome. I want you to let me be your Teddy Bear—specifically I want to play Brick in *Cat*."

"Well," Tennessee said. "That's a startling casting idea. At least you won't have to fake a Southern accent."

"No one can play a Southern boy like Elvis," the singer said. "The part has my name written on it. I want a meaty role. I'm tired of all this shit Colonel Parker tosses my way. I can't go through the rest of my life shaking my butt and swinging my hillbilly pecker—covered in pants, of course—in front of a lot of screaming teenage gals."

[*"Colonel" Tom Parker, a former circus roustabout with a shady background, became Elvis' rapacious business manager. He consistently demanded (and got) a fifty percent agent's fee, and a hell of a lot more. In essence he functioned as Elvis' crooked Svengali.*]

"I, for one, would be delighted to see you on the screen as Brick," Tennessee said. "But from what I hear of this colonel of yours, he won't let you do it."

"Fuck Colonel Parker," Elvis said, flashing anger. "I'm seriously pissed off at him. There are just so many movies I can do like Loving You."

"I'm all for you," Tennessee said. "I find you very charismatic, but I must say I fear the deal can't be worked out."

"You leave that to me," Elvis said. "I've got clout in this town." He settled back with his drink on a large sofa.

"I hear that cute little Jew boy, Paul Newman, is also up for the role," Elvis said. "But he ain't Southern. Newman's got Yankee written all over him. It takes a guy like me to stand up to both Maggie the Cat and Big Daddy."

"Paul has been talked about," Tennessee said.

"I think he's too old," Elvis said. He's ten years older than me...at least."

"I don't make casting decisions in films...regrettably," Tennessee said.

"I hear Newman's a nice guy, and I think he and I can settle this competition the way we do it in Memphis," Elvis said.

"You mean, duke it out?" Tennessee asked.

"Not quite," Elvis said. "I thought of a little contest between me and Newman. Of course, we both could invite Marilyn Monroe over, and each of us could plug her. Then she could award the prize to the best man for a roll in the hay."

"I'm sure Marilyn would find that most intriguing," Tennessee said.

"Actually, I had another contest in mind," Elvis said. "Both Newman and I are world class beer drinkers. What I'm suggesting is that I have him over, and that we both fill up on brew. Then when we want to get rid of some of the suds, we go out into my moonlit garden. Let my boys be the judge. We stage a pissing contest like we do in Memphis. Whoever can piss the farthest gets to play Brick."

"I won't say this is a first for Hollywood," Tennessee said, "and I can't say it's not been done before, but this is a most intriguing contest. I'm a bit of a voyeur, if you'd like me to judge the contest."

"I don't think me or Paul could trust you when we whip out our dicks," Elvis said. "We've heard stories."

"You're probably right. I wish you luck in throwing the largest arc of golden showers."

Tennessee remembered that sometime during the remainder of the evening, he and Elvis each passed out from drink and drugs. Two members of the Memphis Mafia eventually placed Tennessee in the back seat of his car for the ride back to his hotel.

A few nights later, Newman called: "Good news. I won the pissing contest that Elvis came up with. I'm your Brick."

Weingarten called the following day with a different slant on casting. "Tenn, I've got to be upfront with you. Years ago, Elvis wanted to star in Inge's Picnic, but Col. Parker nixed that idea, too. Now, he's forbidden Elvis to appear on the screen as Brick. He claims you're the biggest queer in Hollywood, and that you've crafted the role as a 'fucking piece of shit about a repressed homosexual.' Those are his exact words, of course, not mine. He claimed that if Elvis appears in *Cat*, it'll destroy his fan base. He had more to say on the subject, too, giving me a lecture about sex."

"What exactly are the Colonel's views about sexual relations?" Tennessee asked.

"Okay, if you must know!" Weingarten said. "The Colonel told me, in his words, that 'God made a man and a woman. He gave a man a dick and a bitch a hole. God's intention was to have a man stick his thing in a cunt and make babies. It was not God's intent for a man to stick his thing up another man's ass. Assholes are made for shitting, not fucking.' Then the Colonel went on to say, 'As long as I'm able to smoke a cigar, my boy, Elvis is not appearing in this perverted piece of crap.'"

"Sounds like a New York drama critic to me," Tennessee said.

At around midnight, Tennessee had fallen asleep in front of his TV set. Then a call came in from Richard Brooks in his capacity as the director of *Cat*.

"Forget Grace Kelly," Brooks said. "Forget Vivien Leigh. Forget Lana Turner. MGM has its Maggie the Cat to play opposite Paul Newman. I've just returned from a late night meeting with the brass. A contract has been signed. Miss Elizabeth Taylor Todd is your Maggie. No doubt, she'll soon be meowing after you."

Elvis Presley was willing to take on serious dramatic roles written by "those two queer playwrights," a reference to Tennessee Williams and William Inge.

But Elvis' manager, Col. Tom Parker, frequently and consistently sabotaged such casting. "I don't want to ruin my boy's image."

"Not as long as Mike Todd is still alive," was Tennessee's immediate response. "I know Elizabeth. She'll make a great Maggie, although I think I might have preferred Marilyn Monroe."

"Dream on," Brooks said. "Marilyn is the Queen of Fox. We want the role to go to MGM's Queen. With this role, Elizabeth is a sure-fire Oscar winner."

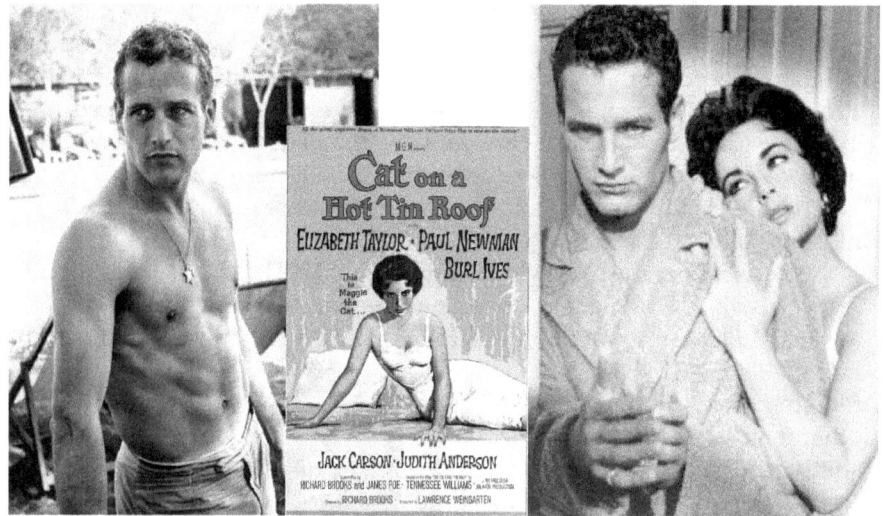

Paul Newman could be convincing as a sexy babe magnet, but Tennessee wondered if the audience could believe he was a repressed homosexual.

Boudoir games and dynastic politics dominated the screen when **Elizabeth Taylor** tried to lure her husband, Brick (**Paul Newman**) into bed. But he was drinking too much, and pining for his lost love, the football hero, Skipper.

Chapter Two

Broadway Remembers

THE UNTOLD STORY OF HOW
DARWIN PORTER
HOSTED A SPECTACULAR BLACK-TIE RECEPTION AT
MAGNOLIA HOUSE
IN HONOR OF TALENT SCOUT, PRODUCER, & EARTH MOTHER

AUDREY WOOD

CALM, EFFECTIVE, SOOTHING, & UNDERSTATED,
SHE WAS ONE OF THE MOST INFLUENTIAL
LITERARY & SHOW-BIZ AGENTS IN THE HISTORY OF
THE AMERICAN THEATER

Audrey Wood, the then-most-famous literary agent on Broadway, with her temperamental client, "ongoing project," and friend, **Tennessee Williams.**

During the peak years of Broadway, Audrey Violet Wood (1905–1985), one of the theater industry's most successful and influential literary and theatrical agents, represented some of America's most famous playwrites.

Through her invitations and intercessions, entire worlds opened up for Darwin, who attended plays with her, advised her on scripts and revisions they needed.

Through Audrey, he met established stars and writers of yesterday (Lillian Gish); today (Robert Preston); and tomorrow (John Kerr).

Her roster of important theatrical associates was already a legend when Darwin met her. Tennessee Williams claimed, "Audrey plucked me from oblivion." Katharine Hepburn said, "She was a tireless and imaginative caretaker for writers—a mother, a sensitive ear."

Elia Kazan found her "always supportive and so patient with the difficulties an embattled director might be having."

Robert Anderson, author of *Tea and Sympathy*, said, "Globe-trotting Audrey was always on the lookout for new talent. She found me in 1945 on a battleship in the Pacific."

Kitty Carlisle Hart called her "a trailblazer, mother, and nurse to talented people."

Among the actresses she represented was the famed Broadway star Eva Le Gallienne, who interpreted Audrey as "a delight—wise, witty, tough, and kind."

[Known as "America's Sarah Bernhardt," Le Gallienne was famous before she was twenty-one for her interpretation of roles that included Peter Pan and Hedda Gabler. She once told Audrey, "I'm a step ahead of the century."]

A new talent who popped up in Audrey's life was the playwright, Arthur Kopit. She represented his first play in 1962, and even tried to persuade Tallulah Bankhead to star in it. "Oh, *dah-ling*, Tallulah responded: "Without some bourbon and branchwater, my throat would get parched just repeating the title."

Opening in February of 1962, it was entitled *Oh Dad, Poor Dad, Momma's Hung You in the Closet and I'm Feelin' So Sad: A Pseudoclassical Tragifarce in a Bastard French Tradition.*

[Described by Kopit as a "farce in three scenes," it involves a deranged, domineering mother who travels to a luxury resort in the Caribbean, dragging her browbeaten son and her deceased husband, embalmed and in his casket, with her.]

Jo Van Fleet starred in it Off-Broadway. On Broadway, Hermione Gingold was featured, and when it was adapted into a film released in 1967, only Rosalind Russell would do.

***

On a cold December night in the late 1970s, in honor of Audrey's many brilliant Broadway succcessess, Darwin hosted a glittering party at Magnolia House. The theatrical elite of Broadway arrived in formal wear, nearly all the women in fur coats. The men, mostly actors, in black tie. One member of Darwin's staff was solely responsible for stoking each of the building's thirteen fireplaces, keeping them ablaze throughout the duration of the evening. Darwin's mother—briefly in residence at the time— designed formal costumes for the waitstaff.

DRINKS, DINNER, and DIVAS: Magnolia House's memorable reception, that long-ago night, in honor of Audrey Wood and fifty of her invited guests.

As part of the evening's entertainment, actress Sylvia Miles presented scenes from her one-woman show.

As Audrey confessed to Max Wilk, the author of one of her early biographies, "My work as a literary and theatrical agent was a peculiar and precarious, filled with a certain amount of success, many disappointments, and frequent disasters. I'm not sure how I keep at it—it's far from easy. But I've been an agent for a long time, and I intend to continue for as long as my sense of humor stays with me."

ONE OF AUDREY'S MOST FAMOUS CLIENTS,
THE TORMENTED MID-20TH CENTURY PLAYWRIGHT

WILLIAM INGE
THE HEART WANTS WHAT THE HEART WANTS.
BUT DOES IT EVER FIND IT?

"Little Sheba Is Dead and Never Coming Home Again."

Audrey often talked about the well-known playwright, her client, Bill Inge, telling her biographer, Max Wilk, "Bill was tall and quite shy, soft-spoken and enormously gifted. He was modest, often inarticulate.

For more than a decade, from 1950 until the mid-1960s, critics and playgoers applauded his work. At the time, he was considered one of the most successful young playwrights on the American stage. His deeply sympathetic observation of small towns and their inhabitants afforded his sophisticated metropolitan audiences an entirely different and possibly more sympathetic attitude toward their neighbors in the heartlands. On the screen, his plays were usually even more successful than they'd been on Broadway. But then Bill went into an almost total eclipse, both professionally and personally, and seemed to just shut down."

In the early 1960s, at Sardi's in Manhattan, Audrey introduced Inge to Darwin, and the two very different writers struck up a friendship that endured until Inge's tragic death.

Darwin later published many of his insights and revelations about Inge in some of the biographies he crafted through Blood Moon,, including *Paul Newman, The Man Behind the Baby Blues* (2009) and *Marilyn (Monroe) at Rainbow's End* (2012).

***

The world was a vastly different place when William Inge was born in 1913 in Independence, Kansas. Even as a boy, he dreamed that one day he'd write plays, but as he matured, he supported himself with work on a road gang maintaining highways in the bleak western part of Kansas.

Later, he got a better job announcing the news at a Wichita radio station. After he graduated from college, he taught English and drama at a high school in Columbus, Kansas, in the isolated and very rural southeastern corner of the state.

His best job yet came midway through the course of World War II, when he became a drama critic for the *St. Louis Star-Times.* "I loved drama, watching it and hoping that maybe one day I'd create my own."

He was assigned the task of interviewing a young, emerging play wright, Tennessee Williams, who was in St. Louis at the time. The men bonded and for a while, at least, became lovers, even though they'd soon become rivals for the attentions of theater audiences on Broadway.

"Before I met Tennessee, I was trying (unsuccessfully) to become the American

William Inge, then one of the two or three most famous and influential playwrights in America.

version of Noël Coward," Inge told Darwin. "I know that sounds ridiculous, but after I saw Tennessee's *The Glass Menagerie*, my outlook changed. Tenn took inspiration for his dramas from his own life, especially from his pathetic sister and devouring mother. He knew how to create art from his own life, and I felt I could do the same in depicting what goes on behind the closed doors of small town America."

Tennessee expressed lavish praise for Inge's first play, *Farther Off from Heaven*. After Inge finally emigrated to New York, he introduced him to Audrey, who would guide him through well-reviewed Broadway productions of many of his plays, and also selling their movie rights.

Come Back, Little Sheba
BURT LANCASTER
Chasing After What He Couldn't Have

As his agent, Audrey was the guiding light behind Inge's first hit play, *Come Back, Little Sheba*, the story of a loveless, deadening marriage that's rocked when a beautiful young woman rents a room in the modest home of the middle-aged couple that owns it. [*The title derives from the family's beloved lost dog, Sheba, who as it turns out, ran away years ago and never returned.*]

In 1950, it ran for 190 performances on Broadway, winning Tony Awards for its stars, Shirley Booth and Sidney Blackmer.

Audrey sold its film rights to producer Hal B. Wallis, who hired Daniel Mann in his directorial debut. The film version was eventually released in 1952.

Wallis offered several big name actresses the lead role but each of them told him, "Only Shirley Booth can do it justice." These ladies were correct: Booth eventually won an Oscar for her bravura in interpreting its female lead. Her co-star, Terry Moore, the mistress of Howard Hughes, was nominated for an Academy Award as Best Supporting Actress.

Who played the tormented male protagonist? Burt Lancaster telephoned Wallis and almost demanded the lead role of the alcoholic chiro-

One critic said "Burt Lancaster made himself a middle-aged, perilously reformed alcoholic with such suppressed tension that he eclipsed all of Shirley Booth's fluttering as his wife."

practor.

"At first, I considered Burt completely wrong for the part," Wallis said. "Physically, he had nothing to do with the part. He was far too virile to play a weakling. So we dressed him in a sloppy, shapeless sweater, padded his torso to flab out his waistline, put him into a pair of baggy pants, and let him grow a stubble of beard. Still we had a problem covering up that magnificent physique of his."

One afternoon, Inge himself showed up on the set, and Lancaster engaged him in a long conversation. As he later relayed to Wallis, "Inge is a sad and lonely man, obviously unfulfilled but seeking some kind of satisfaction and not finding it. I knew he was a homosexual, and, from what he said, he was attracted to guys who'd never consider giving him a tumble. Finally, because I wanted the role he'd created, I volunteered. 'Come back to my dressing room where I'll let you suck my cock,' I told him He followed me like a puppy dog with his tongue hanging out. I felt better after it was done, because the look on his face told me I'd given him the thrill of his life."

[In 1977, in a TV remake of Inge's original script, Laurence Olivier played the Burt Lancaster role, with Joanne Woodward cast in the Shirley Booth role, that of his dowdy wife. Star Wars' Carrie Fisher filled in for Terry Moore.]

WARREN BEATTY
"A Wreath Hung on an Erect Penis"

Both Audrey and William Inge had high hopes for his latest play, the 1959 *A Loss of Roses*. For the first time, Audrey talked about film rights even before getting the play launched on Broadway.

"I can see it now, starring Marilyn Monroe with that divine boy you introduced me to last night."

She was referring to the soon-to-be-sensational movie star, Warren Beatty. In time, he would be hailed as "The Sexiest Man Alive."

He aggressively embarked on a campaign to live up to his reputation. Over a period of years, he seduced Jacqueline Kennedy Onassis, Joan Collins, Natalie Wood, Leslie Caron, Julie Christie, Diane Keaton, Michelle Phillips, Candice Bergen, Vivien Leigh, Cher, Jane Fonda, Angelica Huston, Bianca Jagger, Christina Onassis, Lee Radziwill, Vanessa Redgrave, Diana Ross, Jean Seberg, Carly Simon, and Mamie Van Doren and dozens of other lesser-known (or completely unknown) other partners. And we must not leave out Elizabeth Taylor and Barbra Streisand.

Madonna, however, gave him a bad report, publicly defining him as "a pussy. He's a wimp."

Beatty's biographer, Ellis Amburn, wrote: "The gay preoccupations of playwrights James Leo Herlihy, the novelist, who wrote *All Fall Down*, and William Inge—self-absorption, rebellion against convention, narcissism—jibed with Warren's own psyche and enabled him to summon up a passable performance."

It was Inge who was enlisted to craft a screenplay for the 1962 film adaptation, directed by Joshua Logan, of Herlihy's novel, *All Fall Down*. Logan later claimed, "Inge fell for Warren the moment he set eyes on him, but it was so hopeless that I felt sorry for him. Inge was a shy Midwesterner with thinning hair, and he wasn't young anymore. He also looked like a god damn insurance salesman in an ill-fitting suit that needed to be sent to the cleaners. He eventually became Beatty's 'fairy godmother,' writing *A Loss of Roses*, *Splendor in the Grass*, and the screenplay for *All Fall Down [each of which Warren starred in]* before Warren dropped him and moved on to greater glory."

Burry Fredrick, the stage manager, said, "It was sad to see Inge slurp

Broadway's version of *A Loss of Roses*. In the words of one critic, "It was a tense triangle with Oedipal overtones about a young gas station attendant living with his mother in Depression-era Kansas.

Three time-sensitive views of **Warren Beatty.**

over Beatty. Although he'd had success with some other leading men, with that stuck-up star, Inge was out of his league."

Meanwhile, Beatty didn't need Inge for sexual relief. Joan Collins eventually flew in from Hollywood to keep him company during rehearsals.

In the aftermath of their affair, Collins, nicknamed "The British Open," delivered her own evaluation: "Warren could proposition a chair if it looked at him sideways. Three, four, even five times a day, every day, were not unusual for him, and he was able to accept phone calls at the same time."

Hollywood agent Sue Mengers said, "God! I must be the only woman in Los Angeles or New York that Warren hasn't tried to shtup."

Depicted above is Broadway star **Shirley Booth** in 1960 as *Hazel the Maid* in that hit TV series.

As regards Warren Beatty's onstage sexual antics, Ms. Booth—Beatty's onstage mother— was neither amused nor impressed, and vocalized it so loudly that she eventually left the show.

***

A Loss of Roses is set in a small Kansas town during the Depression of the 1930s. Helen Baird, a widowed nurse, lives with her son, Kenny (as portrayed by Beatty), who's filled with youthful ardor. Their lives are about to change with the arrival in town of Lila, a tent-show stripper whose troupe has gone belly up. She used to be Kenny's babysitter.

As one critic phrased it, "*A Loss of Roses* is a bittersweet and brooding drama, heavy with regret, pain, and fleeting beauty. Expect inter-generational strife, the loss of innocence, and the fragility of weaving all that through the story."

Right from the beginning, Beatty conflicted with Shirley Booth, who starred as his mother. For her previous appearance in a film adaptation of an Inge drama (*Come Back, Little Sheba*; 1952), she'd won an Oscar.

She objected to Beatty "using his sex appeal to get anything he wants from Inge. Our playwright seems head over heels crazy about this young buck. Inge told me that Warren is a 'young colt who's out in a new green pasture,' whatever in hell that meant. If his boy wanted a line changed, Inge obeyed. Frankly, Beatty and I were not harmonious. I thought the play would fail. I wanted out—and I bailed. TV's Hazel the Maid lay in my future."

During the arguments that preceded her departure, Booth had informed Inge, "I don't like the morals of the people in your play."

As her replacement, a lesser-known but very competent actress, Betty Field, was given the role. *[Later, she was awarded a co-starring role in Inge's Picnic. Known for her sad, sultry eyes, Field had first appeared on Broadway at the age of sixteen. Of her many film roles, she'd been the disturbed daughter of Claude Rains in* Kings Row *(1942), starring Ronald Reagan in his only memorable movie.]*

"So ya wanna put a laurel wreath on Warren Beatty's WHAT??!"

Beatty made his stage debut on October 29, 1959 at the National Theater in Washington, D.C. Ironically, four years earlier, he'd been hired by the same theater as an exterminator to chase out the rats.

A *Loss of Roses* opened on Broadway at the Eugene O'Neill Theatre on November 28, 1959, where it ran for three weeks.

The New York Times called it "earnest and attractive." The Daily News hailed Beatty as a new arrival in the ranks of juvenile leads. Kenneth Tynan, writing for the New Yorker, cited Beatty for being "sensual around the lips, with a pensive brow."

Walter Kerr found Beatty "attractive, sensitive, mercurial, and excellent." Judith Crist admitted to "being bowled over." Another writer asserted that "a wreath should be hung on his erect penis."

What was Beatty's opinion?

"I'm glad everybody thought I was hot shit. But I'm sorry the play flopped. Bill took it real bad."

"The only one who came out looking like roses was Warren," Inge said. "I predict a bright future for him. With his looks, he's destined to become a bigtime movie star, perhaps in the tradition of James Dean or Marlon Brando."

Inge was right.

Audrey reflected, "I had a hell of a time. I was the agent for warring factions: Inge, Shirley Booth, Warren Beatty, and the director, Daniel Mann."

[Retitled as The Stripper, *A Loss of Roses* made it to the big screen in 1963. It starred Joanne Woodward and Richard Beymer.]

BILL INGE'S "MIDSUMMER ROMANCE"
PICNIC
A HOBO DRIFTER SETS HEARTS FLUTTERING IN CORN COUNTRY

Flush with the success of Come Back, Little Sheba, William Inge was hard at work on his latest play, *Women in Summer*. He sent its first draft to Audrey Wood, who suggested that although it had the makings of a Broadway hit, it needed more work and deeper characterizations.

Retitled as Picnic, the action takes place on Labor Day as the people of a small town turn out for a picnic.

The choicest of the female roles is that of Madge Owens, a beautiful girl just bursting into the bloom of her womanhood. She lives with her sister, Millie Owens, and her mother, Flo. Madge is engaged to a handsome, rich, but dull young man, Alan Seymour.

Into town come the drifter, Hal Carter, who emerges as the real star of the play. After hopping off a train, he looks up his old school chum, Alan.

A high-octane stud, Hal emerges as a testosterone dynamo who stirs up the hormones of the town's females, including those of a lonely, unmarried, middle-aged schoolteacher, Rosemary Sydney, who is renting a room within the Owens' home. She has spent many unsuccessful months trying to maneuver her boyfriend, Howard Bevans, into proposing marriage.

Joshua Logan was called in to direct, selecting Ralph Meeker to play Hal, the sexy drifter; Janice Rule [*married at the time to actor Ben Gazzara*] for the role of Madge. Kim Stanley played her younger sister, Millie. Eileen Heckart starred as the sexually frustrated schoolteacher. The role of Alan went to Paul Newman. It was during rehearsals that he met the actress who became his second wife, Joanne Woodward, who was an understudy for Kim Stanley.

In Broadway history, Picnic became almost legendary for shining a first-time spotlight on three future stars: Paul Newman, Joanne Woodward, and Kim Stanley, who would later be labeled as "the female Marlon Brando."

That spotlight seemed particularly poignant for Stanley: Saturday Review added her name to the list of the most distinguished postwar American actresses, other members of whom included Geraldine Page, Kim Hunter, Maureen Stapleton, Barbara Bel Geddes, and Julie Harris.

Through Darwin's links with industry players who included producer Walter Starcke, Inge, Tennessee Williams, and others, Darwin got to meet and in some cases, develop ongoing dialogues with these fine actresses. He became especially close to Kim Stanley during the course of her longtime affair with his boss in TV advertising, Brooks Clift, the older brother of Montgomery Clift.

Darwin came to view Kim as a tragic figure. Arthur Laurents claimed, "If not for her demons, Kim Stanley would have become the greatest actress in America."

Kim recalled her first meeting with Joanne Woodward: "I found her charming and ambitious with two major goals: To become a big-time movie star, and to take Paul Newman away from his wife."

***

Before Logan announced the final cast of the stage version of Picnic, actors on Broadway had jockeyed for each of the roles — even the minor parts. Word was out that Inge's play would morph into the hit drama of the season.

Audrey Wood was working to generate all the pre-opening publicity she could.

Through Audrey and Inge, among others, Darwin learned what was going on behind the scenes before the cast was even selected.

Its tantalizing story, focusing mostly on Paul Newman and Joanne Woodward, was detailed in his award-winning biography, *Paul Newman, The Man Behind the Baby Blues*, published by Blood Moon Productions in 2009.

Two views of the Broadway actors who emerged as stars from their gigs in William Inge's *Picnic*: Top photo: **Paul Newman.**

Lower photo: **Kim Stanley** in mock combat with **Ralph Meeker.**

PAUL NEWMAN
An "Impossibly Handsome" Blue-Eyed Neophyte Auditions on the Casting Couch

> *"Paul Newman had so many lovers in his early days that he should have kept his pants unzipped for quickies."*
> —Rod Steiger

Newman, who lived at the time less than two blocks from Magnolia House on Daniel Low Terrace in an apartment he shared with his then-wife, Jackie, put on his seersucker suit and, in the stifling midsummer heat, walked the 12-minute downhill slope to the Staten Island Ferry. Boarding it, he embarked on its transit across the murky waters of New York Harbor to the canyons of Lower Manhattan. With him, he carried a baloney sandwich for his lunch.

He summoned his courage and reached for that business card that he'd been carrying around in his wallet. Without an appointment, he arrived at the cluttered offices shared by Audrey Wood and her husband, William Liebling.

Liebling not only remembered Paul from a play he'd performed at Yale but agreed to see him. But first, Paul had to spend more than an hour sitting on a bench without a cushion in the agent's outer office.

In times past, or in the future, many future stars would get their start by warming this same bench, including Cloris Leachman, Eli Wallach, Julie Harris, Cliff Robertson, and even Montgomery Clift, who'd already moved on to stardom in Hollywood.

Fifteen minutes into his interview with Liebling, Paul realized the agent was serious about finding work for him. "I deal only in star parts," Liebling told Paul. "I don't book walk-ons for actors. There's nothing that I know of for you right now. But William Inge has written what I think will be the hit of the coming season. It's a play called *Picnic*. I think I can get you something juicy in it. Let's stay in touch."

"In the meantime, I've got mouths to feed, including my own and one on the way," Paul said.

"I suggest television," Liebling said. "It's booming. There are tons of jobs for handsome actors. I'll get you an appointment with my friend, Maynard Morris at MCA. He discovered Gregory Peck and Barbara Bel Geddes. Maynard, or one of his agents, gets work for actors in television. I'm a stage agent."

True to his word, Liebling arranged an appointment for Paul with Morris at MCA, Inc. The interview was successful, and Paul signed with the agency. He was turned over to John Foreman, who would eventually become Paul's business partner.

Foreman found work immediately for his new client, whom he described to casting directors, especially the gay ones, as a "Greek god."

Late in 1952, after only two months of training at the Actors Studio, the call Paul had been waiting for materialized. Liebling had arranged for him to read for Inge, who had finally finished his Broadway-bound play, *Picnic*. The drama would change Paul's life for all time.

On his way to Inge's apartment, insecure and nervous, he encountered a woman on the street who stopped him. "You're Marlon Brando, aren't you?" she asked. "I loved you in *A Streetcar Named Desire*. Could I have your autograph?"

This was just the beginning of such requests from fans who, throughout the 50s, mistook him for Brando. Dutifully, he signed Brando's name and headed into the apartment building and up the elevator and into the apartment where Inge waited for him.

He checked his appearance in a tiny mirror near the elevator buttons. Author Charles Hamblett described what he looked like at that time in his life: "His eyes could have come straight from an identikit (sic) picture of Monty Clift, his mouth was a refinement of Victor Mature's Magyar leer, and the shade of John Garfield hovered around the thrust of his jaw."

Kansas-bred Inge came from the same Midwestern roots that had given birth to Paul. He was familiar with the nervousness of an aspirant young student actor and offered Paul a drink. "I've already had five drinks in the past two hours, so you need to catch up with me."

The drink put Paul at ease. As a prelude to his reading from the script, Inge spoke of his hometown. "I'll always remember Independence, Kansas. A beauti-

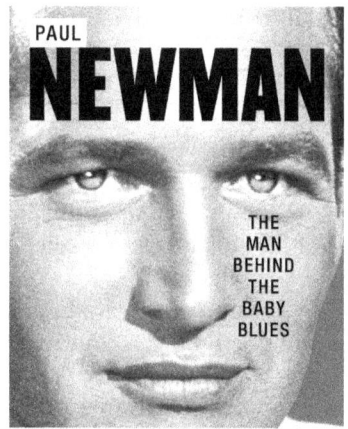

"One can only wonder how he managed to escape public scrutiny for for long."

Upper photo depicts the front cover of Blood Moon's widely reviewed biography of Paul Newman

Lower photo shows **Newman**, by now an actor fimly in control of his "crotch acting," in *Hud* (1963)

ful little town with enormous shade trees and lots of fine spacious homes. I've been to Shaker Heights [*i.e., Newman's home town*]. Our towns have much in common. I recall the celebrations of Halloween and the city park. We had a sad old river there. There was an old wives' tale that the Indians had left a curse on the river and that it would take one life a year in vengeance on the white man for having usurped their land."

When Paul was sufficiently at ease, Inge asked him to read the part of Hal, the leading male role. He later claimed, "I was awful but Inge was very indulgent."

In Key West years later, Inge told Tennessee Williams, "Paul messed up bigtime, but I found him exciting. First, he was a beautiful man. I just wanted to strip off his clothes and tongue him from head to toe. I'd never seen an actor with this particular type of male beauty. And he was also a nice guy with unbelievably good manners. I was determined to have him at all costs."

At the end of Paul's bad reading, Inge congratulated him. "You're very talented as an actor," he said, not meaning it. "Forgive me, but I must ask you to pull off your shirt. On stage Hal appears shirtless in pivotal scenes, and the actor who plays him has to have a certain build."

Without being asked again, Paul stood in front of Inge and pulled off his shirt and underwear top. "Inge asked me to walk around while he devoured my chest," Paul later told Kim Stanley, "I felt like a piece of meat being inspected. But I'd do anything to get cast in a Broadway play. Inge knew just how far I'd go."

With the passage of years, the story of just how Paul parlayed his good

Left: **Paul Newman**, an object of affection, and perhaps obsession, too, of both (right photo) **William Inge** (left) and **Tennessee Williams** (right).

Both would write star-building plays in which Newman would star and from which he would, professionally speaking, leap onward to greater glory and profit.

looks into success as an actor became widely known on Broadway, but because of the fear of libel, it couldn't be described in print at the time. In 1996, writing while Paul was still alive, biographer Lawrence J. Quirk cited Paul's "climbing the lavender ladder" en route to success on Broadway.

"I knew what Inge wanted, and he was going to get the prize," Paul later confided to Kim. "We song-and-danced each other that day. Or should I say that the cat toyed with the mouse? When he invited me for a romantic dinner the following night, I knew what was coming, and I proved to be the man for the job. God damn it, Inge was like a suction pump. I don't think there was one orifice left unexplored. When I got on the 2AM ferry back to Staten Island, I was drained dry. But Inge had promised to arrange an audition for me with Joshua Logan, who was to direct Picnic."

The next day, Liebling called Paul and wanted to meet with him shortly before noon in his office. He'd received a call from Inge praising Paul's talent, although warning that the producers might give the role to a bigger star like Marlon Brando should he become available. "I'll personally lobby for Paul," Inge assured Liebling. "Even if Paul loses out on the role of Hal," Inge promised, "I'll do what I can to get him one of the other parts."

As Paul was leaving Liebling's office that day, he had a chance encounter with one of the agent's former clients. It was Montgomery Clift, who had recently flown in from Los Angeles. Paul seemed dazed by that actor's stunning beauty. He'd seen him in Red River opposite John Wayne and had been mesmerized by his screen image. He'd also been enthralled watching Monty in the screen's most clinging embrace, the goodbye scene between Elizabeth Taylor and him in the 1951 *A Place in the Sun*.

Like many of the actors Paul was meeting, Monty was very direct, making his intentions known. "Where has God's gift been hiding all my life?"

In spite of himself, Paul blushed. Monty took his hand and did not release it for the longest time. "You're the greatest," Paul managed to mumble. He was clearly awed and could have cursed himself for appearing like some gangly schoolboy fan in front of Monty. "I . . . I . . . don't know what to say."

"I've got to run now," Monty said. "Just give me permission to get your phone number from Liebling. Let me call you. It's not every day I meet up with a man who's more beautiful than I am." Monty kissed Paul gently on the lips. There was just a flicker of tongue.

***

A closeted homosexual, director Joshua Logan suffered from frequent bouts of manic-depression. On the day he met Paul, Logan was in an uncharacteristically ebullient mood.

Paul was immediately impressed with this man of the theater who had emerged out of Texarkana, Texas to become president of the drama group at Princeton. Its players included Henry Fonda, Margaret Sullavan, and James Stewart. In the 1930s Logan had actually visited Constantin Stanislavsky in Moscow.

In 1958, when Logan was directing *Blue Denim* on Broadway, a play by gay author James Leo Herlihy, Logan confided to the playwright, "I not only wanted to direct Paul in Picnic, I wanted to sample what was actually in his picnic basket. As you know, I've had many actors in my day, but Paul was exceptional and that was immediately apparent when he walked into my apartment. His arms and legs moved in perfect rhythm. The fact that he was a bit shy made him all the more adorable. Long, lean, and muscular, his body radiated a power that back then he hadn't yet tapped. His nose was well formed and aquiline, as if he had patrician ancestry. His hair was thin but the kind you wanted to run your fingers through. He was extraordinarily handsome with clear blue eyes, bluer than an alpine lake in summer. He had perfectly formed lips. And when he smiled, he revealed strong white teeth. There was just a stubble of beard, which appeared like golden flecks against his perfect skin."

"Sounds like you fell in love," Herlihy said.

"I did indeed," Logan said. "I always go for the unobtainable. That way I can revel in my depression at the inevitable rejection."

Top: **Montgomery Clift** and (lower photo) his loyal but less famous brother, **Brooks Clift,** a frequent visitor to Magnolia House and a romantic partner of Kim Stanley.

Paul read for Logan that day, and, overcome by the moment, the director promised Paul the lead role of Hal, a juicy part that would have been ideal for Brando. The role of Hal was that of a drifter, an uninhibited stud who was "Inge's jerk-off fantasy," in Paul's view. Entering into a small Kansas town where women were deprived of men, leading lives of strained sexual relations and quiet desperation, the character of Hal was like a firecracker, igniting long-suppressed emotions and yearnings.

That night when Paul returned to his apartment on Staten Island, he told Jackie, his wife, "I'm going to be a Broadway star. It's happened at last!"

Lost in the fantasy of overnight stardom, Paul got a jolt of reality when Liebling called him with the bad news. Apparently, Ralph Meeker had become available, and Logan, having changed his mind, had cast Meeker in the role of Hal instead. Brazenly macho, Meeker was obviously more suited for the part than Paul.

Logan had worked with him in Mr. Roberts, for which Meeker had received a Theatre World Award, and he'd taken over the role of Stanley from Brando in the Broadway version of *A Streetcar Named Desire* after Brando grew tired of the grind. Meeker also had a number of screen credits under his belt.

Broadway director **Joshua Logan**. Closeted, insecure, and predatory.

Paul was bitterly angry with both Logan and Inge but promised Liebling he'd conceal his fury. "Losing the role of Hal was one of the hundreds of disappointments I would eventually experience in my long career," he later said.

Despite Paul's upset, other news from Liebling wasn't all bad. For a salary of one-hundred and fifty dollars a week, Logan would hire Paul as Meeker's understudy and also give him a one-line walk-on role. Paul would play "Joker," a slightly menacing gas station jockey who would make a pass at Madge, the play's heroine, which would be played by the very beautiful Janice Rule.

While waiting for his debut in Picnic, Paul met with John Foreman, his new agent at MCA, who promised work for him in television series. One morning Paul's meeting with him ran longer than an hour, even though the agent had a young blonde-haired actress waiting outside to see him too. As Foreman opened the door to his office to let Paul out, Joanne Woodward jumped up from her seat. Foreman introduced her to Paul, who apologized for "eating into your time. We got carried away."

"Oh, that's okay," she said in a cornpone Southern drawl. "I've spent all my life waiting for one man or another."

There were no great sparks, no love at first sight.

"My introduction of these two was a historic moment in theater and film history," Foreman recalled. "They couldn't have seemed less interested that day. Who could have predicted what was to come?"

***

"I hated him on sight," Woodward later recalled. "He was pretty and neat like an Arrow Collar ad. He looked like a snobby college boy type in an unimpressive seersucker suit, the kind insurance salesmen wore in summer making the rounds in my native Georgia."

Like Paul, Joanne had been born a winter baby but not into freezing weather. When she entered the world on February 27, 1930, it was 70 degrees Fahrenheit in Thomasville, Georgia, a town that had once flourished as a winter resort, lying only ten miles north of the Florida border.

With her blonde hair and pixie face, she looked at the world through inquisitive green eyes. By the age of five, she had become an avid movie-goer. She told her parents, Wade Woodward and Elinor Trimmier Woodward, that she wanted to grow up to become an actress like Bette Davis and Joan Crawford. Ironically, at the time of her birth, her mother had wanted to name her after Joan Crawford, but after prolonged wheedling, her Southern relatives succeeded in getting the child named Joanne instead. A brother, Wade Jr., had been born earlier.

More aggressively macho than Paul Newman, whom he replaced in a role Newman coveted, here's **Ralph Meeker** (right) with **Barbara ("Bloody Babs") Stanwyck**.

The movie they appeared in together was *Jeopardy*, released by MGM in 1953.

When Elinor took Joanne to see Laurence Olivier playing the melancholy Heathcliff in Wuthering Heights, Joanne developed her first serious crush.

That same year of 1939, when the newspapers announced that the premiere of *Gone With the Wind* was to be held in Atlanta, Joanne begged her mother to take her.

In Atlanta, she even convinced her mother to wait outside the hotel where Olivier was staying with Vivien Leigh, who played Scarlett O'Hara in the film. When the door to their limousine opened, Joanne, aged nine, jumped inside, landing on Olivier's lap.

In school it was revealed that Joanne had a high I.Q., and she excelled in her grades. Life seemed so happy in the Woodward household that she later said she was devastated when her parents announced that they were divorcing. "It took years for me to adjust to that," she said. Her father went to New York, where in time he became vice president of Scribner's, the publishing house.

When Joanne and her mother moved to Greenville, South Carolina, the future actress had not abandoned her dream of life in the theater. She began to attract attention in high school productions. Weighing 117 pounds, she had measurements of 32-24-34, which attracted the interest of some of her male classmates. She generally ignored their glances, and continued to do so during her two years at Louisiana State University.

Returning to Greenville, she appeared in a local production of Tennessee Williams's *The Glass Menagerie*—ironically, the same play in which Paul had appeared during his own school years in Ohio. Years later, Joanne would star in a film version of that same play, directed by none other than Paul himself.

Persuading her mother to let her go to New York, Joanne arrived there by train at the age of twenty-one. Until she got work in the theater, she planned to support herself on the sixty dollars a month her father gave her. Almost immediately she enrolled in the Neighborhood Playhouse, which, like the Actors Studio, trained the aspiring stars of tomorrow.

Joanne Woodward dispaying one of the *Three Faces of Eve* (1957).

At the playhouse, she studied under the great dramatic coach, Sanford Meisner, who warned her to "get rid of that Southern drawl, or you'll appear only in plays by Tennessee Williams."

Like Paul, Joanne signed with MCA, under whose management she pursued roles in live television dramas. She appeared in an original teleplay, *Penny*, which aired on June 9, 1952. Other live television roles followed.

Between jobs, Joanne liked to hang out with her fellow actors, talking about the theater. She had long cups of coffee with Rod Steiger, a newly made friend of Paul's. She even befriended a young aspiring actor, James Dean, hardly knowing that he was sleeping on occasion with her future husband.

Her big goal involved starring on the Broadway stage, and she avidly followed casting calls. As a result of attending a cattle call, she was summoned to appear before Joshua Logan, who asked her to read a scene from the upcoming play he was directing, *Picnic*. Amazingly, he liked her reading and hired her to understudy both Janice Rule, playing Madge, and also Kim Stanley playing Millie, Madge's younger sister.

When Joanne reported for work the next day, Logan introduced her to Paul. "We've met before," she said.

Paul claimed he didn't remember their initial encounter in Foreman's office. "I meet so many aspiring actresses," he said. That remark didn't endear Paul to her and confirmed her earlier impression that he was a conceited snob.

"I had all the lovers I could handle at the time," Paul later confided to Rod Steiger. "I wasn't about to take on another, even though I could tell that Woodward was attracted to me. Besides, I had a wife at home, a son, and a baby on the way. Maybe Jackie thinks that by becoming a baby factory she can hold on to me. Or else my rubbers had big leaky holes. I'm practically a walking sperm factory."

Paul wasn't exaggerating about all those lovers. According to Steiger, "He should have kept his pants unzipped for quickies. In those days, he was one busy boy."

***

Backstage, Logan introduced Paul to a relative newcomer, character actress Eileen Heckart, who had been cast in *Picnic* as a schoolteacher named Rosemary. Eileen and Paul chatted amicably until Logan tapped him on the shoulder. "There's another cast member here. She says she knows you and is waiting for you in her dressing room." For some reason, Logan was being mysterious. Walking up to the dressing room, Paul knocked on the door.

"Come on in, it's open," came a voice that sounded familiar, though he wasn't sure.

Opening the door, he encountered Kim Stanley in bra and panties, with her feet propped up on her dressing table. "Come on in, big boy," she said to him, "and lock the door behind you. We've got some unfinished business. Now come over here and take care of momma."

[By chance, they had met before and had had a fast fling.]

Before its premiere on Broadway, *Picnic* went on the road, opening in such cities as Cleveland. During its tour, Joanne began to look at Paul with a different point of view. "He wasn't conceited at all. In fact, I found him rather modest for such a good-looking boy. He had a protective wall around him when I met him, but deep down he was a sensitive man with the soul of an artist. He just didn't want the world to know that."

On the road, Paul began to "date" Joanne in a casual way. They often met for a cheap lunch in some dreary coffee shop or treated themselves to a late-night dinner together after the evening's performance. They talked about the weakness of the play's third act and how Logan was fighting with Inge to rewrite it. Sometimes Paul didn't tell Joanne good night until two o'clock in the morning.

In the beginning of their relationship, Paul claimed he did not view Joanne as a romantic attachment but as a good and like-minded friend. They talked about books they'd read, Method acting, movies or plays they'd seen. When not emoting in Picnic, they often attended a movie matinee together.

"I have no doubt but that they were sexually attracted to each other, but weren't admitting it, not even to themselves," said Stanley, who was jealous of Joanne.

"Kim was looking for a series of good fucks during the long run of *Pic-*

nic," Logan later said. "She told me that her greatest fantasy was to have a three-way with both Newman and Brando. I don't know if Paul was paying secret visits to Joanne's hotel room—or not. But it wasn't a question of if they'd start fucking, but when."

***

Paul's lucky break came when Logan decided that the actor playing Alan Benson, Hal's roommate in college, was dull and slowed down the action of the play. Firing him, Logan hired Paul as his replacement. Alan, the rich boy, loses his girl (Janice Rule) to the more seductive jock, Hal, as played by Meeker.

After rehearsing Paul for three days in his new role of Alan, Logan began to feel that he'd made a mistake. "Paul has no fire either," Logan cofessed to William Inge. "He's pretty and has a sexy body, but he doesn't know how to use it."

"Let's seek an outside opinion," Inge told Logan. "We're both hung up on Paul and can't be objective."

Called in to watch Paul's performance as Alan were Tennessee Williams, Elia Kazan, and Dorothy McGuire, who had scored a box office hit in *Gentleman's Agreement*, in 1947.

After Paul's performance, both Kazan and Tennessee congratulated Paul, although McGuire remained noncommittal.

"You are not just beautiful," Tennessee exclaimed, embracing Paul, "but spectacularly beautiful. Up to now I thought Marlon was the most beautiful man I'd ever seen on the stage. Now you come along, making my fickle heart waver. With you on the stage with Ralph Meeker, all homosexuals will have a difficult choice. Do they want to see sexual menace or do they want to worship at the altar of male beauty?"

Paul was embarrassed at Tennessee's adulation, but he returned the compliment. "It's an honor to get a seal of approval from America's greatest playwright."

"With a compliment like that," Tennessee said, "all you have to do is blow in my ear and I'll follow you anywhere. One of these days, I'm going to write a role for you, one so great you'll always be remembered for it."

"A promise I'll hold you to, Mr.

Kim Stanley as Cherie the Stripper in the Broadway version of William Inge's *Bus Stop*.

When it was later adapted into a movie and released in 1956, Slanley's role—much to her rage—was assigned to Marilyn Monroe.

Williams."

After Kazan and Tennessee had each approved of Paul for the role of Alan, Logan decided to head to Broadway with Ralph Meeker and Paul as his male stars. Even so, Paul complained to Logan. "I'll do what I can with Alan. But he's an unreconstructed square. Meeker eats me alive on stage in his juicy part. I play Madge's boyfriend, but it's obvious to the audience I'm going to lose her to Meeker's more threatening sexuality. Alan is a thankless role for any actor."

"All of us must start somewhere," Logan told him.

Paul also complained to Inge. "Could you rewrite Alan a bit? I mean, he's without depth or resonance. Give me a chance." Inge turned a deaf ear to him, as he was angry with Paul, who had refused to become the playwright's off-duty stud.

***

Meeker evolved into Paul's rival both on and off the stage. The more experienced actor had virtually ignored Paul during tryouts on the road. One day he called Paul to his dressing room, where he was relaxing in his boxer shorts while drinking a beer. He offered Paul one, which he gladly accepted.

Paul sat down next to Meeker, who carefully evaluated his understudy. "So you think you're man enough to replace me as Hal in case I get sick or go on vacation?"

"You're great in the part," Paul said. "I couldn't really replace you. Of course, I'd try to give an adequate performance. Perhaps I'd feel the same way you did when you replaced Brando in *Streetcar*."

"That faggot," Meeker said with contempt. "Brando's a big fucking asshole. I was much better in the role of Stanley than he was. But he got all the credit."

"Who said life is fair?" Paul took a big gulp of his beer.

"I've called you here to give you one acting tip, and only one," Meeker said. "And you'd better listen and listen good. When you walk out on that stage, you've got to make every faggot in the audience dream of sucking your big dick. You've got to make every horny bitch in the audience want to get plowed by your whopper. If you don't have a big dick like I do, you've got to convince the audience you do."

"That beats everything I've ever learned at the Actors Studio," Paul said. "I'll heed your advice."

"Ever since you've met me, you've been salivating every time I come around," Meeker said. "Tonight's your lucky night. I didn't get any pussy last night, and I'm horny as hell." He reached inside his shorts and pulled out his penis. "Try this on for size."

"You've got the wrong bitch," Paul said. "I'll summon Kim Stanley for you." Paul slammed down his beer and headed for the door.

"Fuck you, faggot," Meeker called after him.

Years later Paul told Shelley Winters, "Meeker gave me a hot acting tip. But I don't think I ever really followed his advice until I made Hud."

The following afternoon Logan decided to rehearse his two understudies, both Paul and Joanne, in a slow jitterbug to the tune of "Moonglow." "This was the sexiest moment in the play," Logan told his actors. "While Hal is dancing with Madge, I want him to virtually fuck her—symbolically, that is."

After Joanne and Paul had gone through the routine three times, Logan grew frustrated. "With Meeker and Janice Rule, I get sizzle. With Woodward and Newman, I get fizzle. Let's do it again."

Paul still didn't please Logan, who urged him to "do some dirty dancing. Wiggle your ass more." The director put his hands on Paul's buttocks and moved them in rhythm to the music. "I had almost given up on them, and then all of a sudden they got it. They moved into each other like some sort of erotic mating dance. They were falling in love just like in Inge's script. But it wasn't play-acting. This was for real. After that dance that afternoon, I knew that Jackie had lost her husband."

Over a drink that night, Joanne confessed the truth to Logan. "I've set my hat for that guy. Married or not, I'm gonna get him."

***

Long ago, and Once Upon a Time on Broadway, it seemed important that a collection of producer Joshua Logan's peers were assembled to determine if then-neophyte actor Paul Newman was sexy enough to be assigned a leading role in William Inge's steamy "midsummer romance," *Picnic*, about sexual repression in a small midwestern town.

Their verdict? Whereas **Elia Kazan** (left) and **Tennessee Williams** (right) approved (Williams effusively so), **Dorothy McGuire** (center), recent star of *Gentleman's Agreement* (1947), was noncommittal.

Thanks to his promotion to the status of a featured player, Paul earned two hundred dollars a week. With trepidation, he approached the Broadway opening night for the Theater Guild's production of *Picnic*, which premiered on February 19, 1953, at the Music Box Theatre. Although Meeker, Kim Stanley, and Janice Rule stole the night, Paul's role as Alan did not go unnoticed. The critic, Richard Watts, Jr., cited his "excellent work" in the Inge play.

For the most part, critics praised Inge's latest stage play. Brooks Atkinson of *The New York Times* found it "more admirable than *Come Back, Little Sheba*." *The New York Post* cited its "gift for looking into the human heart." *The World-Telegram* claimed, "It draws its roots from the American soil."

One underground paper in Greenwich Village noted that "Horny women and homosexuals are flocking to see Bill Inge's *Picnic* just for a gander at Ralph Meeker. He struts his stuff in tight pants and boots, with his shirt off for most of the evening."

Walter Kerr was more ironic, writing in the *Herald-Tribune*: "Since Marlon Brando last appeared in these parts, the male is no longer male unless he is stripped to the waist, covered in sweat, and given to communicating by grunts, stammers, and the practice of spitting through his teeth."

***

Picnic would run for fourteen months and 477 performances, eventually winning the Pulitzer Prize.

During the run of Picnic, Paul had been seeing more of Joanne than his wife Jackie. Officially Paul assured fellow cast members that he and Joanne were "just friends." But no one, especially Kim Stanley or Logan, believed that. It was suspected that Paul had occasional sleepovers at Joanne's apartment on Fifty Sixth Street at Madison Avenue in Manhattan. It was a five-flight walkup.

A female cast member recalled that one day when she dropped in on Joanne, she found both Paul and Joanne stark naked, and painting the ceiling and walls of her cheap rental. Joanne wore a shower cap to protect her hair.

As Paul hurried to the bathroom for his clothes, Joanne claimed that they didn't want to spill paint on their street clothes.

***

When Ralph Meeker announced he was leaving on a two-week vacation, Josh Logan came to Paul and said, "Here's your big chance. At last you get to play Hal."

Paul was elated about his first big break on Broadway, until Logan punctured his balloon. "Frankly, I don't think you're sexy enough for the part. Meeker is very sexy on stage or off, from what I hear. But you're an uptight college boy, which is okay for the role of Alan, but not for Hal. Meeker acts from his crotch. You move across the stage like you don't even have a dick. Brando in *Streetcar* was a crotch actor. For this role you've got to be white, trashy and sleazy—a low-down sexual menace."

"I can do that," Paul said. "Give me a chance. I'll study. I'll work with you. I'll do anything."

"Okay, I'll take you out to my house for the weekend, but you've got to do everything I tell you to do. If you'll learn and cooperate, I'll mold you into Hal. I might even let you play Hal in the road show version."

Logan drove Paul to a friend's house in Connecticut, where they could be alone and undisturbed for the weekend. Details of what actually happened on that weekend are sketchy, the only surviving account being what Paul later confided to Shelley Winters. Reportedly, Logan insisted that Paul strip naked for the entire weekend, presumably to "get in touch with your crotch." Completely nude, Paul was rehearsed in how to walk like a stud, stand like a stud, and move like a stud. In spite of his initial reluctance to appear nude before Logan, he grew more comfortable under the director's tutelage. "Even though you're wearing pants, I want the audience to be aware of your crotch at all times."

Paul told Shelley it was "a boot camp initiation. I wasn't happy satisfying the voyeuristic pleasures of a closeted homosexual, but I knew he could teach me something—and he did. I know I've got a lot to learn. I just can't do sexual menace like Meeker and Brando. Maybe it'll come to me."

Of course, Shelley asked the obvious question. "Did you guys get it on?"

"In a very one-sided way," Paul said. "I figured that if I could give it to Inge, I might as well pump it to Logan. He had such praise for my dick that when we drove back to Manhattan that Monday morning, I felt it was fourteen inches long."

Years later, Paul gave a highly edited version of his experience with Logan to a reporter from *The New York Times*. "At that time in my career, I probably wasn't a sexual threat like Logan suggested. When he told me to get in shape, I thought he meant spend six hours in the gym every day. I went to work to build up a muscled physique, which I've been working on ever since and certainly have shown off plenty of times on the screen. That 'lack of sexual threat' comment still rankles me, though. I've been chewing on that one for almost thirty years."

***

Word had gone out along Broadway and had even reached Hollywood that a hot new star was appearing on Broadway, taking over for Ralph Meeker in Picnic. "It didn't match the excitement that Brando had generated," Shelley Winters said, "during his performance in *Streetcar*, but the word was out to catch Newman's act."

Movie studios, even potential stars wanting to play one of the parts, arrived nightly. Paul didn't need to make any phone calls to alert potential producers or directors. The New York papers widely publicized his appearance.

Just before one of his performances, during his second week as Hal, he was alerted by both Inge and Logan that Frank Sinatra and Marilyn Monroe were in the audience. "I wasn't just nervous that night, I had butterflies coming out of my asshole," Paul told Geraldine Page. "I wasn't so afraid of Marilyn, but of Sinatra. For some reason, I thought he'd make fun of me. I knew he hated Method actors like Brando."

Backstage, Marilyn chose not to be herself that night, but appeared as all that was good, bad, glamorous, and phony about a movie star. "She was beautiful and tacky at the same time," Paul later told Shelley Winters, her former roommate.

After wrestling **Paul Newman** away from his then-wife and troubled son, **Joanne Woodward** became fifty percent of Hollywood's then-most-photogenic working couple.

With that breathy voice and exaggerated sexuality, she came on strong, kissing Paul on the lips as part of his introduction to Sinatra. "She was playing the bubble-headed innocent number she did in *Gentlemen Prefer Blondes*, but I knew right from the beginning that she was one smart cookie," Paul said.

Sinatra was still depressed and almost suicidal over the recent breakup of his marriage to Ava Gardner. But, in spite of Paul's fears about meeting him, he warmly extended his hand and congratulated Paul on his performance. "You're great, kid," Sinatra told him. "Originally Logan wanted Brando for the part. That jerk would have fucked it up big time."

"Now, now Frankie," Marilyn said. "Marlon has his nice side."

"Yeah, right," Sinatra said.

Paul accepted their invitation for an après-theater dinner. Every head in the restaurant turned to watch Marilyn slither across the restaurant floor. Paul and Sinatra were virtually ignored by the rubber-neckers.

Over drinks and dinner, Paul deciphered the real purpose of the visit. Marilyn was lobbying for the role of Madge in the movie version of *Picnic*. "Janice Rule would be okay," Marilyn said, "but no sex appeal. In the movies, you've got to have sex these days to lure them away at night from The Box."

"If you say so, sugar," Paul said, feeling tipsy from the wine. Being in the presence of two fabled stars, and accepted by them as an equal, was going to his head even more than the wine.

Shortly after midnight the party was over, and Sinatra suggested they go back to his hotel suite for a nightcap. Marilyn giggled and Paul readily accepted.

En route to Sinatra's hotel, Marilyn whispered in Paul's ear that Sinatra was so horribly depressed over Ava that she was trying to help him get over her.

"You're the gal to do it," Paul assured her.

Back in Sinatra's suite, the champagne flowed. Marilyn didn't like the hard stuff. She gave them a detailed description of how she'd play Madge differently from Janice Rule's interpretation. Shortly after 1:30AM, Sinatra rose to his feet. "I'm going to leave you kids alone for some fun while I hit a late-night spot with some buddies of mine." He leaned over and kissed Marilyn, patting Paul's cheek. "Take good care of our gal," he told Paul. "For this, you're gonna owe me big time."

When he was gone, Marilyn giggled and snuggled up close to Paul. "Now I want to know something."

"Ask me anything," he said.

"What does the most beautiful boy on Broadway do with the most glamorous star in Hollywood when they're alone together?"

"I can answer that," he said, as his lips came down on hers.

PICNIC SEGUNDO
(I.E., THE MOVIE)
WILLIAM HOLDEN STRIPTEASES FOR CINEMASCOPE

Audrey Wood sold *Picnic's* film rights to Columbia Pictures, where studio mogul Harry Cohn scheduled it for a big-budget movie adaptation and a CinemaScope release in 1955.

Many male stars were considered as candidates for the male lead, Hal Carter. For reasons of his own, Cohn did not evaluate either of the actors then appearing in *Picnic's* Broadway version (Ralph Meeker and Paul Newman) as suitable.

"Charlton Heston," according to Cohn, "certainly has the body for it. So does Burt Lancaster, but Tony Curtis is too, too 'The Bronx.' We need someone wholesome. Warren Beatty could do it."

Despite his earlier considerations, Cohn eventually decided to offer the role to William Holden. "He can play that drifter who hops off a freight train and sets all the female hearts in this one-horse town fluttering."

Holden was eager to fulfill his contract to Columbia: "Cohn has abused me for years, taking advantage," he said. As the vehicle that would wipe out his contractual obligations, all parties agreed that Holden would be paid only $35,000, a figure much less than the usual $250,000 he'd been getting for his involvement in most other film projects.

Although he was still in good physical shape, Holden believed that at the age 37, "I'm a bit too ripe for striptease."

[Over the years, Holden had never showed qualms about stripping down for certain ladies—most notably Jacqueline Kennedy, who was married at the time to a Senator from Massachusetts who was dreaming of running for President of the United States one day. Holden had also deflowered a number of screen goddesses, beginning with Barbara Stanwick and moving on to Grace Kelly, Audrey Hepburn, Lucille Ball, Shelley Winters, Dorothy Lamour, and Susan Hayward.]

Marilyn appears here in a movie star moment, singing her all-time most famous musical number, "Diamonds Are a Girl's Best Friend," in *Gentlemen Prefer Blondes* (1953) opposite Jane Russell.

Marilyn, however, wanted more dramatic roles like *Picnic, Baby Doll,* and *Cat on a Hot Tin Roof.*

Holden was informed that for "artistic reasons," the film's producers had demanded that he shave off his body hair every morning. Its director, Joshua Logan, would send a young man from the makeup department, for whom he'd remove his clothing, "down to your pubic hair, which you're allowed to keep. After all, there are censors. But this Little Miss Nancy will insist that you strip completely nude for him every morning."

Although Janice Rule had screen-tested for the movie version of the role she had successfully interpreted on the stage, Cohn wanted his relatively new discovery, Kim Novak, as the film version's female lead.

Susan Strasberg would portray her younger sister, "a tomboy with brains and an artistic vision."

Betty Field would play the long-suffering, rueful, and heartbroken mother who, as a young girl, had run off with a man much like Hal Carter.

Rosalind Russell, in a memorable performance, was cast as the sexually frustrated teacher who had been waiting and waiting for her boyfriend, Howard Bevans (Arthur O'Connell) a cornpone store owner, to propose marriage. [Of all the stars in the film version, O'Connell would be the only one nominated for an Oscar (as Supporting Actor), losing the award to Jack Lemmon for his portrayal of the lead character in Mr. Roberts.]

In the contest for Best Picture of the Year, *Picnic* was bested by Marty, starring Ernest Borgnine, who also won the Best Actor Oscar. Logan lost the award as Best Director.

At the Academy Awards presentation, *Picnic* was nominated for six Oscars, winning for Best Art Direction, Best Set Decoration, and Best Film Editing. Also, the musical "Theme from Picnic" morphed into a hit that reached number one on the Billboard charts of 1956.

Rosalind Russell's most dramatic scene, one of the most insightful into the much-repressed 1950s, occurred when as a sexually frustrated spinster, she rips off Holden's shirt, then bitterly denounces him as a bum.

Nick Adams, dating Natalie Wood at the time, played Bomber, a small-town newspaper delivery boy. He had been a close friend (some witnesses said "more than close") of both James Dean and Elvis Presley.

Holden delivered his own review of the screen version of *Picnic*: "Rosalind Russell is vividly scary as an older schoolteacher who foolishly lunges after Hal. Betty Field is just right as Madge's wistful, once-beautiful mother."

In his review, he left out any mention of Novak, his leading lady, but said to Russell, "She has absolutely no sense of humor. She's ice water."

He later told Harry Cohn at Columbia, "Novak's a pain in the ass, but from what I hear, you know more about her ass than I do."

Holden's performance won almost universal praise, Variety writing, "As the drifter, he is sometimes ribald, partly sympathetic and colorful, and giving a forceful interpretation all the way."

In 1966, critic Stephan Holden (no relation) reviewed the restored film, writing, "Today, it probably wouldn't be worth more than a PG-13 rating, if even that, but in 1954 the 'Moonglow Dance' between Holden and Novak and the torn shirt sequence were about as steamy as Hollywood could get in evoking explosive sex."

Picnic has been remade twice, first in 1986 with Gregory Harrison and Jennifer Jason Leigh, and again in 2000 as a made-for-TV version with Josh Brolin and Gretchen Moll.

A PLAYWRIGHT'S FINAL CURTAIN

Darwin had dinner with William Inge on one of his last nights in New York.

"It wasn't exactly a dinner," Darwin said. "All he would eat was red cherry Jello."

"The New York critics had driven him to despair with their hostile reception of his latest play, *Natural Affection*, even though it had a top director, Tony Richardson, and a first-rate star, Kim Stanley.

It had opened at the Booth Theatre during a devastating newspaper strike that severely limited its advance publicity and pre-opening buzz. Adding to the strikes against it, *Time* magazine reviewed the play as "a roiling, quivering hysteria of a child's uncontrollable tantrum."

"It's time for me to get out of Dodge to avoid more bullets aimed at my weak heart," Inge said. "I'm not coming back. I know you visit Los Angeles. Drop in on me to make sure I'm still alive. I see Warren (Beatty) has done very well without me."

That same year (1963) Inge faced another disappointment with the release of the horribly named movie, *The Stripper*, which was based on his play, A Loss of Roses.

Jerry Wald, its producer, had promised Audrey Wood that it would be configured as a star vehicle for Marilyn Monroe and singer Pat Boone.

But by the time the film went into production, Monroe was dead [suicide or murder—take your pick], and Boone had rejected any involvement in the film "for moral reasons."

Richardson replaced Monroe with Joanne Woodward. Supporting players included Claire Trevor, Carol Lynley, and a real stripper, Gypsy Rose Lee.

The character defined as "the young man"—originally portrayed in its stage version by Warren Beatty—was awarded to Richard Beymer, who had scored a bit hit in *West Side Story* (1961).

Over the next decade, Darwin visited his long-time friend whenever he flew to Los Angeles. "He seemed to be sinking deeper and deeper into depression and alcoholism," Darwin said.

On the night he saw Darwin for the last time, he gently reached for his hand, shaking very nervously.

"I wish you a long and happy life," Inge said to him. "Of course, like the rest of us, you can't expect one, but it's the wish that counts."

"Thanks, Bill. The theater will be reviving your plays for the next two centuries, at least."

"My talent for writing has vanished," Inge said. "Tennessee keeps turning out crap, but I've given up."

At the age of sixty, Inge committed suicide by carbon monoxide poisoning on June 10, 1973.

William Holden with Kim Novak in the 1955 film version of William Inge's play, *Picnic*.

In Memory Of Darwin's Brilliant, Tormented, and Under-Appreciated Friend,

WILLIAM INGE
(1913-1973)

Rest In Peace

Chapter Three

JOAN BLONDELL
A Magnolia House "Regular"

PORTRAIT OF A MOVIE STAR

The James Cagney "Gun Moll & Gold Digger."

She Seduced Hollywood, Errol Flynn, & Clark Gable & Married Dick Powell & Mike Todd.

Surviving a long and sometimes lustrous career, while leading a life of passion and heartbreak, **Joan Blondell** was a leading lady of the 1930s. Although her heyday ended, some said, in the mid-1950s, she continued to work in movies for the rest of her life.

She was known for her luminous saucer eyes, "my big knockers," her "cello" voice, and her megawatt smile.

She appeared with, and often seduced, her leading men: Humphrey Bogart, James Cagney, Errol Flynn, Leslie Howard, Clark Gable, and Dick Powell (she married him.) She also wed Mike Todd before Elizabeth Taylor snared him.

She also held her own against such formidable stars as Jean Harlow, Bette Davis, Barbara Stanwyck, Loretta Young, and Margaret Sullavan.

"Blondell was the screen's sexiest female, and I've bedded Ava Gardner"
—George C. Scott

Darwin bonded with the legendary Joan Blondell at the end of her national tour in the James Leo Herlihy play, *Crazy October*. "Of all the movie stars I've interviewed or known, she was that special someone," he said, "a great lady who'd seen and done it all. I adored her, especially when she came to stay with me at Magnolia House during her stopovers in New York. In Hollywood, I became her guest. A good cook, she even got me addicted to her favorite vegetables, rutabagas mashed with potatoes."

Joan Blondell was a hugely important movie star from vintage, pre-Code Hollywood.

But like a revered classic film, she remained hip, emotionally generous, and thoroughly modern, especially during her many visits to Magnolia House.

"The reason I agreed to take the second lead in *Crazy October* was that it gave me the chance to work with the great Tallulah Bankhead," she said. "But after I joined the cast, I was terribly disappointed in her. She appeared on stage drunk most of the time—one of the most unprofessional and foul-mouthed actresses I've ever starred with. After our first tryout, she realized I had the better part, and was getting the most laughs, and she resented me for it."

"I'd been cast in the play as an over-the-hill actress, remembering the loves of yesterday that seemed to have been blown away by the summer wind. And as the tour moved on, I became more sympathetic to Tallulah. She was a lonely and depressed woman, staging a kind of last hurrah. On one desperate night, I'll always recall, she confessed that she wanted to die."

"Crazy October was anything but a masterpiece, but we soldiered on," Joan said, "playing to packed houses. We found our most receptive audience in San Francisco. Tallulah is virtually a gay icon."

During Darwin's frequent conversations with Joan, she supplied him with much insider information that went into his biographies, especially The Secret Life of Humphrey Bogart (1899-1931), published in 2003, and Humphrey Bogart: The Making of a Legend, published in 2010.

"Joan was filled with revelations, including her on-again, off-again affair with Bogie, as well as information about some of her co-stars, notably

Errol Flynn and Clark Gable," Darwin said. "She discussed her ill-fated marriages to showman and producer Mike Todd and later, to the singer, actor, and director, Dick Powell. She also supplied fascinating tidbits about her frequent co-star, James Cagney, and her own decades-long career as a hoofer and later as a major-league star."

Blondell made seven films with Cagney. "Wherever I go today, I'm always asked, 'What was Cagney really like?'"

She also made nine films with her second husband (Powell) and two each with Ginger Rogers and Barbara Stanwyck.

In Three on a Match in 1932, Joan appeared with the emerging stars Bette Davis and Ann Dvorak. "Bogie had the male lead."

Warners cast her with saucy Glenda Farrell, a former hooker, in eight separate movies, marketing them as "snappy, wise-cracking broads."

Her male co-stars included Clark Gable, Errol Flynn, Bing Crosby, John Wayne, and William Powell. "I had affairs with most of them," she admitted.

Born in New York in 1906 to a vaudeville family, Joan was originally known as "Rosebud Blondell."

With her family, she spent six years in Australia before moving to Texas, where in 1926, she became "Miss Dallas."

"A year later, I almost became Miss Universe," Joan said, "and I was fourth runner-up representing the Lone Star State in the Miss America competition."

Joan Makes Her Screen Debut With
JAMES CAGNEY,
Former Drag Queen & Hoofer

Joan's goals involved becoming a stage actress, so she relocated to New York City. There, she met James Cagney, with whom, in the 1930s at Warner Brothers, she would co-star in seven movies.

In 1929, Joan and Cagney appeared together at the Fulton Theatre in Penny Arcade, a three-act drama about murder and bootleggers against the backdrop of a seedy amusement park.

Al Jolson went to see the play and bought its film rights for around $25,000, later reselling them to Warner Brothers.

The studio imported Blondell and Cagney to Hollywood for a three-week work gig, paying each of them a salary of $250 per week. The title the studio eventually selected for the play's rebirth as a movie was Sinners' Holiday. Emerging from all that was a studio contract, and the two hoofers soon developed niches for themselves at Warners that would continue until the dawn of World War II.

The movies had learned to talk, and many of the stars from the silent screen had voices that were judged as "unusable," and in some cases, "laughable." Some of the players barely spoke English.

An influx of stage actors was surging into Hollywood. They included Barbara Stanwyck, Katharine Hepburn, Kay Francis, Bette Davis, Claudette Colbert, Miriam Hopkins, Ruth Chatterton, Sylvia Sidney, and Ann Harding.

Contrary to rumor, Joan never had an affair with Cagney. Her lover became Lewis Warner, the son of studio mogul, Harry Warner. Their affair lasted for four months but ended with his death from pneumonia at the age of twenty-two.

Cagney admired Joan's talent. "She looked like a tootsie, so I called her Grandma. It was a joke, of course. If she didn't look so hot, she might have gotten better roles than the crap that Warners dished out. I don't mean she could have played Lady Macbeth but she might have made a fine dramatic actress. She later proved herself in the '30s. Before that, Jack Warner cast her as a floozie, a gun moll, a gold digger, or as the sister of the leading lady."

Before Sinners' Holiday was released, Joan was rushed into another quickie film, *The Office Wife* (1930), starring the largely forgotten star, Dorothy Mackaill. Mackaill played a secretary who gets involved with two men simultaneously. With dark hair, Joan played her sister. "In my opening scene—remember this was still the era of pre-Code—I'm pictured rolling out of bed to meet the dawn. I perform a kind of striptease, taking off my lingerie and heading for the bathtub."

When Jack Warner first saw Joan on the screen, he fired off a memo to producer Hal Wallis. "We must put a brassière on Joan Blondell and make her cover up those big tits, or else her pictures will be banned. I like to see

When film historians talk about **Blondell and Cagney** (as in photo above), it's in the context of OLD, ART DECO, PRE-CODE Hollywood--the equivalent of discussing a Rembrandt or a Vermeer ("An Old Master") in the art world.

a dame show off what she's got, but we can't let it spill out like those milk jugs of Blondell. By the way, while you're at it, change her name to Inez Gomez."

Joan usually followed orders, but she rejected the name of Inez Gomez. "Blondell is a great name for the marquee," she claimed—and she was right.

Joan and Cagney teamed up to film *The Public Enemy*, a gangster flick released in 1931. "I had to compete with two of Jimmy's mistresses, Jean Harlow and Mae Clark."

One scene in the movie became one of the most iconic in film history. Bored with his mistress, Kitty (as portrayed by Clarke), Cagney shoves a grapefruit into her face. Bosley Crowther of *The New York Times* wrote: "This was and remains one of the cruelest and most startling acts ever committed on film."

Despite its cruelty, it shot Cagney's fame to the moon, and it shot adrenaline into the career of its female star, the platinum blonde, Jean Harlow, too. Coming in as "also rans," Blondell and Mae Clarke were cast as *a pair of "night club tarts." [A year before, in 1930, Harlow's career had enjoyed a significant boost from her performance in* Hell's Angels, *a technically complicated film produced by her lover at the time, Howard Hughes.]*

After *The Public Enemy*, Joan was teamed with Cagney in *Blonde Crazy* (1931), another pre-Code drama in which she plays his very blonde and frequently wise-cracking partner in crime. Cagney informs her that "the age of chivalry has passed. This is the age of chisery."

In one scene, he toys with her bra and panties, perhaps evoking memories of his early start in show business when he was a drag queen.

"Cagney was such a tough guy on the screen, a man handy with his fists. I was surprised when he told me that early in his career that he was a female impersonator. Then he showed me pictures of himself in drag…There he was, for all the world to see."

That's a tough drag queen! Left photo shows **James Cagney** smashing grapefruit into the face of **Mae Clark**; right-hand photo show him (third from left) in a **drag review**.

BLONDELL: Portrait of a Golden Age, Pre-Code Movie Star

Cagney and Joan co-starred yet again together in *The Crowd Roars* (1932) with Ann Dvorak in a supporting role. In it, Cagney played a daring race-car driver. His younger brother, Eric Linden, cast as Eddie, meets a young woman named Ann (Joan). He falls in love, but Cagney labels her as "a racetrack broad not worthy of you."

As Ann, Joan delivered her opinion of men: "You can take those hard-drinking, hard-riding men and put them in a truck and shove them over a cliff."

Joan met her second husband, Dick Powell, when she and Cagney starred together in *Footlight Parade* (1933) with Ruby Keeler.

Joan played Cagney's secretary, waiting for him to come to his senses and "realize I'm the gal for him."

Facing her rival, Claire Dodd, Joan delivers her best-known line of the 1930s. After tossing her out on the street at 3AM, she says, "Outside, Countess, as long as they've got sidewalks, you've got a job."

Also paired together in that film were Powell and Keeler, the co-stars of *42nd Street*. One scene—an aquacade—depicted a hundred bathing beauties placed into geometric, artfully re-arranging patterns of legs, limbs, and torsos that evoked a kaleidoscopic view of flowers bursting into bloom.

Joan's final picture with Cagney was *He Was Her Man* (1934). The dynamics of the script were something of a cliché: He played a gangster, and she was cast as a (reformed) prostitute.

After making all those 1930s films with Cagney, Joan rarely saw him after their run of films was over. They did meet again after World War II. By then, he'd begun spending enormous amounts of his free time with Audie Murphy, the most-decorated hero of World War II.

"I'm trying to make Audie a movie star," he said, "but it's an uphill battle. The other day, I tried to teach him the waltz clog *[a popular stage dance at the time]*, but failed. I've taken some full-frontal nudes of him to see how his body photographs. They're only for my private collection, of course. I also have nudes of Errol Flynn and Johnny Weissmuller."

"Audie is the son of Texas sharecroppers, and he has this hayshaker walk. But he's a dear boy."

Joan was left with the distinct impression that Cagney was attracted to the war hero, but, as she later said, "I'm sure it was a love unfulfilled."

Three huge stars of their era: top moving down: Ruby Keeler, James Cagney, and Joan Blondell in *Footlight Parade* (1933).

BLONDELL & THE KING OF HOLLYWOOD

"I Can't Replace Carole Lombard In Your Life"
—Joan Blondell to Clark Gable

In *Illicit* (1931), Joan's first picture with Barbara Stanwyck, she was cast as Dukie, a roughneck playgirl pal to the star. "I was told to be a good-natured gal who'd seen and done it all," Joan said.

She and Stanwyck became friends during the shoot, although Joan told Cagney and others, "I think Barbara wants to carry it a little beyond the friendship realm into something more personal. But I'm not that kind."

The film ran into censorship problems because of its depiction of premarital sex.

Two views of **Audie Murphy,** who--rather clunkily and with a lot of bumps, grinds, and psychotic moments--tried to leverage a Hollywood career from his status as the most-decorated veteran of World War II.

Thinking it was good publicity for future war efforts, the Department of Defense did everything it could to help.

Joan was also cast with Stanwyck in *Night Nurse* (1931), playing the star's insolent, gum-chewing sidekick.

In *Night Nurse*, Clark Gable, in one of his early films, was cast as an amoral chauffeur. "I swooned when he came on the set," she said. "He had such animal magnetism. I shacked up with him that night. I don't know if he ever got around to Stanwyck or not. And although he went on to dozens of other seductions, he was not gone from my life completely," she said.

After Gable returned from World War II, Joan played the third lead in his comeback picture, *Adventure* (1945), co-starring Greer Garson.

As an airplane pilot, Gable had flown dangerous missions over Germany. He told Joan, "Hitler wanted me to be captured alive. As I was told, he planned to exhibit me nude like a caged animal, mocking my image as King of Hollywood."

"On the screen, Greer Garson was his lover, but she and Clark had no chemistry at all," Joan said. "Offscreen, he made love to me, not Greer."

"Clark adored women but not in a lechy way. He worshipped beauty.

His eyes would sparkle when he saw a beautiful woman, and he'd set out to get her. Usually, he succeeded."

"He was boyish yet manly, a brute—all kind of goodies. When he grinned, you melted. He had the hormones of any gal working overtime unless she was dead, and then I'm sure he could have revived her with a kiss."

In the late 1940s, during her marriage to the movie producer Mike Todd, Gable phoned Joan and set up a private dinner with her. He'd heard how violent Todd was, and he urged her to divorce him.

"Even though she'd died in an airplane crash in 1942, Clark was still mourning the loss of his wife, Carole Lombard."

"I found that he was very lonely, so I kept inviting him over when Mike was away. I still remember those juicy steaks he brought from his ranch and even fresh milk for me."

"On occasion, he turned to me for love-making, asserting that I was the only woman in Hollywood who reminded him of Carole. I felt he was not making love to me, but to his long-gone wife."

"One night, he even proposed marriage, but I turned him down—imagine, Miss Rosebud Dallas turning down the great Clark Gable. But I did. I told him that no other woman, not even me, could replace Carole Lombard in his life."

Clark Gable with Blondell in *Night Nurse*. He played a woman-abusing, rough and tough chauffeur. *Film Daily* claimed that Blondell walked off with the picture, in part because of her wisecracking and comedy antics.

Barbara Stanwyck and Blondell appear in a Pre-Code scene in *Night Nurse* with vaguely lesbian overtones. *Hollywood Reporter* said the best thing in the movie was Stanwyck and Blondell stripping two or three times.

More **Blondell with Gable** on the set of *Adventure* (1945), a romantic drama made a few months after World War II.

She played a slightly giddy blonde who goes for sailors, particularly Gable. *Motion Picture Herald* called her "a sheer delight."

BOGIE & BLONDELL

"I Got Him Before Lauren Bacall."
—Joan Blondell

It was Friday night and everyone in Hollywood except Humphrey Bogart seemed to be having a good time. His wife, Mary Phillips, had said that during their separation he was free to date. So far, he'd met no one.

He then remembered that bouncy blonde bombshell, Joan Blondell, with whom he'd appeared in that Ruth Etting flick, *Broadway's Like That* (1929). He searched through his papers until he found her number.

Feeling a bit shy, he went to the phone. It was probably a useless gesture. A woman as sexy as Joan Blondell probably had guys lining up at her door, especially on a big date night like Friday in Hollywood. "What the hell," he said, deciding to ring her up anyway.

This publicity shot was widely distributed by the studio in 1939 after **Gable and Lombard** returned from their honeymoon.

Blondell, as a "great broad" who recognized the importance of love, graciously relinquished Gable.

***

"Say hello to Miss Dallas, honey," the expressive face with the pop eyes said to Hump as she pulled up in front of his apartment house to find him already waiting on the sidewalk. "I'm Miss Dallas, Texas, and I've got the pictures to prove it."

"Good to see you out here in Hollywood," Hump said, leaning in to kiss Joan on the lips. "Here we are: Two stars of tomorrow."

"Get in, handsome." Her big smile and big blue eyes lured him into the passenger seat of her secondhand 1927 Dodge, with its dented fenders and ripped canvas hood tied down with a rope to keep it from flapping. "As you can see, this ain't no Gloria Swanson limousine," Joan said.

She drove toward Santa Monica where she knew a small and charming Italian restaurant where they could dine quietly. On the way there, he brought her up to date on what was happening—or not happening—to his career at Fox.

With a youthful exuberance lighting up her kewpie doll face, she told him about her own career. "I've been out here long enough to know that Warners has got me pegged as a brassy, gum-chewing, wise-cracking blonde floozy. But better that than no work at all."

"I hear that back East a lot of us thespian hacks are out of work," he said. "They call it a Depression."

"Jimmy Cagney and me are going to try to make the world forget its troubles," she said. "They signed us both to five-year contracts. He gets the big bills. I get the small change. But it's a job. I'll take any part they want me to play. The only thing I'm fighting is my name change."

"I think Joan Blondell is a great name for a movie star," he said. "What did the Warner friars come up with?"

"Inez Holmes."

He burst into laughter and reached for a cigarette, offering her one.

"Don't laugh too loud," she said. "You don't think Fox is going to let you keep 'Humphrey,' do you? Bogart is okay, but 'Humphrey?'. I'm sure they're going to change it to something like Dale or maybe Cary. What about Brad?"

"Hell with that," he said. "It's going to be Humphrey Bogart or nothing. Don't let them rename you Inez Holmes. Warners will take enough from you. Hold onto that name, girl."

Over dinner he got to know her for the first time, as, except for a one-night sexual encounter back in New York, they'd hardly gotten acquainted.

Before the spaghetti was served, he'd learned that her father, Ed Blondell, had been one of the original Katzenjammer Kids. Joan was a true "born in a trunk" show biz woman, reared on vaudeville stages, having made her first appearance at the age of three months when she was brought out before the lights as a "carryon" in the play, *The Greatest Love*.

"I grew up on the stage," she said. "I've taken more baths in train station toilets than anyone."

"How did you get the nickname, Rosebud?" he asked.

"We toured everywhere," she said. "Ed even took the Blondells to China. My big

Bogie with Blondell in *The Stand-In (1936)*.

According to Blondell, "I liked him more than a lot. He should have married me instead of Mayo Methot. Of course, there was a problem. I was also in love with Dick Powell."

Blondell with Leslie Howard in a scene from *The Stand-In*. She stole the picture from both Bogie and him when she performed a savage travesty of Shirley Temple singing "On the Good Ship Lollipop."

number was called 'In a Rosebud Garden of Girls.' Since then, only my intimates are allowed to call me Rosebud. But before the night is out, I hope you'll be calling me that." She leaned over and planted a light kiss on his lips.

"Before this night is over, I hope your rosebud and I are on intimate terms," he said.

"Now, now," she said. "No need to get vulgar. Let's keep it clean."

The waiter arrived with the veal parmigiana

After dinner they went for a walk along the Santa Monica pier, noticing the boats rocking from side to side as the water was choppy. He spotted a drunk throwing up over a railing.

"I'm living with Kenneth MacKenna," he said, "and my brother-in-law is visiting from the East Coast," he said.

"And I'm living with three broads and sharing the rent," she said. "But there are ways."

"What do you mean?" he asked.

"Have you ever tried it in the back seat of a broken-down Dodge?"

***

Bogie escorted Joan to the premiere of Night Nurse and later spoke about her to his best friend, actor Kenneth McKenna.

"She's my kind of broad. I like her tremendously, but I'm not in love with her. She's loyal, dependable, warm, loving, and forgiving when I stand her up."

"I don't think she'll ever become a big star. Neither will I. She takes every part Warners throws her way, never complaining. A real trouper. Sometimes, she makes two movies at once, rushing from one sound stage to another."

"In person, she has the same vitality she displays onscreen as a gold digger. She's brazen and fun to be with, and she doesn't take herself too seriously, like most Tinseltown dames. When I bed Joan, she makes me

Perhaps Joan Blondell had been prepped for the horrors of breaking into Pre-Code Hollywood by her vaudevillian father, **Ed Blondell**, whose image is positioned above.

Her father was one of the original "Katzenjammer Kids," based on the popular comic strip. Both of her parents, Ed and Katie, were overweight vaudevillians, hitting the stage in elaborate costumes with carefully rehearsed *schtick*.

The four of them, including sister Gloria, toured Honolulu, Australia, and New Zealand. Joan remembered the white sand beaches of Hawaii, running through a rice field wearing only a bra and a "shredded wheat skirt."

In Australia, she briefly fell in love with the son of a hotel manager.

There were horrors on the road as well. While driving through New Zealand, they came upon a scene where several black men were being lynched.

feel ten feet tall."

In *Three on a Match* (1932), Joan was pleased that Bogie was also in the cast, which otherwise starred Bette Davis and Ann Dvorak. In the late 1920s, Davis had been her classmate when they attended the Robert Milton/John Murray Anderson Theatre School in Manhattan.

On the set of *Three on a Match,* Davis approached her. "I'm miffed. Your part is better than mine."

[At that time, Warners thought that Blondell would become a bigger box office star than Davis. How wrong they were. The balance eventually swung in Davis' favor. In 1934, Davis, not Joan, was selected as Cagney's co-star in Jimmy the Gent. Adding to the perception that Davis was supplanting Joan in box office appeal, Bogie, too, would make several pictures with Davis, notably *The Petrified Forest* in 1936.]

***

On the set of *Big City Blues* (1932), Bogie told his co-star, Joan, that "I'm pissed off that our damn director, Mervyn LeRoy, has given me such a small part. I'm billed after you, Eric Linden, Jobyna Howland, Ned Sparks, and even Guy Kibbee. I'm a leading man, not a bit player."

Bogart later told LeRoy, "The only good thing about working on this turkey is that I can resume my affair with Blondell."

In *Big City Blues,* Joan was cast as Vida, a street-wise Manhattan gold digger who's tangled with too many Stage Door Johnnies in her day. She says, "Chorus girls used to get diamonds and rubies. But with the Depression, they now have to settle for a corned beef sandwich."

Both Bogie and Blondell got second-tier billing to a bigger star, Edward G. Robinson, when they appeared together in *Bullets or Ballots* in 1937. She played a shady nightclub owner in Harlem. The picture ran into trouble with the censors, and cuts had to be made before its release.

Her fourth appearance with Bogie—or fifth if you count that 1929 short—was the romantic comedy, *Stand-In* (1937). Joan played a character called Lester Plum, a cheerful former child star cast in the film as a stand-in for the actual star.

Leslie Howard was cast in it as a straight-arrow financial advisor who runs the studio. Bogie played a boozy producer trying to get a picture made called Sex and Satan.

Over lunch one day, Howard told Bogie, "I plan to seduce Blondell tonight."

The next day, Joan did not admit he'd achieved that goal, but reported, "Leslie is a little devil. He might be holding your hand while his other hand is going up the girl's dress who's sitting next to him. All the while, he's listening for his phone to ring to signal him that his wife is arriving at the gate."

Throughout the next few months, Joan and Bogie—both of whom were married to other people at the time—occasionally got together for a secret liaison. He told McKenna, "Sex with Joan has become what it's like between a married couple who've been going at it for a number of years. It's comfortable and safe, but completely without fireworks."

In 1938, during a farewell dinner with Joan, he told her, "Let's be friends…I mean pals, not lovers. Maybe we'll get together every other year or so for old time's sake. In the meantime, both of us have a lot of living to do, and Hollywood is riddled with temptation. It's around every corner."

"You've got yourself a deal, big, boy," she answered.

ERROL FLYNN
The Perfect Specimen

The tyrannical director, Michael Curtiz, was set to direct Errol Flynn in a movie entitled *The Perfect Specimen* (1937), which—of course—he was.

The role of its female lead—Mona Carter, a newspaper reporter—had already been offered to and rejected by Marion Davies, Carole Lombard, Rosalind Russell, Miriam Hopkins, and Olivia de Havilland. As for the male lead, before Flynn received his copy of the script, it had been turned down by Robert Montgomery. In defiance of the trend, after Joan read the script, she told Curtiz, "I'm game."

Written by Samuel Hopkins Adams—the author of the hugely successful *It Happened One Night*, a film that won an Oscar for Best Picture of 1934—The Perfect Specimen would mark Flynn's debut in a comedy.

In The Perfect Specimen, Joan crashes her car through the fence of an estate where Errol's character of Gerald Beresford Wicks has been kept a virtual prisoner from the real world.

His tyrannical aunt, as played by May Robson, treats him like a hothouse plant. Joan pulls him into the real world.

For a boxing scene, Errol had to go on a rigid diet, dropping twenty-five pounds to a weight of 175 pounds. Although he informed Joan that he had represented Australia as a boxer in the 1928 Olympics in Amsterdam, "That turned out to be just another of Errol's tall tales," she said.

"When I first met him on the Warners lot, his reputation had preceded him," Joan said. "As he shook my hand, I noticed that his eyes were flecked with gold. By the late 1930s, he was already known by his own assessment as 'The Phallic Symbol of the World,'"

"He'd married the French actress, Lili Damita, but that didn't stop him from seducing every beautiful woman he met," Joan said.

As a bisexual, the list of his sexual intimacies was already legendary. He'd already seduced Howard Hughes, Robert Taylor, Tyrone Power, Joan

Bennett, tobacco heiress Doris Duke, Hedy Lamarr, Ann Sheridan, and Evita Perón of Argentina. He told Joan that Lupe Velez had developed a quirky habit of crossing herself three times in advance of every time she had ever fellated him.

Jack Warner said, "You know Flynn: He's either fighting or fucking."

"I'm not a breast man," he told Joan, "although I see you're more endowed than all these no-tit gals like Ann Sheridan at Warners. I'm a leg man myself, and I could really go for those gams of yours. As you've heard, I have no trouble getting girls. My problem is escaping from them. I often come home at night to discover that three or four of them have broken into my house and are hiding under my bed. And often, usually when I'm relaxing in my dressing room reading the newspapers, three or four girls will arrive to devour parts of my naked body."

When Joan asked him about the secret of his celebrated sexual prowess, he said, "A bit of cocaine on the tip of my penis before intercourse does the trick. What else could it be?"

"Errol and I had a great rapport. We struck up a friendship right away, and he told me fascinating tales of his early life in the South Pacific. He claimed that for a while in New Guinea, he'd been a slave trader."

"I'm known for being a great swordsman," he said. "Actually, I'm not, except in one department. On the screen, during dueling scenes, I come across as a top swordsman. But between you and me, I stink. I'm horrible at fencing, afraid my opponent will cut off my most vital part. I won't tell you his name, but one of Warners' uncut actors was accidentally circumcised during the filming of a duel with me."

After their first afternoon of working together, he invited Joan to come home with him. "I'm as horny as a three-peckered billy goat."

"What a flattering invitation," she said. "I accept."

The next day, she confided to her frequent co-star, Glenda Farrell, "Every gal, at least once in her life, should have the chance to go to bed with Errol Flynn and enjoy his manly charms. And, at the rate he's going, every gal will get that chance."

In *The Perfect Specimen*, **Flynn** played a body beautiful "reared like a hothouse plant" until he encounters sexy **Blondell**, a newspaper reporter who sets out to teach him the facts of life.

MARRIAGES THREE
JOAN BLONDELL'S ILL-FATED NUPTIAL TRIO:
GEORGE BARNES, DICK POWELL, & MIKE TODD

"Three strikes and I'm out. As for Dick (Powell) & Mike (Todd), June (Allyson) and Elizabeth (Taylor) are welcome to them."
—Joan Blondell

HOW JOAN'S HUSBAND NO. 1 (GEORGE BARNES) INTRODUCED HER TO BACK ALLEY ABORTIONS

George Barnes was already a famous icon in Hollywood, hailed as its greatest cinematographer. Born in Pasadena in 1892, he'd been nominated for an Oscar at the dawn of the Academy Awards for his behind-the-camera work on *The Devil Dancer* (1927), co-starring Clive Brook and Gilda Gray, before the movies had learned to talk.

Over the course of his professional life, Barnes would be nominated for his cinematic skill a total of eight times, but he won only once, and that was for Alfred Hitchcock's *Rebecca* (1940), co-starring Laurence Olivier and Joan Fontaine.

At the last minute, Samuel Goldwyn phoned Joan and asked her if she could fill in for Carole Lombard, who had dropped out of Barnes' upcoming film, *The Greeks Have a Word for It*. [Its original title had been *The Greeks Have a Word for Them*, but censors found that title too provocative.]

Directed by Lowell Sherman, who also cast himself in the movie, the picture starred such reigning stars of that

Errol Flynn poses in the living room of his home on Mulholland Drive, an address where it was said that more orgies took place than at any other address in Hollywood.

His portrait hangs above the fireplace, the work of artist John Decker, the founding father of "The Bundy Drive Boys," a coven of broken-down booze-soaked actors, writers, and artists. Their ranks included John Barrymore.

day as Madge Evans, Ina Claire, and David Manners.

There was also a small role in it for a then-unknown newcomer (Betty Grable)whose career during World War II blossomed into a pin-up icon and later, "Queen of the Box Office." In fact, Joan Blondell first spotted her future husband during one of his exits from Betty Grable's dressing room.

"George was buttoning up his trousers," Joan said. "From that day forth, I set my hat for him," she said. "I'd never been attracted to a man like him. My goal, and it was a big one, was to take him away from 'Legs' Grable."

"You know what? During the war, Grable's left leg was voted the loveliest in the world. Okay, she had better legs than mine, but I jutted out in the best bosom war."

"At last, George started to notice me. One day, he told me he was working diligently to capture my beauty on camera. What actress wouldn't love a man who told her that?"

"We began to date. Was I impressed! Hollywood was a small town in those days, and an important guy like George knew the Hollywood elite."

"During our second date, he took me to a dinner party at the home of Ronald Colman, one of my screen idols. A suave, urbane English gentleman with that seductive voice and those impeccable manners."

"One by one, Miss Nobody from Dallas was hanging out with all these big stars. No one was a bigger name than 'The Great Profile' himself, John Barrymore. He invited me for a walk in the garden. There, he unbuttoned and showed me his penis. I ran back into the house."

"Over the next few weeks, as George and I dated, I met George Arliss (Bette Davis was welcome to him); Wallace Beery (a ghastly brute), Ruth Chatterton (a big snob who insisted she be billed as Miss Ruth Chatterton), Adolphe Menjou (the best-dressed man in Hollywood), and even Slim Summerville. That ugly former Keystone Cop was the least likely movie star ever to hit Hollywood. Slim told me that he began his career in Hollywood emptying cuspidors in men's latrines, but ended up starring with John Barrymore and with Little Miss Lollipop, Shirley Temple—what a brat!"

"My favorite times with George were private dinners alone with him. He was still married but going through his third divorce. That should have been a warning to me, but I was too much in love to notice. Samuel Goldwyn warned me about George, telling me this 'two timing Lothario' will break your heart."

After his divorce came through, Barnes and Joan were married in January of 1933 in Phoenix, Arizona. In a bizarre and perhaps drunken fit of misguided indiscretion, Joan's father, Ed Blondell, a vaudeville comedian, told her future husband that Joan, at the age of eight, had lost her maidenhead backstage in an accident involving the jagged edge of a costume trunk.

In advance of their marriage, Barnes never discussed the possibility of their having children, but a month after their wedding, he stridently insisted that he did not want to have any kids.

"Yet he did not practice birth control, asserting that protection reduced the sexual sensation for him. It was inevitable that I'd get pregnant several times. He introduced me to a series of back alley abortionists. One quack nearly killed me."

Once, I refused to have an abortion, and our son, Norman, was born. But George was indifferent to him. Later I had a daughter with Dick Powell. We named her Ellen. Dick adopted Norman and changed his name to Norman Powell. My son grew up to become a producer, director, and TV executive, my daughter a studio hair stylist."

"George never got over the resentment of my giving birth to our son," she said. "He often fought with me, insisting that I loved Norman more than I loved him. It was dreadful."

"As we drifted along with our marriage, he began to shut himself away from me," she claimed. "He would sit for hours looking off into space, and he became furious if disturbed. Slowly, ever so slowly, I began to fall out of love with him. And whenever we worked together, he insulted me, complaining how hard it was to shoot 'a god damn cow.'"

"The final straw came when I found out he was having an affair with Glenda Farrell, with whom I'd made all those movies. I felt betrayed on two levels. That squinty-eyed bitch, Glenda, had pretended to be my friend. Finally, I could take it no more."

In 1936, Joan appeared in divorce court. She cited Barnes' increasing alcoholism, his mental cruelty, and how he'd subjected her to frequent humiliation. She also claimed that he refused to pay any of the household expenses, and that she was supporting the family alone. She asked for no alimony, only the custody of Norman. The judge granted the divorce.

What she didn't tell the judge was that she'd fallen in love with Dick Powell, and that she would marry him later that year.

Blondell with her obsessively possessive Husband #1, **George Barnes**.

Suffering mental troubles, the great cinematographer fought with directors whenever he insisted on filming Blondell "only from the neck up."

After years of reflection, Blondell confided to Darwin at Magnolia House that Barnes never wanted to share views of her ample bosom and sexy curves with other males.

***

In May of 1953, Gloria Blondell, Joan's actress sister, phoned to say that George Barnes, Joan's first husband, had died at the age of sixty. By that point in his life, he had been married seven times, and had worked on 142 movies.

A Sad Song for Joan:
DICK POWELL
Life With A Crooner

Joan was strolling toward the commissary when she encountered her future husband, Dick Powell. Both of them were new to the Warner Brothers' lot.

They struck up a conversation, and he invited her to lunch. She found him "amiable, boyish, and bursting with energy." Born in Arkansas in 1904, he had dark, wavy hair and dimples. He'd been a crooner and a bandleader before landing a contract at Warner Brothers.

As one critic later claimed, "Dick Powell's most lasting image is still that of the wide-eyed hoofer, face alight with lewdness, tunneling through the splayed legs of Busby Berkeley's chorines in 42nd Street (1933)."

Another critic referred to him as "Warners' crooner-in-residence glowing with a kind of gosh-and-golly ebullience that wasn't to be taken seriously."

Joan didn't know at the time of their inaugural meeting that she'd co-star with him in nine movies.

After an unsuccessful first marriage to Mildred Maund, a childhood friend, Powell would eventually become a fixture in the bedrooms of such legends as Marion Davies, the mistress of William Randolph Hearst. He would go from there to seduce Ruby Keeler when they co-starred in *42nd Street*, and Ginger Rogers, his co-star in *20 Million Sweethearts* (1934). Evelyn Keyes and Ida Lupino each lay in his future.

Joan first worked with Powell in *Gold Diggers of 1933*, where she spent most of her off-screen time talking to Ginger Rogers, as Powell and Keeler disappeared during luncheon breaks into his dressing room.

This became the most famous Depression-era musical. In it, Busby Berkeley directed a swirling kaleidoscope of all-girl dancers who were reviewed as "intoxicating."

Joan rendered her famous and most stirring song, "Remember the Forgotten Man," with 150 male extras cast as hobos unfairly thrown out of work. It was later defined as the most socially compelling of any song to emerge from the Great Depression. *[Another, more cheerful, hit song from that film was "We're In the Money."]*

Powell appeared with Joan again in *Footlight Parade* (1933), except that this time, James Cagney was the star. Some critics have hailed this movie as "the best of the Depression-era musicals." The second leads were played by Keeler and Powell. *[Once again, Keeler and Powell scheduled their sexual trysts in his dressing room between takes.]*

Along with Adolphe Menjou, Joan was given top billing in *Convention City* (1933). Powell, along with Mary Astor, was a supporting player.

Exhausted from overwork, Joan didn't want to make the picture, but Jack Warner threatened her with suspension. Back on the lot, she was grateful to be reunited with Powell in yet another movie. "He was looking better and better every time I saw him," she said. "I kept wondering if he and I might hit some high notes."

Convention City ran into trouble with the newly formed Production Code, its board members interpreting the characters as "amoral." Cuts were demanded before it could go into general release.

In 1934, Joan and Powell were reteamed in *Dames,* once again with Ruby Keeler. "It seemed I couldn't shake this little dancing fool," Joan said.

Joan had a cat-and-mouse number in which she, cast as a cat, suggests to a rodent, "Come up and see my pussy sometime," aping the line that Mae West had made famous. Censors immediately yelled, "CUT! CUT! CUT!"

Any time she was on the screen, veteran actress ZaSu Pitts stole the show by interjecting her familiar "flibbertigibett" routine, using her fluttering and expressive hands and quavering voice.

Joan came on strong in the movie as a cutsie-pie blackmailer.

Another Busby Berkeley hit, *Dames* could easily have been retitled as *Gold Diggers of 1934*. At the time that it was being filmed, Production Code censors were avidly campaigning against "Hollywood smut."

Joan's most memorable number was "The Girl at the Ironing Board," in which the clothes she's pressing come to life with the help of thin, carefully concealed wires.

Since she was pregnant at the time, she had to be filmed at special angles to conceal her waistline.

In September of 1934, she went on maternity leave. Still married to George Barnes at the time, she named their infant son Norman Barnes, selecting "Norman" for its association with Claudette Colbert's husband, actor-director Norman Foster, a friend of the family.

In *Colleen* (1936), Powell and Keeler were co-stars, with Joan and Jack Oakie in supporting roles. "We might have been just the support, but Jack and I stole the picture," Joan said.

"Before filming began, I had to go on a diet," Joan said. "Orry-Kelly designed a beautiful dress for me, but I bulged at the seams. I dropped fifteen pounds before shooting began."

It was supposed to have been shot in Venice, Italy, but during its planning stages, its locale was moved to Venice, California.

Joan fought with Warners until the studio raised her salary to $1,600 per week.

It was cold during the shoot, and I was wearing this sheer gown, but Dick (Powell) wore red flannel long johns. He was banging me at the time, and I always made him take them off. In Colleen, and for the first time in real life, too, Dick and I played a romantic couple. Call it Art imitating Life!"

Joan was cast as Minnie, "an adenoidal, chocolate-dipping swindler," as the script defined her character. "I had to add wit to compensate for Keeler's dull *persona*," Joan said.

By September of 1935, Joan and Powell were dating steadily, even though her divorce from Barnes would not come through until 1936. The press took notice.

Around Warners, the couple were known as "Big Tits and Dopey." The

"**Ruby Keeler** (left) got to sample the manly charms of my future husband, **Dick Powell**, before I did," **Joan** (right) said.

"He was mine for some time until he met that nympho, June Allyson, falsely billed as 'America's sweetheart.' The bitch, who slept around a lot, was ANY man's sweetheart."

nickname fitted her, but Powell was no dope, as his later career as a director and as a tough guy star on screen would prove.

"We rushed through the shoot because we were to get married in a showcase wedding on September 11, 1936." During filming, she fell and "nearly broke my ankle," she claimed. "And my darling crooner came down with a case of laryngitis."

Hundreds of their fans showed up for their wedding. For some odd reason, her dress designer, Orry-Kelly, told the press, "Joan has the most beautiful mouth in Hollywood."

According to Joan, "He certainly didn't know from having engaged me in any lip-lock, as he was gay."

Cary Grant, Orry-Kelly's former lover, said, "Orry has the most overworked mouth in Hollywood, and seems to get around to servicing every male on the crew, even the straight ones."

"When you marry someone, you learn their bathroom secrets," Joan said. "Dick certainly had a problem."

She was referring to the fact that he had been born without a sphincter. Since he could not control his bowels, he had to live in cycles dominated by two different medications—one to induce constipation, the other, laxatives to purge himself.

***

Busby Berkeley cast Joan with Powell once again in **Stage Struck** (1936). Warren William had the third lead.

"Williams had been a big deal in films of the early 1930s," Joan said. "He often played suave rotters, and he looked like a combination of Mischa Auer and Basil Rathbone."

His leading ladies had included both Dolores Costello and Bebe Daniels. In *Gold Diggers of 1933*, he had played a millionaire who falls for Joan, cast as a showgirl.

"Off screen, he propositioned me, but I turned him down," Joan said. "In some way, working with him again, I saw my future. Big star today, and a 'has-been' in the years to come."

William ended his career in small roles in films churned out by Monogram Pictures, a studio usually trivialized as part of "Poverty Row." He died of bone cancer in 1948.

In 1937, Joan appeared once again with Powell in *Gold Diggers of 1937* with her by now familiar sidekick, Glenda Farrell. Busby Berkeley was at the helm, but, as the world was drifting to war, the "girls and glitter" theme had become a bit threadbare and passé.

In the end, it was all too suggestive and subliminally erotic, and **Joan** was just too deeply entrenched within the then-current wave of what was perceived as "immorality."

Censors from the Production Code swept the old, café-society hints and winks aside for a cleaner, less "decadent" look and style, and Hollywood got less fun and less prone to party.

Joan, amazingly, managed to continue her career, albeit in more restrained roles for wiser, older women.

After their first two years of marriage, and finding that they had very little in common, Powell and Blondell began to drift apart. "We were married for years, but he was more like a big brother to me than a husband. I was having an occasional fling on the side, and I suspected that he was, too. Eventually, we slept in separate bedrooms. I didn't want to be in the same room with Dick when he had to go to the toilet after those laxatives kicked in."

"He spent more and more time in his study, listening to the music of Bing Crosby, my former lover when we'd made East Side of Heaven in 1939 for Universal."

Joan's final co-starring role with Powell was at Paramount in the aptly named movie, *I Want a Divorce* (1940). "I think Paramount was trying to tell me something," Joan said. "They didn't invite me back for the next twenty-five years."

As the war-torn 1940s rolled in, many of Joan's rivals from the 30s had evolved into big stars, especially Barbara Stanwyck, Ginger Rogers, and Bette Davis, who had become the Queen of Warner Brothers.

In his review of *I Want a Divorce*, Bosley Crowther of *The New York Times* suggested that Joan stick to those "old-fashioned bed-and-board movies of the 1930s that she'd made for Warner Brothers."

"During my marriage to Dick, our best friends were Ronald Reagan and his wife, Jane Wyman. We dined with them either at their home or at our house at least once a week," Joan said. "Dick and Ronnie always talked politics, while Jane and I caught up on Hollywood gossip."

"She told me that Ronnie, at least in private, had this wild idea that he might run for U.S. President one day."

"What kind of First Lady do you think I would make?" Wyman asked.

"Certainly not one like Eleanor Roosevelt," Joan answered.

Joan sometimes had her movie wardrobe designed by **Orry-Kelly** (right), one of the leading dress designers in Hollywood. When **Cary Grant** was known as Archie Leach in New York, he was the designer's kept boy.

According to Orry-Kelly, "Leech was the right name for him, "because that's what he was—a goddamned leech."

As her marriage continued to unravel, Joan saw less and less of her husband. She learned that he was slipping around and seeing June Allyson, being billed at the time as "America's Sweetheart," usually opposite the gay actor, Van Johnson.

Soon, Powell and Allyson's sexual affair became more visible, thanks in part to their many appearances as a loving couple at the Mocambo, Ciro's, Chasen's, and Romanoff's.

Joan's divorce from Powell followed her appearance in court on July 15, 1944. "Actually, as the years went by, I began to feel sorry for Dick for having married that nympho, Allyson. I kept up on the gossip. She had replaced me at those dinners with Jane Wyman and Ronnie. Not only that, but she was having an affair with John F. Kennedy, too."

During their marriage to Powell, Allyson bedded some of her leading men, notably, Peter Lawford when they made *Good News* in 1947 and James Stewart when they shot *The Glenn Miller Story* in 1954.

Allyson also maintained side affairs with the bisexual actor, Alan Ladd, and later with Dean Martin, whom she asserted was "the love of my life other than Alan Ladd."

There was always bad blood between Joan and Allyson. But, as so often happens in Hollywood, rivals get cast in the same picture. Such was the case when "Joan & June" starred together in *The Opposite Sex* (1956).

In spite of their failed marriage and many betrayals, and despite the forceful objections of Allyson, Joan attended Powell's funeral on January 2, 1963.

Mourners reported that Joan was teary eyed at the services, and that she was greeted by Richard and Patricia Nixon, James Stewart, Walter Pidgeon, Barbara Stanwyck, and Ronald Reagan. Some eight hundred mourners, including the elite of Hollywood, attended.

Razzmatazz and Death Threats
Joan's Marriage to Showman
MIKE TODD

Around the World in 80 Days with Mae West

Elizabeth Taylor Waits in the Final Port

"I'll never marry an actress," claimed Mike Todd, the theater and film producer. "To live with an actress, you gotta be able to worry about her hair. When her bosom starts to drop, she gets panicky. You gotta pay all those bills from the headshrinker."

Obviously, Joan Blondell and Elizabeth Taylor changed his mind about marrying actresses.

In film history, Todd is known mainly for the 1956 release of *Around the World in 80 Days*. Its all-star cast included, among others, Frank Sinatra and Marlene Dietrich.

Here's the rundown that Joan Blondell delivered to Darwin Porter at Magnolia House about the unhappy trajectory of her marriage to Mike Todd, aka "Mr. Elizabeth Taylor."

The studio billed it as a comedy, but partly because of the realities whirling around her marriage to Dick Powell at the time, **Joan Blondell** (depicted above in *I Want a Divorce*) didn't think that any of it was particularly charming or funny.

Neither did audiences.

***

In 1943, Joan—married at the time to Dick Powell—ran once again into Todd. She thought that Damon Runyon's description of him was accurate: "A short, chunky and dark kind of guy, a human dynamo with a big cigar hanging out of the corner of his fast-moving lips, spitting out orders to his flunkies."

Born in 1909 in the unlikely locale of Minnesota, Todd was one of nine children reared in poverty. His father was an Orthodox Jewish rabbi. Young Todd came up the hard way, taking whatever jobs he could to survive: newsboy, soda jerk, even a shoeshine boy.

As an adult, he became a building contractor, working for studios in Hollywood. The Depression bankrupted his company, and he lost a million dollars, the equivalent of $15 million in today's currency. "I've been broke many times," he said, "but never poor. Poor is a state of mind."

His dream was to become a flamboyant Broadway producer in the style of high-flying Billy Rose. After many a failure, but with some big successes, he managed to produce seventeen Broadway shows.

Dick Powell and June Allyson making their offscreen affair very very visible in films like T*he Reformer & the Redhead (1950).*

Joan had met him in 1943 when Todd was trying to talk her husband, Dick Powell, into starring in a Broadway show, *Beat the Band.*

That casting didn't work out, but in its aftermath, Todd had informed his cronies: "I've met my dream girl, sexy Joan Blondell. When I saw this hot blonde with those big tits, I knew then and there I had to have her. God damn it, I'm gonna get her, too."

World War II was raging in Europe as the Allies desperately battled Hitler's Nazi empire. In the Pacific, Americans and their Allies were dying in their march, island to island, toward Japan.

Todd paid little attention to the war, as he had two simultaneous hits on Broadway, Star and Garter starring America's most famous stripper, Gypsy Rose Lee, and Something for the Boys, a frothy musical that showcased "The Belter," Ethel Merman.

During a meeting with Joan, Todd asked her if she'd star in the road show version of *Something for the Boys.* She was reluctant to do so, because she did not have Merman's vocal range, but she eventually accepted. *[As anticipated, critics noted "Joan Blondell is no Ethel Merman."]*

At the end of its run, Todd returned to Blondell with another offer, asking her to star in *The Naked Genius,* a backstage murder mystery written by Gypsy Rose Lee.

Again, Joan was reluctant to accept, but as she said, "that conniving little devil talked me into it. He did more than that. When I visited him at his hotel in New York, he ripped off my bra and attacked my breasts. My bloomers were the last to go. I was his willing victim. When he mounted a woman, he wasn't a man—he became a machine."

During rehearsals of *The Naked Genius,* she halted abruptly during one of her song and dance routines: "Mike, for god's sake, would you quit ogling my tits and concentrate on the number?"

Still married to Powell, she phoned him nightly, concealing her affair with Todd by constantly referring to him as "an A-1 jerk."

The Naked Genius opened at the Plymouth Theater on Broadway in October of 1943. Although its reviews had been hostile, the theater filled up every night. Audiences seemed to want to take their minds off the war, which at the time was going badly for the U.S. and its Allies.

"I'm humiliated every night I have to go on in this turkey," Joan told Todd.

Even though doing good business, he shut down the show but not before he sold its movie rights to 20th Century Fox.

Through her agent, Joan wanted to star in the movie, but to her chagrin, the role went to Vivian Blaine. A former "Big Band" singer, she delivered a bowdlerized *[i.e., selectively edited and sanitized]* version of Cole Porter's song, "Something for the Boys." Today, Blaine is best remembered for her film interpretation of Miss Adelaide, the brassy, nasal-voiced nightclub singer in the 1955 film version of Frank Loesser's hit, *Guys and Dolls*.

Todd tried to console Joan over the critical attacks on her performance in *The Naked Genius*: "All of life is just one big chance. Sometimes you lose, maybe quite a lot, but oh, how sweet it is when you win, which is just what I'm doing with you."

***

In 1944, back on Broadway and around the same time as his involvement with Joan, Todd geared up for another big smash, *Catharine Was Great*. It had been written by, and starred, the "one and the only" Mae West.

[The morning after its opening, critic George Jean Nathan wrote: "The scene in Mae West's Catharine Was Great *involving Mae and one of the actors in a bed was one of the dirtiest scenes shown on the New York stage in years, yet the mayor did nothing about it.*

The Herald Tribune said, "Mae West came to Broadway last night, decked out like a battleship in a swimming pool."]

Todd told his backers, "Mae will wiggle her way onto the stage as the Russian empress with the exaggerated zeal of a drag queen—and the audience will shout and hoot. The only down side for me is that she demands my fat Jewish dick at least once a day."

Apparently, that wasn't enough for Miss West. After surveying the men in the cast, she

The Hays office of blue-nosed censors levied a ban on much of the original script of *Belle of the Nineties*.

In their estimation, it was "vulgar and obscene, a glorification of crime and prostitution."

They went on to say that "Its general sympathies are on the side of Evil and Crime."

demanded that he fire some of them—"they're too effeminate"—and bring in some bigger, better-looking, and more studly young men."

"I can't," Todd protested. "We're in a war, and they're all in the Army."

At the end of every show, after the applause had subsided, West strutted forth to address her audience. "Catherine once ruled over thirty million Russians and took on 3,000 lovers. I can't match her in that number, but I can knock off at least a platoon in just two hours."

The audience burst into wild applause peppered with wolf whistles.

When that died down, she said, "C'mon, boys…come up and see me sometime."

***

By 1946, America had entered the post-war era. Dick Powell was a figure in Joan's past, but Todd was still married to Brenda Freshman. He'd fallen in love with her when she was only 14, back in Crown Point, Indiana. He'd married her on Valentine's Day, 1927. Two years later, Mike Todd, Jr. was born.

But over the years, Todd's love for Brenda had faded. In part because of his constant "womanizing," he was rarely at home with her.

One night in their kitchen, he told Brenda that he was divorcing her. She picked up a kitchen knife and lunged toward him, aiming at his heart. She slipped and fell, the knife plunging into the wooden door frame. As it did, its blade cut into her hand, severing a tendon.

Bleeding profusely, she was rushed to the Santa Monica Hospital. Doctors frantically tried to save her life during surgery, but she died on August 12, 1946 from what doctors defined as a collapsed lung.

An autopsy was ordered, and police grilled Todd about the knife attack. Many members of the police thought that it had been Todd, not Brenda, who had wielded the knife. He was known for his violent outbursts and he had a history of abuse with Brenda.

But no evidence was found, and charges against him were dismissed. However, for the rest of his life, there were rumors that he had murdered her.

***

On July 5, 1947, at El Rancho, the oldest hotel on The Strip in Las Vegas, Todd married Joan. It was a second chance at

Mike Todd: Before Elizabeth Taylor began dominating his every move, he had emotional space for a marriage to..... **JOAN BLONDELL**, depicted above on the right.

wedded bliss for each of them.

Almost immediately, Todd flew (alone) to New York. Meanwhile, Joan reported to the studio to co-star with Tyrone Power in *Nightmare Alley*, a film released in 1947.

Nightmare Alley was a bizarre departure from roles usually interpreted by Tyrone Power. In the movie, as noted by *Time* magazine, "He climbs a ladder made of ladies. On Rung No. 1 is Zeena (Joan Blondell), the midway's mentalist. He plays cozy with her just long enough to swipe a pseudo-telepathic formula through which he can graduate to the big time."

When Todd returned from New York, he and Joan had a violent confrontation. He'd heard rumors that she'd had sex with her co-star, Power, a Hollywood icon whom members of the press had defined as "a living doll."

A few weeks later, Joan was seen dining with Ronald Reagan, her good friend from the days of his marriage to Jane Wyman and her marriage to Dick Powell. As she later claimed, "It was a harmless lunch during which he mostly talked about his painful split from Jane Wyman, whom he continued to define as 'the love of my life.'"

"He seemed to be recovering by dating blondes," Joan said. "He'd proposed marriage to Adele Jergens and had given her a diamond engagement ring. But when he went to pick her up on the set of *Ladies of the Chorus*, he switched his affection to her co-star, Marilyn Monroe."

When Todd heard that Joan had lunched with Reagan, he demanded to know what happened later that same afternoon. "Did he take you to some sleazy motel? I've known that you and Reagan have been going at it for years, even

"In the offbeat *Nightmare Alley* with **Tyrone Power**, I played a counterfeit seer," **Joan** said. "Ty, a darling man, was a carnival hustler clawing his way to the top."

"He desperately wanted for the movie to overcome his image as a bedroom swashbuckler."

An altogether different kind of Nightmare: Todd and Taylor as a romantic unit. Where did that leave Joan Blondell?

BLONDELL: Portrait of a Golden Age, Pre-Code Movie Star   89

when he was married to Wyman. Everybody in Hollywood knows that for a fact."

That night, Joan suffered one of Todd's most violent beatings.

The remaining months of her marriage to Todd were characterized by arguments over infidelity, violent rages, mental deterioration (on his part), and his continued public humiliations of her. *[Loudly, and in public, he frequently called her an "old hag" and "a has-been."]*

In 1950, she sought refuge in a divorce court. Throughout the rest of her life, Joan denied the perception that Elizabeth Taylor had stolen Mike Todd from her.

"That's ridiculous," she said. "When he married the very beautiful Miss Taylor, Mike and I had already been divorced for seven years. I just hope the bastard treats her better than he did me."

"I'm Still Here! Still a Trouper, So Bring on the Roles!"
—Joan Blondell

"Even when I was just cutting my teeth at Warners, stories appeared in the press that each new starlet who signed on was destined to become 'the next Joan Blondell.' I wanted to tell those damn press boys that Joan Blondell was still here, ready and raring to go on for my next feature. But all things, of course, come to an end."

She would always remember her mournful last day on the Warners lot, as she stood facing an empty sound stage with her friend, Jane Wyman. On January 7, 1939, a messenger arrived with her final paycheck for $2,916.65.

As she relayed to Wyman, "It looks like a war is coming, and I feel the 1940s will call for a very different type of movie star than what I represented. I predict bigtime stardom not only for you, but perhaps for Rita Hayworth and Betty Grable, too. I fear I'll go down in film history as one of those Depression-era blondes that rose up between the World Wars."

Joan's high visibility in the 1930s had made her one of the best-known faces in cinema. Her biographer, Matthew Kennedy, wrote: "She was full of surprises, one moment as tough as Joan Crawford, the next as fragile as Margaret Sullavan, and the next as saucy as Mae West."

"She could cry on cue, a talent sorely envied by Bette Davis. Joan excelled in a wide variety of genre pictures, including mysteries, romantic comedy, film noir, musicals, westerns, screwball comedies, family dramas, and satire."

"In the fifty-three movies I made for Warners in the 1930s," Joan said, "I learned how to swap dialogue with screen gangsters, impersonate a whore, play a wise-cracking blonde floozie, tangle with on-screen cops, hustle stage managers...whatever."

Ironically, in contrast to her fears in the early 40s, her greatest performances lay in her future.

Two of her favorite roles came at war's end, when she starred in *A Tree Grows in Brooklyn* (1945), directed by Elia Kazan and based on Betty Smith's bestseller. Joan's role was that of Aunt Sissy, a generous-hearted soul who had suffered hard knocks.

In 1947, to her surprise, 20th Century Fox offered her the co-starring role in *Nightmare Alley* with Tyrone Power. It was to be directed by Edmund Goulding and produced by George Jessel, the ex-vaudevillian.

"Both Ty and I played two carnival hustlers, with me cast as Zeena, a mind reader...sort of. As a carnie heel, he delivered one of his best performances in years."

As an amoral carnie, as noted by *Time* magazine, "Power climbs a ladder made of ladies. Rung No. 1 is Zeena (Joan Blondell), the Midway's mentalist. He plays cozy with her just long enough to swipe a pseudo-telepathic formula through which he can graduate to the big time."

"I found Ty very attractive, but we did not have an affair," she said. "He was too busy satisfying both female and male libidos. He sure dated A-listers: Lana Turner, Judy Garland, Howard Hughes, Errol Flynn, Robert Taylor, Rock Hudson, Noël Coward, Rita Hayworth, Linda Darnell, Loretta Young, and even Evita Perón of Argentina.

***

The greatest role of Joan's career didn't come until she reunited with her old friend, Jane Wyman, to make *The Blue Veil* (1951). In the movie, Blondell played a neglectful show-biz mother of a twelve-year-old. One writer said, "Blondell added vinegar to a movie drowning in molasses."

For their performances in The Blue Veil, Wyman and Joan were nominated, respectively, for Best Actress and Best Supporting Actress Oscars. Wyman lost to Vivien Leigh for *A Streetcar Named Desire* and Joan lost to Kim Hunter for her performance as Stella in that same film. "I should have won," she told Darwin. "It was my only chance."

In 1965, Joan co-starred with Steve McQueen in *The Cincinnati Kid*, a movie about gambling with a supporting cast that featured Tuesday Weld, Karl Malden, Ann-Margret, Rip Torn, and Cab Calloway.

On the set, Joan had a reunion with Edward G. Robinson, with whom she'd last worked in *Ballots or Bullets* in 1936. He told Joan, "McQueen comes out of the tradition of Bogie, Gable, and Cagney, and myself. He's a stunner."

In her role as "Lady Fingers," Joan impressed McQueen with her humor. During their discussions about Bette Davis, Joan told him that Davis had married "Four Skins," referring to the fact that each of them were Gentiles.

Joan told Darwin Porter at Magnolia House, "Even though Steve Mc-

Queen was friendly, I don't think he liked to hang out with women. He much preferred the company of men. He liked women for only one thing, I gathered. I told him that whatever he did with women, he should never do what Mike Todd did to me. He gambled away all my life's savings and then, in Manhattan, he hung me by my ankles out an eighth-floor window until I turned my last thousand dollars over to him."

Mike Todd and Elizabeth. Taylor, out and in love with each other, and with the possibility of maneuvering their boat into any port.

In 1972, Joan published a novel, *Center Door Fancy*, a not-so-thinly-disguised autobiography. *[In her words, "Only the names were changed to protect the guilty."]*

Joan herself was the inspiration for its female protagonist of "Nora Marten." "David Nolan" was a thinly disguised reference to George Barnes. "Jim Wilson" was a pseudonym for Dick Powell, and "Jeff Flynn" was a codeword for Mike Todd.

As she relayed to Darwin, "I was introduced to a whole new generation when I played a supporting role in *Grease* (1978). In it, I was surrounded by poodle skirts, bubble gum, ducktails, and rock 'n roll."

"I was a soda shop lady, serving high schoolers, although they were a bit long in the tooth for teenagers: John Travolta, then aged 24; Olivia Newton John, 29; and Stockard Channing—would you believe 34?"

For a 1979 release, Joan appeared in a remake of Wallace Beery's *The Champ* (1931). In her role of a blousy blonde wisecracker, she co-starred opposite Jon Voight and Faye Dunaway.

***

Joan was offered one of her last film roles when producer Jerry Wheeler and Darwin visited her in Hollywood. Wheeler wanted her to play the second lead in a film based on Darwin's best-selling drama, *Butterflies in Heat*.

She would have played Tangerine, a lovable "gopher" and companion of a decayed, massively egocentric fashion diva, Leonora de la Mer. At the time, Gloria Swanson had been announced as the actress who'd portray Leonora in the film.

To everyone's regret, Joan asserted that she was "just too tired" to accept, and the role went to veteran actress Pat Carroll.

Coincidentally, as the movie was being shot in Key West, Joan died on Christmas Day, 1979.

Depicted above is **Darwin Porter** from the period of his most intense and most frequent dialogues with Joan Blondell at Magnolia House.

REST IN PEACE

Magnolia House Superstar

JOAN BLONDELL

1906-1979

Today a cult classic, **Butterflies in Heat,** a novel authored by Darwin Porter, is hailed as "the gay version of both *All About Eve* and *Sunset Blvd.*"

For its film adaptation (entitled *The Last Resort),* Joan was offered one of its key roles, that of "Earth Mother & Universal Confidante" Tangerine, but was too ill to accept it, the part going to Pat Carroll. Also configured into key roles were the era's top male model, Matt Collins, along with Eartha Kitt and Barbara Baxley.

Lower tier of photos: Right, the Blue Library--a room at Magnolia House where Joan Blondell felt comfortable, proud, appreciated, unapologetic, well-respected, and at home.

Left: **Magnolia House** as photographed for the NYC tax census in 1940, Joan Blondell's heyday.

ASK JOAN!

Joan Blondell Discusses Aging, Acting & Acceptance

"It takes all the talent you've got in your guts to play unimportant roles. It's not degrading, just tough to do. It's fine to start out as a curvy biz-whiz, but unfortunately, when you can't do those roles anymore, people think you're finished. I accept change. I say 'It's all right, it's a new generation growing up.' So you support the young kids, and you have great respect for them because that's the way you were at one time." (Source: *Life* magazine, 1971).

"The only right thing I ever did was when I looked at myself in the mirror in 1951 and the rosebud lips weren't quite as upturned and there was that line between the eyes. I told my agent to get me anything that said 'aged'. I'm not going to have anything lifted so, why not, I might as well play fallen-faced dames." (Source: *NY Post*, 1972).

Chapter Four

Murder Ahoy!
Widely & Publicly, Tennessee Williams Suggests to Darwin Porter & an Enthralled Corps of Fans:

"Did Bette Davis Murder Her 2ND Husband?"

As the conniving "witch, not a bitch," playing Regina Giddens (left photo) in Lillian Hellman's *The Little Foxes* (1941), **Bette Davis** looks like she could murder anyone.

Tallulah Bankhead had played Regina on Broadway, but lost the movie role to Bette. Later, confronting her at a party, Tallulah said, "So you're the woman who gets to play all my parts in the movies. And I play them so much better."

Bette Davis faced a murder investigation during the darkest days of World War II. Surely, we're talking about on-screen Bette Davis, not the star in private life? Perhaps we're rehashing one of her famous movie plots, such as W. Somerset Maugham's *The Letter* from 1940.

But in 1943, in addition to the dramas unfolding around each of the heroines she played on screen, the real Bette came very close to being charged with the murder of her second husband, Arthur Farnsworth Jr. Instead, under murky circumstances, she was never charged.

Some tantalizing background on this strange case emerged during interviews that Darwin conducted with Jim Dougherty in the 1970s. Ostensibly, they were meeting to discuss his former wife, Norma Jean Baker (aka, Marilyn Monroe). But as a longtime officer of the Los Angeles Police Department, Dougherty had other tales to tell about Hollywood and its stars, including Miss Bette Davis. *[Davis had appeared with Dougherty's former wife, Marilyn, in the memorable 1950 film, All About Eve.]*

Dougherty reported that on one slow afternoon as he was going through police files, he came upon a thick document labeled BETTE DAVIS, later revealing that he read the complete file "for voyeuristic pleasure." The screen's greatest *tragedienne* at the time had been investigated on a charge of murder in the mysterious death of her second husband, Arthur Farnsworth Jr., whom she called "Farney." She'd met this handsome New Englander when she was on vacation at Peckett's Inn in Franconia, New Hampshire, where he was assistant manager.

She immediately became infatuated with him

Cutting the wedding cake: **Bette Davis** and her new husband, New Englander **Arnold Farnsworth Jr.** (she called him "Farney"), were a vision of domestic bliss. But not for long.

The marriage started to unravel during their honeymoon. She married him on December 31, 1940, when he was a perfect male specimen, in robust good health. He died on August 25, 1943 under suspicious circumstances.

and invited Farney to come back with her to Hollywood, which he did. At the time, Bette was at the pinnacle of her career, making her most successful movies for Warner Brothers. Love bloomed and eventually, Miss Bette Davis, 31, married Farney, 33.

Like all of Bette's marriages, this one started to fail almost from the beginning. Farney had a lot of male charm which he turned on other ladies as he indulged in a number of secret affairs. Bette wasn't exactly the faithful wife either. She was also having affairs with actor John Garfield, her "chum" at the Hollywood Canteen, and with the director Vincent Sherman, who was to guide her through two of her most critically acclaimed films, *Old Acquaintance* (1943) and *Mr. Skeffington* (1944).

On the afternoon of August 23, 1943, Farney lunched with Bette's lawyer, Dudley Furse. After lunch, which ended at 2:30pm, he strolled down Hollywood Boulevard toward his car. In front of a cigar store, he suddenly screamed—"a blood curdler," reported an eyewitness. He fell backward onto the sidewalk with a dull thud, hitting his head. David Freedman, the owner of the cigar store, rushed to his aid, discovering Farney "bleeding profusely from both ears and nostrils." An ambulance was summoned.

In the hospital, Farney lived in a coma for two days until his heart gave out. The news of his death flashed around the world. From the very beginning, it had an unsettling air of mystery about it. How could a young man in apparent good health die so quickly? Of course, the public interest in Farney existed only because of his marriage to the woman who at the time was the world's most famous movie star.

At a Hollywood nightclub in 1941, **Bette and Farney** (right) seemed like a happy couple. But later that night, he accused her of having an affair with Errol Flynn, and she denounced him as a lush.

Months later, she would discover that he was spending the money she earned at Warner Brothers on other, even more glamorous, women.

A few days after his death, an inquest was called in front of a six-man grand jury. The autopsy surgeon, Dr. Homer Keyes, claimed that his collapse onto the sidewalk was not the immediate cause of his death. He charged that Farney had suffered an earlier blow on the head from "some unknown party."

Called to the witness stand, Bette appeared properly dressed in black mourning clothes, playing the grieving and heart-broken widow, "a performance worthy of an Oscar" as she would later tell Sherman. She was questioned about a possible blow to Farney's head, and did she know anything? In her testimony, she recalled that in June, about two months before, her husband had begun a descent of the stairs of her summer home [Butternut, in New Hampshire], with his feet clad only in socks.. She claimed that he fell from near the top of the stairwell, landing on his head. "Although he complained of severe headaches for a day or two, he seemed to recover quickly and never consulted a doctor," she testified.

Dr. Keyes disputed Bette's story, charging that the blow to Farney's head with "some blunt instrument" had not occurred in June, but had been sustained "no more than two weeks" before his untimely death.

He stated, "The blood in the fracture was black and coagulated, not merely purple and partially congealed as it would have been if the blow had been received only last Monday [i.e., from Farney's fall on Hollywood Boulevard]." The report went on to say, "After receiving some blow to his head [i.e., prior to his death], Farnsworth had been walking around ever since with the condition fructifying until it eventually caused his death."

A Dr. Moore, a personal friend of Bette's who also happened to be physician to both Farney and Bette, took the stand, confirming Bette's description of the fall on the stairwell. Ironically, he had no direct, firsthand knowledge of that alleged fall and had not examined Farney since early January of that year. Nevertheless, the jury sided with Dr. Moore and Bette, rejecting the report of the autopsy surgeon. It was later revealed that the starstruck jury consisted of men who were ardent fans of the star.

Bette walked. Months later, perhaps over pillow talk, she told a startled Sherman that she made up the entire story. "It never happened."

Sherman was not a man to keep secrets. He later reported that Bette told him a completely different story. She claimed that Farney had accompanied her to the train station where she was traveling alone to Mexico. It was later learned she was meeting Sherman there to continue their adulterous affair.

Farney (above) was not as lonely as this photo suggests. He accused Ann Sheridan of betraying him with Ronald Reagan and charged his wife with having an affair with John Garfield at the Hollywood Canteen.

To get even with both of them, he launched a (not-so-secret) affair with that Southern belle, Miriam Hopkins, Bette's co-star in *Old Acquaintance* (1943) and her off-screen arch enemy.

On board the train, Bette and Farney got into an argument over the exact purpose of the trip. She said the train started to move, and she couldn't get Farney to disembark. At that point she told Sherman that she pushed her husband off the platform. As the train left the station, she reported seeing him fall to the ground, but get up as he rubbed his head.

There was one major flaw in Bette's second story, according to detective Dougherty. Farney was in another part of Los Angeles that day consulting with a private attorney about bringing divorce action against Bette. Ignoring his own clandestine affairs, he had discovered her romance with Sherman.

In 1961, Bette came up with another version of what really happened to Farney. She was in Chicago at the time, appearing as the stage star of Tennessee Williams's *The Night of the Iguana*. The playwright urged Bette, after she'd had a few drinks, to tell him about how Farney died. Also present at this late night social gathering were Frank Merlo (Tennessee's longtime companion) and Darwin Porter.

In her new version, Bette said that she came home early from the studio one day, having had to take off from shooting at Warner Brothers because of a "splitting headache." When she came into her living room, she heard sounds coming from her bedroom. Going to investigate, she opened the door, discovering Farney deep into intercourse with some woman.

The object of Farney's affection turned out to be the original "Oomph Girl," who, along with Bette, was also a top star at Warner Brothers and one of the most famous women in the world in the 1940s. It was the actress, Ann Sheridan.

Grabbing a sheet, Ann fled from the bedroom and raced toward her car parked outside. That left the temperamental Bette alone in the bedroom to confront Farney. She confessed that she picked up a wrought-iron lamp on a nearby nightstand and crashed it into "Farney's two-timing skull."

Death came to him ten days later, in front of the above-noted cigar store on Hollywood Boulevard. The story (the third of the three tales she'd recited) coincided with the findings of the autopsy general.

Tennessee asked Bette if she had any lingering guilt for delivering such a damaging blow to her husband's head. She denied having any remorse, primarily because she discovered after his death that Farney had been spending her money on expensive gifts for other women.

According to her, her only anxiety came when Farney's relatives obtained a legal order to exhume his body where she'd buried it in New Hampshire. "I thought they were going to demand another autopsy and reopen the case. As it turned out, they wanted Farney's

Columnist Walter Winchell nicknamed **Ann Sheridan** (lower photo) "The Oomph Girl."

In addition to Farney, she sustained an affair with **Ronald Reagan**, her co-star in *Juke Girl (1942*; They're depicted together in that film in the upper photo*)*.

Fortunately, Reagan's wife, Jane Wyman, never found out. Since she considered Sheridan her best friend, she'd probably have felt double betrayed.

body shipped back to their family vault in Rutland, Vermont."

Dougherty felt that the red stamp imbedded on Bette's secret police file said it all: CASE CLOSED.

Locals, proud of Farney's New England origins, dedicated a plaque (lower left) to him. Cast in bronze, it referred to him as "the keeper of stray ladies," a title originally bestowed upon him by Bette.

In old age, a reporter asked **Bette** for some specific details about Farney's death. Her answer? "No comment."

Bette? A Murderess? Could It Be True?

If some of the bloodthirsty characters she played during the long course of her spectacular career have anything to say about it, the idea of Bette as a killer isn't new.

Movie stills from her cinematic past reveal an actress who was capable of entertaining the idea, at least, of a woman who could conceivably have gotten away with murder.

Above, left to right, show Bette shedding blood (or contemplating it) in *The Letter* (1940), *What Ever Happened to Baby Jane?* (1962); and *Hush, Hush, Sweet Charlotte* (1964).

Chapter Five

WHERE PROSTITUTES WERE NAMED AFTER FLOWERS

How Truman Capote's Avant-Garde, All-Black Cast Danced the Mambo All the Way to Broadway

Black stars rule a Haitian world of prostitution and voodoo magic in the Broadway adaptation of Truman Capote's novella, **House of Flowers**, which became part of New York's *avant-garde* news in 1954.

On the right, the talented Trinidad-born dancer, **Geoffrey Holder**, portrays a witch doctor to **Diahann Carroll**'s take as Ottile, a symbol of Creole sensuality whose innocence somehow remained unsoiled.

It all began in 1948, when Truman organized a vacation in the Caribbean to celebrate his success as a novelist after the publication of *Other Voices, Other Rooms.* *[Darwin had first met Capote at a literary soirée at the Greenwich Village apartment of Anaïs Nin, the diarist and novelist.]*

Based on the increasing fame of Haiti among the avant-garde *[and the growing cognizance of its role as the cradle of Caribbean art]*, *Harper's Bazaar* commissioned some of the costs of Truman's trip to Port-au-Prince, Haiti's capital, where he worked on a travel article. That article later evolved into a short story, which he entitled "House of Flowers."

In the wake of his discovery that local nightlife didn't really exist in Haiti in any format he understood, he began to visit the local brothels, many of which were positioned amidst lush foliage on Bizonton Road.

Capote had no interest in seducing any of the local prostitutes, yet he found them charming, *piquante*, coquettish, and culturally fascinating, and he enjoyed their company. Most of them sat on rocking chairs waiting for customers to come along, an occasional black man but more often white foreign tourists, usually from either France or the United States.

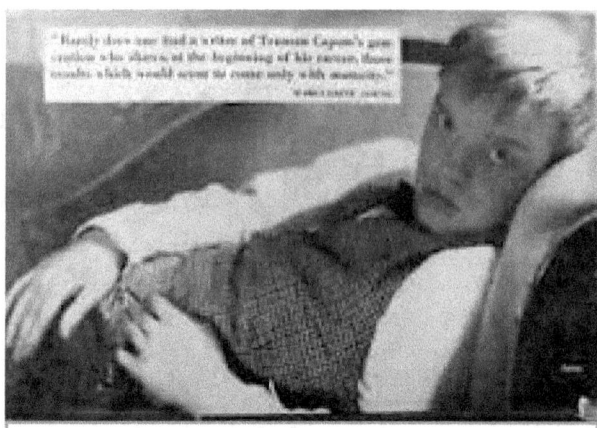

This is the back cover of the original first edition of Capote's **Other Voices, Other Rooms.**

Detractors said that **Truman** used his resemblance to an underaged and very precocious teenager to spark both controversy and sales, perhaps among pedophiles.

Cafe Society: In 1955, at the Blue Angel in New York City, a very gay **Truman Capote** entertains heiress **Gloria Vanderbilt** (left) and the star of his play, **Pearl Bailey**.

He brought lots of cold beer for the girls to drink and learned that they had each been assigned French-language nicknames based on flowers or flowering shrubs such as Jasmine, Bougainvillea, Pansy, Tulip, Gladiola, and even Wisteria Lilac. The working girls would drink his beer and fan themselves with cardboard-backed illustrations of Jesus Christ.

His favorite of the impoverished city's many bordellos was called "The Paradise" (in English), run by a three-hundred-pound businesswoman, "Madame Fleur." She advertised her establishment as "a place that can satisfy any desire known to man."

Although **Porfirio Rubirosa** (left) married **Doris Duke**, the tobacco heiress and richest woman in the world, he preferred the whores of Haiti.

Truman wasn't surprised that the *putas* were usually retired by Madame Fleur before they reached the age of twenty. "Most of my customers, especially those from the States, like them young," Madame Fleur told him. "*Très jeune, m'sieur.* In some cases, not even ten. I pick up a lot of kids at the border town, Dajabón."

[Dajabón, a blood-soaked market town on the northern end of Haiti's shared border with the Dominican Republic, with a population of about 10,000, is located on the Djabón River. That waterway is also known as the *Fleuve du Masacre* because of its connection to the genocidal Parsley Massacre of an estimated 20 to 30 thousand Haitians ordered by the Dominican dictator, Rafael ("The Goat") Trujillo in 1937.]

"There's a thriving market in Dajabón for both young boys and girls," she said. "It takes all kinds to make up God's world."

"Right now, I have only one young boy working for me," she said. "But when winter comes and business picks up, I might have three or four." She went into a back room and returned with a little boy who looked no older than ten.

"He was slender, with large brown eyes, rather frightened,"

The murderous dictator of Haiti, **François Duvalier ("Papa Doc")**, sets out with members of his dreaded private paramilitary, the **Tontons Macoutes**, to murder or castrate, or perhaps both, his enemies.

HOUSE OF FLOWERS: How the Literary Avant-garde Brought Haiti to Broadway

Truman said. "He seemed traumatized and, in spite of his profession, was very shy, afraid really. He wore a sleeveless undershirt, and there were bruises on his arms and back."

"His name was Juan, and he greedily devoured the candy I gave him," Truman said. "I made it clear to Madame that I was not a child molester. 'I much prefer Mandingos,' I told her."

"Well, I have plenty of those I can round up," she said. "Just give me the preferred height, weight, and the size of the whanger preferred—inches, not centimeters. I can round up what you want by midnight, even if I have to drag the stud from the bed of his wife."

"Not tonight, Joséphine," he answered.

"*M'sieur*, my name is not Josephine," she said. "If you must call me by my first name, it's Rosa. I was a working girl myself until I turned twenty and put on all this fat."

She looked down at Juan. "His mother died and he went to live with his grandmother, who didn't want him, She sold him to me for fifty U.S. dollars. For one of my girls for an hour, I charge tourists five dollars. Unless he's a Haitian man, and then I charge him only one dollar. Because Juan here is so special, I can ask as much as ten dollars."

In the course of one evening, Truman met the "prettiest girl among a lot of ugly ones in those rocking chairs."

"She was olive-skinned and an import from the old colonial city of Santo Domingo," he said. "She had three gold teeth and five silk dresses. Her name was Ottilie."

"Madame Fleur sold her every night as a virgin," he said. "How she managed to pull that one off I don't know. She said it was a special secret of hers, a secret she'd learned from her voodoo priest."

On another night, Madame Fleur was hysterical. She told Truman that Porfirio Rubirosa was flying in from Santo Domingo (Ciudad Trujillo) to talk with the *[terrifying, to Haitians]* Haitian dictator, François Duvalier.

"There is some shit about a border dispute," she said. "When Monsieur Rubirosa is in town, he always visits my Paradise."

Of course, gossipy Truman was well acquainted with the reputation of the legendary playboy, who had married Doris Duke, the tobacco heiress and the richest woman in the world. Nearly all of the conversation centered on his mammoth penis. He was also nicknamed "Rubber Hosa."

He'd once been married to Flor de Oro Trujillo, Generalissimo Rafael Trujillo's whorish daughter.

In Hollywood, Rubi's list of sexual conquests had become part of his legend. They included Joan Crawford, Dolores del Rio, Ava Gardner, Susan Hayward, and Veronica Lake. He'd also seduced such prominent personages as Eva Perón, co-dictator of Argentina.

Rubi had once told a reporter, "I consider a day in which I make love only once as virtually wasted."

"I'd love to see that stud in action," Truman told Madame Fleur.

"You can, but it'll cost you twenty dollars," she said. She led him to a dark back room. There was a two-way mirror that opened onto her most elegant boudoir, a room with an elaborately carved four-poster bed.

"Rubi likes to keep the light on, so if you stand here, you'll be able to see everything."

Madame Fleur lived up to her promise. "She arranged for Rubi to seduce three of her youngest and prettiest gals," Truman said. "He put on quite a show—in fact, the best show of my life. The handsome gigolo lived up to his reputation. All the stories about him were true. Three years later, Doris Duke, at a party in the Hamptons, told me that Rubi's penis was the most magnificent she'd ever seen."

[Doris Duke (1912—1993) the America heiress, hedonist, art collector, and philanthropist, was the whimsical, imperious, and autocratic daughter of an almost unimaginably wealthy tobacco tycoon. In the lurid aftermath of her death, she left a fortune estimated at 1.3 billion and a carload of outrageous anecdotes and references.]

"I agree with you," Truman told Doris at that party in the Hamptons.

Duke looked at him. "And how in hell would you know?" Then she retracted her question. "Don't tell me. I don't want to know."

Although Truman didn't tell Duke, he announced to the world the size of Rubi's penis. He was quoted in print as saying, "It was six inches in circumference, an eleven-inch octoroon dick." He then whispered an aside. "A skilled fellator such as myself could even get it to stretch two or three more inches."

Truman's whisperings were based on the fact that he later introduced himself to Rubi at Madame Fleur's. Both of them shared a taxi back to the Hotel Oloffson—the best hotel in Port-au-Prince at the time, a seedy 19th-century gingerbread palace evoking something from a Charles Addams fantasy—where they were staying.

The next morning, a maid found Truman in Rubi's bed. Truman later said, "If it were late enough at night, Rubi didn't care what legs were open to him."

MEANWHILE, IN PORTOFINO:

The "Lavender Hill Mob" Discusses a Broadway Adaptation of Truman Capote's *House of Flowers*

Early in 1954, the influential American-born Broadway producer, Albert Saint-Subber, wanted to mount a Broadway play based on Truman's short story, "House of Flowers." After a long confab, Truman agreed.

Saint-Subber was most persuasive, and he was the "angel with the dough."

[Previously, Saint-Subber had traveled to Taormina (Sicily) to urge Truman to write a stage adaptation of his The Grass Harp, *which had been published in 1951, and eventually adapted into a vehicle for Broadway in 1952. It wasn't until 1995 that* The Grass Harp *appeared as a movie. The cast was more impressive than the drama: Walter Matthau, Jack Lemmon, Sissy Spacek; Charles Durning, Roddy McDowall, and Piper Laurie could not rescue it.]*

From the beginning of the stage adaptation of *House of Flowers*, Truman imposed a lot of demands. He wanted the distinguished English director, Peter Brook, to helm it; Virgil Thomson to write the incidental music, and Cecil Beaton to design the sets and costumes. Both "Saint" [as Saint-Subber was nicknamed] and Truman lobbied hard to convince those Silent Screen duennas, Dorothy and Lillian Gish, to appear in the lead roles of Dolly and Verena Talbo.

None of those original visions worked. Robert Lewis replaced Brook as director; the Gish sisters gave way to Mildred Natwick and Ruth Nelson. And even though Brooks Atkinson of *The New York Times* interpreted the final product as both "effortless and beautiful," *House of Flowers* never generated much business at the box office.

[Whereas Truman was completely inexperienced in creating a Broadway musical, Saint was very experienced, having previously won a Tony for Kiss Me, Kate, *a musical based on Shakespeare's* Taming of the Shrew. *It ran on Broadway from 1948 to 1951. Later, he'd produce seven Neil Simon plays, including* Barefoot in the Park, *and in 1973, he'd help launch the theatrical version of* Gigi *by Alan Jay Lerner and Frederick Lowe.]*

During the late spring of 1953, Truman and his lover, Jack Dunphy, planned to travel to Positano on the Italian Riviera where Dunphy would try to complete a novel and where it was understood that Truman would begin work on his stage adaptation of *House of Flowers*.

Prior to their departure for Positano, John Malcolm Brinnin, the poet and critic, attended a party that was conceived as both a celebration of Harold Arlen's birthday and a *bon voyage* party for Truman and Dunphy. Arlen, the creator of "Over the Rainbow" for Judy Garland, had agreed to write the musical score for *House of Flowers*. *[Brinnin, a close friend of Capote, came to live in Key West, two blocks from where Darwin also maintained a home.]*

"I remember Truman sitting on the floor, his head resting, using Arlen's knees as a cushion," Brinnin recalled. "In the corner was Marlene Dietrich encircled by the arms of Montgomery Clift. They were mutually transfixed and exchanged monosyllables now and then. But for the most part, they simply stood there, staring into one another's eyes. Dietrich wore a dress that was less like fabric, more like molten silver. Clift's suit was too big for him."

[Through the fabled European chanteuse, Greta Keller, Darwin got to entertain Marlene Dietrich on several occasions.]

Once they reached the Italian Riviera, whereas Dunphy liked to be alone most of the time, Truman loved company. In Portofino, there were plenty of famous names with whom to associate, including the port's two most famous residents, Rex Harrison, and his wife, Lilli Palmer. Passing through town was a parade of stylish visitors, including John Gielgud and Truman's friend, Cecil Beaton. A coven of gay couples arrived, including Tennessee and Frank Merlo; Paul Bowles "with some Arab boy;" Noël Coward with Graham Payn; and Hugh (Binkie) Beaumont with John Perry (Gielgud's ex).

Truman labeled these homosexuals "The Lavender Hill Mob." With the exception of the snobby Gielgud—who was turned off by "that ghastly little voice, the world's longest fingernails, and dirty shorts,"—most of them gravitated to Truman.

In letters to friends in the States, Truman had comments about the resort's gaggle of other illustrious visitors. These included the Duke and Duchess of Windsor ("utter morons"); Henry and Clare Luce ("morons plus"), and Laurence Olivier and Vivien Leigh ("Apparently, Scarlett O'Hara has been released from the madhouse"). A surprise visitor was Greta Garbo, "who looked like Death with a suntan." *[Darwin was a long-time friend of the former child star, Philippe de Lacy, who invited him to the Manhattan apartment of Greta Garbo. As a child actor, De Lacy had co-starred with Garbo in the silent film, Love.*

On another occasion, Tennessee, at a social event attended by Darwin, wanted Garbo to star in a script he'd written, which would have marked her comeback. Garbo listened patiently as he read it. Finally, she rose from her chair and said, "Not for me, but it would be a wonderful vehicle for Joan Crawford."]

After Garbo's visit, Truman wrote to one of his best friends, Cecil Beaton, who had returned to New York. Truman fully understood how close Beaton was to Garbo. Nonetheless, he wrote: "Darling Cecil, I'm afraid Greta will never be a satisfactory person because she is so dissatisfied with herself, and dissatisfied people can never be emotionally serious. They simply don't believe in anything—except their own limitations." He later revealed that Garbo had spent most of their time together complaining about a pain in her neck.

[Truman encountered Garbo again in February of 1955 in New York and wrote to Beaton: "She was looking extremely well—though her hair seemed a peculiar color: a sort of blondish lavender. I think she must have dyed it."]

Back in Positano that summer of 1953, Truman complained that Noël Coward was trying to steal Jack Dunphy from him.

Eventually bored with Portofino, Truman announced to his friends there that he was leaving for Switzerland to visit Charlie Chaplin and his wife, Oona. She was one of his best friends.

During the Red Scare in America, Chaplin—who had remained a British citizen through the peak of his Hollywood fame—was charged with being a communist. Shortly after that, he flew from semi-retirement in French-speaking Switzerland to London for the premiere of his last American film, *Limelight* (1952). While there, the U.S. State Department told him he would not be allowed to return to the States.

After their visit with the Chaplins, Truman, with Dunphy, flew to Paris, where he found the city "dull and yellow" at that time of year.

In November of 1953, Truman wrote to his scholarly former lover, Newton Arvin, of John Gielgud's arrest, in October of that year, in London. An undercover police officer had apprehended Gielgud in a men's toilet in Chelsea, based on a charge of sexual solicitation of a male.

Carson McCullers, author of one of America's greatest novels, *The Heart Is a Lonely Hunter*, is seen here with her suicidal gay husband, **Reeves.**

Truman called it "a dreadful rumpus over gents who interfere with gents. I'm terribly fond of John, and I talked with him on the phone last week. He seemed to be bearing up with a good deal of bravery and style. Still, it was a shocking thing to happen, malicious and stupid."

At his hotel, Truman was summoned to the phone. "It's Mr. Sister," Dunphy said. He and Truman always referred to Reeves McCullers as "Mr. Sister," because he had confessed to them that he was a homosexual.

On the phone, Reeves seemed on the verge of a nervous breakdown. He told Truman that his wife, Carson McCullers, had flown back to New York, leaving him with no money. Truman invited him for dinner, but he never showed up.

[Darwin had met Carson McCullers, a fellow Southerner and one of his favorite novelists, through Tennessee. McCullers was the author of the memorable The Heart is a Lonely Hunter.]

The next morning, Truman learned that Reeves had committed suicide by overdosing on liquor and barbiturates. Truman was among the handful of guests who attended his funeral in Paris, although he'd requested to be buried in Georgia.

Bad news came in pairs. Shortly after

Truman Capote's friendship with **Greta Garbo**, who's depicted above, was not very widely publicized.

At one point in 1949, he was going to travel to Paris with her for her comeback picture, its plot based on Balzac's 1834 novel, *La Duchesse de Langeais*, but the deal fell through.

that, Truman received a call from New York, informing him that his mother, Nina Capote, had also committed suicide.

He decided to fly back for his mother's burial, leaving Dunphy and his dogs in Paris, where it was understood that they'd later catch a ship back to the Port of New York.

On the pier, as Truman told Dunphy goodbye, he lamented, "My youth is gone."

***

After the failure of *House of Flowers* on Broadway, Truman was not interested in continuing friendships with its cast and crew. However, he did maintain a relationship with its set designer, Oliver Messel. *[In the spring of 1960, Messel's nephew, Anthony Armstrong-Jones, became the Earl of Snowdon based on his marriage to Princess Margaret.]*

In London, Truman dined with Messel and his Danish companion, Vagn Riis-Hansen. In the aftermath, he wrote Cecil Beaton, fully aware that Beaton and Messel were bitter rivals.

"Darling Cecil, I dined with Oliver and his dear friend, a Dane. They were thrilled—absolutely thrilled—to be given 10,000 pounds to do Liz's clothes for *Cleopatra*."

[At the time, in 1963, Elizabeth Taylor and Richard Burton were in Rome, filming the horrifically expensive Cleopatra. *Later, in Rome, the epic film's director, Joseph Mankiewicz, fired Messel from any further association with* Cleopatra's *costumes and set designs.]*

When he later met with Beaton in New York, Truman claimed that because of Messel's new links, through his nephew, to Buckingham Palace, and because of Truman's friendship with him, "I expect the gates of Buckingham Palace will be open to me as well. So far, the Queen—perhaps the poor dear has forgotten—hasn't invited me for tea. But it's only a matter of time. I'm sure she admires my work."

"Through Oliver, I was invited to this swanky party in Mayfair," Tru-

> Although Haitian whorehouses were not his *forte*, **Oliver Messel** (photo above) England's most acclaimed theatrical designer, agreed to create the sets for Truman's *House of Flowers*.
>
> His usual commissions involved designing and decorating houses for uber-jaded and uber-famous owners of houses in the U.K., Barbados, or the Caribbean Island of Mustique, where Princess Margaret maintained a vacation home.
>
> In Messel, Truman found "a man after my own heart--we're two bitches in heat ready to set the world on fire."

man continued. "I met Prince Philip, who practically drooled over me. That man, I'm sure, has the hots for me. If he ever gets me alone, I know—I just know—that he'll rape me, and I will be forced to give in to his demands. The word around London is that Philip is extremely well hung. I can't wait to be deflowered, like one of my gals in *House of Flowers*."

MARLENE DIETRICH'S "LIP LOCKS" WITH PEARL BAILEY

In Manhattan, in 1954, *House of Flowers* was ready to go into production. Saint *[its producer]* and Truman huddled together to select its creative team and to cast it. Once again, Truman wanted Peter Brook, the English *Wünderkind*, to direct. *[Previously, he'd wanted him to direct* The Grass Harp, *but didn't get him.]*

As Saint and Truman were soon to discover, whereas Brook vividly understood how to direct virtually any play by Shakespeare, he was utterly lost in his attempts to direct a musical, especially one with an all-black cast. In England, he'd successfully directed such plays as *Romeo and Juliet* and *Love's Labour's Lost*. He had also directed productions at the Royal Opera House in Covent Garden, including the staging of Strauss's *Salome* with sets by Salvador Dalí, and he'd also staged Puccini's *La Bohème* using sets created in 1899.

[In time, Brook would become famous for staging the controversial and very avant-garde work of the Franco-Greek playwright and laudanum addict, Antonin Artaud and his Theater of Cruelty. A prime example included the London premiere of Artaud's The Spurt of Blood.

Before coming to Broadway, Brook had directed John Gielgud in both The Winter's Tale *and* Measure for Measure. *None of this prepared him for what he'd encounter on Broadway, including Truman Capote, whose voice and effeminate mannerisms struck him as "peculiar."]*

Oliver Messel, the world's most acclaimed theatrical designer, agreed to design both the sets and costumes. Harold Arlen had already signed to write the play's musical score. As the crowning gem of *House of Flowers'* A-list associates, the great George Balanchine eventually signed on to choreograph the play's dance numbers. *[Darwin's friend, the Russian ballerina, Tamara Geva, had been married to Balanchine, and introduced him to Darwin years after her marriage to the great choreographer had ended.]*

Both Brook and Truman agreed that Pearl Bailey should play the lead, Madame Fleur, who ran the play's namesake bordello..

[Bailey had made her Broadway debut in 1946 in St. Louis Woman. *In 1968, Bailey would win a Tony Award for her starring role in an all-black production of* Hello, Dolly! *A staunch Republican, she would be appointed in 1970 as "Amer-*

ica's Ambassador of Love" by President Richard Nixon.]

Before casting even began, Truman was a bit taken back by Brook, who seemed apprehensive. "I am not familiar with people of the Negro race. Do they require any special handling?"

Both Brook and Truman were surprised, even shocked, when Marlene Dietrich constantly showed up backstage, practically serving as Bailey's wardrobe mistress during the short run of the play.

As Marlene Dietrich's biographer, Steven Bach, wrote: "Marlene found time to make a few recordings of songs by Harold Arlen, on whom she doted and who doted back. She served as den mother and charlady for the cast of *House of Flowers* when it was in trouble out of town, advising Pearl Bailey to wear on stage jewelry of big rhinestones, not small diamonds. She rushed to Arlen's bedside when he was hospitalized in New York, persuading the police department that her missions of mercy to the man who wrote 'Stormy Weather' required an escort complete with screaming sirens."

Truman was at least mildly surprised when he walked into Bailey's dressing room and discovered Marlene and Bailey in a passionate lip-lock. He excused himself for intruding and departed. Later, he told Saint that "if Tallulah Bankhead can seduce Hattie McDaniel, then Marlene is entitled to Pearl."

Brook, Truman, and Saint rounded up the best black performers in New York, mainly dancers. These included Alvin Ailey; Carmen Da Lavallade and her husband, Geoffrey Holder; and Arthur Mitchell. Juanita Hall, who had leaped to fame as Bloody Mary in the Broadway version of *South Pacific*, was selected to play the pugnacious madam of a rival bordello. The beautiful Diahann Carroll, cast in the role of the play's love interest, Ottilie.

[*Darwin had met Carroll when she posed for*

"During **Marlene Dietrich's** affair with Pearl Bailey, she mothered both of us," Truman recalled. "After the show, she'd invite us back to her apartment, where she made the most divine omelettes for us. I'd leave at around one in the morning, letting Pearl and Marlene enjoy a sleepover.

"For a brief time, Pearl and Marlene were known along Broadway as the odd couple. But in show business, all sexual combinations are possible."

The performers in *House of Flowers*, especially Pearl Bailey, claimed that its director, **Peter Brook**, "treated us like slaves on the plantation. He knew Shakespeare, and he could direct Gielgud, but he was not the man to put us through our paces."

HOUSE OF FLOWERS: How the Literary Avant-garde Brought Haiti to Broadway

pictures for his boss, Stanley Haggart. Haggart knew a lot of African American entertainers, notably the great dancer, Alvin Ailey, Pearl Bailey, and the Trinidad-born painter and dancer, Geoffrey Holder. Darwin eventually bought two of his paintings, one of them a portrait of Holder's wife, dancer Carmen Da Lavallade.]

Holder remembered meeting Truman at the time of the cast's first script reading. "He carried a large bouquet of red roses. Hopping, skipping, jumping around the theater, he gave each of us a rose. 'Pearl, a rose for you, *Dah-hanne* [Diahann Carroll], honey, a rose for you.' It was all so sweet—like a little elf."

Immediately, the show ran into trouble. Balanchine was not familiar with Caribbean dance traditions. "It took him hours until we finally figured out that he wanted us to do the God damn mambo," Alvin said. "Why didn't he say so in the first place?"

Brook kept addressing the cast as "You People," which they resented. He constantly and loudly reaffirmed that, "I am not prejudiced against African Americans," which elicited a collective groan from the cast.

Herbert Ross replaced Balanchine when he bolted. Ross would go on to greater successes on Broadway, including involvements in both *Funny Lady* with Barbra Streisand, and in *Tovarich* with Vivien Leigh.

He would become more famous in 1988 when he married Lee Radziwill, sister of Jackie Kennedy. Radziwill, for a time, would become Truman's closest friend.

After *House of Flowers'* first tryout in Philadelphia *[November 24, 1954]*, Brook assembled the all-black cast for a meeting:

"Before leaving London, I was told that all you blacks were a lazy, shiftless lot, and that I'd have massive trouble working with you. After watching your performance last night, I think all of you should be sent back to Barbados or Africa, or wherever it is you came from."

In the immediate aftermath of the director's diatribe, Bailey stormed out of the theater, vowing never to speak to Brook again, and the rest of the cast was filled with

Two views of **Pearl Bailey**, whose character in *House of Flowers* (Madame Fleur, who lost her virginity before she was 12,) dominated the stage

seething hostility.

As the show limped toward Broadway, Truman told his friend, Brinnin, "*House of Flowers* has become an extended one-woman vaudeville act for Pearl Bailey."

But Arlen remained optimistic, telling Brinnin, "I just love Truman Capote. He's one of the most enchanting souls I've ever encountered."

The songs kept the show going, at least for a while. The audience heard such tunes as "A Sleepin' Bee," "Two Ladies in the Shade of de Banana Tree," "One Man Ain't Quite Enough," and "Don't Like Goodbyes."

On December 30, 1954, *House of Flowers* opened to lukewarm reviews on Broadway. Because of all the big names associated with it, and the music, it ran for 165 performances. Nevertheless, it was still viewed as a failure. Messel's "wild and wonderful" sets came in for some of the highest praise. Critics also praised Arlen's music, but attacked Truman's script.

"It's one of those shows where everything seems to have gone wrong," wrote Walter Kerr in the *New York Herald Tribune*.

Truman was also attacked for being "a clumsy lyricist and an even worse librettist." Other critics found the show "as funny as an ingrown toenail." Yet another wrote, "There was too much gilding of the lily—too much manner for the matter."

Many found racist overtones in the show, which some people claimed depicted black people as stupid.

After reading the reviews, a drunken Truman called Saint at around three o'clock in the morning. "The fault is Pearl Bailey. We should replace her with somebody…help me name someone."

"Eartha Kitt, perhaps," Saint said. "She looks like she knows her way around a whorehouse." [*Eartha Kitt, the singer, spent a lot of time with Darwin Porter when she starred in a movie, The Last Resort, which was based on a novel* (But-

Dancer **Alvin Ailey** was broke throughout most of his life.

When he was one of the co-stars in *House of Flowers*, it would be beyond his imagination that one day a street in Manhattan would be named in his honor, and that a dance troupe would be established in his name.

Two talented Trinidadian dancers, **Carmen Da Lavallade and Geoffey Holder,** fell in love and got married, one of the better things that spun out of *House of Flowers*.

Truman had assured them that their appearances in his play would make each of them an overnight sensation.

HOUSE OF FLOWERS: How the Literary Avant-garde Brought Haiti to Broadway

terflies in Heat) *that Darwin had written.]*

"I think we should give it to a white Broadway musical star—take Mary Martin, for example. She could appear in blackface."

Despite Truman's drunken (and terrible) idea, Pearl Bailey retained her starring role until the end of the run.

Before departing for Europe, Truman assembled the cast and sang to them.

*"My house is made of flowers,
and fireflies climbed into my dome."*

House of Flowers, which would later be revived, is remembered today as one of Broadway's legendary failures, where great talents didn't manage to create the masterpiece that it could have been.

A 2003 review by critic John Kenrick stated, "It's high time that musical theater buffs stopped pretending that *House of Flowers* is a theatrical gem. After several disastrous productions, it is pretty clear that this musical stinks—and it always has."

Years after the demise of *House of Flowers*, **Eartha Kitt** starred as the outrageous transgendered hooker, Lola La Mour, in ***The Last Resort***, based on Darwin Porter's cult classic bestseller, **Butterflies in Heat.**

Chapter Six

AVANT-GARDE, GENDER-FLUID, PINK, AND CRAFTED BY GORE VIDAL,
MYRA BRECKINRIDGE
BECAME AMERICA'S FOREMOST LITERARY TRANSSEXUAL

Left photo: **Raquel Welch** in the film **Myra Breckinridge**, "pulls down my bloomers to show these guys what a real woman looks like. Except she's not a real woman at all."

In the right photo, Myra prepares to stick the dildo to the school stud, Rusty Gadowsky, played by actor Roger Herren in his fifteen minutes of fame on the screen.

[Of all the "reports from the front" delivered to him by members of the "Pink Triangle," none was more eagerly received by Darwin than Gore's tale about the making of the most controversial film of the year, Myra Breckinridge *(1970).]*

Howard Austen, Gore Vidal's longtime companion, once claimed that the inspiration for his controversial novel, *Myra Breckinridge*, actually came after Gore had sat through a 1949 movie, *Siren of Atlantis*, a frothy romance co-starring Maria Montez, the sultry actress from the Dominican Republic, and her French husband-at-the-time, Jean-Pierre Aumont.

To Gore, the so-called "Queen of Technicolor" represented all that was campy and false about Golden Age Hollywood and the motion picture industry. His iconoclastic novel, published amid the social turmoil of 1968, was his attempt to satirize it.

Written in the form of a diary, the novel, according to Gore, was inspired by "the megalomania of the Anaïs Nin diaries."

In *Myra Breckinridge*, Gore's most outrageous fictional endeavor, he satirized such themes as transsexuality, deviant sexual practices, and feminism—each of them filtered through the lens of an aggressively campy sensibility.

His character of Myra was a recreation of the ultimate Hollywood *femme fatale*.

Even though Myra is a fantasy conglomeration of silicone and hormone injections, Gore claimed that her laugh is better than Carole Lombard's; that she has more warmth than June Allyson, she's sweeter than Irene Dunne, she whispers better than Phyllis Thaxter, and her smile is more winning than Ann Sothern's.

To recreate the role of Myra, Gore Vidal found inspiration in the screen image of **Maria Montez**, "the Queen of Cinematic Camp."

Shortly after Myra arrives in Hollywood, she imposes a legal claim on the land holdings of Buck Loner, a retired horse opera star. She cites her status as the widow of Buck's nephew, Myron Breckinridge, even though, in fact, "she" is Myron himself. In the aftermath of a "gender reassignment, he has been reincarnated as an uber-glam female.

With a dose of self-delusion, she declares that, "No man will ever possess Myra Breckinridge," insisting that it is she who will possess men in her "own good time and in ways convenient to my tyrannous lust."

She unleashes herself (and her stated goal) on the sexy, macho, and unwaveringly heterosexual Rusty Godowsky. Earlier, he had arrogantly flaunted his manhood in front of her. After subjecting him to a series of sexual humiliations, she straps him to a table and triumphantly straddles him with a dildo.

"I am a dish, and don't you forget it, you motherfuckers!" Myra proclaims. Then she shares some of her sexual fantasies with the readers of her diary, admitting that she maneuvered her way—in her incarnation as a woman—through a lesbian phase of her past, crushed between the heavy breasts of Lana Turner.

Myra goes on to announce that she abandoned her lesbian past after being exposed to the manly charms of James Craig, a dashing actor who, in the 1940s, was widely promoted as the next Clark Gable.

"For years," the lush and beautiful Myra declares to her viewers and fans, "I practiced self-abuse, thinking of Craig's voice, those broad shoulders, those powerful thighs thrust between my own. No matter what condition James Craig is in today, decrepit or not, Myra Breckinridge is ready to give him a good time for old time's sake."

A subplot for the film spins around the character of Leticia Van Allen, an aging, sexually voracious talent scout who virtually invented the casting couch. As a workaday accessory, her office boasts a four-poster bed.

Myra meets Leticia and they become friends. Leticia confides that her studs provide her with "small attentions a girl like me cherishes, like a lighted cigarette stubbed out on my derrière, or a complete beating with his great thick heavy leather belt."

Mae West said that she detested the sex symbol, **Raquel Welch**, who responded, "The feeling is mutual."

With some reluctance, and alert to the fear that a backlash might be imminent, Little, Brown Company published *Myra Breckinridge* in book form in February of 1968.

Critiques included lavish praise from Christopher Isherwood and harsh attacks from William Buckley, Jr., who denounced Gore as a pornographer.

Critic Dennis Altman wrote: "*Myra Breckinridge* is part of a major cultural assault on the assumed norms of gender and sexuality, which swept the western world in the late 1960s and 1970s. It is tempting to argue that Vidal did more to subvert the dominant rules of sex and gender in *Myra* than is contained in a shelf of queer theory treatises."

MYRA — HOW DID SHE HAPPEN?

In 1968, shortly before the official release of *Myra Breckinridge* as a novel, Gore Vidal sent a copy to the controversial expatriate director Joseph Losey. Gore thought he'd would be ideal as the director of his book's movie adaptation.

Losey had been blacklisted in Hollywood during the 1950s for having joined the Communist Party in 1946. Subsequently, he left the United States and moved to Europe, where he made the remainder of his films, mostly in England. Losey's previous so-called radical associations didn't frighten Gore at all, as his own left-wing views had often incited people who disagreed with him to label him as a communist.

In the late 1960s, Losey had formed a working relationship with playwright Harold Pinter, and had directed two films based on that writer's screenplays, including *The Servant* (1963) and *Accident* (1967). Each was lavishly honored with awards from, among others, the British Academy Film Awards and the Grand Prix Special du Jury Award at the 1967 Cannes Film Festival. These movies examined the politics of sexuality and gender in the 1960s. Collectively, they seemed to make him the ideal candidate as director of an actress in a transgendered role.

Losey's response to Gore's proposal was immediate and enthusiastic. He'd not only read the novel twice but had already developed strong ideas about how to cast it. He wanted Elizabeth Taylor to play Myra Breckinridge, and he felt Anne Bancroft would be ideal cast as Leticia Van Allen. He'd just seen her film, *The Graduate* (1967), and he thought she'd be perfect playing a sex-hungry film talent scout who liked to bed studs more manly than Dustin Hoffman.

After Losey managed to contact Bancroft by telephone, he learned that she, too, had read the novel and would be "delighted to sink my teeth into the role of LeTITia Van Allen." *(West later demanded that the TIT in her character's name be chaned to TIC.)*

Unable to reach Elizabeth Taylor on the phone, he wrote her a letter, dating it December 26, 1968, and addressing it to her chalet in Gstaad. With Richard Burton, she was staying there over the holidays.

"I've been re-reading *Myra Breckinridge* by your friend, Gore Vidal, who served you so magnificently with the script he prepared for you for *Suddenly, Last Summer*, where you gave a performance that should have won the Oscar. Done properly, *Myra Breckinridge* could make millions. You could afford not to work again, and I don't care—or, rather, we should put it the other way 'round. I could afford it (!) and you don't care."

When Elizabeth later encountered Gore at a Hollywood party, she said, "Under different circumstances, I might have considered it. But Losey's letter came at a very bad time for me. Of course, no one would have believed me as a trannie. But, what the hell, it would have been a lark. In that scene where I stand on a table and lower my lace panties to those guys, I would not have worn a sex-hider. With my back to the camera, I would have had great fun showing them the Full Monty."

When she read Losey's letter, Elizabeth was behind schedule in the shooting of *The Only Game in Town*, a movie in which she was wrongly cast in a story about the romance of a chorus girl and a gambler, as played by Warren Beatty. After shooting in Paris, she would have to fly to Las Vegas for

When Gore Vidal visited **Mae West**, he was shocked that she thought she had been cast as the very young Myra.

the final location sequences. This was the last film shot by director George Stevens, who had previously directed Montgomery Clift and her in *A Place in the Sun* (1951).

Overweight, especially for an actress playing a chorus girl, Elizabeth was also in constant pain because of her spine, and was taking a lot of painkillers. She was on pills and consuming a lot of liquor. Richard Burton often found her "incoherent and sloshed as a Cossack."

Burton later said, "I tried to get her to read Vidal's novel, but she wouldn't even finish reading the script for *The Only Game in Town*. I thought that if Losey directed it, I might put in a turn as Buck Loner, the part that eventually went to John Huston. I mean there was another problem. The ol' girl had just had her uterus removed."

Burton also said that although she didn't exactly tell Losey to "Fuck off," she "didn't give a rat's fart if she ever made another movie. But Losey didn't give up. That spring, he was asking both of us, or either of us, if we wanted to star in Edward Albee's *A Delicate Balance*. He got a firm NO for that offer as well."

***

After the release of the movie adaptation of his novel, *Myra Breckinridge*, Gore Vidal denounced the film as "an awful joke."

Trouble had begun with the casting of Mae West, who had last appeared on a movie screen in the box office disaster *The Heat's On*, released by Columbia Pictures during the dark days of war-torn 1943.

Although Gore had rejected an offer to write the screenplay of *Breckinridge*, he did accept an invitation to visit Mae at her residence in the Ravenswood Apartments (on North Rossmore Avenue) in Los Angeles.

The movie's producer, Robert Fryer, had called Mae to offer her a role in the film for $100,000. She mistakenly thought he was offering her the lead, and she was initially outraged that he wanted her to star in a movie for only $100,000.

She told him that she would agree to a role in the movie only if she was given top billing, a free hand in rewriting her scenes, and $300,000.

At first, 20th Century hesitated, but they eventually agreed to her price. In response, she notified Fox executives that they had waited too long. She now demanded $350,000. Finally, they agreed to that, too, believing that the publicity of including her

Mae West, pictured above next to **Raquel Welch**, played an aging talent agent who invented the casting couch for studs.

would be worth it at the box office.

***

Gore relayed to Elizabeth Taylor the litany of his (disastrous) experiences with Mae during the filming of *Myra Breckinridge*. "The wisest thing you ever did, Elizabeth, was to turn down the role."

When Gore had visited Mae, he recalled that she was dressed entirely in white, including her furs and diamonds. She blended in with her all-white apartment. "She was so heavily made up and so flamboyantly gowned that I had no idea exactly what was lurking behind all that artificial glamour," Gore recalled. "I feared a very old lady who had helped Lincoln draft the *Emancipation Proclamation*."

"Mae looked like a living refugee from the waxworks," he said. "No wonder Billy Wilder originally offered her the role of Norma Desmond in *Sunset Blvd*."

"Beneath all that war paint, I sensed a tireless trouper from yesterday, a born entertainer who loved to perform, and a consummate publicity agent promoting only one product—herself, in all her faded glory."

Although she hadn't made a movie in twenty-three years, she wanted it clearly understood that she didn't want Fox to bill this picture as her comeback. "It's a return, not a comeback," she told him, parroting a line from *Sunset Blvd*.

"I'm still a star, one of the really big ones, right up there with Charlie Chaplin," she told him. "He was a little guy, but one with a big prick. I'm also a playwright. Speaking of playwrights, there are only three big ones—Tennessee Williams, Eugene O'Neill, and me."

"I can still undulate these old hips of mine, even if they date from the 19th Century," she told him. "I'm such a big name that I can carry the picture myself. They'll come to see me. Every birthday, I get so many phone calls from well-wishers that I practically shut down the phone lines with overload."

Before agreeing to participate in the project, she had definite requirements.

"First, I never play a character older than twenty-six," she told him. "Not only that, but I write my own lines, each guaranteed to get a laugh."

"When I went into her all-white bathroom to take a piss, I was shocked to see this large blowup, a frontal nude, of Jack Dempsey," Gore said. "She had a thing for boxers, especially if they were as black as Gorilla Jones, another of her lovers."

["Gorilla" Jones (aka William Landon Jones (1906-1982), was an African-American, Memphis-born boxer and twice NBA Middleweight Boxing Champion of the World.]

"Earlier, she'd told me that when management had objected to her having black boxers come and go, she bought a large interest in the building and lifted the ban on Negroes."

Seated opposite her once again, Gore learned that she wanted to perform three or four musical numbers within the context of the upcoming movie. "She even sang a few lines from a song from one of her long-ago road shows. It was called 'Rub-a-Dub-Dub, Three Fags in a Tub.' I convinced her that that exact title might not be appropriate."

"After two of the most fascinating hours of my life, Mae announced that she had to retire for her afternoon beauty sleep so she would be in condition to rock 'n' roll around the clock till dawn breaks," Gore said.

"God, these young men of today are so demanding," Mae said. "They just can't get enough."

Gore kissed her diamond-laden hand and wished her luck with the movie.

He remembered her parting words to him: "Fox is sure lucky to get me in the picture. It'll increase sales of that novel of yours. I tried to read it but couldn't get through it. With me in the picture, it'll become a classic."

Some of her final words were filled with a certain nostalgia. "I never loved another person the way I loved myself, and I have no guilt about it. I'm in a class by myself. I have no regrets."

"How about you, Vidal?" she asked. "Did you ever love?"

"Only once in my entire life, and he was slaughtered by the Japs on the beaches of Iwo Jima."

***

Before the final cast of *Myra Breckinridge* was announced by 20th Century Fox, Candy Darling, the emerging superstar from the entourage of Andy Warhol, began to pursue Gore, even though he insisted with her that he had no say over casting. She didn't really believe him.

She was aggressively lobbying for the role of Myra. "Why get one of those Hollywood whores with a smelly vagina when you can cast a 'Trans woman' like me?" she asked. "I AM Myra Breckinridge. I understand her to my scarlet-painted toenails."

When she first came to call, Gore paid her a lot more attention, since he'd written a book (that was about to be adapted into a movie), about a transsexual.

She revealed to him that while she was growing up as James Lawrence Slattery (nicknamed Jimmy) in Queens (New York City), she had identified with Myra Breckinridge. Like the heroine of his novel, she was addicted to old movies.

She confided that she learned the mysteries of sex from a salesman (a child molester) in a local children's store.

Her mother confronted her one evening with rumors she'd heard that her son was a cross dresser. Jimmy went to his bedroom and emerged an hour later as "Hope Dahl," a name she later changed to Candy Darling.

The name was chosen because of her love of sweets.

"I knew then that I couldn't stop Jimmy," her mother, Theresa Phelan, said. "He was too beautiful and talented. His beauty rivaled that of any girl I knew. I also knew that every red-blooded male in America would want my son in bed."

Gore, in time, heard all of Candy's stories, including details about some movie stars who had seduced her, including one who was the macho King of Hollywood at the time.

Pictured on the left in this photo are **Raquel Welch** as Myra Breckinridge and film critic **Rex Reed** as Myron Breckinridge, what she had looked like before her gender re-assignment.

The two figures on the right are **Mae West**, born in 1893, and director **John Huston**, born in 1906, sharing memories of yesterday.

"I'm not going to name him, but movie buffs of the early 70s will know exactly who I mean."

Finally, Gore grew impatient, having by now heard all of Candy's revelations. He quit accepting her phone calls. She reacted by appearing on his doorstep several times late at night.

Finally, in exasperation, he threw open his door to confront her. "Fuck, Candy, let me get some sleep. If you want to play Myra, head over to Richard Zanuck's house and suck him off." Then he slammed the door in her face.

He never saw her again but was saddened to learn of her death on March 21, 1974 of lymphoma. "She truly lived up to the motto of young people: Live fast, die young, and leave a beautiful corpse."

***

At long last, the cast of *Breckinridge* was announced by Fox. Raquel Welch was designated as Myra, and Mae West as Leticia. According to Mae, "The Leticia role was tailor made for me, that of a sexually predatory talent scout who auditions only studs."

Director John Huston signed on for the role of Buck Loner after promising Fox that, "I won't try to take over as the director. Think of me as a piano player in a whorehouse."

Producers David Giler and Robert Fryer assembled a very talented cast, with Roger Herren cast as Rusty Godowski, who is dildo-raped by Myra. The character of Rusty was described "as the last stronghold of masculinity in this Disneyland of perversion."

The movie critic, Rex Reed, was cast in a very brief cameo as Myron Breckinridge—that is, Myra "before she had it cut off."

Farrah Fawcett played Mary Ann Pringle, Rusty's girlfriend. Some very talented character actors filled out the bill, including Jim Backus as the Doctor; John Carradine as the Surgeon, Andy Devine as Coyote Bill, and Tom Selleck in an early role as "The Stud."

The surprise from Fox involved the hiring of the relatively unknown director, Michael Sarne, whose contract gave him total control over the expensive project. He did not set out to make "one of the fifty worst films of all time," but he succeeded in doing just that.

Sarne had previously directed a film, *Joanna* (1968), about a young country girl entangled in the murky morality of swinging London. Fox hired him as the film's director, hoping to capture a youth market which had never before heard of Mae West.

A reporter asked Mae how she felt about the casting of Raquel Welch as Myra. "Who?" Mae asked. "Never heard of her." Consistently throughout the course of filming, Mae never called her by her name, but constantly referred to Raquel as "The Little Girl."

"'What's her face' has one or two little scenes in the movie—so I've been told," Mae said.

She was also asked if she'd heard rumors that both Gore Vidal and Rex Reed were homosexuals. "Gay lib?" she asked. "The gay boys? Looks like they're practically taking over. I think they invented the word 'gay' back in 1927 when I wrote a homosexual comedy called *Drag*. The gay boys have always adored me, and they're always imitating me. They know talent when they see it."

She was passionately opposed to the director's idea of defining the entire film as a fantasy. "It's like someone tells you a story and gets you all interested. Then they say, 'I woke up to find it was all a dream.' You want to smack 'em in the face!"

It was agreed that Mae would appear only in black-and-white outfits, her gowns designed by Edith Head. When Welch showed up for a photo shoot dressed in black, a feud was launched.

Behind Raquel's back, Mae was lobbying

A transsexual, **Candy Darling,** wanted to play Myra. "I'm the real thing."

Gore Vidal later said, "Candy might have given the movie the shot of testosterone it needed."

One night at Studio 54, she told Sylvia Miles and Darwin Porter, "My goal is to become the Kim Novak blonde of the trannie world. Andy Warhol said he finds me 'surprisingly *femme*.' He thinks I 'evoke ambulatory archives of ideal movie star womanhood.'"

to have her replaced, even though she was the world's reigning sex symbol at the time. Mae wanted a homosexual—"maybe like this Candy Darling that Gore Vidal was telling me about—cast as Myra instead of a biological woman. Only a homosexual can play the role."

Sarne informed Mae that in one sequence, she'd appear in front of a chorus line of African-American men, each of them dressed in white tie and tails. She issued a warning: "They must never touch me—because of all those rednecks in the South, you know."

When Gore heard that, he remarked, "In her private life, Mae never had any objection to being touched by a black man—that's touched, not fucked."

Raquel had her own views about Mae West, her casting, and the script itself.

"If you can buy the fact that a woman of 77 can send a 22-year-old stud to the hospital to recuperate after a night of sex, then you can buy anything in this picture."

At one point, Mae was introduced to Farrah Fawcett. "Oh, you play the lesbian lover of Myra Breckinridge," Mae said. "You certainly look the part. I guess you're quite familiar with mattresses."

[Mae's put-downs always contained a double entendre. She'd previously seen Fawcett advertising Beautyrest mattresses on TV.]

Sarne tossed out nearly all of Mae's quips, which seriously angered her. She later claimed "the movie would have been sure box office if they'd kept in my one-liners and some of my musical numbers."

[One of her memorable lines in Myra Breckinridge is delivered when she auditions a row of good-looking men. One in particular strikes her fancy. "Cowboy," she asks. "How tall are you?"

"I'm six feet, seven inches," he replies.

"Well, never mind the six feet—let's talk about the seven inches."

Gore read some of Mae's quips that she'd submitted for inclusion in the movie. "She must have gone down memory lane and opened an old stage trunk when these

Newcomer **Farrah Fawcett** challenged Raquel Welch as a sex symbol, and Ryan O'Neal was in her corner.

Also emerging as a male sex symbol was **Tom Selleck**. When Mae West spotted him, she said: "That's the kind of man I'd like to invite to come up and see me sometime."

one-liners were first written. I think Theodore Roosevelt was in the White House. A typical sample would be, 'I don't expect too much from a man—just what he's got!'"]

In subsequent releases of Myra Breckinridge, some of which were heavily edited, many of the best scenes were cut, including when Rex Reed, as Myron, confronts the Surgeon, played by John Carradine. He's ready to undergo "the cruelest cut" in his attempt to transform himself into Myra.

"You realize that once we cut it off, it won't grow back?" Carradine warns Myron. "How about circumcision instead? It'll be cheaper."

Raquel and Mae, during a rare break in their frequent battles, agreed on only one point: Sarne should be fired and replaced with the gay director George Cukor. But finally, they decided that even Cukor wouldn't be able to save this picture.

Michael Sarne, the director of Myra Breckinridge, said, "Raquel and Rex Reed didn't want Mae in the picture, and they also launched a hate-fest against me."

***

When Myra Breckinridge opened in 1970, it was an immediate flop, and Fox soon withdrew it from circulation. It was one of two X-rated films that Fox released that year, the other being *Beyond the Valley of the Dolls*.

Movie critics at *Time* magazine pounced on it, asserting, "Myra Breckinridge is about as funny as a child molester. It is an insult to intelligence, an affront to sensibility, and an abomination to the eye."

Vincent Canby of *The New York Times* denounced filmmakers who go to "great lengths to try to be different and dirty. As for Mae West, she possesses a figure of a cinched-in penguin and a face made of pink-and-white plaster in which little holes have been left for her eyes and mouth."

Author Simon Louvish wrote: "The problem derives largely from the original material: Gore Vidal's mock-trashy vision of a morally and physically polluted America, drawn through the transsexual's eyes—and in particular, the subculture of Los Angeles, inhabited by a rogue's gallery of phonies and grotesques. George Cukor would have floundered as deeply as Michael Sarne, who survived the movie without being assassinated."

The film also attracted unwanted attention from Golden Age movie stars. From the Fox archives, footage of movies filmed in the 1930s had been inserted to punctuate the jokes, and as a spoof of the film's climatic dildo-rape scene. During the latter, images of Myra getting invasive with Rusty fade as footage from Shirley Temple's 1937 film *Heidi* appears on the screen. The 1937 clip showed Shirley (as Heidi) getting squirted with milk during her attempt to milk a stubborn goat. The symbolism of ejaculation in her face is quite clear.

Objections to the scene reached all the way to the White House. "Shirley's face, symbolically at least, is being sprayed with semen," claimed Richard Nixon, of all people.

For reasons known only to himself, Nixon had requested a screening of *Myra Breckinridge* at the White House. The morning after he saw it, he telephoned Richard Zanuck in Hollywood, asking him to remove the Shirley Temple footage from the context of the larger film, fuming, "Shirley is a staunch Republican and, as an ambassador *[to the United Nations in 1969; to Ghana in 1974; and to Czechoslovakia in 1989]* will represent the United States."

Loretta Young successfully sued to have old film footage of herself removed from the picture.

After the film's release, Gore picked up a copy of the *Los Angeles Times* to read a letter to the editor written by one J. Correll. "Mae West has become a tiresome old bore, forever talking about how wonderful she was—and she thinks she still is. At almost eighty, she's a gabby girl, but not the Mae West of forty years ago, when I was a fan of hers. She belongs to the past, and only the past, an old lady who thinks of herself as a sex symbol. It is sad and somewhat revolting."

Gore showed the letter to his breakfast companion, Howard Austen. "I couldn't have said it better myself."

The story may be apocryphal, but years later, Gore heard that Sarne was working as a waiter in a restaurant. "God does exist," he said.

In spite of its initial reception, the film version of *Myra Breckinridge* has, since its release, become a cult classic.

MYRA/MYRON TRADES PLACES WITH COBRA WOMAN

Despite the dismal reception of the movie, in 1974, based on the best-selling success of his 1968 novel it had been based on *[Myra Breckinridge]*, Gore released a sequel, *Myron*, which was published shortly after an anti-pornography crackdown by the U.S. Supreme Court. To show his contempt for specific members of the Court, Gore satirized their names by inserting them at unexpectedly salacious points within his manuscript. *[Example: "He thrust his enormous Rehnquist deep within her Whizzer White."]*

In the sequel, *Myron*, Gore went wild with the he/she fluidity. As literary critic Robert F. Kiernan encapsulated the novel: "Obscenities and recriminations shoot freely back and forth as the antagonists (Myra battling Myron) settle down to a stalemated war, and tweezered eyebrows, padded brassieres, and raw oysters become delightful beachheads in their battle for sexual supremacy. Myron threatens Myra that he will take male hormones and turn the Breckinridge body as hairy as a tarantula, and she threatens him that she will dance the *tarantella* in a Maidenform bra on his grave."

Maria Montez, the sultry Dominican star of such movies as *Cobra Woman* (1944), figures into the newer novel. One night, while watching *Siren of Babylon* (Gore's satire of Montez's 1948 movie, *Siren of Atlantis*), Myron/Myra is transported to a 1940s film set via his/her television set.

For the Myra aspect of the protagonist's character, this is a dream come true; for Myron, it's his worst nightmare. As he desperately tries to escape from the film set, he encounters Richard Nixon seeking a hideaway from the Watergate scandal.

Gore also used this novel to "send up" his critics. Its character of Whittaker Kaiser is clearly inspired by author Norman Mailer. From Kaiser's mouth emerges this declaration: "Look, every man wants to make it with another man, but the real man is the one who fights off his hideous weak fag self and takes one woman after another without the use of any contraceptives or pill or diaphragm or rubber, just the all-conquering sperm, because contraception of any kind is as bad as masturbation."

At the novel's climax, a former cowboy actor in the film, now a transsexual, has been elected as the Republican Governor of Arizona. The episode was an obvious spoof of Rex Bell, the former celluloid cowboy who became the Lieutenant Governor of Nevada who (unhappily) married the emotionally unstable silent screen vamp, Clara Bow.

Kiernan summed up the two Breckinridge novels: "They are preposterous, droll, and gaudily offensive—although altogether triumphant and altogether wonderful."

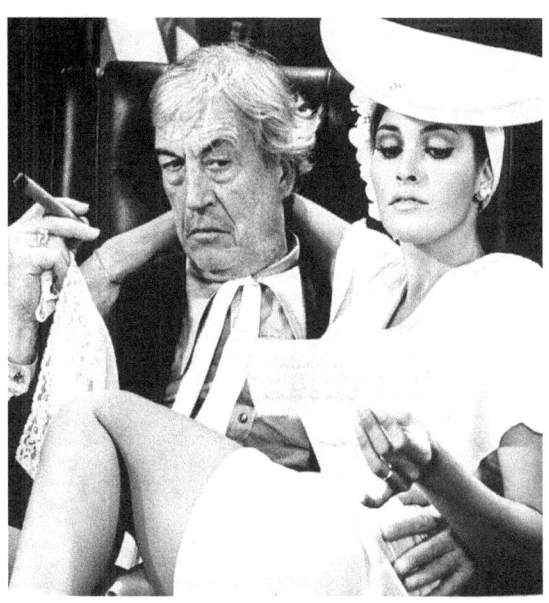

Could It Be Love?

Depicted above in this scene from *Myra Breckinridge* is major-league film director **John Huston**, impersonating the most decadent over-the-hill roué in Texas.

Huston has just authorized a substantial blackmail payoff to Myron or Myra (**Raquel**), depending on how you interpret his (or her) character.

Left photo: **Maria Montez** as Cobra Woman graces the cover of a paperback containing both of Gore's "transsexualized" novels.

Right photo: "**High Testosterone Raquel**," as Myra, "clanking balls," and lower photo: **Gore Vidal** in a publicity photo for the then "unbelievably shocking" *Myron* as part of a nationwide book tour.

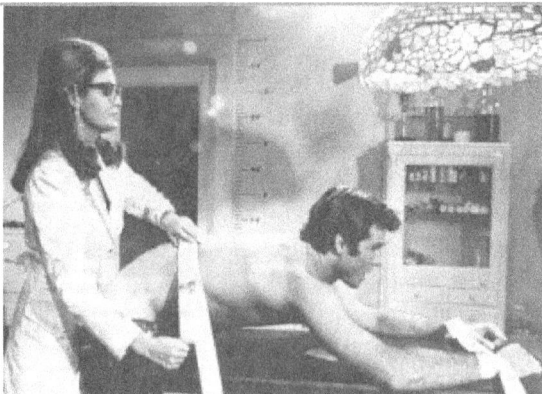

Gore Vidal in a publicity photo for the then "unbelievably shocking" *Myron (a sequel to Myra Breckinridge)* as part of a nationwide book tour.

Yet another view of the role-playing ironies exposed in the cinematic version of Gore Vidal's *Myra Breckinridge*.

Who is doing what to whom in this "medical examination" by Myron or Myra (**Raquel Welch**) to the former high school football hero, Rusty Gadowski (**Roger Herren**)?

Chapter Seven

CRAZY OCTOBER

TRICKING, TREATING, AND ON THE ROAD, TOURING
WITH THREE BRILLIANT STAGE, SCREEN, & SOCIAL DIVAS

TALLULAH BANKHEAD,
JOAN BLONDELL, & ESTELLE WINWOOD

The play by James Leo Herlihy, **Crazy October** (1958), introduced Darwin to the crazy world of the theater. He formed lifelong friendships with not only the playwright, but with two of its stars, **Joan Blondell** and **Tallulah Bankhead.**

Tallulah, in wedgies and rolled-down red socks, played Daisy, the owner of a wayside inn in West Virginia.

During his extended gig as a Bureau Chief (1957-1960) for *The Miami Herald*, Darwin Porter was assigned to interview producer Walter Starcke, playwright James Leo Herlihy, and the indomitable star, Tallulah Bankhead. Each of them had retreated for some much-needed R&R in Key West after their nationwide tour in Herlihy's black comedy, *Crazy October*.

Starcke was the first Broadway producer Darwin had ever met, and they became instant friends. He knew a host of Broadway luminaries and relayed stories to Darwin about the legends and lore of "The Great White Way."

Years before, Starcke had been the long-time sexual *protégé* of John Van Druten, the English playwright and theater director who had died in 1957.

One of the most successful playwrights of his era, Van Druten sold the rights to many of his plays to Hollywood pro-

One of the theater's most popular playwrights, **John Van Druten** (right), more or less adopted **Walter Starcke**, depicted on the left in his later years, as a *protégé*.

Under his guidance, Starcke produced *I Am a Camera* in 1951, which later reached the screen as a musical, *Cabaret* (1972), starring Liza Minnelli as Sally Bowles.

ducers for adaptations into movies. These included such classics as *Old Aquaintance* (1943) with Bette Davis and Miriam Hopkins; *The Voice of the Turtle* (1947) with Ronald Reagan, and *Bell, Book, & Candle (1958)* with James Stewart and Kim Novak.

In 1951, in collaboration with Broadway producer Gertrude Macy, Starcke had produced Van Druten's hit play, *I Am a Camera,* a stage adaptation of Christopher Isherwood's *Berlin Stories,* a biographical saga about Isherwood's life and risqué adventures in pre-Hitler Berlin. *I Am a Camera* was later adapted into the hit Hollywood musical *Cabaret* (1972), starring Liza Minnelli as the incomparable and insouciant Sally Bowles.

It had been Starcke who had introduced Darwin to the playwright, James Leo Herlihy, who became his best friend for many years.

Born to a working-class family in Detroit, Herlihy had studied at Black Mountain College in North Carolina, and at the Yale University Drama department. He was also an actor, appearing on stage at the Pasadena Playhouse.

In 1945, at the end of World War II, he'd enlisted in the U.S. Navy.

His highly successful play, *Blue Denim,* premiered in New York City and was later staged in Scandinavia, Germany, Italy, and France. In 1959, it morphed into a hit film starring Brandon de Wilde and Carol Lynley. Actually, although the theme of the film was abortion, that word was never spoken—not even once—throughout the entire course of the film.

Ever since Herlihy had seen Tallulah in a revival of *A Streetcar Named Desire,* he'd been enchanted with her and wanted to write a play for her.

After finishing his first draft of *Crazy October*, he arranged to meet her through her agent. At her home, he read all the parts for her.

At the end of his reading, she ordered her "caddy," Ted Hook, to bring her another bourbon, and she lit a cigarette. "A perfectly dreadful play, *dah-ling*, but I find you charming," she said. "Let's be friends."

"As for your play, *dah-ling*, it's just another one of those downbeat, down-trodden, degenerate Southern *thaangs!*"

They became friends for life, and he finally overcame her objections to her play. As one of the female leads, she agreed to embark on a nationwide tour with *Crazy October*, beginning in New Haven and ending in San Francisco.

Over time, Herlihy became a frequent visitor to Darwin's penthouse apartment in Greenwich Village, and Herlihy became the first visitor to Darwin's new home (Magnolia House) on St. Marks Place in Staten Island.

During that visit, Herlihy's second novel, *Midnight Cowboy*, was being filmed in Manhattan. Herlihy's social call began a long tradition of Darwin's entertaining of celebrities, mostly from the theater or from Hollywood, at Magnolia House.

According to Darwin, "You never knew who the very charismatic Herlihy would show up with: Perhaps Angela Lansbury, Edward Albee, Geraldine Page, or Truman Capote—even the diarist, Anaïs Nin."

Through Herlihy, Darwin was also introduced to Stanley Haggart, who had a home in Key West. He had been the scenic designer for *Crazy*

Key West residents and fellow playwrights, **James Leo Herlihy** (left) and **Tennessee Williams,** came from completely different worlds, but bonded as friends. For reasons known only to himslf, Tennessee called the playwright "The Hun."

TED HOOK'S
BACKSTAGE
"New York's Most Theatrical Restaurant"
Lunch • Cocktails • Dinner
• Late Nite Snacks
Sunday Brunch Commencing At Noon
318 West 45th Street, New York City
(212) 581-8447

When Sardi's got "too touristy," an aging actor and chorus boy, Ted Hook, opened **Backstage** in the theater district. It became a gathering place for the theatrical elite, ranging from Carol Channing and Ethel Merman to Richard Burton and Laurence Olivier.

Hook once tried to handle the personal affairs of Tallulah Bankhead, who dismissively referred to him as "my caddy."

October, and had been friendly with its star, Tallulah Bankhead, for years. On their first meeting, she had come on to him.

In time, Haggart would hire Darwin as a business partner at his TV advertising company, and as an associate in his publishing ventures.

Darwin had originally launched his friendship with Tallulah in Manhattan, and eventually became a frequent visitor to her townhouse on East 62nd Street in Manhattan.

"You never knew who would be sitting in Tallulah's living room," he said. "Adlai Stevenson, Eleanor Roosevelt, Rock Hudson, and invariably the veteran English actress, Estelle Winwood. Born in England in 1883, she had decided at the age of five that she wanted to be an actress. Years later, she played the third female lead in *Crazy October* during its nationwide tour with Tallulah.

At the time of his first meeting with Estelle, in Tallulah's living room, she told him, "You can kiss my hand, dear heart," she said. "I'd like to introduce you to Montgomery Clift. He's a former stage star but now a Hollywood movie star. He sucks cocks, you know."

Tallulah butted in. "He's never sucked *my* cock."

"I just adored Estelle," Darwin said. "I found her very outspoken. She told me she'd married four times, once to the film director and producer, Guthrie McClintic."

"I don't recall that I ever went to bed with any of my husbands," she told me. "They were always off somewhere with their boyfriends. I detest appearing in films. I do it only for the money. Movies are a medium beneath me."

Among Winwood's many screen roles was an appearance opposite Marilyn Monroe in *The Misfits* (1961) and another with Bette Davis in *Dead Ringer* (1964). She had also starred in *Camelot* (1967) with Richard Harris and Vanessa Redgrave, and in Mel Brooks' *The Producers* (also 1967).

[Estelle died in 1984 at the age of 101.]

***

During her declining years, Tallulah seemed to either be looking for work in the theater or flamboyantly rejecting roles that were offered to her. Tennessee Williams arrived one night to ask if she'd star in a revival of his play, *Sweet Bird of Youth*. *[It had already been filmed as a showcase for Geraldine Page, with Paul Newman as her gigolo.]*

"Mr. Williams, how dare you insult me by offering me such a ghastly role, that of an aging, drunken, broken-down has-been whose better days are long gone? She's forced to pay for sex from a male hustler. *Dah-ling*, no wonder you created such a role, later changing the gender of its key player. *YOU*, Mr. Williams are Alexandra del Lago. Your play about the aging star is totally autobiographical. And it's YOU who's devoted of hustlers—not me!"

Tennessee was disappointed that Tallulah had rejected (brutally) his proposal for her involvement in the revival of his play, but later reported that she had once expressed interest in starring as Violet Venable in *Suddenly, Last Summer*. *[That role eventually went to Katharine Hepburn.]*

"Hepburn, that dyke with the dreadful voice, is a New Englander," Tallulah said. "PLEASE, *dah-lings*. She doesn't know how to play a Southern lady like I do. Whereas she'd look ridiculous, the world would believe ME as Violet, knowing I'd like to lobotomize Elizabeth Taylor."

Tennessee also revealed that Tallulah had also rejected an offer to appear in *What Ever Happened to Baby Jane?* (1962).

Estelle Winwood, sometimes to great effect, played "down on their luck" English ladies flaunting their eccentricies and upperclass speech patterns.

In the photo above, she appears as a panhandler with **Marilyn Monroe** and **Clark Gable** in their last film, *The Misfits* (1961), written by Monroe's estranged husband, Arthur Miller.

The part she'd been offered went instead to Bette Davis, who starred opposite her arch rival, Joan Crawford. "No one wants to go see those two old hags," Tallulah said, viciously. "Besides, I've never forgiven Davis for stealing my great stage role in *The Little Foxes* and also for impersonating me as Margo Channing in *All About Eve.*"

One night, Darwin joined playwrights Herlihy and James Kirkwood, Jr., for a visit to Tallulah. She had been offered a role in a new play by Arthur Kopit, *Oh Dad, Poor Dad, Momma's Hung You in the Closet, and I'm Feeling So Bad.* Both men were actors, and Herlihy and Kirkwood read the script to her, taking all the parts.

Tallulah listened impatiently. When they were finished, she lit a cigarette and called for Ted Hook to "get your well-used ass in here with another bourbon."

"I was reared in a proper home in Alabama as a respectable Southern lady with a distinguished father. Despite many vile rumors, I am still a respectable grand lady of the Old South, the one that's *Gone With the Wind*. I should have played Scarlett O'Hara! You can tell Mr. Kopit that he should offer the role to Shelley Winters. She's cornered the market on playing tramps and whores, no doubt drawn from personal experience."[a]

Upper tier, right: **Tallulah Bankhead,** as a stage actress, and (*upper tier, left*) **Eleanor Roosevelt**, the First Lady, worked together duirng World War II to launch the first canteen in Washington, D.C. It was open to all enlisted men, with top politicians or visiting stars of stage and screen serving food, washing dishes, or else, like George Jessel, providing entertainment. When the canteen threw open its doors, Tallulah boasted that she was the first person to dance with one of the enlisted men.

In the mid-1950s, Tallulah and Eleanor joined forces, politically, making joint appearances at, for example, this civil rights rally in Madison Square Garden. Between them *(lower tier)* sits activist **Autherine Lucy** (the first African-American to attend the University of Alabama), and on the far right sits **Rosa Parks**, an organizer of the Montgomery (AL) bus boycotts.

Even in their later years, **Tallulah and Eleanor** remained close friends and avid supporters of the Democratic Party. Eleanor, on one occasion accompanied by Darwin Porter, sometimes visited Tallulah in the era when both women were living in the same neighborhood of Manhattan's Upper East Side.

Despite their huge differences in background, presentation, and style, the two women seemed to understand and respect one another on very deep levels, and Eleanor could always overlook Tallulah's outrageous behavior.

For example, directly off the the living room of Tallulah's Manhattan apartment was a bathroom from the depths of which Tallulah would continue talking loudly to Eleanor even if she had to urinate, keeping the door open and—in some cases, the television's soap opera blaring—as she "took a horse piss" (her words).

If other guests were present (as was Darwin, one long-ago afternoon), Eleanor benignly sipped her tea, dismissing the antics and ribald dialogue of the actress with the simple but wise adage: **"THAT'S TALLULAH!"**

Chapter Eight

MIDNIGHT COWBOY

THE FIRST X-RATED MOVIE TO WIN AN OSCAR

James Leo Herlihy's first novel, *All Fall Down (1960)* was turned into a screenplay by William Inge and eventually starred Warren Beatty, Eva Marie Saint, Karl Malden, and Angela Lansbury.

When Herlihy released his second novel, **Midnight Cowboy**, in 1965, his agent told him that it could never be adapted into a film because of its sexual content and blatant homosexual overtones. "Let's face it," the agent said. "It's the story of a love affair between two men."

The novel chronicles the flight from Texas to New York of Joe Buck. In Manhattan, he plans to sell his huge endowment to love-starved rich women longing for "a real man," a stud-for-hire. On the grimy streets, he meets "Ratso" Rizzo, a crippled con man who's eager to function as Buck's pimp. Director John Schlesinger thought it would make a terrific film, and bought the rights, adapting it into a favorite at the 1969 Academy Award Ceremony honoring that year's cinematic achievements. It won awards as Best Picture, Best Director, and Best Adapted Screenplay.

The photo on the left was taken by Stanley Mills Haggart, a long-time associate of Darwin Porter and one of Herlihy's best friends.

When Darwin moved into Magnolia House on St. Marks Place on Staten Island, the first friend to arrive on his doorstep with a housewarming gift was James Leo Herlihy.

In 1965, he'd published his second novel, *Midnight Cowboy*, to disappointing sales. But John Schlesinger, at the time, one of the world's leading directors, picked up a copy in an airport bookstore and read it *en route* to London.

From England, he phoned Herlihy's agent and optioned the property, later hiring Waldo Salt to write the screenplay. A native of Chicago, Salt wrote nineteen films over the course of his career, beginning with *The Bride Wore Red* (1937) starring Joan Crawford and her husband at the time, Franchot Tone.

Salt's string of hits was halted when he was blacklisted during the McCarthy witch hunts. But he came back, not only winning an Oscar for his script of *Midnight Cowboy* (1969) but one for *Coming Home* (1978), starring Jane Fonda and Jon Voight. Salt was also nominated for an Oscar for *Serpico* (1973), starring Al Pacino.

Scenes from the movie were shot in Manhattan, starring Voight as Joe Buck, a male prostitute wandering the streets around Times Square, and Dustin Hoffman as Ratso Rizzo, a streetwise con man smart enough to know how to survive in a cruel world.

Although Voight's fame for younger generations rests mainly on his being the father of Angelina Jolie, *Midnight Cowboy* launched him into the bigtime. Later, he delivered other powerful performances, too, notably in *Deliverance* (1972) with Burt Reynolds and again when he played a paraplegic Vietnam veteran in *Coming Home* (1978). This picture with Jane Fonda earned him a Best Actor Oscar. He was also notable as a pen-

Here's Joe Buck (**Jon Voight**), a disillusioned hustler, and his unlikely ally Ratso (**Dustin Hoffman**), both of them cold, hungry, bitter, and wondering if all of this is worth it.

A post-coital cowboy getting a grip on the difficulty of his dream—becoming NYC's hottest hustler.

Executive hipster **Brenda Vaccaro**, bored with the everyday singles scene in the big bad Apple, wonders if Mr. Buckaroo was worth the time, money, and trouble.

When **Prostitute A (Jon Voight** as Joe Buck) shacks up with Prostitute B (as portrayed by an aging **Sylvia Miles**, a real-life *protégée* of Andy Warhol), one can only wonder:

"Who's Hustling Whom?" and "Who's the more hardened hooker?"

niless ex-boxing champion in a remake of *The Champ* in 1979.

Hoffman evoked a dyed-in-the-wool New Yorker during his performance as Ratso, even though he'd actually been born in 1937 in Los Angeles. Over the years, he won a reputation for versatile portrayals of anti-heroes and unexpectedly vulnerable men working through ironies and dilemmas. *[Life magazine once joked that "if Dustin Hoffman's face where his fortune, he'd be committed to a life of poverty."]*

Before his involvement in *Cowboy*, his breakthrough role had been as Benjamin Braddock, the title character in *The Graduate* (1967). His co-star had been Anne Bancroft, who accepted her part after Doris Day turned it down.

[Later in his career, beginning in late 2017, seven women accused the actor of sexual misconduct or assault over the course of several decades.]

That night at Magnolia House, Herlihy and Darwin talked into the wee hours, as the novelist told him about the dramas associated with the casting of Hoffman and Voight.

Joe Buck had been publicized among the actors who competed for the part as "the sexiest role of the year," and Ratso was viewed as a character role so stunning that whomever played it was "guaranteed" to win an Oscar.

Sal Mineo was the first major star to

FANS CALLED IT "AN X-RATED MORALITY TALE"

Here's **Jon Voight** as Joe Buck: The sex appeal of a callow cowboy from friendlier climes doesn't necessary work in the sexual cesspools of urban and blighted New York.

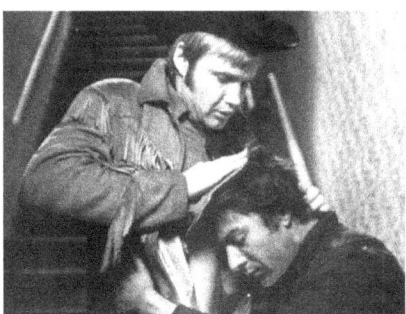

The Ironies of Love: Joe comforting a very sick Ratso in the filthy stairwell of a bordello.

Love and Death: Although their dream of an escape from the grime of Times Square has lured them away from their urban and existential traps, Ratso (**Hoffman**) dies en route to their utopian dream in Florida.

Midnight Cowboy

read the novel and apply for a role. He flew to Key West to meet with Herlihy to discuss the nuances of the part. Preoccupied with buying the movie rights to the original novel, he wasn't able to raise the cash to acquire them. As he told an interviewer at the time, "the book's fuckin' fantastic, man."

Mineo spent the weekend in Key West, and Herlihy later admitted that he had sex with him. "He was like a firecracker. Paul Newman might kick him out of his bed, but Sal could put his shoes under my bed any night he wants."

When Darwin expressed amazement that Sal thought he could play Joe Buck, Herlihy quickly corrected him: "No, no. no. Sal wants to play the streetwise Ratso. The kid's from the Bronx. He'd be terrific as Ratso. He's hip enough to realize that my novel is really the love story of two men, Ratso and Joe Buck."

To many of Sal's fans, the role ultimately went to Hoffman, who delivered one of the most brilliant performances of his long career.

Warren Beatty was the next to weigh in. At the height of his sexual allure, he wanted the juicy role of Joe Buck for himself. Beatty had already appeared in the film adaptation of another of Herlihy's novels, *All Fall Down*.

Although Herlihy thought Beatty would be ideal as Joe Buck, the ultimate decision lay with the film's director (Schlesinger), who rejected him. Schlesinger told Herlihy that Beatty was too well known and too sophisticated to play a naïve hustler whose primary ambition involves selling his sexual favors to women.

Then Paul Newman entered the contest, contacting Herlihy in New York through Arnold L. Weissberger, a famous theatrical attorney who represented such clients as Marlene Dietrich and

John Schlesinger on the set of *Midnight Cowboy*.

He expressed regret that four of "the hottest scenes" in the Waldo Salt script had to be cut. He was told, "The world is not ready for them yet."

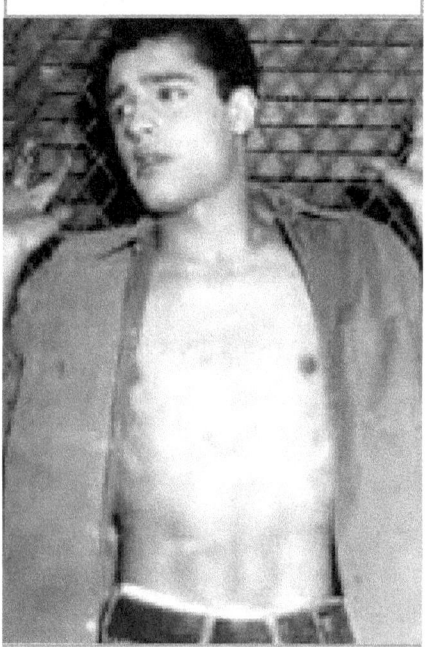

When **Sal Mineo** saw this picture of himself, he told a publicist, "In this photograph, I'm baring both my heart and soul."

For more on the suitability of Sal as Ratso Rizzo, refer to the final pages of this chapter.

Elizabeth Taylor. Herlihy was astonished to receive the call and hastily invited Newman up to his rather cramped and uncomfortable bachelor pad in the East Village, a walk-up whose bathtub was configured as part of its kitchen.

"I'd always resented Newman," Herlihy confessed. "I used to think that the movie in which he'd starred, *Hud* (1963), was a bit of a rip-off of my novel, *All Fall Down*. But whereas my movie had starred Brandon de Wilde with Warren Beatty, *Hud*, of course, had starred Brandon but with Newman this time. And whereas *Hud* did very well at the box office, *All Fall Down* did not. I have to admit I was rather jealous of the success of *Hud* over my own work."

"Newman was all charm and graciousness when he walked up to my little hippie pad," Herlihy said. "'Mr. Newman' became 'Paul' after a few beers. He had that winning smile that captivated me at once. I could really go for him, and I think he knew that. He talked a lot about my character of Joe Buck, and both of us clearly understood that the character I'd created was a lot younger than Paul."

"Eventually, Paul devised an unusual, slightly different interpretation of the movie character he was interested in playing," Herlihy said. "He believed that if Joe Buck planned to hustle older, rich women, these ladies wouldn't want to be seen out in public with a young Buck but with an older, well-preserved Buck. 'No fifty-five-year-old woman wants to show up at a party in New York with a man young enough to be her son . . . or her grandson,' Paul told me. He had a point. I realized that a smooth, urbane guy like Paul would be more convincing as a New York stud than some young kid who just got off the Greyhound from Texas."

"Before the night was over, I was rooting for Paul, but I hadn't a clue as to what Schlesinger would think," Herlihy said. "At the time Paul was also up for the lead in *Butch Cassidy & the Sundance Kid* (1969). He couldn't seem to make up his mind which role he really wanted. A real cowboy like Butch Cassidy or that of a *faux* cowboy like Joe Buck. In some ways, I think he wanted to do both pictures. He wondered if *Midnight Cowboy* could be delayed until he finished

Three gay playwrights, Herlihy, William Inge, and Tennessee Williams each helped launch the film career of sexy **Warren Beatty** with the following scripts: *All Fall Down*, *Splendor in the Grass*, and *The Roman Spring of Mrs. Stone*.

Although Beatty was never offered the role of Joe Buck, he came under heavy consideration.

Paul Newman strutting his volcanic sexuality and striking good looks in *Hud*. He later demonstrated to Herlihy how, up close and personal, if he were awarded the role of Joe Buck, he'd interpret it.

shooting *Butch Cassidy*. I didn't know the answer to that."

"Throughout the evening, Paul and I had been sizing each other up," Herlihy said. "I'd heard that he was bisexual, and I made it clear I wanted some action. I didn't have to come out and proposition him. We were too subtle for that, even though both of us were drunk. When I invited him to spend the night, he readily agreed. And when we both decided we'd be more comfortable if we pulled off our clothes, the night was ours."

"We liked it so much that we went at it again the next morning," Herlihy claimed. "I thought we were so hot together, both drunk or sober, that he'd surely call again, but he never did. Even worse, he seemed to have completely lost interest in both Joe Buck and me before the end of the following day. However, there's a footnote to the story. He gave the novel to his friend, Tony Perkins. That weekend the *Psycho* man himself called me. He'd read the novel, and now he wanted to play Joe Buck."

"As far as my love life was concerned," Herlihy continued, "I thought I'd died and gone to gay heaven. First, Sal Mineo. Then Paul Newman. Then Tony Perkins. Too bad I never got to audition Warren Beatty. My friends, Tennessee Williams and Bill Inge, thought Beatty—and Newman, too—belonged in the pantheon of Greek Gods."

***

Published by Blood Moon in 2010, about a year after the death of its impossibly handsome and famous subject, this was a pioneering biography of a charismatic icon of Tinseltown whose rule over the hearts of American moviegoers lasted for more than half a century. It's loaded with never-before-published revelations that look behind the innocent-looking baby blues that enthralled the movie-going public.

Paul Newman became one of the most potent, desirable, and ambiguous sex symbols in America, a former sailor from Shaker Heights, Ohio, who parlayed his ambisexual charm and extraordinary good looks into one of the most successful careers in Hollywood. It's all here, as recorded by celebrity chronicler Darwin Porter—the dirt and the glory, the bad and the beautiful, the giddy highs and the agonizing lows of a great American star.

This title won an honorable mention for biography from the NEW ENGLAND BOOK FESTIVAL.

When Herlihy eventually rendezvoused with Tony Perkins in a discussion about the role of Joe Buck, he encountered an actor who desperately wanted the part. He feared that he'd be destined to play remakes of *Psycho* for the rest of his life unless he dramatically changed his image with the movie-going public. "Joe Buck is the kind of cowboy character who could do that for me," Tony said.

Herlihy had avidly followed his career ever since he saw him on Broadway in *Tea and Sympathy*, where he played a student accused of being gay. But after Alfred Hitchcock cast him as the skinny, quivering wacko in *Psycho* (1960), he was forever identified as Norman Bates.

"I found my soulmate in Tony," Herlihy claimed. "Both of us were a little mad, but we brought out the best in each other. The first night I met him in Key West, I took him to Tony's Bar. We were both high on pot. I learned that Tony wanted to be a singer. He stood up in front of a roaring crowd and sang 'Midnight Swim.' The guys loved him, and so did I later in that evening."

"Tony talked about Paul Newman all the time," Herlihy claimed. "Year after year throughout our long drawn-out, on-again, off-again affair. He seemed obsessed with Newman and measured his success on the screen—or lack of it—with that of Newman's. He had obtained the stardom that Tony wanted, and he resented it, even though he continued to maintain a long friendship with both Newman and his wife."

He relayed to Herlihy many of the details associated with his affair with Newman in the '50s. "He's just as gay as I am, but he won't come out of the closet. He uses that so-called great marriage of his to conceal his true desires."

[Ironically, Perkins lived deep in the closet throughout most of his life, too.]

In marked contrast to Herlihy's enthusiasm, Schlesinger would not even consider the concept of Tony Perkins playing Joe Buck for more than a few seconds. "It's about the worst casting idea I've ever heard," Schlesinger bluntly told Herlihy. "Norman Bates as Joe Buck! You guys have been smoking too much pot."

Despite their mutual disappointment,

Once one of the premier candidates for roles written for young, vulnerable, painfully sensitive men, **Tony Perkins**—around the time of his appearance (lower photo) in Alfred Hitchcocks ***Psycho*** (1960)— appeared on the cover of film magazines throughout Europe and North America

Tony Perkins portraying a murderous psychotic in 1960. Would he have made a convincing Midnight Cowboy?

(Heterosexual) love at last: Husband-and-wife team of **Berry Berenson** with **Tony Perkins.**

Perkins and Herlihy remained friends, rendezvousing in secret and going to out-of-the-way gay bars in New York.

In the years to come, Perkins continued to sleep around and kept Herlihy abreast of his many affairs. His relationship with Tab Hunter had long ago ended, and from this point onward, he pursued famous bed partners only rarely. An exception involved a torrid affair with Rudolf Nureyev, the ballet dancer. For the most part, Perkins preferred hustlers, beautiful young Thai men, and lots of tall, thin male dancers, many of them from Broadway.

"Tony was kinky," Herlihy admitted. "He'd pay guys to climb through his bedroom window, tie him up with ropes, and rape him."

Author Truman Capote, who knew Herlihy only casually, chastised him for hanging out with Perkins. "Personally, I don't like blood even though I wrote *In Cold Blood*," Capote told Herlihy. "Tony's a sadist. He likes to see blood. I mean, he *is* Norman Bates."

Although Herlihy himself had not seen aberrant behavior like that in Perkins, he'd heard stories.

Later in life, Perkins approached Herlihy and asked the writer if he'd help him pen an autobiography. "Random House will give me a hundred thousand bucks for every dick I say I sucked."

As it happened, Perkins never aggressively pursued the project and ultimately rejected every offer for a personal memoir. In contrast, his former lover, Tab Hunter, however, agreed to write a detailed overview of their love affair, but only after Perkins had died.

Perkins told Herlihy an amazing story: After Newman got him a role in *The Life and Times of Judge Roy Bean* (1972), he had grown tired of listening to Tony rant about how much he wanted to go straight. Responding to Tony's expressed intentions to "become heterosexual," Newman urged him to have an affair with Victoria Principal, who was also starring in the movie. "Don't knock it until you've tried it."

Newman pointed out to Perkins that he'd had very satisfactory relationships with both men and women. "Each one is a different thrill in its own way. Instead of getting off on soft breasts, you learn to dig a hard chest, or vice versa. Instead of a hole to plug, you get plugged. The thrills are there in either case."

Tony took Paul's advice and seduced Victoria Principal, who would go on to become a household word when she starred in the long-running CBS nighttime drama, *Dallas*, from 1978 to 1987.

As Tony later admitted to *People* magazine, his intimacies with Principal produced a "spontaneous combustion" and launched a four-day sex binge. "I was a virgin before I met her," admitted the forty-year-old actor.

"In asserting his virginity, he seemed to have forgotten all the dozens of men he'd slept with," said Herlihy, "including

Victoria Principal (remember her?) in 1982 on the cover of the French edition of *Playboy*, during the glory years of her gig as Pamela Ewing on the hit TV sitcom, *Dallas*.

me. I can personally testify that Tony was no virgin when he met Principal."

Tony's biographer, Charles Winecoff, claimed that after Tony's cherry-popping sex binge with Principal, the actor "became a real man."

In his attempt to go straight, on August 9, 1973, he married Berinthia ("Berry") Berenson, an American photographer, actress, and model. *[Berenson was the granddaughter of fashion designer Elsa Schiaparelli.]* The union produced two sons, actor/musician Oz Perkins (1974) and folk/rock singer/songwriter Elvis Perkins (1976).

[Yet throughout the course of his marriage, according to Herlihy, Perkins would continue his intimacies with male prostitutes. It was from one such prostitute that he acquired AIDS.

In 1990, he sued the National Enquirer *for writing that he'd tested positive for the AIDS virus. Later, to his horror, he found out that the tabloid was right. A lab technician had sold the results of his blood test to the paper. Tony did have AIDS, from which he would die two years later.*

Perkins' widow, Berry Berenson, was among the passengers aboard one of the airliners that was deliberately flown into the North Tower of the World Trade Center by terrorists on September 11, 2001.

Newman never wanted to discuss Tony or the disasters that occurred to his widow. He referred to both deaths as tragedies and preferred to conceal his memories of his long friendship with the troubled actor whose fear of exposure helped seal his own doom.]

***

There was a footnote to the casting of *Midnight Cowboy.*

Schlesinger told Herlihy that all his casting plans had been tossed out the window after Elvis Presley called. "This guy wants to play Joe Buck."

WALDO SALT: ACKNOWLEDGING THE UNDER-APPRECIATED SKILLS OF AN OVERLOOKED SCREENWRITER

What do all of these (fascinating) films share in common with *MIDNIGHT COWBOY*? Their screenplays were all crafted, over a sweep of more than thirty tumultuous years, by the same gifted screenwriter, **Waldo Salt.**

Midnight Cowboy

Herlihy thought Elvis in this truly serious role might be a sensation. "I can just see Elvis walking down Times Square dressed as a cowboy hustling his dick. The public would go wild."

But within two weeks Schlesinger called Herlihy again. Once again, his domineering manager, Col. Tom Parker, had intervened. "There's no way I'm gonna let Elvis play a fag cowboy," Col. Parker told Schlesinger. "Sometimes I think my boy doesn't have enough sense to come in from out of the rain. No wonder…he's doped up all the time." Then Col. Parker slammed down the phone.

Finally, Schlesinger "turned down all other applicants" [his words] and cast Jon Voight into the role of Joe Buck. Herlihy was hardly delighted but had neither a vote nor any veto power in the actual casting.

Starved for meaty roles extending beyond the usual cinematic fluff foisted upon him by Col. Parker, **Elvis** let it be known that he'd be terrific as a sidewalk stomper (Joe Buck) turning tricks in NYC

As part of their dialogue within *Midnight Cowboy*, Ratso and Joe Buck argued about cowboys, Ratso claiming that, "Cowboys are fags." Joe counters, "John Wayne is a cowboy. Are you calling John Wayne a fag?"

In a touch of irony, both Voight and Hoffman would eventually be nominated for Best Actor Oscars for their performances in *Midnight Cowboy*. Ironically, each lost to none other than John Wayne himself for his performance in *True Grit* (1969). *Midnight Cowboy* as a film, however, would become the first X-rated movie ever to win a Best Picture of the Year Oscar. In addition, Schlesinger carried away the Best Director Oscar.

The very talented Sylvia Miles played a hooker in the movie, for which she was later nominated for a Best Supporting Actress Oscar, even though she'd been on screen for only six minutes. She was a friend of Darwin's and made many tightly scheduled appearances with him, popping in and out of multiple social events in Manhattan during the highly social 1970s.

Schlesinger won an Oscar for Best Director, with Waldo Salt going home with the gold for Best Screenplay from Adapted Material.

As for awards associated with *Butch Cassidy and the Sundance Kid*, it was nominated for both Best Picture and Best Director but would lose both. For their respective performances, Newman and Redford would each be ignored by the Academy, but not by the movie-going public. Newman had predicted that the film might take in as much as $50 million. Soon after its release, it doubled that figure and continues to make money to this day.

***

After his initial social call at Magnolia House, Herlihy invited Darwin to dinner a few evenings later in Manhattan. There, in a restaurant, he met Voight, Hoffman, and Schlesinger.

Hoffman had little to say and seemed distracted, but Voight was quite articulate in discussing his role, which he suspected might be career-making.

He had recently completed the filming of a scene within *Midnight Cowboy* in which he was showering in Boondock, Texas, dreaming of success in New York, where he planned to "hustle my meat" to horny, rich women.

"But, according to Waldo's script," he said, "I first get my cock sucked in a seedy movie theater on 42nd Street, and then, after that, I pick up this woman *[Sylvia Miles]*, and escort her back to her apartment where I screw her. And when we're through, she wants ME to pay HER, as she's a hooker herself."

"*Midnight Cowboy* is a love story," Voight continued. "Well, of sorts. Mostly it's about loneliness and insecurity—and what that does for alienated people cut off from the world. I don't know anything about homosexuality, about transferring feelings I have for women to certain situations I might feel for a man."

"As a struggling actor in New York, I never had to sell my ass like Joe Buck or this Ratso character here," Voight pointed to Hoffman. "My parents, thank god, provided for me, although they wanted me to become a lawyer...perhaps a golf pro."

"I know one thing...I'm at the peak of my male beauty and sex appeal, and I'm damn aware that neither of those qualities last forever."

During the shooting of *Midnight Cowboy*, Herlihy escorted Schlesinger—who had begun his career in British films as an actor—to dinner at Magnolia House. Darwin was most impressed with him, having been enthralled by his films, *Billy Liar* (1963) and *Darling* (1965), which had starred Julie Christie. Darwin also was a fan of some of Schlesinger's later films, notably *Sunday, Bloody Sunday* (1971) and *Marathon Man* (1976), which had once again included Hoffman, this time co-starring with [Lord] Laurence Olivier.

Schlesinger later—perhaps partially in jest—defined *Midnight Cowboy* as "a woman's picture, with Hoffman playing Joan Crawford sacrificing herself for a blonde stud."

THE LEGACY OF *MIDNIGHT COWBOY*

Midnight Cowboy is still seen across the nation today and also internationally. At the 42nd Academy Awards nominations, it won for Best Picture, Best Director (John Schlesinger), and Best Adapted Screenplay (Waldo Salt).

Both Jon Voight and Dustin Hoffman were nominated as the year's Best Actor, perhaps splitting the vote and canceling each other out. That paved the way for John Wayne to win for *True Grit*.

Sylvia Miles, as the prostitute who successfully hustles Joe Buck, was nominated as Best Supporting Actress, but she lost that Oscar to Goldie Hawn for her performance in *Cactus Flower*.

Miles was enraged when the Golden Globe Award Committee overlooked her and nominated Brenda Vaccaro instead as Best Supporting Actress. (She lost.)

Reviews were mostly positive. In the *Chicago Tribune*, film critic Gene Siskel wrote: "I cannot recall a more marvelous pair of acting performances in any one film. In 1994, at the 25th anniversary retrospective, Owen Gleiberman of *Entertainment Weekly*, said, "*Midnight Cowboy*'s peep show vision of Manhattan lowlife may no longer be shocking, but what is shocking in 1994 is to see a major studio film linger this lovingly on characters who have nothing to offer the audience but their lost souls."

Made for $3.2 million, *Midnight Cowboy* grossed nearly fifty million at the box office, a hefty sum, for United Artists in those days.

It has been positioned as #36 on the American Film Institute's list of the 100 Greatest Films of All Time. The Library of Congress has deemed it "culturally, historically, or aesthetically significant."

Even though it was X-rated, Schlesinger had to alter large portions of the novel to make it acceptable for general release. For example, in an early scene in Texas, Joe is sadistically raped by a big gay half Indian fat man and a local hustler named Perry. In the original script, Waldo Salt included a dream sequence where Joe Buck runs nude down Times Square.

The director also wanted to show a nude Miles and Voight in bed having at least simulated sex. She told him, "I think you should allow Voight to penetrate me for greater authenticity." Schlesinger rejected the idea "as a bridge too far."

Ironically, Voight's character in the movie was completely out of his element as a sex worker on the sidewalks of Times Square, even though Voight himself was a native New Yorker. In contrast, Hoffman, who on film portrayed a wise-cracking and very street-smart urban infighter, was actually from Los Angeles. To get the role—a career maker—Voight agreed to work for the Screen Actor's Guild minimum wage.

At first, *Midnight Cowboy* got an "R" rating, but the Motion Picture Association changed its rating to an "X" because of "its homosexual frame of reference." That was later restored to an "R," since by today's standards, it hardly shocks as it did in the late 1960s.

Glen Campbell's hit song, "Rhinestone Cowboy," was said to have been inspired by the Joe Buck character in Midnight Cowboy.

SAL MINEO
Living Fast and Dying Young:
A Scandalous Life

To his lasting regret, Mineo was not awarded with the Dustin Hoffman role ("Ratso") in the movie version of *Midnight Cowboy*. His glory days in cinema had ended, and he struggled along finding work wherever he could, including on the stage.

Today, he is best remembered for his role of Plato opposite James Dean in *Rebel Without a Cause* (1955). He also lives on in Hollywood lore for his mysterious murder at the age of thirty-seven in 1976.

He rose to fame in the 1950s where he was viewed as a heartthrob. Born in the Bronx, he was the son of Sicilian immigrants. As he matured, he had this sultry-eyed look with a tight, muscled body that he didn't mind exhibiting.

At the age of eleven, he appeared on Broadway in Tennessee Williams' *The Rose Tattoo*, starring Eli Wallach and Maureen Stapleton. He was Prince Chulalongkorn in the original Broadway production of *The King and I*, starring the bisexual Yul Brynner.

Mineo later claimed that the bald-headed star frequently molested him during rehearsals and during the production itself. However, Brynner was far better known for his seductions of some of the century's leading female stars, including Marlene Dietrich, Tallulah Bankhead, Ingrid Bergman, Joan Crawford, and Marilyn Monroe. We must not leave out a young Nancy Davis (later, Reagan).

As his career wound down in the late 1960s, Mineo was quite open about his homosexuality, at least to his friends. "I like them all—men," he said, "and a few chicks now and then. Everyone's supposed to be bi. What's wrong with that?"

His most controversial stage play was the grim 1967 prison drama *Fortune and Men's Eyes*, which he directed and in which he also starred. *[Its most controversial scene was his rape of an eighteen-year-old actor named Don Johnson, who later scored big with the leading role in the long-running hit TV series* Miami Vice *which debuted in 1984. Johnson later said, "Sal was gay by his own admission, but he wasn't completely gay. He was also with women."]*

When word got out that Mineo was appearing frontally nude during some of his appearances in *Fortune and Men's Eyes*, the production began attracting huge numbers of gay men. Rave reviews of both the theme and the quality of the performances later led to more diverse audiences, too.

In February of 1976, Mineo was set to open in James Kirkwood's *P.S., Your Cat is Dead*, in which he played a bisexual burglar. He also became engaged in an affair with Kirkwood, who interpreted

In *Rebel Without a Cause*, teenaged **Sal Mineo** fell hopelessly in love with James Dean, both on and off the screen. The first rushes of Dean with Mineo horrified the censor, Geoffrey Shurlock. In a memo to producer Jack Warner, he warned, "It is, of course, vital that there be no inference of any questionable or homosexual relationship between Jim and Plato."

Meeting Dean was one of the highlights of Mineo's life. "I realize that from the moment I met Jimmy, my whole life took on a completely different meaning. It was only years later that I understood I was incredibly in love with him."

In addition to director Nicholas Ray, Mineo had many other male lovers, including Rock Hudson and Peter Lawford. He even spent a "nude weekend" with (of all people) Mickey Cohen, the Mafia mobster.

All that Cohen ever said about that notorious weekend was, "Sal Mineo is a fine young man." But to his gangster pal, Johnny Stompanato, he said, "That kid's got a great ass on him!"

him as "most alluring."

Coming home one evening from rehearsals, he was fatally stabbed in an alleyway behind his West Hollywood apartment. His death inspired lurid headlines across the nation.

ONSCREEN WITH SAL MINEO AND JAMES DEAN:
THEIR SEXUAL CHEMISTRY

In his own words, whenever Sal Mineo wanted a role, he pursued it "no holes barred." Sometimes, it worked…but often it didn't. At the time of his auditions for *Rebel Without a Cause,* Mineo was already a film industry veteran, having appeared in two movies, *Six Bridges to Cross,* and *The Private War of Major Benson,* both released in 1955.

Yet the director of *Rebel Without a Cause,* Nicholas Ray, kept rejecting him for the role of Plato. Ray was very frank: "There is just no chemistry between you two guys." But finally, he relented, inviting both Jimmy and Mineo to his suite at the Château Marmont.

Mineo arrived wearing pegged pants, a skinny tie, and a jacket. Jimmy showed up in jeans and a T-shirt. "They were from different planets," Ray said.

Mineo later revealed what happened that late Sunday afternoon. "At first, Jimmy and I were awkward, and I gave a bad first reading of the script. Perhaps Ray was right: We had no sexual chemistry. But I was determined to play Plato and begged for a chance to do it over. Ray tried to get us to relax with each other. Instead of reading the script, we were told to improvise."

"Suddenly, Jimmy and I were talking to each other, and he was fascinated to learn I'd been a street kid from the Bronx. We relaxed—and how! He even started to wrestle me, which ended up in a long, passionate kiss. We stripped down to our underwear and continued to wrestle some more until both of us got erections. Off came our panties."

"Right in front of Ray, I came on to Jimmy like gangbusters. Ray was all eyes. Jimmy and I really went at it. When I looked over at our director, he'd whipped it out and was jerking off. I got the role of Plato, and I later got Ray. But by then, I was already in love with Jimmy."

"Something happened during the making of *Rebel,*" Mineo said. "It was as close as you could get to a spiritual experience. Jimmy was the focus of all of it. Everything that happened was a result of his presence."

During the first week of his involvement with *Rebel,* Jimmy told Mineo that he couldn't sleep and that he was overcome with a nervous anxiety. He went to three sessions with a psychiatrist. "This headshrinker told me to love my father. What a stupid assignment! I could have told him that fifteen years ago. The fucker should have tried to love my father himself."

"Whatever's inside me makes me what I am. Cut me open and take it out, and let in the light, and it might kill my acting talent. Tennessee Williams calls it 'creative malady.' Sometimes, it's the wackos who create the greatest art. Make them normal, and they may lose that neurosis that drives them to create in the first place."

James Dean (left) with **Sal Mineo** in 1955's testimonial to teenaged love, alienation, and rage, *Rebel Without a Cause*.

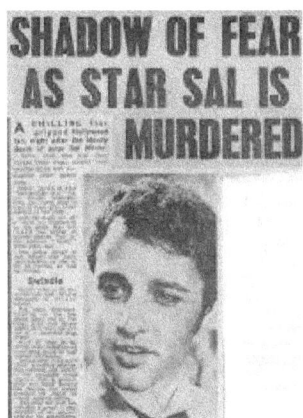

Sal's murder catalyzed news reports throughout the nation.

Fortune and Men's Eyes. It opened in 1967 as an avant-garde play by John Herbert. In 1971 it was adapted into a film.

It was about a young man's experience in prison, exploring themes of homosexuality and sexual slavery. The title of the play comes from William Shakespeare's Sonnet 29, which begins with: "When in disgrace with fortune and men's eyes...". It has been translated into 40 languages and produced in more than 100 countries. Actors in the earliest days of the stage play included **Sal Mineo**, depicted in the center photo above raping the character then played by a young neophyte actor named **Don Johnson**.

Midnight Cowboy

REST IN PEACE
JAMES LEO HERLIHY
(1927-1993)

After *Midnight Cowboy,* Herlihy wrote a series of "left-wing" political essays, but when they were compiled into non-fiction book, it was rejected by eight major publishers before he abandoned it.

His final novel *The Season of the Witch* (1971) generated bad reviews and poor sales.

As the autumn leaves were falling outside his Silver Lake, Los Angeles, residence, he committed suicide, viewing his life as "a total failure."

At the age of 66, he was found dead after an overdose of sleeping pills.

One of his final works, *A Story that Ends in a Scream* (1967), was dedicated to Darwin Porter.

As the Key West Bureau chief of *The Miami Herald,* Darwin covered the shooting of *All Fall Down.* The novel on which the film was based had been written by Darwin's friend, James Leo Herlihy.

Darwin met and interviewed everyone in the cast, including its stars (left to right in left-hand photo), Angela Lansbury, Karl Malden, Eva Marie Saint, Warren Beatty, and Brando De Wilde. Not pictured in either of the photos above was Barbara Baxley, who would later star in the film *(The Last Resort)* based on Darwin's novel, *Butterflies in Heat.*

The right-hand photo above shows Eva Marie Saint emoting in *All Fall Down* with Warren Beatty. Its filmscript was written by playwright William Inge, who confessed to Darwin that, "I've fallen madly in love with Warren."

Chapter Nine

WHEN DIVAS CLASH

The Fight Over
ROBERT TAYLOR
When
TAMARA GEVA
The Great Russian Ballerina and ex-wife of George Balanchine is Assaulted Backstage by
BARBARA STANWYCK
Plus the Tormented Sexual Involvement of
HOWARD HUGHES

Known as "the ice-cold blonde from Russia," the great ballerina, **Tamara Geva,** defected from the Soviet Union during a tour of Germany in 1924. In the 1970s, she was escorted to many events and parties in Manhattan by Darwin Porter and spent time at Magnolia House.

When she was only fifteen, in Russia, she'd married the great dancer and choreographer George Balanchine. "Today that is called child molestation," she later said.

Above, are two views of her performing in Leningrad (St. Petersburg) in the 1920s.

Born in 1907 in St. Petersburg, Russia, the great ballerina and choreographer, Tamara Geva, was Darwin's frequent houseguest at Magnolia House in the 1970s.

As a little girl, she grew up in a house that was constructed in the 1700s with its own small theater and a museum of Russian theatrical memorabilia.

As a teenager, she attended the Kirov School of Ballet in Leningrad. After the Csar was overthrown during the Revolution, she was enrolled at the Theater School of Soviet Ballet. Here, she met a dancer and later choreographer, George Balanchine, who at the time was teaching classes in ballroom dancing.

He fell madly in love with her, marrying her in 1923 when she was only fifteen years old. Their union survived until 1926.

In today's dance world, Balanchine (1904-1983) remains a legend, hailed as the father of American ballet. He co-founded the New York City Ballet and remained its artistic director for thirty-five years.

He was said to have ruled the City Ballet as a feifdom, with a *droit du seigneur* among his privileges. The older he became, the more consuming his love affairs with young ballerinas.

After his divorce from Tamara, he married three more times, always

VERY AVANT-GARDE: **Tamara Geva** dancing with her then-husband, **George Balanchine**, in 1923 in Russia.

AND THEN THERE WAS HOLLYWOOD, where she competed as an actress, with a slew of B-rated films to her credit, with ratings far less prestigious than those awarded to her rival, Barbara Stanwyck, at the time the highest-paid woman in America.

with dancers: Vera Zorina (1938-1946), Maria Tallchief (1946-1952), and Tanaquil LeClercq (1952-1969). So far as it is known, he never fathered any children in spite of his numerous affairs.

When he died on April 30, 1983, writer Clement Crisp eulogized Balanchine: "He created 465 works and extended the traditions of classical ballet. His teaching technique is still in use today. He is one of the 20th Century's best known choreographers, and his style and vision of ballet may remain for many generations to come."

Two more husbands and numerous affairs with both men and women loomed in Tamara's future. After her divorce from Balanchine in 1926, Tamara married Kapa Davidoff, an actor and fashion designer born in 1897. He had previously been married to the enigmatic Russian-born Lucia Davidova.

Lucia became intimate friends with her ex-husband's new bride, and the two of them, former and present wives, were seen everywhere with Davidoff. Rumors spread that they were a *ménage à trois*.

Ironically, Lucia Davidova was described as Balanchine's "best platonic woman friend," a relationship that lasted for half a century. She was present at every one of his performances. She was also a close friend of Igor Stravinsky, the Russian-born composer who immodestly identified himself as "the inventor of music."

As a teenager, Tamara became a professional ballet dancer, appearing in concerts and dance recitals throughout the Soviet Union. During a tour through Germany, Diaghilev

Tamara was an emerging ballerina in the orbit of the great Balanchine when she posed for this portrait in Russia.

She was hailed as "The Next Anna Pavlova (1882-1931). Tamara danced some of Pavlova's greatest roles, notably *Le Cygne* composed especially for her by Michel Fokine, and the only piece she ever choreographed herself, *Autumn Leaves*.

Late-in life portrait of **Tamara Geva** during the era when Darwin was escorting her in and out of gala functions in NYC of the early 1980s.

approached Balanchine and Tamara and asked them to join his Ballets Russes. Together, they made the life-changing decision to defect from the Soviet Union. They remained with the Ballets Russes in Monte Carlo until 1926.

After a visit to America, Tamara decided this country would be her future home. In 1927, although divorced by then from Balanchine, she introduced his choreography to New York City.

Work as a dancer on Broadway followed, and she was featured in such musicals as *Three's a Crowd* (1930), *Flying Colors* (1932), and *Whoopee* (1934).

She and Balanchine remained friends, and by 1935, she was performing with American Ballet, the predecessor to the American Ballet Theater, in Manhattan.

George Balanchine in 1965 during a rehearsal in Amsterdam with the NYC Ballet.

Tamara eventually evolved into an actress, appearing in plays by George Bernard Shaw and Jean-Paul Sartre, delivering a magnificent performance in London opposite Raymond Massey in Robert Sherwood's anti-war play, *Idiot's Delight*.

On Broadway, her most notable role in 1932 paired her with Ray Bolger in *On Your Toes* by Rodgers and Hart. Bolger today is known for playing the scarecrow in *The Wizard of Oz* (1939) opposite Judy Garland.

It was in *On Your Toes* that she danced one of the most famous dance sequences of all time. Called *Slaughter on Tenth Avenue,* it was a balletic parody that won rave reviews in *The New York Times.*

She also starred in several films during the late 1930s and throughout the war years. Her movies are largely forgotten today, except by Darwin, who cited his favorite role when she played the Countess Olga Karagin in *Night Plane from Chungking* (1942). Starring Robert Preston and Ellen Drew, it was a remake of *Shanghai Express* (1932) with Marlene Dietrich. "Our cast and director found Dietrich a tough act to follow," Tamara said. "If I recall, the character I played was caught spying."

Before that, she'd been cast as Madam "Charlie" Charlizzini in *Manhattan Merry-Go-Round* (1937), a musical starring Phil Regan, Leo Carrillo, and Ann Dvorak. In supporting roles were Cab Calloway and his Cotton Club Orchestra and baseball great, Joe DiMaggio as himself.

In 1941, she starred in Euripides *The Trojan Woman*. In 1947, she flew to Los Angeles to perform in Jean-Paul Sartre's *No Exit*. In one of her most unusual roles, she played the character of a sarcastic acrobat in the Manhattan revivial of George Bernard Shaw's *Misalliance*, co-starring with Roddy McDowall and Richard Kiley.

In the 1940s and '50s, Tamara was offered a number of film roles, most of them mere fluff and unworthy of her remarkable talent. *Orchestra Wives*, a 1942 musical for Fox, starred George Montgomery, Ann Rutherford (Scarlett O'Hara's sister), Lynn Bari, Carole Landis, Cesar Romero, and Tamara. The movie was the last to feature the Glenn Miller Orchestra.

While making that film, she fell madly in love with its star, "the rugged, handsomely masculine" George Montgomery, who was both a boxer and an interior decorator, an unusual combination.

She met him right after he'd co-starred with Ginger Rogers in *Rosie Hart*, and right before he appeared with Betty Grable in *Coney Island* (1943).

Montgomery was one of fifteen children born to immigrant parents from the Ukraine. Arriving in Hollywood, he found immediate work as a stuntman in Greta Garbo's *Conquest* (1937).

When Montana-born Montgomery was having an affair with Tamara, he was seeing Hedy Lamarr every other night. At the time, Hedy was being hailed as "the world's most beautiful woman." Lana Turner had also staked him out.

"If you wanted George in your bed, you had to stand in line," Tamara lamented. Ultimately, he would ditch all these glamour queens and marry singer Dinah Shore in 1943, a union that lasted for two decades.

Tamara Geva dancing with Ray Bolger in 1936 in the then very novel and innovative *Slaughter on Tenth Avenue*.

***

Tamara met and fell in love with another actor, John Emery, who was known on Broadway as "the poor man's John Barrymore." At the time she met him, he was still married to the formidable Tallulah Bankhead, her one and only marriage. "Once is enough, *dah-ling*.

Emery had a long theatrical background. His grandfather,

Tamara, during her balletic heyday. Memories, stardom, husbands, lovers, and agility lost.

Sam Emery, was said to have been the first interpreter of Charles Dickens on the English stage. His mother had played Little Eva in *Uncle Tom's Cabin*.

At the age of eleven, he was more or less "adopted" by John Barrymore and his then wife, Katherine Harris. There were rumors that the boy was Barrymore's illegitimate son.

Tallulah and Emery had married on the last day of August in 1937, a union that almost from the beginning was destined to fail. The following day, Tallulah announced that David O. Selznick had agreed to cast her as Scarlett O'Hara in *Gone With the Wind* (1939). Obviously, he changed his mind.

When Tamara became involved with Emery, he was still married to Tallulah, although they were no longer living together. He told Tamara that during their marriage, she often insisted that a man or woman join them in bed together.

Hedy Lamarr with George Montgomery.

"I'm tired of talking about myself," she said. "Now you tell me how beautiful you think I am."

Tamara and Emery began living together during the final months of his marriage to Tallulah. Their divorce did not come through until 1941.

Tallulah made Emery agree not to marry Tamara until a year had passed. "It would wreck my career, dah-ling, if word got out that I was dumped for another woman." He agreed to her terms.

A reporter for *Time* magazine asked Emery what married life was like with Tallulah. "Like the rise, decline, and fall of the Roman Empire," he answered.

A year later, he married Tamara. Days before the marriage, Tallulah phoned Tamara: "Dah-ling, I must warn you that the weapon may be of admirable proportions, but the shot is indescribably weak."

"Maybe with you, dear one," Tamara answered. "But not with me. It's like a blast-off to the moon."

One night when Darwin and Tamara were dining together at the Algonquin Hotel in Manhattan, she told him of a party she'd attended at Tallulah's apartment.

"We both arrived and Tallulah opened the door," Tamara said. "She gave us each deep French kisses, with tongue, and invited us in. A bevy of Broadway performers were there, including Estelle Winwood, Ethel Barrymore, Mildred Dunnock, Donald Cook, Robert Ryan, and Florence Eldridge—even Elia Kazan and Fredric March."

Tallulah had been drinking heavily, and about an hour into the party,

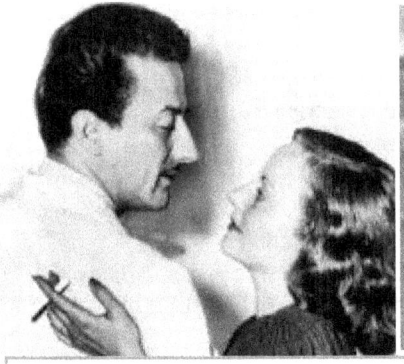 

John Emery (with the Barrymore nose) and two of his three wives: (left) **Tallulah Bankhead** (married 1937-41), and (right) **Tamara Geva** (married 1942-64)

as she was standing beside John, she suddenly unzipped his trousers and removed his penis. "DAH-LINGS!" she shouted at the room, filled at the time with her stunned guests. "Take a real good look. It's a two-hander that grows a foot."

During the final years of Tamara's marriage to Emery, the couple were estranged and lived apart. She divorced him in 1963.

From 1961 to 1964, Emery was romantically involved with the sultry brunette movie star, Joan Bennett. She cared for him during the final days of his illness, which led to his death in New York City at the age of 59 on November 16, 1964.

"The Only Man I Ever Loved Was Robert Taylor"
—Tamara Geva

One November night at Magnolia House, as the cold winds blew outside, Tamara Geva sat with Darwin beside one of the fireplaces and spoke lovingly of her on-again, off-again affair with matinee idol Robert Taylor. It had endured for more than fifteen years.

"We were hardly faithful to each other because we were married to other people during much of our love affair," Tamara confessed. "But he turned to me because I was more than a lover. I was also, at least in my view, a substitute mother and a psychologist. He feared he might be a homosexual, and indeed, he'd had a number of affairs with men."

"I was one of the few women with whom he could talk about his desires for men, knowing that I would understand, never condemn, and that I would protect his image and career. Bob had to live a private life in secret, using his marriage to Barbara Stanwyck as a cover. Of course, she had a lot in her own life to cover up as well, including her lesbianism."

Strikingly handsome, Taylor was destined to join that pantheon of movie idols that blossomed in the late 1930s and '40s. They included not only Taylor, but Clark Gable, Errol Flynn, and Tyrone Power.

Three of these men were bisexuals, all except Gable who in his early days was more "gay for pay," advancing his screen career by sleeping with director George Cukor and William Haines, about the biggest box office draw in America in 1930.

Taylor had been a drama student at Pamona College in Claremont, California. In the school production of *Journey's End,* on December 2, 1932, Taylor appeared in the pivotal role of Captain Stanhope set during World War I. A talent scout for MGM was in the audience and he held out the possibility of a studio contract.

Once in Hollywood, Taylor was launched on the road to screen glory, becoming one of the biggest stars in the MGM stable, a position he held for twenty-five years.

He performed in such classics as *Magnificent Obsession* (1935), *Camille* (1937), *A Yank at Oxford* (1938), *Waterloo Bridge* (1940), *Johnny Eager* (1942), *Quo Vadis?* (1951), and *Ivanhoe* (1952).

Over the years, he worked with a stunning roster of leading ladies: Irene Dunne, Janet Gaynor, Loretta Young, Barbara Stanwyck, Joan Crawford, Greta Garbo, Jean Harlow, Eleanor Powell, Vivien Leigh, Margaret Sullavan, Myrna Loy, Hedy Lamarr, Greer Garson, Norma Shearer, Lana Turner, Katharine Hepburn, Ava Gardner, Arlene Dahl, Elizabeth Taylor, Deborah Kerr, Joan Fontaine, Eleanor Parker, Ann Blyth, Janet Leigh, Dorothy Malone, Julie London, Cyd Charisse, Shelley Winters, Anita Ekberg, and Rosalind Russell, plus many, many others—an array of female

In *Camille* (1936), **Greta Garbo** played Marguerite Gautier and **Robert Taylor** her lover, Armand Duval.

In an iconic boudoir scene, she kissed him all over his face forehead, cheeks, neck, chin, and then full on the lips.

The same year, in *The Gorgeous Hussy,* **Joan Crawford and Robert Taylor** brought a cinematic glamour to their boudoir scenes that were more in the style of 1936 than 1828, where the film was set..

co-stars almost unmatched in the history of Hollywood.

The year of 1936 was pivotal in the life of Taylor, because his first male lover, the silent screen star, John Gilbert, had died. At one time, he was having affairs with Greta Garbo, Marlene Dietrich, and with Taylor himself. Hollywood biographer Mart Martin wrote, "Gilbert often attended gay parties where he danced with men, frequently in the company of Robert Taylor."

Except for Taylor, nearly all of Gilbert's affairs were with women, often famous ones, such as Mary Pickford, Clara Bow, Jeanne Eagels, Miriam Hopkins, Barbara La Marr, Carole Lombard, and Lupe Velez.

Gilbert at one time had hoped to marry Garbo, but she stood him up. Ironically, Taylor had a brief fling with Garbo when they co-starred in *Camille* (1936). She later said, "He was so beautiful—and so dumb."

He had a different spin: "Working with her was a magnificent experi-

Barbara Stanwyck (left) with (on the right) matinee idol **Robert Taylor,** whom she'd married in 1939. Their unhappy but long-enduring union lasted for years, because each of the stars needed the other to cover up their attractions to their own gender.

When Tamara Geva began a longtime affair with Taylor, word reached Stanwyck, and she developed a lifelong hostility toward the ballerina.

Darwin became painfully aware of that when he escorted Tamara backstage to Lincoln Center to greet Stanwyck. When Stanwyck encountered Tamara again after all those many years, her hostility toward the ballerina was still strong. As Darwin was being introduced, Stanwyck hauled off and slapped Tamara's face.

"Those bygones between the two had not been buried, but were still toxic," Darwin said. "Barbara Stanwyck had long been among my very favorite screen goddesses, and I was looking forward to spending an evening with her, as I had been promised by Tamara would happen. Instead, hugely embarrassed, we had to make a hasty retreat."

ence. I was just a scared kid of twenty-five, and she was thirty-one—and in full bloom, already a fantastic legend."

Privately, Taylor told Tamara, "George Cukor was about the best director who ever guided me through a film. He brought out the best in both Garbo and me. What I didn't like was his daily visits to my dressing room, where I had to put out for him. He certainly wasn't my type—give me Tyrone Power any day."

According to Tamara, "I met Bob in the late 1930s, and we hit it off at once. It was the beginning of a long affair, although there would be long spells where we never saw each other. My affair with him lasted about as long as his marriage to Stanwyck. They finally divorced in 1952. Bob was a great shield for her, covering up her romances with Joan Crawford, her great love, and Marlene Dietrich."

"I had never seen Bob's picture with Joan Crawford, *The Gorgeous Hussy* (1936), Tamara said. "One night he set up a screening, and I got to see them emote. The press later asked, 'Which one of them does the title infer?'"

"During Crawford's ill-fated marriage to actor Phillip Terry, I think Bob spent more time in bed with her husband than Crawford herself did," Tamara claimed.

When Taylor and Stanwyck starred in *His Brother's Wife* (1936), their romance was in full swing. He told a reporter "Miss Stanwyck is not the kind of woman a boy would meet in Nebraska."

Stanwyck told the press, "I will never marry Robert Taylor. Got that? NEVER! And I'm a woman of my word."

Obviously, by 1939, when the couple got married, she'd changed her mind.

According to the Hollywood grapevine, it was a "lavender marriage."

Taylor often shared with Tamara the conflicts in his marriage to Stanwyck. "In many ways, she reminds me of my mother, Ruth, a neurotic hypochondriac who tried to run my life...make that *ruin*. She wanted me to be at her side and never have anything to do with another woman."

"Even though Barbara did not sexually desire me, and was also disparaging the size of my penis, she didn't want me to get it elsewhere," Taylor told Tamara. "After a few years with her, and even

During an air raid over London in World War II, a handsome soldier (**Robert Taylor**) meets a beautiful ballerina, **Vivien Leigh**.

It's only later, as the plot of ***Waterloo Bridge*** unfolds, that he discovers she's a prostitute.

though we still stayed married in name only, my penis got tired of hearing put-downs from Barbara—and never rose to the occasion again."

Tamara also revealed that Taylor always lived in fear of his "pretty boy" reputation, thinking that it might backfire and cause speculation that would end his career. As Tamara recalled, "He grew a mustache to make himself look more manly."

Once, when Stanwyck was on location, Taylor invited Tamara to his home. "I wasn't surprised when I found out those two slept in separate bedrooms. At that time, Bob had to work me in between his affair with Lana Turner when they were co-starring in *Johnny Eager* (1941)."

Once, when Taylor was making *The Bribe* (1949), he slipped away with Tamara for a rendezvous in a bungalow in the rear of the Beverly Hills Hotel.

"He told me of his affair with the luscious Ava Gardner," Tamara said. "To keep our affair secret, I conducted it in the home of my mother, Ruth."

Taylor confessed "I viewed it as a 'safe house.'"

Gardner's biographer, Lee Server, said that one night, post-coital, "Taylor slipped out of bed and ran straight into his mother, who had words with him. Ava, wrapped in a sheet, heard Taylor pleading, 'Mother, would you rather I go to a cheap hotel?'"

The next time Taylor met with Tamara "for a roll in the hay" (as they called it in his native Nebraska), he said, "irony of ironies, Ava and Barbara starred in the same movie together, *East*

Star-crossed lovers **Greta Garbo and John Gilbert** co-star in *A Woman of Affairs* (1928).

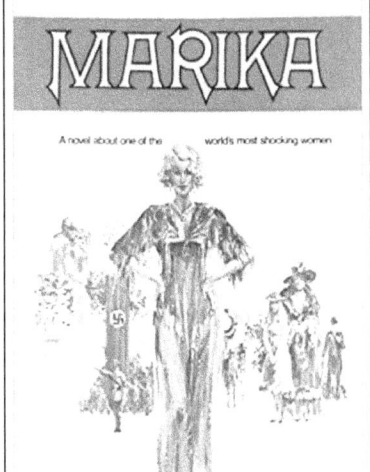

At the time of her death, Tamara Geva was re-reading a novel by Darwin Porter. Coroners who hauled her body away from its site of death discovered a copy of it beside her bed.

Here's how Amazon.com described it in its sales materials:

"A fabled superstar from the glamorous era of Garbo and Dietrich, **Marika** was a fascinating mixture of elusive sensuality and bold innocence."

"Soaring from the depths of poverty to the brilliant decadence of Berlin and the sweet temptations of Hollywood, she is haunted by the looming betrayal of her own secret past!"

Side, West Side (1949). Their co-star, James Mason, who is bisexual, told me that Barbara at first was very attracted to Ava, even suggesting that they share the same dressing room. But word soon leaked to her that Ava had an affair with me. Mason told me that Ava is now on Barbara's murderous list forever. Ava was gone from my life soon after she'd entered it. There was Robert Walker, there was Howard Duff, plus a fling with Gregory Peck during the time they co-starred in *The Gambler* (1948)."

"One of the last times I saw this divine man, Bob was making *The Conspirator* (1950) with a very young Elizabeth Taylor," Tamara said. "He told me that in love scenes with her, he always got an erection, and he had to ask the cameraman to photograph him from the waist up."

"By this time, I knew it was time for me to move on, and I never saw Bob again. But we had some good memories," Tamara confessed. "The next thing I heard, he was dating actress Ursula Theiss, which led to marriage and two children. From what I hear, he's found contentment at last, at least I hope so."

Old Wounds Never Heal

TAMARA GEVA vs. "BLOODY BABS" STANWYCK

One of Darwin's all-time favorite actresses was Barbara Stanwyck. He escorted Tamara to Manhattan's Lincoln Center to see her onstage at a Lifetime Achievement Gala. Naively, before they made their way backstage,

"I was just a teenager when **Bob Taylor** made love to me, both on and off the screen in *The Conspirator* (1949)," **Elizabeth Taylor** said.

"Would that be called child molestation?"

When **Ava Gardner and Robert Taylor** starred in *The Bribe* (1949) they had a secret affair—"away from my ball-busting wife" (his words.).

Tamara assured him that she had arranged to introduce him to the screen goddess, whom she said she knew well "from long ago." Their reunion didn't go well.

When Miss Stanwyck saw Tamara in the lobby of Lincoln center and in front of dozens of embarrassed witnesses, she slapped her face. Stanwyck had apparently never forgiven her for sustaining a long affair with her former husband, matinee idol Robert Taylor. Darwin's hoped-for introduction to Stanwyck ended disastrously, a morass of resentment.

TAMARA GEVA: A POSTSCRIPT

On December 9, 1997, Tamara Geva, aged 90, died in her Manhattan apartment from natural causes, leaving an indelible imprint on memories at Magnolia House. She was 90 years old. In 1972, she had published her highly sanitized autobiography, *Split Seconds*.

Darwin may have been among her last visitors. By her bedside was a copy of a novel he had written in 1977, *Marika*, a *roman-à-clef* loosely inspired on the lives of Marlene Dietrich, Tamara Geva, Hedy Lamarr, and Pola Negri.

"Your characterization of your heroine, Marika Kreisler, reminded me of my long life," Tamara said. "So much pain and sorrow always accompany moments of love and triumph. I've had all four in full measure, but one grows weary after a time."

Three views of stage, screen, and dance star

TAMARA GEVA
(1907-1997).
REST IN PEACE

ROBERT TAYLOR

His Tangled Bisexual Love Affairs with Aviator
HOWARD HUGHES

And With the Husband and Wife Team of

JOHN GILBERT & VIRGINIA BRUCE
Whose Lives Inspired the Plots and Remakes of
A STAR IS BORN

The affairs depicted in this section occurred when a young Robert Taylor, relatively new to Hollywood, was seducing actress Virginia Bruce and her husband, the legendary John Gilbert, the handsome silent screen icon who fell in love with Greta Garbo, both on and off the screen.

When not bedding both Bruce and Gilbert (always on separate occasions), Taylor was also being seduced by Howard Hughes.

[In time, rich and well-connected Hughes would sustain sexual interludes with many ambitious, career-obsessed Hollywood film stars, among them Gary Cooper, Randolph Scott, Jean Harlow, Errol Flynn, Bette Davis, Tyrone Power, Susan Hayward, Ava Gardner, Lana Turner, and eventually Marilyn Monroe and Katharine Hepburn.]

Many of the events discussed in this sub-section occurred during four years before the 1939 marriage of Robert Taylor to

In the original *A Star Is Born*, **Janet Gaynor** played an actress whose career is soaring as her husband, portrayed by **Fredric March**, fades.

Barbara Stanwyck during the filming of *Society Doctor* (MGM, 1935), which starred Chester Morris, Virginia Bruce, and Robert Taylor.

Some film historians believe that the plot of the original *A Star Is Born* was based on the marriage (1932-1934) of Bruce and Gilbert.

That early film starred Janet Gaynor as a rising young star and Fredric March as a fading, alcoholic actor of yesterday. *[Bruce was the inspiration for Vicki Lester in the movie, Gilbert for the character of the bitter and competitive has-been actor, Norman Maine.*

At the time, the full extent of Robert Taylor's private involvement in the lives of Bruce and Gilbert could not be depicted on the screen since even the mention of homosexuality was rigorously silenced by his era's Production Code.

Gilbert was not alive to see the film his marriage to Bruce had inspired. He died of acute alcoholishm and a heart attack at his home in Bel Air on January 9, 1936 at the age of thirty-eight.]

Mourners at his funeral included Marlene Dietrich and Gary Cooper, . He

HOW DID BOOKSELLERS DESCRIBE THE BLOOD MOON PRODUCTION FROM WHICH THIS EXCERPT WAS REPLICATED?

"From his reckless pursuit of love as a rich teenager to his final days as a demented fossil, Howard Hughes tasted the best and worst of the century he occupied. Along the way, he changed the worlds of aviation and entertainment forever."

"This biography reveals inside details about his destructive and usually scandalous associations with other Hollywood players, including ROBERT TAYLOR."

"This book give an insider's perspective about what money can buy—and what it can't."

Blood Moon's widely reviewed, widely publicized biography of Hollywood's most eerie film mogul, billionaire **Howard Hughes**, was researched and written by Darwin Porter at Magnolia House in 2003, and published to widespread reviews in the *New York Daily News* and *The Times of London*.

The section that immediately follows (i.e., the story of the sexual and emotional links between Howard Hughes and superstar Robert Taylor) first appeared in this ground-breaking *exposé*. Set in Hollywood of the 1930s, this tale of tangled loyalties, straight and gay, traced what happens when a demented billionaire becomes an aggressive, predatory, and well-funded player in Hollywood.

bequeathed his ex-wife, Bruce, $364,000 the equivalent of $6.6 million in 2019B dollars.]

The handsome but tight-lipped actor, Chester Morris, "with the patent leather hair," was startled to receive a phone call from Howard Hughes. Even though he had awarded Chester with a long-ago role in his film, *Cock of the Air*, with Billie Dove, the two men hadn't spoken since. During the shooting of the film, they had not bonded.

Virginia Bruce with her then-husband, **John Gilbert** in *Downstairs* (1932)

[Howard had let it be known that he was terribly disappointed at the poor box-office returns of Cock of the Air, *placing the blame for the picture's failure on Chester and not on his lover at the time, Billie Dove herself. In fact, however, Howard's picture was so bad that it practically marked the twilight of Billie's film career.]*

Even though Chester Morris has been almost forgotten, he starred opposite some of Howard's most memorable girlfriends, in-

One critic wrote, "**Chester Morris** (left) move on, make room for a young **Robert Taylor** (right).

cluding Jean Harlow and Carole Lombard. He's remembered mainly as "Boston Blackie," the retired safecracker and amateur detective in more than a dozen 1940s-era B movies.

HOW DID ROBERT TAYLOR FIRST BECOME INVOLVED WITH HOWARD HUGHES?

Early in his career, Chester had been directed in three separate films (*Alibi* and *Bat Whispers*, both in 1930, and *Corsair* in 1931) by the eccentric and autocratic director, Roland West.

Since then, Chester and West had become best friends, often hanging out together at a club that Roland West had established with actress Thelma Todd, who'd had a brief but disappointing encounter with Howard during the casting of *Hell's Angels*.

The club, Thelma Todd's Sidewalk Café, evolved into the most popular restaurant and nightclub in Hollywood, regularly attracting such patrons as Clark Gable and Charlie Chaplin.

Hughes had seen Thelma on several occasions since she'd married his friend, Pat DeCicco, in 1932. Hughes had never been to her club, however. Suddenly, he wanted to go there with Chester, suggesting that, "We'll arrive stag and pick up some girls once we're there."

At the club both Thelma and West warmly welcomed the Aviator, although each of them appeared startled to see him show up with Chester. *[At that point, Pat DiCicco was not appearing at the club very often, because his marriage to Thelma was on the skids.]*

Billie Dove, whom Howard Hughes cited as the woman who infected him with syphilis, was once hailed as "The World's Most Beautiful Woman."

Eventually, Chester figured out Hughes' motive for inviting him. Casually, Howard suggested to Chester that he might like to include the handsome young actor at MGM, Robert Taylor, at their table. Howard obviously knew that Chester was starring in a film, *Society Doctor,* that featured him.

Eight years before his death in 1970, Chester in an interview said that Robert rejected Howard's first two invitations, claiming "I find him creepy."

But according to Chester, "Howard could be very persistent, and after badgering us both, Robert finally consented to visit Thelma's and to sit at his table. Perhaps for his own protection, he insisted on inviting Virginia Bruce, with whom he was having an affair."

Virginia was married to John Gilbert at the time. Her career was on the rise but John's was fading. Sounds like the plot for *A Star is Born.*

Chester also revealed that unknown to Virginia, Robert Taylor was having an affair with her husband, John Gilbert, on the side.

"It was hardly any secret in the Hollywood of the Thirties," Chester said. "Both Robert Taylor and John Gilbert were the poster boys, as we call it today, of the bisexual world. Not me. I didn't go that route, though I got a lot of offers back then. I don't think Vir-

Howard Hughes, still handsome, still young, in vivid contrast to the reclusive fossil he eventually became.

ginia knew that her husband was sleeping with her lover, Robert. It was very Hollywood. Triangles like that were going on a lot back in those days, and I guess they still are in the Hollywood of today. Except I'm out of the loop."

"Howard knew that Robert was making only thirty-five dollars a week, and he played up to the actor's ego," Chester said. "He said he had big plans for both of our careers. Personally, I thought it was all bullshit. He was using the same lines on us that he used on chorines. Once I got Howard launched with Robert, I knew he'd never call me again. I was right. When my career began to slip, I phoned him several times, and the shit never returned one of my calls."

"Robert and Howard had several private talks at Thelma's Club, and apparently established some sort of rapport," Chester said. "I think that Robert was not sexually attracted to Howard, but went along for the ride to see what he could get. Call it a form of hustling if you like. I guess Robert figured that if Clark Gable could get his start this way, so could he. Besides, I always knew that money and power are great aphrodisiacs. How else could you explain all those German women throwing themselves at Adolf Hitler. Certainly not for his body!"

The next thing that Chester learned before he'd finished shooting *Society Doctor* was that Robert and Howard were taking weekend trips together. "I even heard they went hunting somewhere," Chester claimed, "and someone told me that Howard hated hunting. I guess to get his man, he'd go to great lengths."

***

Hughes was not impressed with Virginia Bruce and accurately predicted that her star, unlike that of Robert Taylor, would not rise over Hollywood. If she's remembered at all today, it is for her eighteen-month marriage to John Gilbert. *[Movie buffs taking a trivia quiz still recall that in the 1936 film,* Born to Dance, *she introduced the Cole Porter standard, "I've Got You Under My Skin."]*

Toward the end of her life, the Minnesota-born, pale-eyed blonde, who often played "the other woman," had become dottily eccentric and tactlessly outspoken from her home at Woodland Hills, a retirement community in California favored by aging movie personnel. She truly detested Howard and didn't mind admitting it. At first, she didn't want to talk about either Robert or Howard, and certainly not about John Gilbert.

She was more interested in discussing her appearances in Turkish films, few of which had ever been seen in America. Amazingly, she'd married the Turkish producer, Ali Ipar, in 1946, divorcing him in 1952. She remarried him in 1952 shortly after the divorce papers were finalized, that bond lasting until 1964 when she divorced him again.

Bruce still seemed proud that she was one of the 20 original Goldwyn

Girls. *[The others included Betty Grable, Lucille Ball, and two of Howard's former girlfriends, Paulette Goddard and Ann Dvorak.]*

"I knew Robert Taylor was bisexual," she finally admitted. "I was madly in love with him and wanted to marry him as soon as my divorce (from John Gilbert) came through. At one point I had introduced Robert to my husband, John, who was drinking heavily at the time. I didn't know until years later that John was sleeping with Robert on the side. It got very complicated. Robert told me that of all the movie stars in Hollywood, he wanted most to become the next John Gilbert. Maybe, and this is a bit far out, Robert felt that by sleeping with John he could assume his *persona*. How in hell do I know?"

She claimed that Robert would have married her if Howard hadn't entered the picture. "Between John (Gilbert) and Robert (Taylor), my life was complicated enough. Enter Howard Hughes and that made an already explosive situation become a field of dynamite. As for John, he was still in love with Greta Garbo when he married me, with Marlene Dietrich waiting in the wings. How could I compete with those two?"

"In the years before he married that dyke-bitch, Barbara Stanwyck, Robert was very open with me about his bisexuality," Virginia said. "We often talked about getting married one day. He said he would be true to me, the only woman in his life, but he wanted to be free to have relations with men. And I agreed to that. I was so desperately in love with him, I felt I didn't have much choice."

***

Suddenly, despite the fact that he was making almost no money at MGM, Robert Taylor appeared around Los Angeles in a new car and with a new wardrobe.

"We had several fights over Hughes," Virginia claimed. "Robert admitted that he didn't like having sex with Hughes. As men go, Hughes was not his type. But he wasn't adverse to accepting gifts. Robert had never had money before, and suddenly he was flying in private planes, sailing on one of the world's greatest yachts, and drinking champagne and eating caviar, with a house filled with servants to iron his underwear. Hughes even presented him with a dozen pair of the most beautiful handmade alligator shoes I'd ever seen and a pair of diamond cufflinks. And he was driving a new Duesenberg. I must say Hughes was very generous to him. He really turned Robert's head. At one point, Robert was convinced that Hughes was going to offer Louis B. Mayer one-hundred thousand dollars to buy out Robert's contract and put him on a salary of five-thousand a week."

"Robert did not conceal his relationship with Hughes from me," Virginia said. "How could he? It was so obvious." Then she leaned back in her bed and hesitated before her next statement. "But what really won

Robert for Hughes was not the expensive gifts but a common bond they shared. Those two, from all I gathered, spent a lot of time talking about their mothers. Believe it or not, Hughes seduced Robert with all this mother talk!"

***

Because of the way their overly protective mothers had forced them to dress, both Howard and Robert had been taunted as sissies by their boyhood schoolmates. Sam Rudel, a schoolmate, claimed that Robert "looked more like a girl than a boy, especially because of the way his mother combed his curly hair. Actually, back then, we knew him as Spangler Arlington Brugh."

Spangler, the future Robert Taylor, was born on August 5, 1911, in Filley, Nebraska. His father, Spangler Andrew Brugh, was a doctor of Pennsylvania Dutch extraction. His mother, Ruth Stanhope Brugh, was descended from Scotch-Irish parents and was a virtual invalid because of a weak heart. Although her illness was real, she was also a hypochondriac like Allene Hughes, the mother of Howard.

In the prairie environment in which young Robert grew up, his mother inappropriately dressed him in black velvet knickers and stiffly starched white lace shirts. Like Hughes himself, he was mocked as Little Lord Fauntleroy. School bullies used to knock him down and splatter him with Nebraska mud so that he would go home dirty. When not attending school, the "pretty boy," as his classmates called him, spent long hours practicing the cello. He suffered so much ridicule from his classmates that he developed a bad speech impediment by the age of eight. He was shy and insecure, just as Howard had been.

After her husband's early death in October of 1933, Ruth Brugh became totally dependent on her young son. She obsessed about his every action or movement, even after they moved to California and he started to mature. She selected not only his clothes, but his companions and warned him to stay away from girls "because the hussies can ruin a young man's future." She wanted Robert to spend his nights at home with her. She handwashed his underwear, even ironing them for him. Unlike Allene, however, she did not check his stool daily.

"Ruth Brugh was the biggest mother hen protecting her pretty young chick in Hollywood," said actress Lois Wilson. *[Lois had been cast with Robert in Universal's* There's Always Tomorrow *(1934)].*

Two years later, Joan Crawford appeared opposite Robert Taylor in *The Gorgeous Hussy,* prompting her to privately tell Billy Haines that "Robert Taylor and Howard Hughes are just two mama's boys."

[Wags at the time speculated about which of the movie's two stars had been cast as The Gorgeous Hussy: *Joan or Robert.]*

At Muirfield, Hughes' residence, housekeeper Beatrice Dowler recalled waking up early one morning and entering the kitchen. There, she discovered Howard in his underwear reading the morning news. Also in his underwear, Robert was at her stove making pancakes. He claimed that he'd learned to make these pancakes from a former landlady, "Auntie Neuhauser," whose house he had occupied when he was six years old in Nebraska.

Howard invited Beatrice to sit down and have a few pancakes. "They weren't bad," she later said. "Auntie must have had some secret."

On some evenings, Beatrice could hear Robert in Howard's library playing his cello. That was followed with Howard presenting a concert on his saxophone.

"To my untrained ear," she said, "both men were lousy musicians."

She later reported a strange happening at Muirfield: As a youth, Robert had wanted to be a doctor like his father and had pursued a career in medicine for a while before switching to acting. "At one point, Mr. Hughes started calling Mr. Taylor, 'Doc,'" Beatrice said. "Mr. Taylor tended to Mr. Hughes' ailments, real or imagined. At one point, six doctor's uniforms arrived for Mr. Taylor. The very next night, Mr. Taylor was seen wandering around Muirfield in one of these uniforms. I assumed he went to Mr. Hughes' room to 'examine' his patient."

Hughes told Noah Dietrich that Robert's personality was "prairie style." Since Hughes didn't like overly sophisticated men, he found that quality in Robert endearing. When Robert began working for MGM, film crews there called him a sissy, using the same kinds of taunts that he'd endured as a schoolboy back in Nebraska. To them, Robert was a pretty boy, an appellation he'd spend years fighting off. Robert became so disgusted on the set at one point that he ripped open his shirt and yelled, "See here, fellows. I've got hair on my chest! I'm a red-blooded man just like the rest of you."

"Oh, princess," one of the grips yelled back at him. "C'mon over here and see the big surprise I've got for you."

"After a tough day's work," Virginia Bruce recalled, "Robert would return to the arms of his mother.

Louis B. Mayer at MGM ordered his star, **Robert Taylor**, to pose for beefcake--"and look more manly showing some hair on your chest."

Later, he might rush over to my protective arms, and, later still, might end the night in Hughes' arms. That was a lot of protection!"

Beatrice recalled that very slowly, Robert began to move more and more of his clothing and personal goods into Muirfield. "One day he showed up with at least ten quilts. He told me that his mother, Ruth, had made each of them. Mr. Hughes preferred his expensive blankets but gave in to Mr. Taylor's demand that each of them be replaced with one of his mother's quilts."

"I remember one night Mr. Taylor opened the door to find two of the best tailors in Hollywood," Beatrice said. "Mr. Hughes had summoned them to make Mr. Taylor his first dinner jacket and tails. They also brought ten top hats for him to try on. Mr. Hughes never told me what the occasion was, but it was this big formal affair in San Francisco. I think William Randolph Hearst was throwing a party."

"Mr. Taylor, as I heard later, actually arrived as Mr. Hughes' date," Beatrice said. "That must have started a lot of tongues wagging when the news traveled south to Hollywood."

Although intense, the Taylor/Hughes infatuation eventually flickered and burned out, as was Howard's tendency with both men and women.

Meanwhile, Robert's romance with Virginia Bruce was unraveling, too. Complicating matters, the handsome young actor had developed a crush on a twenty-year old extra, whom he'd met on the set of *Society Doctor*, in which he was co-starring with Chester Morris. "He was blonde, well built, and very good looking," Chester claimed. "I think his name was Wayne Dedd—close enough."

"I can't remember," Chester continued. "Suddenly, Robert and Dedd were seen everywhere together. I figured that in spite of all his money, Hughes was being pushed aside. What I didn't know until much later was that Hughes had met the true love of his life, a young actor who would eventually evolve into a far bigger star than Taylor himself. When it came to selecting lovers in those days, male or female, Hughes went after the big names. Of course, from what I was told, he still continued to pick up the occasional budding starlet with big knockers or a garage mechanic with a big something else."

In spite of their eventual separation, Robert Taylor and Howard Hughes remained friends. Even though Hughes was no longer sleeping with him, he was still interested in news about his love life. To keep him abreast of any new develop-

Richard Nixon with Thelma...at least that was her name when Robert Taylor first seduced her.

ments, Howard had Robert trailed.

At one point, even though she'd married Lew Ayres, Howard found out that Robert was secretively dating Ginger Rogers. Howard found this amusing and wasn't angry at all.

During the filming of *Small Town Girl* for MGM in 1936, the gossip columnists were busy writing about a romance between Robert Taylor and his co-star, Janet Gaynor. This was fictional, as Janet was far more interested in members of her own sex than she was in Robert.

Taylor then became momentarily taken with an attractive female extra, Thelma ("Pat") Ryan, and started to date her. But for some reason, each of them decided to keep their romance secret.

Years later, Pat, now First Lady of the United States, Mrs. Patricia Nixon encountered Robert on a visit to the White House. In front of witnesses, she said, "I had an awful crush on you, Bob Taylor, when I worked on *Small Town Girl*. I had my eye on you all day and dreamed about you at night." Both of them shared a public laugh over that.

At the time it was happening, however, back in the 1930s, Hughes' detectives described a very different scenario. They were reporting back to Howard that Pat was seen leaving Robert's bungalow many times at around three or four o'clock in the morning. Later in life, Howard snidely remarked to Hughes' assistant, Noah Dietrich, "I wonder if Dick Nixon ever found out his wife wasn't a virgin when he married her?"

***

Back in the 1930s, it was early afternoon and all the flowers were in bloom at Muirfield as Howard wandered alone in his garden, dreaming dreams known only to himself.

Suddenly, he looked up to see his housekeeper, Beatrice Dowler, leading his on-again, off-again sleeping partner, Randolph Scott, into the garden. He was locked arm in arm with a handsome, debonair looking man that Howard instantly recognized as the dashing Cary Grant.

"Mr. Hughes," Randolph said, rather formally. "May I introduce you to my roommate, Mr. Cary Grant? He's British."

Normally he didn't like to shake hands, but Howard eagerly extended his hand to Cary. "I know who this young man is, and I've been eager to meet you. Call me a fan if you wish."

New man in town, **Cary Grant**

Two views of the increasingly demented movie producer and billionaire **Howard Hughes**, above left as an experimental aviator, above right with the tempestuous **Ava Gardner**, with whom he often fought, sometimes violently

Cary Grant with his lover, **Randolph Scott**, building their careers and waiting out the worst of the anti-gay sentiments of Hollywood.

Chapter Ten

From Russia With Love/Tales of Tatar Tail
RUDOLF NUREYEV
His Links to Gore Vidal & the Literary Avant-Garde

Dance world mega-star **Rudolf Nureyev** (left photo) with **Margot Fonteyn**, and (center photo) with one of his lovers, the Danish ballet star **Erik Bruhn**, shortly after Nureyev's defection from the Soviet Union.

The right-hand photo depicts one of the lions of America's middle-and-late-20th Century, the acerbic, "never suffered fools lightly" gay essayist and novelist, **Gore Vidal**.

[As the years went by, Darwin always looked forward to a New York visit from Gore Vidal. His adventures with world celebrities were tantalizing, especially his early and later involvement with the fabled ballet dancer, Rudolf Nureyev.

For much of his life, Rudi—born in Russia in 1938—lived in fear that KGB agents would kidnap and extradite him to Russia.

"That wasn't paranoia on Rudi's part," Gore said.

As it was later revealed, Rudi was in far more danger than he ever thought. At one point, Nikita Khrushchev issued an order demanding that Soviet agents assassinate Rudi.

The dancer never let his fear interfere with his sexual exploits.

James Toback, a film director and close friend of the dancer, said, "Rudi had a sex life that was probably as wide-ranging as anyone's in this century."

He cited a long and varied list of sexual partners that included Cecil Beaton, who said, "In many ways, Rudi reminded me of Greta Garbo, that same wild and untamed quality of genius."

Other seductions included Leonard Bernstein, Dame Margot Fonteyn, Tab Hunter, Anthony Perkins, fashion designer Halston, Mick Jagger, Freddie Mercury, and Lee Radziwill, the sister of Jacqueline Kennedy.]

***

Ever since the late 1940s, Gore Vidal had been a *balletomane*, seeking out dancers such as John Kriza and Harold Lang and seducing them. He'd also studied ballet himself, though he was not particularly good at it.

In 1961, Gore was mildly intrigued when he read in the newspapers that the premier Russian ballet dancer, Rudolf Nureyev, had defected to the West, turning himself over to police officers in Paris and asking for asylum.

Gore read that Nureyev had been born on a Trans-Siberian train racing across the Soviet Union to meet his father, a Red Army political commissar.

Gore Vidal. His passionate interest in politics, ballet, and the American and Soviet concepts of Empire made it almost inevitable that he'd begin a pursuit of the most fascinating Russian dancer in years, Rudolf Nureyev.

Some of his fans and fiercest critics claimed he'd been reincarnated from the soul of an ancient Roman emperor.

The papers claimed that Nureyev was known for "his rebellious character and non-conformist attitude." Suspecting he might defect, KGB agents in France, using a ruse, tried to lure him back to Moscow. But quick-witted Nureyev knew he was being lied to and suspected that if he returned to Russia, he'd be imprisoned.

As Gore remembered it, he was in Paris when he read an article by Oliver Merlin in *Le Monde*, describing Nureyev, who was being increasingly referred to as "Rudi" in the press:

"I will never forget his arriving running across the back of the stage, and his catlike way of holding himself opposite the ramp. He wore a white sash over an ultramarine costume, had large wild eyes and hollow cheeks under a turban topped with a spray of feathers, bulging thighs, immaculate tights. This was already Nijinsky in *Firebird*."

As Gore proclaimed, "I've got to possess this ballet god."

Rudi, within a week of his defection, signed up with the Grand Ballet du Marquis de Cuevas, and Gore attended a performance of Rudi's *The Sleeping Beauty* with Nina Vyroubova.

Gore went backstage and was introduced to Rudi by the theater manager, who told him that Gore was a famous American writer and "the brother of Jackie Kennedy."

It was suggested that Gore's connection to the recently elected American president, John F. Kennedy, might be helpful to Rudi's quest to become an American citizen. As such, Rudi desperately wanted to meet this author with such close ties to Kennedy's White House. He accepted Gore's invitation, and returned with him to the author's hotel suite in Paris.

Over champagne, Rudi told Gore that, "My creativity as a ballet dancer is very much akin to my sex drive."

Gore found this stimulating. He was even more aroused when Rudi pulled off all his clothes and performed a scene from *Le Sacre du Printemps (The Rite of Spring)* that Vaslav Nijinski had performed at the Théâtre des Champs-Élysées in Paris in 1913.

Rudi recreated the role of a nymph and, like Nijinski in the original, he danced an act of masturbation. But whereas Nijinski (on stage, at least) had only mimed masturbation, in front of Gore, Rudi actually masturbated.

"Before his dance had ended, I had already planned its climax," Gore later claimed.

That evening marked the beginning of other nights that would be played out around the world, mainly in New York, London, and the Amalfi Coast of Italy.

"We were on-again, off-again lovers," Gore said. "I knew better to want more from him, and I also knew that I would never possess him, as he'd know many other lovers, perhaps even some female ones, in his future."

"On our second night together, Rudi went into the bathroom and emerged from it naked," Gore said. "He lay down on his stomach on the thick carpet. 'Take me,' he commanded."

After it was over, Gore claimed that Rudi had wanted to have sex with him like that "just to show off my back [his words]. It is very beautiful, *non*?"

"Yes, you have an incredibly beautiful back," Gore told him. "But with an ass like that, who in hell looks at your back?"

Gore said, "Rudi considers taking off his ballet tights as the beginning of foreplay. He likes to be taken when he's all hot and sweaty."

Within weeks, Rudi had fallen in love—not with Gore, but with Erik Bruhn, the Danish soloist ballet dancer at the Royal Danish Ballet in Copenhagen. Gore soon learned that Bruhn and Rudi had become lovers.

Even though he was in Verbier, Switzerland, at the time, Truman Capote was among the first to learn of the Vidal/Nureyev affair. "Gore had the hots for Rudi," Truman claimed. "Word spread through the ballet world. Even though Rudi had taken Bruhn as his permanent lover, Gore showed up at his performances with his tongue hanging out."

Truman wrote Cecil Beaton. "I don't understand Nureyev. What sort of sex life does he have? Is he in love with Erik Bruhn? Myself, I think Nureyev is repulsive. But then Gore and I have never agreed on this subject of what constitutes attractiveness."

"As for Rudi, Gore can have him," Truman siad. "Besides, I understand he fucks like a jack rabbit."

***

Monique van Vooren wrote in her 1981 book, *Night Sanctuary*, "Rudi was tortured and tormented by his sexuality. He was ashamed of being a homosexual."

In Diane Solway's *Nureyev: His Life*, published in 1998, she wrote that he preferred "rough trade, pickups, sailors, lorry drivers, and the like."

"Rudi went in for rent boys and hustlers, but he seduced an amazing number of celebrities, and I include myself on that list," Gore said.

"What especially intrigued Gore were Rudi's rumored Kennedy seductions, including both Jackie and her sister, Lee Radziwill. Even more astounding was an affair with Bobby Kennedy, whom Gore had long suspected of being a deeply closeted homosexual. He later speculated about this in his memoirs.

In *Palimpsest*, Gore claimed that Rudi confessed that he and Bobby "did share a young soldier, American soldier," in Rudi's words.

Julie Kavanagh, who wrote the definitive biography of Rudi, added another RFK/Nureyev link.

Alexander Grant of the Royal Ballet claimed that he and Rudi were having an intimate talk at Arthurs *[the leading nightclub in Manhattan in the 60s]* when Bobby Kennedy approached them.

Abruptly, Bobby asked, "Hey, what's going on between you two? Break this up!"

It seemed that RFK wanted to take possession of Rudi, and he pulled him away and disappeared with him into the night.

***

In Paris, Rudi invited Gore to a screening of his 1977 film, *Valentino*, in which he impersonated that great lover of the Silent Screen, "The Sheik." British director Ken Russell had guided Rudi through a difficult role with many costume changes. His wardrobe included gangster-style pin stripes, flowing Moorish djellabas, and Argentinian-style gaucho pants. The film also included scenes in which he appeared without any clothes at all.

Long after the dying embers of passion's fire had turned to ashes, Rudi and Gore Vidal remained friends, especially after Rudi bought a small, rocky island a short distance off the coast of Positano, along the Amalfi Coast, south of Naples. The islet had previously been owned by Léonide Massine, the great Russian choreographer, who had built a villa there and connected the island to the Italian mainland with a bridge. Gore, of course, lived in the nearby hilltop town of Ravello.

In his memoirs, Gore relates, "I would come down from Ravello to visit him. Then, with seigneurial courtesy, he would come to see me by the sea, where he would let his AIDS-wasted body collapse beside the pool."

"I spent the night with Rudi and was awakened the next morning at nine o'clock," Gore said. "A boat filled with tourists was circling the island, and a woman's voice on a loudspeaker was extolling the glories of Rudi's achievements in ballet."

"After breakfast, we went into a room below, which was covered with ceramic tiles from floor to ceiling," Gore said. "It was crowned with a dome. Rudi told me he wanted to be buried in the center of the room under that dome—this was, in fact, his mausoleum."

"For lunch and dinner, the cook served only potatoes cooked in myriad ways—no meat or vegetables," Gore said. "The cook was fat, Rudi, of course was not."

"I knew Rudi practiced unsafe sex, but he seemed to think he was immune from AIDS," Gore said. "In 1984, he told me that he'd tested positive for HIV, but he didn't change his sexual habits. He kept insisting that, 'There is nothing wrong with me. My Tatar blood is as pure as a mountain stream in Siberia.' But by the summer of 1991, I noticed a remarkable decline in his health. When I saw him in Paris in the spring of 1992, I knew he was dying."

Gore attended Rudi's final ballet performance in *La Bayadère* at the Palais Garnier in Paris. During the ten-minute ovation that followed, Rudi needed help to walk across the stage.

Later that night, he told Gore, "The main thing for me is my dancing. Before it withers away from my body, I will keep dancing until the last moment, the last drop."

In his memoirs, Gore recalled Rudi's final visit to Ravello. It transpired during the August before he died.

Gore remembered that Rudi looked thin and exhausted. "He sat on my sofa, drinking white wine. He could go for hours without talking. He did come alive for ballet gossip."

As Gore reported it, Rudi said, "Peter Martins—he kill wife, no? No. Sad. Saw him when he was sixteen. In class. Big cock hangs here. I make move. Erik Bruhn say, 'No, too young. Go to jail.'"

[Peter Martins, the very talented and hard-driving Danish classical dancer and choreographer and one of the luminaries of the ballet world, served for many years as the artistic director of the New York City Ballet.]

Gore claimed that Rudi's face was ravaged but still beautiful. "He was still very much the Tatar king. The upper body had begun to waste away, but the lower was still unaffected—legs powerful, and the feet, for a dancer, not too misshapen, no hammertoes."

The last time Gore met with Rudi, the dancer told him, "I will soon be joining Erik Bruhn somewhere, someplace. He and I will dance a *pas de deux* into eternity."

Rudi died on January 6, 1993 at the age of 54. He was buried at the Russian cemetery in Sainte-Geneviève-des-Bois near Paris, a pilgrimage site even today for his still-loyal fans.

On his last visit to Paris, Gore placed yellow roses on his grave and included a note:

THANKS FOR THE MEMORIES
—G.V.

REST IN PEACE

Master Artist and Athlete
& the Greatest Male Dancer of His Generation

RUDOLF NUREYEV
(1958-1992)

The hottest dance sensation in the world, **Rudolf Nureyev**'s widely publicized defection from the Soviet Union generated worldwide attention and added a shot of testosterone to popular conceptions about classical ballet.

In Ravello, Italy, **Gore Vidal** (left) walks along a pathway with his friend, the AIDS-ravished **Rudolf Nureyev** at the twilight of his life.

Chapter Eleven

RUDOLF NUREYEV
Seducing His Way Through the Kennedy Clan

LOVE TRIANGLE In November of 1968, deep in the English countryside, **Lee Radziwill** *(left)*, **Jackie Kennedy** *(center)*, and **Rudolf Nureyev** enjoy the great outdoors.

Even in the presence of these world-class dressers, Rudi managed to appear as the most fashionably attired.

Rudi captivated the hearts of both Jackie and Lee, as well as the hearts of two male members of the Kennedy clan. "When it came to seducing, it was hard to say no to Rudi," said ballerina Margot Fonteyn. "He usually got what he wanted. Even otherwise straight men, or at least some of them, couldn't resist this bundle of Slavic charm." Rudi never kept his affairs with the Kennedys a secret, and often relayed boastful tales about his conquests.

The love of his life was Erik Bruhn, the Danish-born *danseur noble*. "A totally reciprocal deep passion existed between the two men," said Rudi's biographer, Julie Kavanaugh. Rudi was never faithful to Bruhn.

One night at Maxim's in Paris, he told Bruhn: "I was just in New York. I fuck Jackie Kennedy. Now I take you back to hotel, and I fuck you--all night!"

FROM RUSSIA WITH LOVE
TALES OF TATAR TAIL

"I know what it is like to make love as both a man and a woman."
—Rudolf Nureyev

"When you've known Nijinski, you don't want to see Nureyev."
—Coco Chanel

"Rudolf had a street life that was probably as wide ranging as anyone's in this century."
—Film Director James Toback

"I don't care what the magazines say," said ballet star **Rudolf Nureyev**. "I am the sexiest man alive. Just ask Lee Radziwill. Just ask Jackie Kennedy. And if you still don't believe me, ask Bobby and John-John. Nobody in the world can resist me. Everyone who has ever gone to bed with me has fallen madly in love with me."

Rudolf Nureyev was the greatest male ballet dancer of his generation. Along with Nijinski, he was one of the most spectacular ballet dancers of all time.

He had a stunning Slavic physical beauty, an extraordinarily athletic and sexual persona, a prodigious endowment that he liked to exhibit, and oodles of Russian charm.

As a stellar member of the glitterati, he attracted the attention of international café society—specifically Lee Radziwill, Jackie Kennedy, Bobby Kennedy, and John F. Kennedy Jr. In time, he would seduce all four of them.

In 1961, during the darkest days of the Cold War, Rudi was touring Western Europe with the Kirov Ballet Troupe. At Paris's Le Bourget airport, he had been scheduled to board a flight for London. But shortly before takeoff, KGB officials ordered him to board the next plane to Moscow because his mother was dying.

Sensing a trap, the 23-year-old dancer fled into the arms of two French policemen. "Save me! I want to stay."

Later he told friends that he was

carrying a pair of scissors with him. "Had anything gone wrong," he said, "I was prepared to plunge the scissors into my heart."

Rudi knew that if he returned to Moscow, he'd never dance again. The KGB had accumulated an extensive file on him, detailing his homosexual encounters.

He was "born wild" in 1938 on a train chugging beside Lake Baikaal in Siberia. In 1945, at the age of seven, he fell in love with the world of dance when he saw his first ballet. He would dance for the rest of his life.

His father nicknamed him "Ballerina." He despised his son and the world of ballet and frequently beat Rudi.

In spite of his father, Rudi stubbornly insisted on taking ballet lessons. He was an amazing pupil and by 1958, he'd evolved into a sensation within the Soviet dance world. His performances, so the critics claimed, were "erotically charged."

Two weeks after his defection, Rudi was performing at the Théâtre des Champs-Elysées in Paris, to shouts of "traitor" coming from Russians or their sympathizers.

A call from the English ballet diva, Margot Fonteyn, changed his life. She was the aging *prima ballerina* of Britain's Royal Ballet. At a charity event, the offstage and onstage liaison of the 42-year-old ballerina and the young Russian exile began.

Succumbing to Rudi's charms were **Jackie Kennedy** *(upper left)* and her younger sister, **Lee Radziwill** *(upper right)*. In the lower left is **Robert (Bobby) Kennedy**, smiling, but not, at least then, at Rudi.

Bolstered and supported by Peter Lawford, Rudi urged **John F. Kennedy, Jr**. *(lower right)* to become a Hollywood movie star. "You already look like one," Rudi told JFK's impressionable young son. "Why not be one?"

One night, Rudi persuaded JFK Jr. to wear a pair of his purple ballet tights. When he saw how JFK looked, Rudi said, "The way you wear those tights, you'd be a sensation, if only you could dance."

Prince and Princess Stanislas Radziwill saw Rudi perform in London's Covent Garden and were mesmerized by him. While he was trying to find some permanent residence, the Polish aristocrat, married at the time to Jackie's sister, Lee, invited the ballet dancer to stay with them at what was called "the two prettiest houses in England," their townhouse in London and their country home.

In either house, Lee led a privileged life. Her friend, the French actress/dancer Leslie Caron, claimed that Lee was "overprotected, a child-wife evocative of Nora in Ibsen's *A Doll's House.*"

At first, Rudi was suspicious of the Prince and Princess. He told Fonteyn that he thought he was being set up for a "three-way."

"We even have those arrangements in Moscow," he said. As it turned out, Rudi's sexual suspicion was only half founded. Lee was powerfully attracted to him. He would be their guest for seven months, as "Rudimania" swept across London. Arguably Rudi became the first pop icon of the 1960s.

Fonteyn and Rudi were the hottest cultural ticket in the west, creating a sensation in the United States when they performed there in 1960s.

His first American review called Rudi "a cheetah behind bars."

Truman Capote said, "Everybody, man or woman, wanted to fuck with Rudi, and most of them did, even the Kennedys. Whether he was dancing *Swan Lake* or *Romeo and Juliet*, all eyes were glued to Rudi's ample crotch. I sampled it myself. All nine and a half inches of thick Slavic meat."

Lee called Rudi "my eternal flame," and photographers liked to capture them in intimate situations as they danced together. She was caught on film clinging suggestively to him.

Friends reported that Lee was deeply in love with Rudi and "continued her campaign to make him straight." But as Capote warned her, "It was a hopeless undertaking. Once you've enjoyed the taste of cock, you can't keep them down on the farm."

A free-lance journalist, Diana DuBois, claimed: "Lee was put off by Rudi's homosexuality. That was always a bone of contention. He would tell her that he wanted a 'big cock,' and she would react with disgust."

In the early days, Lee was so taken with this ballet dancer that she purchased for him a Russian double-headed eagle of solid

Prince and Princess Stanislaw Albrecht Radziwill (aka, "Stash" and Jackie's younger sister, as she was widely known) enjoy balmy weather at the Half Moon Resort in Montego Bay, Jamaica, during a holiday in March of 1961. JFK had only recently become president of the United States, and Lee was beginning to enjoy worldwide attention as the sister of Jackie and as the sister-in-law of the U.S. president.

Although she was smart, talented, and charming in her own right, Lee often suffered unfavorable comparisons with her more formidable sibling. The press constantly compared them: Which of the sisters was better-looking? Which could more easily attract men? Which was the better-dressed?

gold studded with diamonds and rubies.

Lee allegedly admitted to Capote (at least he claimed so) that she did have sex with Rudi one time. "It was the most athletic experience I've ever known in bed," Capote quoted her as telling him.

Lee visited Rudi on the French Riviera where he'd rented a villa, "Arcadie," in La Turbie, high in the hills above Monte Carlo. In the guest bedroom, she came across pictures of men engaged in sex.

She came to realize that her sexual pursuit of the young dancer was a losing proposition. Yet their friendship survived, and would stretch over some three decades. It began on a note of intense animal passion and developed into an enduring friendship.

When Rudi arrived in America and was introduced to Jackie, Lee found herself competing against her own sister for Rudi's affection. It would not be the first time the two sisters pursued the same man.

Lee was still in love with Rudi, and maybe the problem was that he was much more in love with Jackie than he was with Lee. He thought Jackie had the more alluring personality.

Capote claimed that Jackie fell in love with Rudi on the day she invited him and his dance partner, Margot Fonteyn, to the White House for tea.

Unlike her husband, "Rudi," as Jackie came to call him, admired her passion for the arts and even her choice of antiques. Sitting in the president's old North Carolina porch rocker in the Cabinet Room, he ordered his favorite drink, port with ginger ale, from a White House waiter.

Lee had warned Jackie that Rudi was "ninety-nine and a half percent homosexual," but Jackie wasn't so sure. Rudi was flirting outrageously with her, and she was a notorious flirt herself.

When the room emptied, he impulsively rose from the rocker, grabbed her, and passionately kissed her. "Unlike your beautiful husband, I do not have a bad back," he said. "A strong Russian back made for leaping through the air."

From that point on, according to Capote, Jackie was mesmerized.

After her husband's death, Rudi, on many a night, "warmed the sheets" [his words] of the former First Lady's bed.

Capote claimed that Jackie "stole" Rudi from her sister, Lee, with whom the dancer was temporarily feuding. "She destroyed my baby," he charged to Jackie. "Had it cut in little pieces from her body. But with you, I will make nine beautiful children—five boys, four girls."

"I'm not a breeding factory," she warned him. "Better call Ethel for that."

"But I've already told my friends about the babies we're going to make."

"Don't you dare!" she shouted at him. "Stop this talk about our private relationship! It'll be fodder for the tabloids. Those friends of yours are malicious gossips!"

"But every part of your life has been in print already, although that is not good for the soul," he said.

Rudi not only admired Jackie for her beauty, but for her financial advice. "The first real money Rudi made was under Jackie's influence," said one of his associates. "She's the one who got him to buy gold just before gold shot up to the sky."

Jackie was hesitant to introduce Rudi to either her son or to Bobby Kennedy. At times Rudi could be flamboyantly homosexual. She feared Bobby might be put off by his exhibitionism. Even so, she arranged a dinner between Bobby and Rudi. "I've never seen two men bond in such a way," she told Lee when their relationship resumed. "Bobby seemed fascinated by Rudi." Jackie later admitted that she had no idea at first that Bobby and Rudi were seeing each other outside her home.

She became aware of that when the phone by her bedside rang one night. She was in bed with Rudi at the time. She picked up the phone. "Bobby," she said, her face lighting up.

A sudden look of distress crossed her brow. She muffled the phone. "He wants to speak to you. I must warn you, he's dangerously jealous of any man who gets near me. He must have had you trailed here."

Rudi eagerly took the phone from her. "Bobby, Bobby, you are the greatest American of them all. Fonteyn has taught me a new word for us—*peccadillo.*"

As she made her way to the bathroom, she heard Rudi giggling into the phone like a young teenage girl with her first crush on the star football captain.

Two weeks later, over cocktails with Capote, Jackie said, "I think Rudi systematically plans to seduce every member of my family, even my son when he grows up. Or before he grows up. He's already talking about teaching John ballet at an early age."

"Watch out for that Cossack," the author warned her. "Rudi has enough charm to seduce Richard Nixon. Forgive me for prying—how unlike me—but I must ask. Is it true what they say about Rudi in bed?"

"Afraid so," she said. "On stage, his movements are the most graceful of any man on earth. But in bed I have a nickname for him: *Mr. Jack Rabbit.*"

There were many sightings of Bobby and Rudi at New York night spots, especially Arthur's. The celebrity-haunted joint was the most exclusive disco in New York; it was operated by Sybil Burton, the Welsh actress who'd lost her husband, Richard Burton, to Elizabeth Taylor, that "Serpent of the Nile."

Janet Villeha, a prima ballerina with the New York City Ballet in the 1960s, spotted an arrival one night. "I saw Bobby come in with both Jackie and Rudi. Later on, as I went to make a phone call, I saw Bobby and Rudi in a telephone booth. They were kissing passionately."

All of his lovers knew that Rudi was a devotee of "deep throat" kissing. As one of his boys put it, "He went for your tonsils."

In his famous memoir, *Palimpsest*, Gore Vidal wrote of a revelation Rudi made to him:

> "Between Bobby's primitive religion and his family's ardent struggle ever upward from the Irish bog, he was more than usually skewed, not least by his own homosexual impulses, which, Nureyev once told me, were very much in the air on at least one occasion when they were together.. 'Nothing happen,' said Rudi. 'But we did share young soldier once. American soldier. Boy not lie ... maybe.' Rudi gave his Tartar grin, very much aware, firsthand, of the swirls of gossip that envelop the conspicuous. Yet anyone who has eleven children must be trying to prove-disprove? Something other than the ability to surpass his father as incontinent breeder."

No one encouraged JFK Jr. to pursue a theatrical career more than Rudi. "John-John" shared his dreams with the Russian ballet dancer, who was falling in love with him.

A bit of a mama's boy, JFK Jr. told Rudi that Jackie was "dead set" against his going into the theater.

"Have some balls," Rudi said. "I know you've got a pair on you. We can't always do what mommy says."

John Cohan, who has been a celebrity psychic to the stars for more than three decades, delivered several bombshells when he wrote: *Catch a Falling Star: The Untold Story of Celebrity Secrets*.

One night at New York's infamous Studio 54, he encountered John F. Kennedy Jr. in the company of family friend, Rudi, and New York's "hottest" male prostitute who advertised his services for $1,000 a night.

"This was a threesome I saw with my own eyes," Cohan wrote. "I think John

JFK, Jr.'s straight life, frat boy style, was best chronicled by his former roommate Robert T. Littell in 2005 in his memoir, *The Men We Became*. They first met as freshmen during orientation week at Brown University.

"Going out with John at night was like having a key to the city," Littel asserted. "Doormen bowed and velvet ropes fell when he stepped out of a cab. Sometimes, I felt as though I was with Moses at the parting of the Red Sea."

Littell claimed that their shared apartment was the venue for some strange sexual adventures. One night, one of their friends returned with a female flight attendant and took her to the spare bedroom. Later, Littell and JFK Jr. peeked in on their friend. The door was open a crack.

Inside, they saw their lusty friend rubbing the sheepskin collar of President Kennedy's official commander-in-chief leather jacket across the woman's bare breasts.

Her seducer was getting her excited by informing her that it was "The First Coat" actually worn many times by the assassinated president.

wanted a new experience. He had confessed to me that he became bored with people and things quickly."

"He always talked about an acting career, which his mother adamantly refused to permit," Cohan said. "I used to caution him on many occasions—no race cars, no airplanes, and no scuba diving. I didn't feel good about these adrenaline rushes he got."

At the club, Cohan also warned Rudi, "Leave John-John alone, because this scene isn't his first preference."

"I love the challenge of seducing a straight man," Rudi told Cohan. "That night he did just that."

The male prostitute later tried to sell an exposé article about that night with Rudi and John Jr. But there were no takers—the allegation at the time was too controversial.

In his accusation, the male hustler claimed, "John fucked me, really hard, but when I tried to return the favor, he told me that part of him was 'off limits.' Rudi went down on him later in the evening. John-John was strictly rough trade, but what an evening."

Although Rudi could have seduced some of the most famous men and women on the planet, and did on occasion, he much preferred anonymous encounters in public toilets, New York bathhouses, and other gay cruising venues.

In his dressing room, he often received celebrities in the nude. One night Arnold Schwarzenegger came backstage to congratulate him. Rudi sucked on the muscleman's index finger. "I want to know how you taste," he allegedly said. "I've seen pictures of you nude. I want you to put your cock in my mouth."

Celebrity psychic **John Cohan** wrote a tell-all book in 2008, revealing relatively unknown secrets of the stars. No revelation was more shocking than the romantic link between John F. Kennedy Jr. and Rudolf Nureyev.

As a psychic, Cohan warned JFK Jr. about his possible early death by advising him to avoid racecars, airplanes, and scuba diving.

John patted him on the back. "I'll start calling you my brother, an older brother, who worries a bit too much about me."

Once, when Cohan suffered from a sore shoulder, JFK Jr. offered to massage it. To JFK Jr. Cohan said, "I'm glad I'm straight, because this kind of feely stuff from an attractive, sexy man could certainly tempt the best of them."

JFK Jr. replied with a knowing smile. "I take the fifth."

"You're the sixth person today who has requested that," Arnold reportedly said, retrieving his finger before it was devoured.

Monique Van Vooren, who wrote about Rudi in her 1981 book, *Night Sanctuary*, claimed he "was tortured, and tormented by his sexuality. He was ashamed of being homosexual. And I think he wanted to be degraded." In Diane Solway's *Nureyev: His Life* (1998), she wrote that he preferred "rough-trade, pickups, sailors, lorry drivers, and the like."

One night at one of Rudi's openings (the exact performance unknown), Jackie was in the audience and the stage manager urgently summoned her to come backstage to Rudi's dressing room.

There she found him completely nude. He told her that he was tired of his fans shouting, "We want Rudi in the Nudi," and that he was going to dance one ballet completely naked.

Using the force of her personality, she urged him to put on some purple tights. After holding the curtain fifteen minutes, Rudi agreed to go on, but his tights were so thin they were almost see-through. Jackie later told friends, "His fans got to see him almost naked, but he was covered enough so that the policemen weren't called."

She later became miffed at Rudi. In her working capacity as an editor at Doubleday, she went to him in 1986 and asked him to write his memoirs.

He turned her down. "Jackie darling," he said, "you know I can't write story of life. Story of life must tell what happened . . . I mean, really happened, not pack of lies. It should not be a cover-up, no truth in it. My not writing book will protect you and Bobby. Even your son."

Jackie's face flashed anger. "And what about my son? What did you do to John?"

"Nothing, not so excited. I encouraged him to be an actor. That's all. Nothing else. I swear it!"

Her upset with Rudi didn't last long. He charmed his way back into her good graces.

She was greatly concerned in 1987 when Rudi announced he was returning to Russia to see his ailing mother. She asked Ted Kennedy as a senator to write to the Soviet ambassador in Washington, requesting protection for Rudi.

For twelve years Rudi carried the AIDS virus. His final artistic statement involved the choreography of a production of *La Bayadère*, which opened in February of 1992 at the Palais Garnier in Paris. During the ten-minute ovation that followed, he needed help to walk across the stage. He is quoted as saying, "The main thing is dancing. Before it withers away from my body, I will keep dancing till the last moment, the last drop."

Rudi died on January 6, 1993 at the age of 54. He was buried at a Russian cemetery in Sainte-Geneviève-des-Bois near Paris, a pilgrimage site even today for his still loyal fans.

Chapter Twelve

STAR POWER:

NUREYEV'S HOMAGE TO RUDOLPH VALENTINO

HOW AN INSANELY POPULAR ICON FROM THE 1970S REINTERPRETED THE DOOMED LIFE OF A LEGEND FROM THE 1920S

The homosexual actor from movie-making's silent era, **Rudolph Valentino** *(photo, right)*, darling of millions of women, died mysteriously in New York City during the hot August of 1926. He was only thirty-one years old.

Almost half a century later, a homosexual dancer, **Rudolf Nureyev** *(right)*, was cast as the lead in an ultra-avant-garde movie, *Valentino (1977)*, in an attempt to bring the legend of the silent screen back to life.

The movie, widely and (in most cases) negatively reviewed in the Hollywood press, was a box office failure.

Yet with the passage of time, and through the lens of 21st-Century audiences, it has evolved into one of the great camp classics of the "Me" Decade.

> # *"WE WANT RUDI IN THE NUDI!"*
>
> —Oft-repeated chant of Nureyev's fans, clamoring for him to remove his clothing onstage.

The 1977 film, *Valentino*, starred Rudolf Nureyev playing Rudolph Valentino. It was directed by British director Ken Russell.

Nureyev said that the director had to develop *des couilles en fer* (iron testicles) to guide him through a difficult role where he either appeared almost naked, or in a bizarre combination of gangster-style pinstripes, flowing Moorish *djellabas*, or Argentinian-style *gaucho* pants.

In one of screen history's most exaggerated performances, Leslie Caron appears as Nazimova, a deliberate send-up of the extravagantly theatrical 1920s-era actress known as America's Eleanora Duse.

The movie opened to bad reviews on both sides of the Atlantic. According to film critic Pauline Kael: "There is no artistry left in Ken Russell's work. By now, his sensationalist reputation is based merely on his going further than anybody else. His films have become schoolboy Black Masses, a mixture of offensiveness and crude dumbness. Spitefulness is almost the sole emotion of *Valentino*."

(Two photos above) The real **Rudolph Valentino** *(left)* as he appeared in the early 1920s in the coveted role of the young bullfighter, Juan Gallardo, in the Vicente Blasco-Ibañez blockbuster *Blood and Sand (1922)*.

Rudolf Nureyev *(right)*, in Ken Russell's 1977 remake of the Valentino saga, draws his sword in imitation of that long-ago screen matador.

Valentino's lover, Paul Ivano, once revealed that the silent-screen star wore his Juan Gallardo matador costume as an erotic stimulant in his bedroom, re-enacting some of his bullfight scenes as a prelude to rough sex. On the set of *Valentino* in the mid 70s, Nureyev had a young gay stagehand fellate him before stuffing himself into his matador costume and appearing on set. In one scene, the dancer's erection was too prominent, and the cameraman had to wait for it to deflate a bit.

The "other" Rudi, almost in the Nudi in 1921. depicting Valentino carrying a surfboard,

It was a then-shocking publicity photo for the silent romance *The Young Rajah*.

L'Apres-midi d'un faune
It was so revolutionary that at its premier in Paris, fistfights disrupted the audience.

L'Apres-midi d'un faune:
Valentino (1921) imitating Nijinsky

Nureyev (1976) imitating-
Valentino imitating Nijinsky

In the early 1920s, in a private photo session, Valentino evoked Nijinsky as Nijinsky had appeared about a decade previously in the Stravinsky-Diaghilev ballet *L'apres-midi d'un faune.* Prior to their marriage, Valentino's second wife, a lesbian, Natacha Rambova, asked him to pose for the faun pictures.

And although it was viewed as almost unbelievably pretentious at the time, it was her way of paying homage to Valentino's "Greek god body," and to her Russian compatriot, Nijinsky. When Valentino's first wife, Jean Acker, also a lesbian, filed for divorce, she vengefully introduced these pictures to the press. Headlines immediately blared FAUN PICTURE CAUSES STIR.

In 1977, in a scene from the Ken Russell film, Nureyev played Valentino imitating Nijinsky.

  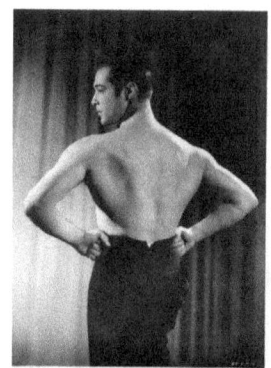

Rudolph Valentino

Rudolf Nureyev

Unlike Rudolf Nureyev, who never married, Valentino took two wifes, Jean Acker, and later, Natacha Rambova. There is strong evidence that neither of the two marriages was ever cosummated. In fact, Acker announced her intention of permanently locking Valentino out of her bedroom only minutes after the marriage ceremony ended.

Other lovers, however, were far more willing to receive *The Sheik (1921)* into their bedrooms, including "Rae" Bourbon, the female impersonator, and Norman Kerry, once a famous silent screen actor. Even Ramon Novarro, the star of the original film version of *Ben-Hur*, fell madly in love with Valentino. Valentino's greatest role remains *The Sheik*, in which he played a swarthy Arab seducer in a film about desert sex and machismo. In theaters across America, women fainted. *The Sheik* would seal Valentino's legend as the World's Greatest Lover. Baring his chest and popping his eyes, Valentino also attracted thousands of gay male fans who knew "he was one of us."

In director Ken Russell's 1977 *homage* to Valentino, another Rudolf (in this case the Russian-born emigré ballet superstar Rudolf Nureyev) played the desert scenes almost nude. Most critics found him far more seductive than the original.

Before Nureyev, and even before Valentino, NIJINSKY
Defined the Way Men Should Move

Of Polish descent, but born in The Ukraine in 1880, Vaslav Nijinsky was the most celebrated male dancer in history. At the age of 18, he garnered leading roles in St. Petersburg's Marinsky (aka Kirov) Theater. It was here that he met Sergei Diaghilev, a wealthy impresario and patron of the arts, who soon after became his lover.

Diaghilev wanted his *protégé* to break free of the Marinksy. As a means to this end, Nijinsky appeared at a performance in honor of Russia's royal family without a jockstrap, an accessory that was otherwise obligatory for the troupe's male dancers. The Dowager Empress Marie Feodorovna complained that his appearance was obscene, and that she could see Nijinsky's penis and testicles in complete detail. As a result, he was dismissed from the company, leaving him available to pursue a more radical (and potentially more profitable) style of choreography within Diaghilev's dance troupe, *Les Ballets Russes*.

In Paris, Nijinsky, having developed a "modern" style inspired by Greek antiquity and radically angular movements, helped define a form of choreography "that was an assault" upon traditional classical ballet. In May, 1913, in Paris, a riot broke out among the otherwise black-tie audience at the Théâtre des Champs-Elysées after he mimed masturbation with the scarf of a nymph during the premiere of a joint Stravinsky/Diaghilev production, *Le Sacre du Printemps* (The Rite of Spring).

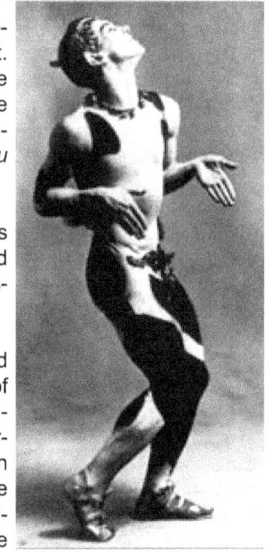

Despite almost universal charges of obscenity, such luminaries as Rodin and the gay author Marcel Proust aggressively and loudly defended the work, and Nijinsky's dance, as an expression of genius.

Much to the jealous fury of Diaghilev, who had not accompanied his dance troupe on a recital tour of South America because of his morbid superstition of drowning during a sea voyage, Nijinsky eventually married Romola Pulszky, an obsessive Hungarian countess who had been virtually stalking him for months. In 1919, he suffered a nervous breakdown. Diagnosed with acute schizophrenia, he spent the rest of his life in and out of psychiatric hospitals. Before his death in a London clinic in 1950, he recorded a bitter exposé of his relationship with Diaghilev.

Born in Soviet Siberia in 1938, Rudolf Nureyev was the greatest male ballet dancer of the 1960s and 70s, expressing himself in both classical and modern roles. Nureyev cut his ties with the Soviet Union on June 17, 1961, seeking political asylum in France at Le Bourget Airport in Paris, just before his scheduled flight back to the USSR and probable imprisonment for his self-defined status as a gay man.

He never married, although he formed several long-lasting relationships with men over the years, especially Erik Bruhn, the Danish ballet dancer.

Trading on his fame and charisma, he became something of a Kennedy family seducer, enjoying intimacies not only with Lee Radziwill but with Jackie-O herself. And if "Rudi" is to be believed, he and Robert Kennedy, one drunken night in Los Angeles, jointly shared the sexual favors of a handsome American G.I.

Looking macho and particularly virile, Rudolph Valentino created a sensation when he appeared as a gaucho in *Four Horsemen of the Apocalypse,* a 1921 film adaptation of the novel by Vicente Blasco-Ibañez. Valentino kept himself busy tending to the needs of his two male lovers at the time, the young Ramon Novarro, working as a nude model, and Paul Ivano, an adviser to the film's battle scenes.

Novarro later confessed that Valentino became "the great love of my life," even though The Great Lover viewed their sexual liaison as "passionate but loveless, mere ships that pass in the night." As a goodbye gift, Valentino gave Novarro a life-sized replica of his penis, a ten-inch Art Deco dildo.

Nureyev's re-enactment of Valentino's portrayal followed the original with flair. The script detailed the plot of a playboy wastrel who evolved into a man thanks to wartime suffering. A Muselman Tartar who had been born in a Soviet Trans-Siberian railway car near Irkutsk, near Vladivostok, Nureyev managed to play an Argentinian rather well.

Cult singer Michelle Phillips

In Russell's film, the willowy blonde singer and songwriter, Michelle Phillips, played Natacha Rambova, the notorious second wife of Rudolph Valentino. In the film, a nude Natacha lures Nureyev (playing Valentino) into her tent. Her provocative poses, and their sexual passion, was a mere screen fantasy. In real life, Natacha spent far more time in the arms of Alla Nazimova, the flamboyant actress (and godmother of First Lady Nancy Davis Reagan) than she did eating Valentino's famous spaghetti.

Phillips is best known as one of the founders of the 1960s pop group "The Mamas and the Papas." She and Nureyev clashed often. "I hope you understand that I have no interest in women," he said to her at the time of their first meeting. After working with her for a week, he told her, "Just because you play cunt in film doesn't mean you have to be cunt in life."

Savvy insiders asserted that Natacha aggressively "steered" Valentino's career and public image. Their stormy marriage reflected the legend of Pygmalian and Galatea--in reverse. The impresario, Jacques Hébertot, once claimed that "Natacha was an absolute cow-- snotty, rude to Valentino in public. She treated her dogs better than she treated him. He told me that he had slept with her many times, but that she always refused to have sex with him." Hébertot also claimed that whenever he was with Valentino, it was he who took care of the actor's sexual needs.

Nureyev, however, while playing the Sheik, never had trouble finding a bedmate. Just ask Cecil Beaton, Leonard Bernstein, Anthony Perkins, actress Ultra Violet, Mick Jagger, Freddie Mercury, Robert Mapplethorpe, and most definitely the designer, Halston. "All I remember of him," said Marlene Dietrich, "was his constant complaints about his legs--he considered them too short. But he was proud of something else which he talked about as if it was longer than it actually was."

Coco Chanel stood virtually alone in utterly dismissing Nureyev, his allure, and his legend: "If you've known Nijinsky, you don't want to see Nureyev."

As the director of *Valentino,* the very flamboyant **Ken Russell** *(right figure in photo below)* hawkeyes the final touches on Nureyev's slicked-down hair before releasing him to the cameras as Valentino.

Before his career as a director, English-born Russell was also a dancer. His third feature film, the X-rated adaptation of D.H. Lawrence's erotic *Women in Love (1969),* made him internationally famous. He took an enormous gamble in casting Nureyev as Valentino, since the dancer had not at the time been proven or tested as a screen personality.

Another of Russell's cinematic gambles failed in the early 1980s, when he insisted that Liza Minnelli play *Evita* in his abortive attempt to launch a film adaptation of the Argentinian dictator's life. That movie, of course, was eventually made by Alan Parker, who cast Madonna in the role instead.

Russell, during various stages of his life, has been variously dubbed as both "England's Orson Welles," and "The Fellini of the North."

Valentino portrayed a scene from its namesake's life wherein Nureyev (playing Valentino) is arrested because his second marriage license was processed before his divorce was finalized. In this enactment of an L.A. prison, female prostitutes attempt to undress him, and male inmates taunt him and threaten him with rape. A warden mixes a diuretic drug into a mug of coffee, which Valentino unsuspectingly drinks. In the film, he tries not to wet his pants, but his bladder eventually, and very visibly, gives up.

During the shoot, Nureyev fought bitterly with Russell about the size of his penis, since the scene portrayed him pissing his pants. To suggest the long length of his penis, Nureyev kept demanding that the hose (a prop) in his pants be pushed farther and farther down the leg of his pants. Finally, an exasperated Russell told his cameraman: "It looks like Rudy is wrestling with a snake halfway down his pants. No one, not even John C. Holmes, is hung like that!"

Rudolf Nureyev imitating Rudolf Valentino, with *(right and also displayed in photo below)* Ken Russell

Rudolph Valentino in *Blood and Sand* (1922)

Margot Fonteyn *(with Nureyev, right)* became the most famous ballerina of the second half of the 20th century, dominating British ballet for more than four decades. She achieved all that before what has been called her "wonderful Indian summer," a chapter of her late career based almost entirely on her association with Rudolf Nureyev.

After his famous leap to freedom in Paris, he shortly thereafter teamed with Fonteyn, who invited him to London as her dance partner in *Giselle*. Their first performance startled the world, and the most celebrated partnership in the history of ballet was born. They were referred to as "The Dream Duo," and their interpretation of *Giselle* "the success of the century."

Despite the 20-year difference in their ages, Nureyev became her friend and occasional lover, exhibiting enormous tenderness to the *duenna* during her bout with terminal cancer.

The Love of His Life

There are those in the dance world who claimed that one of Nureyev''s most compelling motivations for escaping from the Soviet Union involved his fixation on **Erik Bruhn**, the Danish-born *danseur noble*. Born in 1928, Bruhn danced for the Royal Danish Ballet School from 1938 to 1947, eventually evolving during the 1950s into the world's premier male classical dancer.

All of Rudi's antennae were working. From the moment he met Bruhn in 1961, "It was love at first sight. I had to possess him. More than that, I had to move inside his body and take over his soul. I had to inhabit him. I had to work it so that Erik would become obsessed with me--and he did."

Bruhn, 32, and Rudi, 23, were as different as Apollo and Dionysus, yet they were fiercely attracted to each other. Bruhn later referred to their turbulent relationship as "pure Strindberg."

Erik Bruhn

As expressed by Rudi's biographer, Julie Kavanagh, "A totally reciprocal deep passion existed between the two men. Their emotional intimacy coexisted with an extraordinary artistic interchange. They began each day at the *barre*. Home-movie footage shows them working together in a studio, both dressed in black. Erik raises one arm into an arabesque position. Rudolf, facing him, does the same. They study themselves in the mirror, not with vanity but with the self-critical scrutiny of dancers. Then they change sides. Still facing each other, they move in close, their heads almost touching as they begin an arabesque exercise. A faintly homoerotic undertone now emerges, which also plays on the idea of gender reversal as they partner each other."

Of course, there were arguments and a clash of personalities, Erik being his Hamlet-like veiled, inscrutable self, Rudolf filled with a remarkable candor and a child-man impetuosity. In the words of Glen Tetley, "Erik just responded to that very powerful thing in Rudolf, who could suddenly open everything and let you see his soul."

There were even arguments over Bruhn's ballet tights. Rudi was generously endowed, Bruhn was not. Rudi protested that Bruhn embarrassed him on stage and suggested that he use padding to show off more genitalia. In Rudi's words, "For me, sexually in our bedroom, it doesn't matter, since I am a top. But many young gay men attend the ballet just to see the outline of a dancer's genitalia. You don't want to disappoint them, Erik." Despite those blandishments, the Dane steadfastly refused to pad his crotch.

Rudi was never faithful to Bruhn. It was not in the Russian's makeup to be sexually loyal to anyone. He often flaunted his affairs. One night at Maxim's in Paris, he told Bruhn, "I was just in New York. I fuck Jackie Kennedy. Now I take you back to hotel, and I fuck you--all night."

Bruhn seemed to understand his friend's promiscuity. He once said, "I do not like for love to be something possessive. I find it smothering. For me, loving does not mean owning." Bruhn defined his friendship with his lover like this: "My friendship with Rudi has been intense, stormy, and at times, very very beautiful. I have probably done plenty of things that have hurt or upset him. And he has done the same to me. And still, we are very close."

Bruhn died in Toronto of lung cancer on April 1, 1986, leaving Rudi devastated. He even threatened suicide. As he told his long-time dancing partner, Margot Fonteyn, "The only man I've ever loved lies cold somewhere on a marble slab in a morgue. I will never love again. My life ended today."

Rudolf Nureyev never did love again, and tried to blot out the memory of Bruhn in a series of one-night stands with cheap street hustlers or chance encounters in the steam baths of such cities as London.

He continued to perform classical ballet far beyond his prime, making his last public appearance on October 8, 1992, for the premiere of his staging of the Paris Opera Ballet's *La Bayadère*. He ignored critics who carped that he should abandon ballet and retire. "For me, dance and life are one. I will dance to the last drop of blood."

On January 6, 1993, at the age of 54, Rudi died of cardiac complications brought on by AIDS. On the day he died he said, "I will soon be joining Erik somewhere, someplace. He and I will dance a *pas de deux* into eternity."

Nureyev with Erik Bruhn

THE TANGO: THEY DANCED DIVINELY

Director Ken Russell discovered during his research that Valentino had actually taught the tango to the great Nijinsky when the young Russian dancer visited New York at the turn of the (20th) century.

"A re-enactment of that scene would be the most sensual introduction to the picture I know," Russell declared.

Originally, Russell had wanted Nureyev to interpret the role of Nijinsky, and in negotiations to that end, offered a goodly sum for the two-day shoot.

But eventually, Russell realized that **Nureyev** would be even better playing Valentino. **Sir Anthony James Dowell** *(right-hand figure in photo, left)*, who later served as the artistic director of England's Royal Ballet, was cast into the role of Nijinsky instead.

"Nureyev was the living symbol of what Valentino was all about," said Russell. "He was the perfect man for the part. It just *had* to be Nureyev."

Nureyev's Homage to Valentino

Photographed here on the French Riviera, the blonde beauty with the long pedigree as a movie star (**Tab Hunter,** *left*) was enthralled with **Rudolf Nureyev,** whom he described in his autobiography as a "bone white body with blue veins clad only in a sliver lamé swimsuit. Rudi looked like a finely chiseled corpse freshly risen from an ancient crypt, and he walked as if the world was far beneath him."

Eventually, shacked up within Nureyev's exquisitely styled home at 6 Fife Road in the Richmond Park district of London, "Tab & Rudi" abandoned their posturings and got down to some primal intra-male bonding.

Nureyev in those days was known for "fucking like a rabbit." Another of his lovers, Monique Van Vooren, the actress, claimed that Rudolf liked "street boys, toughs, the lowest of the low." Obviously Tab, the ultimate example of a handsome blonde beach boy of the 50s, was an exception to the dancer's usual conquests.

(left), Nureyev with **Margot Fonteyn** in *Paradise Lost*, 1962.

(upper right), In Ken Russell's *film,* film, **Nureyev** is expansive as Valentino.

(lower right) Russell was fascinated with the historical fact that in 1926, at his memorial service, the 31-year-old body of *The Sheik* lay on a block of ice to preserve it in the stifling heat of a New York August. In a separate room, thousands of fans filed by, and fussed over, a wax replica of Valentino's body, thinking that they were paying their respects to the real Valentino. Nureyev, as the dead Valentino, lies in state, oblivious to the adoring crowds.

Chapter Thirteen

How Opera Diva

ELEANOR STEBER

Generated Headlines at a "Black Tie, Black Towel Gala" at a Gay Bathhouse in Manhattan

And How, Between Starring in the World's Greatest Operas, She Dished the Music World's Juiciest Dirt, including

How Adolf Hitler Molested Boys in Bayreuth.

 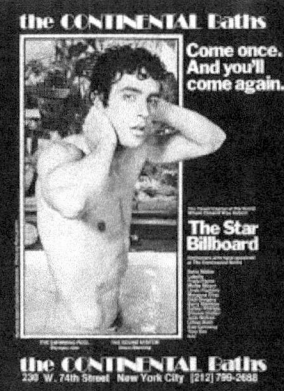 

You never knew who was going to show up to entertain at the raucously extroverted **Continental Baths** in NYC. A steamy recreational playground that combined high camp with high art, it became a "must visit" tourist attraction for thousands of gay men, either jaded, full-time residents of the city or visitors from far away.

Performing on a stage there in front of hundreds of partially undressed and usually GLBT men, Bette Midler would regularly get down and dirty, accompanied by roaring applause. Years later, with wry humor, she said, "When I die, *The New York Times* will surely herald my death by announcing that I got my start at the Continental Baths."

Indeed, Bette was fun, and even when she wasn't performing, there were LOTS of things to see and do at the Continental. But the classiest act at the Baths was the unexpected appearance of the world-class American opera diva **Eleanor Steber** (left and right photos, above.) who delivered an *haute* musical performance there that's still being written about.

A Black Tie Gala at the Baths: Opera Diva ELEANOR STEBER Remembers

Eleanor Steber, one of the world's leading opera divas, will be making a big splash in 2020, as opera lovers around the globe honor the 20th anniversary of her death at the age of 76 in 1990.

Unlike most great opera stars, Steber trained in America and had her greatest success here, although she did perform to acclaim in Germany and Scotland.

Darwin Porter was introduced to her by the fabled Viennese chanteuse, Greta Keller, who first raised a rendition of *Lili Marlene* to international fame.

Eleanor Steber was an honored guest at a book release party that Darwin Porter hosted at Backstage, a theater-district hangout favored by show-biz celebrities. The party marked the adaptation of Darwin's cult classic, *Butterflies in Heat,* into a film whose name was envisioned at the time as *The Last Resort* and later changed to *Tropic of Desire.*

One of the party's featured entertainers was Eartha Kitt. the elegant black movie star and nightclub entertainer.

From the microphone, accompanied by universal applause, she announced that she'd been selected as the film's heroine: Lola La Mour, a blonde transsexual singer who romantically tangles with a male hustler.

"Everyone hustles," she said. "It depends on what price you want to pay—so don't play me cheap. But the one thing I never offer as currency is my soul."

"I like Darwin's character of Lola," Kitt continued. "She has balls."

In addition to Eleanor Steber, another guest at the event Darwin hosted at Backstage was *The Last Resort's* male star, **Matt Collins**, in his film debut.

Widely recognized as one of the best-paid male models in the world, he had been hired to portray Numie Chase, the film's doomed protagonist.

Even Tennessee Williams had something to say about the adaptation of Darwin's novel into a film: "I'd walk the waterfront for Numie anytime."

"Eleanor and I bonded almost from the beginning," Darwin said. "Even though it seemed that at first we had nothing in common, we began an 'odd couple' relationship. Actually, we had a lot more in common than I realized at first. Both of us were born in poverty-stricken Appalachia, she in West Virginia, me in North Carolina."

Once, half-jokingly, they discussed his ghost-writing of her autobiography. As its title, she suggested, *Nothing Operatic Ever Came Out of West Virginia.*

"We often went to where the theatrical elite of Broadway gathered," Darwin said, "a bar popular with show-biz players in the Theater District on Manhattan's West Side. A legend in its time, and managed by my friend, Ted Hook (the gossipy and very gregarious former personal assistant to Tallulah Bankhead), it was called *Backstage*. Everyone always made a big fuss over Eleanor. Once, Richard Burton joined our table and, on another night, so did Peter Ustinov. We had some great evenings back then with Hermione Gingold and also with the very outspoken 'Belter,' Ethel Merman."

After extensive voice training, Steber made her critically acclaimed operatic debut in 1940 at New York's Metropolitan Opera. Her best reviews, and her most legendary performances, all occurred prior to 1961.

During her heyday, audiences and critics raved over her

Richard Strauss

Mozart

Arturo Toscanini

Eartha Kitt.

incredible voice that was described as "large, flexible, and silvery, particularly in the high-lying notes of Richard Strauss" (1864-1949). Steber promoted Strauss, along with Gustaf Mahler, as representative of the late flowering of German Romanticism.

Throughout her career, Steber performed operas from the world's greatest composers under the direction of the top modern maestros.

In 1946, Steber performed Mozart's *The Marriage of Figaro* to wild applause at the Edinburgh Festival, starring as the Countess. This frequently performed *Opera Buffa* was first presented in 1784. *[Talk about artists being misunderstood during their lifetimes: In Vienna, Emperor Joseph II believed that the censors should shut it permanently down.]*

During her heyday, Steber earned especially great success with her renditions of the Strauss opera, *Arabella*, an avant-garde work first introduced in 1933. In 1955, cast into its title role, she sang it in NYC at the Met, marking the first of 58 interpretations of it that various divas delivered over the years.

Steber was equally at home with less controversial lyrical portrayals of heroines created by Mozart, especially through performances of *Die Entführung aus dem Serail*, aka *The Abduction from the Seraglio*.

[In reference to Mozart's mind-boggling musical gifts, Joseph Haydn wrote: "Posterity will not see such a talent again in 100 years.]

Musically brilliant and fervently nationalistic, Richard Wagner composed operas that some critics say helped to define the soul and aspirations of Germany itself.

Wieland Wagner   Adolf Hitler   Wolfgang Wagner

The Nazis tried, with some degree of success, to associate the national aspirations of Richard Wagner and his descendents to their ideologies.

In the photo above, the Nazi *Führer*, **Adolf Hitler**, took pains to be photographed with Richard's musically gifted sons, **Weiland** (who later emerged as one of the most musically gifted and influential directors in postwar Germany), and **Wolfgang.**

In the photo above, **Winifred Wagner,** the widow of German opera's most revered hero, (Richard Wagner) and the mother of Wieland and Wolfgang, welcomes **Der Führer** to Bayreuth, her late husband's musical memorial and shrine.

She was also lauded for her role in the very avant-garde opera entitled *Wozzeck* by Alban Berg (1885-1935). Banned by the Nazis during Berg's lifetime as "degenerate," it combined Romantic lyricism with the twelve-tone scale. *[Wozzeck had been first performed in 1925, and is today considered one of the most startling and important operatic works to have emerged from the 20th Century.]*

"Ground Zero" of the Wagnerian Universe, the **Festspielhaus in Bayreuth** opened in 1876 specifically to perpetuate the music, legacies, and legends of Richard Wagner.

Steber had even been directed by Arturo Toscanini (1867-1957), an Italian conductor who had once been the music director of La Scala in Milan. Her association with him occurred during his appointment (1937-54) as the first music director of the NBC Symphony Orchestra. In 1944, Steber had been the vocal star of their nationwide broadcast of *Fidelio*, Beethoven's only opera, which had premiered in Vienna in 1805.

In 1948, she sang the world premiere of a musical work that she had personally commissioned: Samuel Barber's *Knoxville, Summer of 1915*. A "vocal rhapsody" (her words) to a supposedly slower, more graceful era, it was a collaboration with the Boston Symphony Orchestra under the direction (1924-1949) of its music director, Serge Koussevitsky.

FRIENDS & COLLABORATORS OF ELEANOR STEBER

Gian-Carlo Menotti

Dmitri Mitropoulos

James Levine

In 1953, Steber journeyed to Bayreuth, Germany, for its annual Wagner Festival. Adolf Hitler had defined Bayreuth as "a holy place in the German soul," thanks in part to the operas performed there every year by his favorite composer, Richard Wagner (1813-1883).

Wagner's *Tristan und Isolde* has been acclaimed "for having marked the start of modern music." Wagner's four-opera cycle, *Der Ring des Nibelungen (The Ring of the Nibelungen)* is still performed all over the world.

As her performance piece, Steber had been assigned one of Wagner's more obscure operas, *Lohengrin,* in which the composer had attempted to expose "the consequences of religious intoxication."

[For neophyte opera fans, Lohengrin *is a bit hard to digest. In her role of Elsa, Steber seemed to flee from a "poisonous society" and its false faith, setting out to think for herself. At the end, she is moving into a world where she will be smarter and stronger than before.]*

Decca was in Bayreuth that year to record her performance, which can be heard today.

In 1954, Steber appeared in Florence (Italy) at the May Festival, delivering one of her greatest performances as Minnie in Puccini's *La fanciulla del west,* conducted by Dmitri Mitropoulos.

She had long been a devotee of the operas of Giacomo Puccini (1858-1924), who is hailed as the greatest composer of Italian opera after Verdi. Her favorites were *La Bohème* (1896), *Tosca* (1900), and *Madame Butterfly* (1904).

In 1958, Steber appeared in another opera by Samuel Barber, *Vanessa,* which later won a Pulitzer Prize for the composer. The librettist was Gian-Carlo Menotti under the baton of Dmitri Mitropoulos, with sets by Cecil Beaton, better known for doing the staging of *My Fair Lady* and *Gigi,* the first with Rex Harrison and Audrey Hepburn, the latter with Leslie Caron and Louis Jourdan. Beaton's sets were destroyed by fire in 1973.

Born in Athens in 1896, and dying in 1960 in Milan (age 64), Mitropoulos had made his U.S. debut in 1936 with the Boston Symphony Orchestra. The peak of his orchestral career came in 1949, when he was co-conductor with Leopold Stokowski of the New York Philharmonic.

He told Steber, "I am a homosexual. I feel no need to enter into a cosmetic marriage to preserve my reputation. When I need sex, I call on Leonard Bernstein."

In addition to opera, Steber became better known for her appearances on Radio and TV, notably on the programs *Voice of Firestone* and *The Bell Telephone Hour.* Her records ranged from many popular ballads and operettas to arias and art songs.

In 1973, Steber gave a performance at Carnegie Hall of Strauss's *Vier letzte Lieder (Four Last Songs),* with James Levine conducting the Cleveland Orchestra. They represented the final works of Richard Strauss. He composed them in 1948 when he was 84. He died in September of 1949.

Steber's director, Levine, was a composer and conductor born in Cincinnati in 1943. From 1976 to 2016, he was the widely publicized music director of the Metropolitan Opera in NYC.

[Levine was fired in 2018, based on charges of sexual misconduct, which he adamantly denies. Four young men came forward, airing charges of harassment and abuse from decades ago when they studied music under his direction. Levine thus became the highest profile figure in classical music to have his career upended during the national reckoning of previous, even decades-old, charges of sexual misconduct.]

***

One of the last public appearances of Eleanor Steber was at a press party for one of Darwin's novels, *Butterflies in Heat,* an offbeat love story later adapted into a film co-starring Eartha Kitt. "She was a generous soul right to the end," he said. "At the press party, she attracted more attention than my novel. She also established the Eleanor Steber Vocal Foundation with an annual contest to assist young singers at the dawn of their careers."

Struggling with asthma and alcoholism during her final years, Steber died following heart valve surgery on October 3, 1990 and is interred at Greenwood Cemetery in Wheeling, West Virginia, the town where she was born at the dawn of World War I.

ELEANOR'S OPERA GOSSIP

"Hitler had 'the hots' for Wieland, the grandson of Richard Wagner."

—Eleanor Steber

In 1953, while performing at Bayreuth's *Festspielhaus* (Opera Festival House), a "temple" to the music of Richard Wagner originally built in 1876, Eleanor Seber stumbled upon a dark and embarrassing secret from Hitler's past. The *Führer* had tried to suppress it for years.

Apparently, Seber heard it from one or more of the descendants of Wieland Wagner (1917-1966). *[Wieland was the eldest of the four children produced from the marriage of Richard Wagner's son (Siegfried Wagner) and his English-born wife, Winifred, a close friend and admirer of Adolf Hitler. Talk about a musical aristocracy! Wieland also happened to be the great-grandson of the famous composer Franz Liszt.]*

Bayreuth's annual festival had, for

Wieland Wagner

generations, attracted Wagner fans (and German nationalists) from around the world. Kings had come to Bayreuth, as did music lovers, including composers and conductors such as Liszt, Bruckner, Grieg, and Tchaikovsky. Wagner's *The Ring of the Nibelungen* was always part of the annual repertoire. In the years immediately preceding World War II, young male advocates of the *Hitlerjugend* paraded through the streets singing "Deutschland über Alles."

Steber related a story associated with Bayreuth and one of its most visible conductors (Weiland Wagner, grandson of Richard Wagner) after her return to New York: Hitler, in addition to his other heinous crimes, including the mass slaughter of millions, was also a child molester.

From almost the moment of Wieland's birth, Hitler, a frequent visitor to Bayreuth, focused on the attractive grandson (Wieland) of his musical hero, Richard Wagner. Hitler told his ardent admirer, Wieland's passionate Anglo-German mother, Winifred, "The boy has the bluest of eyes, the sweetest of smiles. He will grow up to be the finest specimen of Aryan manhood. Let me hold him and kiss him." Passionately devoted to Hitler as a cultural hero and promoter of the Wagnerian musical traditions, Winifred gave Hitler free run of the nursery.

Although originally, Hitler had been drawn to Bayreuth for its cult of German heroism, its "super-nationalism," and the music of his favorite composer, in the years ahead, he developed yet another reason to visit Bayreuth: Young Wieland.

As Wieland was growing up, Hitler—every time he saw him—showered him with kisses, telling Winifred, "I'm his surrogate father; he's the son I never had."

Wieland reportedly did not like his own father, Siegfried, an effeminate homosexual famously attracted to SS storm troopers.

As Wieland grew into boyhood, Hitler showered him with gifts, and sometimes sent an armored car to Bayreuth to retrieve him for visits to Berlin.

On his 17th birthday, Wieland, at Hitler's invitation, arrived in Munich, where the most expensive custom-made Mercedes awaited him. Later, he raved about getting to sleep

Depicted above is a detail from a mural (**Lohengrin's Arrival in Brabant**, by Auguest von Heckel (1882-83) in a salon of Bavaria's Neuschwanstein Castle.

It is difficult to overstate the passionate associations of Wagner's music with the Teutonic myths and legends of Germany's primeval past.

in the bed of his *Führer*.

Sometimes, when Wieland visited Hitler at Berchtesgaden, Hitler and the boy, each of them an amateur painter, would retreat together to isolated sites in the Bavarian Alps for inspiration.

Friedelind, Wieland's sister, claimed that her brother "was the victim of Hitler's homoerotic desires," and that their quasi-fanatical mother, Winifred, was part of the conspiracy to seduce the boy.

Decades later, Wieland's daughter, Nike, emerged as an anti-Nazi. She claimed, "The Wagners are an Atreus clan, a many-headed, thousand-footed monster that ponderously rolls through the corridor of our generations."

During the bloody, destructive, and tragic course of World War II, Hitler exempted Wieland from compulsory military service, asserting, "The boy is too beautiful to die." During the war, he was assigned a job at a research institute in Bayreuth that was a satellite of the Flossenburg Concentration Camp.

He and his fellow workers were charged with improving the guidance systems for V-2 rockets raining death down upon London.

In the spring of 1945, as it became increasingly obvious that Germany's defeat was imminent, Wieland embarked on a dangerous journey to Berlin for a final farewell to Hitler as he hid within his bunker. They were locked away together for about half an hour before they separated, Wieland fleeing back to the relative safety of Bayreuth.

In 1948 at a "denazification" hearing in Bayreuth, the Allied interrogators classified Wieland as a *Mitläufer* (a relatively innocuous, low-priority "sympathizer" of the Nazi cause), fining him 100 deutsche marks plus court costs.

In the post-war years, Wieland became the pre-eminent opera director in Germany, noted for the avant-garde introduction of modern (sometimes minimalist) sets to Wagnerian opera, often with an emphasis on the "psychology" of his grandfather's original scores and myths.

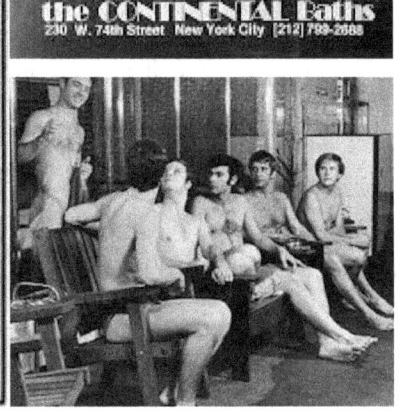

A Black Tie Gala at the Baths: Opera Diva ELEANOR STEBER Remembers

What about Weiland's legendary grandfather? Sometimes noted, alongside the Nazis, as one of the most adroit manipulators of German mythology in the history of the Teutonic World, Richard Wagner spent his final turbulent years as a political exile, embroiled in controversial love affairs, poverty, and repeated flights from his creditors.

How A Fading Opera Diva (Eleanor Steber) Delivered One of the Most Celebrated Performances of Her Career at NYC's Most Notorious Bathhouse

In the 1970s, the basement of the Ansonia Hotel, on the Upper West Side of Manhattan, became one of the hottest entertainment venues in New York City.

Why? It was the site of the Continental Baths. Inaugurated in 1968 on the then-depressed corner of Broadway at West 72nd Street, it was a hedonistic and sprawling gay bathhouse noted for the promiscuity of the interchanges within. But its real fame emerged in the aftermath of its double-duty as an entertainment venue for some of the most sought-after show-biz performances in the world.

Many patrons arrived as run-of-the-mill bathhouse players and *voyeurs* mingling with, and sexually interacting, with other ebullient, scantily clad patrons. Others were primarily interested in the performance skills of, among others, and most famous of all, Bette Midler, among dozens of others. Sometimes, her act was so amusing and stirring that bathhouse clients ripped off their towels and threw them onto the stage. Musically, at least, Midler was usually accompanied by Barry Manilow, who eventually became a big star in his own right.

Other entertainers at the baths included Peter Allen, Sarah Vaughan, Cab Calloway, Alice Faye (Archie Bunker's favorite blonde), and Dorothy Lamour, the sarong girl in all those Hope and Crosby Road pictures.

Additional "Entertainment at the Baths"

Alfred Hitchcock...The great director was both a fan of Eleanor Steber AND a voyeur at the Baths.

was provided by Martha Raye, Julie Wilson, Margaret Whiting, Tiny Tim, Elaine Stritch, Johnnie Ray, Freda Payne, Anita O'Day, Lorna Luft (Judy Garland's OTHER daughter), Kay Starr, Gladys Knight & the Pips, Connie Francis, and Teresa Brewer.

The most unexpected artist to ever entertain at the Continental Baths was Eleanor Steber, the great opera diva, who lived in an apartment within the Ansonia Hotel, upstairs.

RCA Red Seal Records recorded her unexpectedly highbrow performance at the Baths one evening in 1973. The enterprising "show-biz centric" owner of the Continental, Steve Ostrow, said, "All in all, Eleanor Steber was the classiest act we ever had."

Steber treated the audience that evening in 1973 to an evening of Mozart, Massenet, Charpentier, and Puccini. Weeks in advance of her appearance, her "Night at the Baths" had morphed into the hottest ticket in town. Black (instead of the usual white) towels were distributed to the otherwise nude men, and a coterie of the NYC elite arrived, many of the men in black tie; some of the women in *haute couture*.

The patrons in attendance that night almost brought down the house with applause. According to a review in the *Village Voice*, "It was an affair to rank with the coming of Christ, the death of Garland, the birth of the Blues, and the freezing of spinach. The ushers led the tuxes to their $15 seats... Reverence was the order of the evening, and Madame was feeding from the reverence and giving out schmaltz."

Bette Midler..A reigning diva at the Baths.

Dorothy Lamour in a sarong...When this picture was snapped, she was seducing both Bob Hope and Bing Crosby.

New York's *Daily News* wrote: "*Mrs. Leonard Bernstein, Suzy, Patrice Munsel, a lot of Metropolitan Opera Stars, and half of New York society loved it.*"

And the Long Island Press wrote, "*...The steamy atmosphere of the Continental resounded with gorgeous singing and rafter-raising cheers.*"

Mayor John Lindsay cabled his regrets but sent congratulations. *[What prevented him from attending? Al Goldstein, publisher of* Screw *magazine, had previously released Lindsay's nude photo, an embarrassing overview which had been secretly snapped at the New York Athletic Club. It was rumored that, as reported by an aide, Lindsay had said, "All I need now is to get a written description of me at the Continental Baths—no assist for my political career. 'The times, they are a'changin', as Bob Dylan might say."]*

One "normal," non-performance day, an unexpected guest arrived at the Continental: Alfred Hitchcock, who told the management there, "Give me a towel. I'm here just to watch." After he'd seen at least a hundred guys interacting and in various states of undress, he got dressed and departed. After his departure, one young man asked, "Who was that fat guy with the towel, staring at me?"

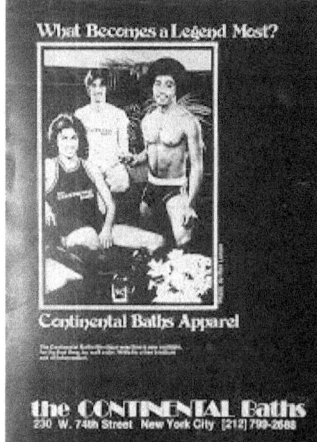

What Becomes a Legend Most?
A Celebrity Sighting at a Bath House!

Tab Hunter, depicted here with Divine in *Polyester* (1981).

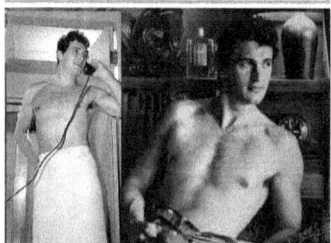

Rock Hudson's unannounced recreational appearance sent frissons through the air, water, and steam.

At the Continental, **Barry Manilow** appeared both onstage and as one of the clients.

Another regular patron said, years later, "I will always remember the night the great but tragic 'torch" singer, Lillian Roth, showed up for a performance at the Continental." *[Susan Hayward, in one of her greatest movie roles, had morphed Roth back into a household name (for a while at least), with her interpretation of Roth in the film* I'll Cry Tomorrow *(1955).]*

"Throughout Roth's performance at the baths," the patron said, "Mick Jagger was sitting in the front row with a skimpy towel, high on drugs and letting it all hang out."

The Continental Baths became so popular that straights were admitted, but only on Saturday nights. It also became a place where movie stars, many of whom were exhibitionists, appeared in various states of undress, long before the advent of cellphone cameras and before nudity became more mainstream and popular on the screen.

At The Continental, an exhibitionistic Lex Barker, part of the Saturday night crop of self-defined straight guys—a former Tarzan and the former husband of Lana Turner—was one of the all-time star attractions.

Other famous personalities showed up to strut their stuff as well. They included former lovers Tab Hunter and Tony Perkins, the long-ago star of *Psycho* (1960). John Ireland and Forrest Tucker vied for whose genitalia was bigger. And Troy Donahue made an appearance one night, as did Peter Lawford and Sal Mineo. Of note too was Rock Hudson, who sent *frissons* through the ranks of on-site voyeurs.

Even John F. Kennedy, Jr. showed up one night, delighting the patrons. *[Both John, Jr. and his father, JFK, had always been known for being bemusedly casual about nudity.]*

The New York Times labeled the Continental as "our most Weimarian nightspot," referencing the decadent notoriety of Germany's Weimar Republic during its pre-Hitlerian heyday.

What happened to end the merry-go-round and carnival?

AIDS come along in the 1970s. By the 1980s, when it began terrorizing the American public, gay bathhouses like the Continental were no longer stylish or chic, or even fun, and many of them were forcibly closed. The party was over. . .

Some Saturday nights, when the Continental was open to "not necessarily gay members of the public," Lana Turner's ex-hibitionistic ex-husband, **Lex Barker,** sometimes appeared in a loincloth, or at least in a state of partial undress. like most of the other men at the Baths.

He'd be immediately surrounded by adoring fans.

In the photo above, he's appearing as Tarzan, the film character he's best remembered for portraying.

But While the Party Lasted, Who Was the Most Visible Pinup at the Continental?

His Name Was *AH-NOLD!* As in
SCHWARZENEGGER!!

And This Was **LONG** Before His Gig as Governor of California

No American immigrant's tale is quite as extraordinary as that of **Arnold Schwarzenegger,** pictured above as a mighty warrior in one of his most famous roles as *Conan the Barbarian (1982)*. Had the laws of the U.S. Constitution been different, this young bodybuilder might have risen from the gyms of Germany and Austria to become President of the United States. As it is, he had to settle for being the governor of the great state of California, even though he could never pronounce it correctly.

On the long road to Sacramento, "*Ah-Nold*" became the greatest bodybuilder in history, and for a while, the number one movie star in the world. And despite his status as a Republican, he eventually married one of the princesses of the Kennedy clan.

His past came back to haunt him during his campaign. For most politicians, an exposé of past infidelities, marijuana use and, even an unknowing cameo in a gay porno would derail their run for office. But not in the case of *The Terminator*.

Chapter Fourteen

LONGTIME RESIDENT OF MAGNOLIA HOUSE AND
"MAD ABOUT THE BOY"

GRETA KELLER

HITLER'S FAVORITE CABARET SINGER,
& EUROPE'S OTHER LILI MARLENE

Greta Keller was a leading chanteuse in the Europe of the 1930s, and in the decades that followed, she remained a cosmopolitan player in the show-biz arts and the subject of endless speculation among the *demi-mondains* of Europe, New York, and California.

She made her stage debut in Vienna in 1929 as the star of a German-language play called *Broadway*.

Marlene Dietrich, in a supporting role, was also in the cast, evolving into Greta's lover and later, a ferocious competitor. According to Greta, as expressed to Darwin Porter during her long residence at Magnolia House, "Later on the night we met, Marlene played the saw for me."

As a boy growing up in Miami Beach, Darwin had been captivated by the *lieder* voice of the Viennese *chanteuse*, Greta Keller. Her voice was said "to carry the charm of the Parisian woman but never lost the heart of the girl from Vienna."

Her fans claimed that her voice "was in a style that evoked Marlene Dietrich."

Actually, it was the other way around. On the Viennese stage in 1929, Greta had been the star of the musical *Broadway*, with Marlene in the chorus line.

Once, at the airport in Berlin, Greta had encountered Marlene carrying her recording. "I'm going to sing in my next picture," Marlene said. "You don't mind if I imitate you? Surely you don't."

Darwin lived in the home of another singer, Sophie Tucker. His mother worked for her, and Sophie owned most of Greta's recordings.

In the 1970s, Darwin, by now living at Magnolia House on Staten Island, heard that Greta was starring at Town Hall in Manhattan. He rushed to buy a ticket to attend Greta's concert.

When it was over, he went backstage to meet his idol, and found her extremely ingratiating, especially when he told her he was her number one fan.

He invited her and her young male companion (from Munich) to lunch at Magnolia House the following day. He would drive into

Conrad Veidt "playing against type" as a Nazi officer in the classic film, *Casablanca* (1942).

It was he who warned Greta to "get out of town, NOW!" after her identity as a "closeted Jew" was unearthed by Hitler's Death Squad.

Manhattan to pick them up.

After their arrival at St. Marks Place, their friendship developed quickly. Before the end of the day, he had agreed to ghost write two books for her—one a cookbook *Food for Love,* based on her recipes from the kitchens of Old Vienna. The other would be her memoirs, with the understanding that it would be entitled *Germany's Other Lili Marlene.*

Within weeks, Greta came to reside at Magnolia House, and he began to interview her, recording their dialogues—most of them a sweeping overview of her life and changing circumstances— on tape.

Born in 1903 in Vienna, Greta became a singer and actress early in life. By the 1930s, she had evolved into one of the most visible chanteuses in Europe, centered in Berlin just as Hitler rose to power. Richard Wagner was his favorite composer, but Greta was his favorite singer.

She became a close friend of many theatrical personalities, including the German actor, Conrad Veidt, a major figure in German silent films because of his sinister, commanding, and rather floridly baroque style. She had an affair with him.

Here are the translated lyrics of
LILI MARLEEN

In the '30s, it was an onstage staple first for **GRETA KELLER**, and later, even more famously for her arch-rival, **MARLENE DIETRICH.**
A deeply emotional ballad, it transcended political boundaries during World War II.

***

Outside the barracks, by the corner light
I'll always stand and wait for you at night
We will create a world for two
I'll wait for you the whole night through
For you, Lili Marleen
For you, Lili Marleen.

Bugler tonight don't play the call to arms
I want another evening with her charms
Then we will say goodbye and part
I'll always keep you in my heart
With me, Lili Marleen
With me, Lili Marleen.

Give me a rose to show how much you care
Tie to the stem a lock of golden hair
Surely tomorrow, you'll feel blue
But then will come a love that's new
For you, Lili Marleen.
For you, Lili Marleen.

When we are marching in the mud and cold
And when my pack seems more than I can hold
My love for you renews my might
I'm warm again, my pack is light
It's you, Lili Marleen
It's you, Lili Marleen.

My love for you renews my might
I'm warm again, my pack is light
It's you, Lili Marleen.
It's you, Lili Marleen.

[Veidt is remembered chiefly today for co-starring with Humphrey Bogart in Casablanca *(1942). Coincidentally, Vera Viola Maria Veidt (Conrad's daughter) would one day live with Darwin during a three-month sojourn at his home in Key West.]*

A bisexual, Greta also launched an affair with the Polish actress, Pola Negri, the former vamp of the silent screen. A long-time rival of Gloria Swanson, Pola sustained affairs in Hollywood with both Valentino and Charlie Chaplin, as well as with her favorite director, Ernst Lubitsch.

Tallulah Bankhead, however, was distinctly not impressed, referring to Pola as "a lying lesbos, a Polish publicity hound. She has a mustache and can't act her way out of a paper bag."

Pola had won a libel suit against a French movie magazine, *Pour Vous,* which alleged that she was the mistress of Adolf Hitler.

After her Hollywood career faltered, Pola returned to Germany and worked for UFA, now under the direction of the Nazi propaganda minister, Josef Goebbels.

[UFA, the abbreviated name of Universum Film-Aktien Gesellschaft*, a Berlin-based movie studio that made technically and artistically outstanding films during the silent era. UFA, for a while, at least, was among the best equipped and most modern movie production companies in the world.*

On the brink of ruin in the aftermath of World War I—to some degree a result of disastrous import/export policies, it was bought in 1927 by Alfred Hugenberg, an ardent supporter of Adolf Hitler. He demanded that UFA devote itself to films

---

Lili Marleen still remains a powerful and evocative symbol of love, passion, and loss throughout the German-speaking world.

Above is a poster advertising a critically acclaimed West German drama film, **Lili Marleen**, released in 1981,

Replicating the tormented politics of the Weimar Republic that ushered in the horrors of the Nazis, it was directed by Germany's most famous bad boy at the time, Rainer Werner Fassbinder, and starred the impossibly brilliant German actress, a household name in Central Europe, Hanna Schygulla.

One evening, a corpulent **Hermann Goering**, one of the most powerful and terrifying leaders of Nazi Germany, dined at the same restaurant as Greta Keller along Berlin's *Unter den Linden.*

She was wearing a carefully tailored Loden coat, one vaguely influenced by the traditions of Styria, in Austria.

Goering rose from his chair and approached her, asking what merchant had sold her the coat. So taken was he with it that he went the next day to order one from the same merchant.

that promoted German propaganda and the Nazi ideal. The Nazi-controlled German government bought UFA in 1937 and thereafter tightly controlled film content through its support of highly politicized directors who included Leni von Riefenstahl, master propaganda artist for the Third Reich. A handful of avant-garde directors were able to produce high-quality, apolitical films within this difficult milieu, but basically, UFA ceased to exist after the defeat of Germany in 1945. A new company called UFA was launched in 1956, but it eventually went bankrupt.]

One day in 1937, while dining in a neighborhood tavern in Berlin, Greta received an emergency phone call from Veidt. He warned her that Goebbels had learned that she was a Jew—something she'd never widely publicized within the anti-Semitic fervor of Germany in the late 1930s—and that she had better leave Berlin (and Germany) at once. "Take a plane anywhere it's going. The Gestapo is searching your apartment now. HURRY!"

The next plane out of Berlin was to Amsterdam, and Greta was on it. Safely outside of Germany, she booked passage aboard a ship sailing to New York.

En route, Greta had a shipboard romance with Ernest Hemingway.

After her arrival in Manhattan, she got an immediate cabaret booking at the Algonquin Hotel. Almost every night, Greta Garbo came to hear her sing, and the two (bisexual) divas had an affair.

Greta Keller had married a musician, Joe Sargent, in 1928, but when his alcoholism grew more visible, they divorced.

She would not marry again until 1942, when she wed actor David Bacon.

His murder the following year is still listed as one of the ten most mysterious murders in Hollywood history. *[For details, see below.]*

The year she married him, Greta was appearing in *Reunion in France*, which starred Joan Crawford and John Wayne. Greta and Joan launched a lesbian affair, Joan taking the opportunity to dish her co-star with statements that included "Get Wayne out of the saddle, and you've got nothing."

"One of the greatest thrills in all my life was to have the world's most beautiful woman (**Greta Garbo,** above) tell me she adored my music," said "The Other Greta" (Keller).

Ernest Hemingway in the late 1930s, around the time he met and sustained a neurotic shipboard romance with Greta Keller.

According to Greta, "It was a desperate and uncertain time, Hitler's rise to power was making all of us crazy, and all of us were careening our ways into uncertain futures—politically, professionally, personally, and artistically."

Meanwhile, Greta's husband, David Bacon, had inaugurated a homosexual affair of his own with the billionaire aviator and movie producer Howard Hughes, who had cast him in his latest film, *The Outlaw*, eventually released after endless delays and complications, and with a different male lead, in 1943.

[After the war, Greta became known as "The Great Lady of Chanson," *appearing in Manhattan frequently at the Waldorf Astoria and later at its competitor, the Stanhope Hotel. In time, she always included Paul Anka's "My Way" in her repertoire of songs.*

That repertoire also included songs by Noël Coward and Cole Porter. She delivered a tender rendition of Jacques Brel's "Ne me Quitte Pas."

In the movie, Cabaret *(1972), starring Liza Minnelli, Greta's by-then aged and cracking voice is heard in her rendition of the song "Heirat" ("Married").]*

THE FAMOUS UNSOLVED MURDER OF THE HANDSOMEST
(AND PERHAPS MOST INDISCREET) MAN IN HOLLYWOOD:
DAVID BACON

Having recently hired publicist Russell Birdwell, the sinister Howard Hughes summoned him to his spooky estate, Muirfield, for a meeting at two o'clock in the morning, standard procedure for Howard, but "bizarre" in Birdwell's view. From the very beginning of their association, the former publicist for *Gone With the Wind* had understood that he was working for an eccentric millionaire. But the pay was good. So if his boss had no regard for the time of day, so what?

Howard revealed to Birdwell that he wanted to make a western based on the private life of Billy the Kid.

Through Birdwell, Howard painfully learned that Louis B. Mayer had already launched production on a competing film, also entitled *Billy the Kid*. Howard's sometimes lover, Robert Taylor, had been cast as Billy.

Howard was furious, feeling he'd been betrayed by both Taylor and Mayer. He vowed never to speak to Robert again—he would later rescind that—and to threaten the MGM boss with a lawsuit.

Birdwell responded by warning Howard

Another puzzle in the unsolved stabbing death of **David Bacon** concerned what happened to the "blackmail" memoir he was writing about his sexual involvement with Howard Hughes.

Greta collapsed in her bed on hearing the news of his death. An estimated forty people came and went from her home in the wake of his murder. When she emerged from her despair four days later, Bacon's manuscript had been stolen.

about what should have been obvious: The saga of Billy the Kid was in the public domain. He also reminded Howard that MGM had previously cast cowboy star Johnny Mack Brown (another of Howard's former lovers) as Billy in an earlier film, and Robert Taylor's most recent version was a remake of the studio's previous picture. Birdwell also pointed out another obvious fact: the character of Billy the Kid was a standard fixture, an oft-repeated theme in dozens of Grade B westerns, called "oaters."

Growing impatient with Birdwell, Howard stood up. "You don't understand. My *Billy the Kid* is going to become the first sex western."

"But, Howard," Birdwell protested, "in westerns men ride off into the sunset with their horses—not the girl. They don't even kiss the girl."

"They'll do more than kiss in my picture," Howard predicted. "Billy the Kid will actually fuck Rio."

"Who's Rio?"

"The gal. And what a gal! The screen will never have seen anything like her."

"Who's the lucky star?" Birdwell asked. "I know them all."

"Some unknown. There's only one requirement. She doesn't even have to know how to act, but she's got to have the hottest-looking pair of knockers in the history of film. Your job is to launch the search to find her."

The Outlaw launched the career of big-bosomed Jane Russell, who ruled as "Sex Queen of Hollywood" until replaced by Marilyn Monroe.

These photos of the slain **David Bacon** and his wife, the Viennese *chanteuse*, **Greta Keller,** appeared in newspapers across the country at the time he was found murdered.

Jane Russell with **Jack Buetel**, the actor who eventually nabbed the role promised to (and coveted by) David Bacon.

Gaspar Bacon Jr. Wins First Role on Screen
By MAYME OBER PEAK

The high-society son of a powerful Boston Brahmin, **David Bacon,** made home-town news with his first Hollywood casting success.

Later, the horrible events associated with his murder made him even more famous. Greta Keller was married to him at the time.

*Greta Keller: Europe's **Other** Lili Marlene* 223

* * *

The next day, a sleepy Birdwell wasted no time in launching the search not only for an actress to be cast as Rio, but for some handsome young man to play Billy the Kid. Only hours before, Birdwell had said to his boss, "I understand what you're looking for in the gal. But what about the actor to play Billy the Kid?"

"I want him to look like he's carrying around a ten-inch cock between his legs," Howard said. "And we're talking soft."

The moment the campaign was launched, Howard's office at 7000 Romaine Street was deluged with glossy eight-by-ten photographs of every aspirant young actor or actress in Hollywood. Some were submissions from agents, others came directly from the hopefuls themselves. "Every handsome gas jockey in Los Angeles, every beautiful gal, sent in their photographs," Birdwell said.

Three weeks later, Howard called Birdwell: "Call off the search for Billy the Kid!" Howard ordered. "I found him last night. Actually, he was sitting alone in the Cock & Bull bar having a drink and looking sad. I came up to him. He knew immediately who I was."

Howard said that the stranger asked him to have a drink with him, and "I accepted his invitation. When I found out he was an actor, I asked him if he'd submitted his photo for Billy the Kid. He told me that he didn't see himself playing in a western. He has a Brahmin accent. Very New England. I told him that I could hire a diction coach to work on his accent. I also told him that I was signing him to a three-year contract. Yeah, just like that. That's how I do business. I also told him that I was going to get you, Birdwell, to start the publicity campaign rolling for him. In his case, we're going to bill him as 'the hand-

Billionaire movie producer and industrialist **Howard Hughes** a few years before his unhappy affair with Greta's bisexual husband, David Bacon.

Notoriously introverted, Hughes is shown here with his leading lady, **Jean Harlow,** the novelty-blonde star of the movie he had a hard time finishing, *Hell's Angels* (1930)

An unknown, **Jane Russell**, became the reigning sex queen of Hollywood with the release of "the First Sex Western," Howard Hughes' *The Outlaw.*

It was a compelling but offbeat story of Billy the Kid that concentrated mainly on Jane's big bosom.

somest man in Hollywood.'"

"Christ, he must really be good looking," Birdwell said.

"He's good looking," Howard said. "In a town known for its male beauties, he may not be the handsomest, but we'll bill him as the handsomest, and the movie-going suckers will fall for it because we said it's so."

"And who's this new guy who's about to become immortal?" Birdwell asked. "What's his name? Tell me because I know we'll have to change it. I bet it's Prescott Reginald Percy the Third?"

"Nothing like that," Howard said. "It's David Bacon. We'll keep his name. David will suggest Michelangelo's statue, and Bacon means pork. Not a bad symbol. Haven't you heard of feeding a gal the pork, as we say in Texas?"

VENICE, CALIFORNIA 1943

It was September 13, 1943. The wind was blowing in heavily from the Pacific, signaling the end of summer. From that same Pacific came news that the war was going badly. The American soldiers and sailors were meeting a formidable opponent in the Empire of Japan.

Although seemingly a perfect physical specimen, actor David Bacon had used the influence of his politically connected family in Boston to escape the draft.

Back in 1915, he'd been born some 3,000 miles away from Venice, California, in the historic town of Barnstable on Cape Cod. Named Gaspar G. Bacon Jr., he grew up as the son of one of the most prominent and socially connected Brahmin families in all of Massachusetts.

"David's family made Kate Hepburn's family look like white trash," Birdwell later said. David's father, Gaspar G. Bacon Sr., sat on the board of Harvard University and would later be elected lieutenant governor of the state. Backed by the support of his close friend, J.P. Morgan, Bacon Sr. encouraged talk that he might one day make a run for the governorship—"even the White House," he told his son.

He never made it to the Oval Office, but he became Ambassador to France under William Howard Taft and Secretary of State under Theodore Roosevelt.

Young David had been a disappointment to his father. Instead of becoming an attorney as his father urged, David had "an insane desire" *[his father's words]* to go to Hollywood and become an actor.

David—or Gaspar Jr., as he was called then—managed to irritate his father all the more when he became involved in a homosexual scandal at Harvard that almost got him expelled. David and his roommate were "auditioning" some of the best bodies on the football team when word of this reached the administration. Only through his powerful father's intervention was David allowed to stay on at Harvard and eventually to graduate. His father had promised the board that he would secure psychiatric help for David "to cure my son of certain anti-social tendencies."

In summer, David deserted his family's summer home and appeared on the stage in amateur productions at Woods Hole on the Cape. His first acting role came with the University Players in West Falmouth. He ingratiated himself with two far more talented young actors, James Stewart and Henry Fonda, and "bunked" with the two men for a time. The director, Josh Logan, who knew all three of the actors, once said "when not dating girls, Jimmy, Hank, and David enjoyed the considerable charms of each other." Logan himself was rumored at various times to have had affairs with all three actors.

After Harvard, young Gaspar Jr. became "David Bacon." Fleeing New England, he arrived in New York where he was financially "sponsored" by William Blair, a wealthy Britisher from a prominent family

FAMOUS FOR BEING FAMOUS, AND WELL-CONNECTED IN BOTH EUROPE AND NORTH AMERICA, GRETA KELLER WAS A CONDUIT TO OTHER CELEBRITIES.

The very grand and very pretentious **Pola Negri,** Greta's friend, was "an acquired taste." No one, before or since, has ever attained her calculated and "not-terribly-sincere" form of camp.

A bisexual, Greta sustained an affair with **Joan Crawford** (depicted above with **John Wayne**) during Joan's filming of *Reunion in France* (1942).

She also sustained a (strictly apolitical) sexual affair with **Leni Riefenstahl**, depicted above and (below) with her patron, muse, and mentor, **Adolf Hitler.**

Depicted here is **Leni Riefenstahl**, propaganda assistant and filmmaker for the Third Reich with **Adolf Hitler**. In the mid-1990s, long after the passions of WWII had at least simmered down, Greta invited Darwin Porter to join her for an intimate dinner at a game restaurant in Austria at which Leni was present.

who was spending the war years in New York, fleeing some sort of scandal back in London. According to David, his family had asked William to leave England, promising to support him in "the New World."

Although David's own father had refused to give him even a stipend during his pursuit of a career in the theater, his patron, William, was most generous. The couple were seen at all the New York hot spots together. Although he'd arrived there with only two hundred dollars in his wallet, David was soon wearing expensive jewelry and appearing at clubs in bespoke tailored suits.

It is not known exactly what happened to end David's relationship with his sugar daddy. William was a bit corpulent, looking somewhat like a 1940s version of Oscar Wilde. In contrast, David was muscular and handsome, standing six feet tall. On the side, he specialized in equally handsome sailors. Apparently, William returned to his apartment one afternoon to find his pampered Brahmin in bed with one of the more well-endowed members of Uncle Sam's navy.

Within the next two weeks David had taken an overcrowded wartime train to Los Angeles to begin a new life.

A month later, he'd met and married Greta Keller.

Following her gig at the Algonquin and hoping to break into films on the West Coast, Greta had migrated to Hollywood. There she renewed her affair with Pola Negri. At a party at Pola's house, Greta encountered "a lost and lonely boy," David himself. "He aroused a latent motherly instinct in me," Greta later said. "Even though I knew he had homosexual tendencies, we began to date. Dating led to a quick marriage. I took him under my wing. It was sort of like Barbara Stanwyck's mar-

David Bacon got to play the *Masked Marvel* in the movies, but the big Hollywood stardom Howard Hughes had promised him never came true.

What did was a fatal stabbing on the beach after he'd willingly posed—perhaps for the person who later stabbed him—for a frontal nude.

The murky circumstances generated headlines everywhere.

Photo above shows **Greta** wth her then-new husband, the cult-quirky just-murdered "Masked Marvel," **David Bacon**.

riage to Robert Taylor. We were beards for each other and didn't ask each other a lot of questions about private matters. David was a bisexual. We were very much in love when I was with him."

Greta had an "understanding" with David, who allowed her to indulge her taste not only in girlfriends but in other men. Some of her young men were shared on the side with David. "He especially liked military men, and there were plenty of those back in Los Angeles in those days," Greta told Darwin as she was dictating her memoirs to him at Magnolia House in the 1970s.

"Suddenly, Howard Hughes appeared on my doorstep," Greta recalled, referring to the mansion she'd rented in Santa Monica, containing nine bathrooms, twelve bedrooms, and a swimming pool on the second floor. "Without knowing any of the details, I was told that David had signed a three-year contract with Hughes. In addition to the Santa Monica mansion where he 'officially' lived with me, Howard had rented a bungalow in the Hollywood Hills as a love nest where David spent a lot of his time, always in the company of his new boss."

Cast as the male lead in *The Outlaw* (1943), **Jack Buetel** was acclaimed as "the sexiest man in Hollywood" by his newly formed fan club. He was written about as "a walking streak of sex," who was lean and muscular and walked with "a cocky gait."

"Even though I didn't think the role of Billy the Kid was right for David, he went ahead with a screen test anyway," Greta said. "I saw the test. It was laughable. David should have been cast in bedroom farces and drawing room comedies like those made in Edwardian England. I could have played the merciless William Bonnie better than dear, sweet David. Even though Howard had a powerful crush on my husband, even Mr. Texas Oil had to admit that there was no way in hell that David could be convincing as Billy the Kid."

David's romance with Howard came to an abrupt end when Howard "fell big, and I mean big, for Jack Buetel," Greta said. "As you and everybody else knows, Jack was eventually signed to play Billy the Kid instead of David. Who wouldn't fall for Jack Buetel?

Although he was still under contract to Howard, David was offered no parts after his failed screen test.

In time, Howard would become infamous for luring actors (or actresses) into ironclad, "exclusive" long-term contracts and then, to their enormous frustration, letting them "stew" in their semi-enslavement, never offering them a role. That, in fact, became his specialty. Eventually, David did get some parts, playing a good-looking college kid in *Ten Gentlemen from West Point* in 1942. In 1943, he appeared in *Crash Dive* (uncredited), *Gals, Inc.*, and the lackluster *Someone to Remember*.

David's first big break came when he was cast as one of the leads in the serial, *The Masked Marvel*, being shot over at Republic Films. The film is sometimes shown as *Sakima and the Masked Marvel*. Accurately perceiving the degree to which his career had collapsed, and resentful of having to work for a "Poverty Row" studio, David grew increasingly furious at Howard and denounced him frequently.

In 1943, he began to write the story of his affair with Howard, knowing that no publisher at the time would touch the material.

"I urged David not to do it," Greta claimed. "But he sat at a typewriter and pounded out almost ten pages a day. I saw some of it. It was very pornographic. There was one very explicit scene where David described in graphic detail just how far Howard would go with him orally."

"My husband never actually planned to offer his manuscript to a publisher," Greta said. "Instead he wanted to show a typewritten copy to Howard Hughes. He said that he was going to demand that his former lover part with forty thousand dollars, which would give Hughes the rights to the manuscript. Of course, Hughes would then burn it."

Through Noah Dietrich, whom David knew, he had what was tantamount to a blackmail threat being delivered directly to Howard. A meeting was arranged between Howard and David.

"I warned David that he was playing with dynamite, making threats to a man as powerful as Howard Hughes," Greta claimed. "But my husband was very stubborn and wouldn't listen. Three days later, he walked out of our house in a white bathing suit and claimed that he was going swimming at Santa Monica Beach. I often knew he met his boyfriends there, but nothing was said between us. I knew that he was getting something outside the home that I couldn't give him. He didn't say for certain, but I believed he was meeting Hughes."

Four hours later, a maroon-colored British-made sports car—a gift to David from Howard—was seen moving along Wash-

Whether she liked it or not, Greta was indelibly associated with the public's beliefs about the decadent indulgences of Germany's Weimar Republic.

Depicted above is **Liza Minnelli** belting out a saucy cabaret number in the hit 1972 film, *Cabaret*.

When its producers decided they needed an authentic-sounding narrator to open the film and set its initial tone, who did they hire? **GRETA KELLER.**

Although she never made an appearance in the film, many of her fans recognized her quavering, heavily accented voice coming, it seemed, either from the edges of the stage or as an eyewitness who had returned from another era.

ington Boulevard in Venice. It was a Sunday. The driver was manning the wheel like he'd had two bottles of whiskey. Fortunately, there were no other cars on the road or else he would surely have crashed in a head-on collision.

Suddenly, the driver slammed on the brakes of the small car and rolled to a stop, jumping the curb. Sheila Belkstein was walking her German shepherd that day and later reported what she'd seen to the police. "I was walking my dog near a field of cabbage. At the sound of brakes, I spun around. My dog barked hysterically. From the car emerged a man wearing only a pair of white bathing trunks which showed blood stains. Across the street was a gas station. The attendant there must have seen the man. He called the police, I learned later. I was a little afraid at first, and I was having a hard time restraining my dog. I moved toward the man. I'll always remember the sunken look of despair on his face. 'Help me!' he said in a very plaintive voice. 'Oh, God, please help me. Please help me!' That was all he managed to say. His eyes rolled back in his head, which seemed to loll to the side like it was separating from his body. Then he fell to the ground. A stiletto was lodged in his back."

A coroner later confirmed that the stiletto had pierced his lung, and that David had bled to death. A thorough examination of his body revealed no bruises, no signs of struggle. Police surmised that David had known his assailant, and that he had driven the car in a position hunched over the steering wheel.

For weeks to come, his death was the talk of Hollywood. Several years later, the youngest-ever editor of *The Saturday Evening Post*, Cleveland Amory, listed the David Bacon murder among the *Top Ten Unsolved Murders in the History of Hollywood.*

Police discovered a leather wallet, soaked with blood, in the pocket of David's bathing trunks. The wallet contained one hundred and fifty dollars, which was remarkable for the time, as few men carried around so much money, especially on a trip to the beach. In the sports car, the police discovered a camera containing a roll of film. The roll was developed by the police. Only one picture had been taken. It depicted David standing happily on a beach completely nude, his white bathing trunks not shown anywhere within the frame. From this, police concluded that David knew the mystery man who stabbed him, and that he had deliberately posed for his murderer.

After the investigation, the nude photograph and the still bloodstained wallet were returned to Greta, although the case was never officially closed. Today, the wallet and the photograph are the property of Darwin.

Greta Keller died in Vienna in 1977, a nostalgic, esoteric, and glamorous figure from a faded golden age. Until the end of her life, she maintained to anyone interested that she knew who stabbed her husband. "I can't prove it, but Howard Hughes murdered David."

CELEBRITY, THE IRONIES OF HISTORY, & FAME
(No one understood them better than Greta)

GRETA KELLER LIVED HERE

For a period of two years, deep into her eighties, preoccupied with the memories generated by her star-studded, ultra-glamorous life, and just before returning to Vienna to die, Greta Keller occupied this bedroom at **Magnolia House** under the care, supervision, and patronage of her friend, Darwin Porter.

It's called "the Roosevelt Room," in honor of the former U.S. President and "Rough Rider" Theodore Roosevelt, who once owned its meticulously crafted bed. It's also been called "the Mendelssohn Room" in honor of the settee once owned, it's believed, by the German composer Felix Mendelssohn.

Many visitors suggest it should be renamed in honor of Greta Keller.

Glam and reveling in an era that's gone with the wind, the photo depicts **Greta** as the toast of Berlin, onstage at the Scala nightclub in the 1930s.

Her "unmasking" as a Jew, she later claimed, was the catalyst that forced her to emigrate to the ironies of Hollywood and the tragedies that awaited her there.

Greta onstage in her native Vienna with singer, songwriter, and poet **Rod McKuen** (inset photo). The world's most devoted fan of the Belgian singer Jacques Brel, McKuen's songs sold more than 100 million copies and his books of poetry sold an astonishing 60 million copies, worldwide. .

REST IN PEACE, GRETA!

Depicted above is the plaque that commemorates the building in Vienna that was occupied by Greta Keller, It roughly translates as:

"In this house for many years lived Greta Keller (1903-1977), singer of lyric-driven songs and vinyl records star"

After leaving her two-year residence at Magnolia House in the mid-1970s, Greta Keller returned to Vienna to die.

Depicted above is her grave in Section 40 of the **Weiner Zentralfriedhof** (Vienna's Central Graveyard). Literally thousands of Viennese remember her still as a revered celebrity.

Chapter Fifteen

WHO'S AFRAID OF VIRGINIA WOOLF?
And Guess Who's Coming to Dinner?

EDWARD ALBEE
AT MAGNOLIA HOUSE

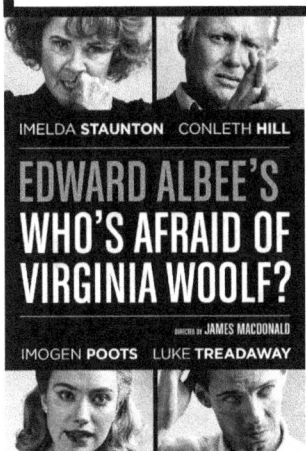  

In February of 1961, *Time* magazine wrote: "**Edward Albee** (center photo) is writing a two-act play that seems unlikely ever to appear on a midtown marquee. Its title is *Who's Afraid of Virginia Woolf?*"

How wrong they were.

"Eugene O'Neill once said you have to have false illusions," Albee said. "*Who's Afraid of Virginia Woolf?* says get rid of them. My play is about the battle (and the love) between George and Martha: the lies, deceits, and futile hopes that have held them together."

Darwin's friend, the actor/writer James Leo Herlihy, flew back to New York after appearing in Paris as a player in Edward Albee's *The Zoo Story*.

At this early point in his life, although he'd already had written several then-unheralded novels, at long last, he had managed to get one of them published. It was *All Fall Down*. There was hope of a movie sale.

He wanted to come over to dine with Darwin at Magnolia House, and in response, Darwin invited him there for the following Sunday at a relatively early hour so that they could catch up on all the latest news.

"If you don't mind, I'd like to bring a surprise guest. We're having a brief fling, a momentary diversion with an expiration date already on it. But even at its worst, it's fun while it lasts."

"Bring him on," Darwin quipped.

When the doorbell rang, and after Darwin threw open the door, he was surprised to see Herlihy standing under the portico with his arm around playwright Edward Albee. They had met at one of Herlihy's performances of Albee's play, *The Zoo Story*, in Boston, before his gig with the same production in Paris. *The New York Times* had recently cited him as "the foremost American playwright of his generation."

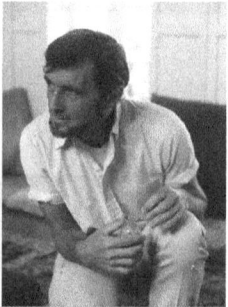

Edward Albee (left) stands proudly in front of a theater marquee advertising one of his plays. Darwin's friend, **James Leo Herlihy** (right photo), appears to be eying him enviously.

That Sunday marked the debut of Darwin's long association with the dramatist. From that day forward, Darwin would attend performances of each of his plays and often met with him, long after his affair with Herlihy had ended, at the San Remo Restaurant and Bar in Greenwich Village.

"To me, Albee had a certain charm in spite of his strong opinions about everything and everybody," Darwin said. "Albee used to say, 'I'm sick and tired of being referred to as a gay writer. I am a writer who happens to be gay.'"

Darwin and Albee found that they had much in common, including the fact that early in their lives, each of them had been put up for adoption. Later, when both were in their early teens, each of them fled from their dysfunctional homes.

Throughout the writing of his most famous play, Albee had **Bette Davis** in mind as the actress he hoped would portray Martha. A friend wrote, "Who's Afraid of Bette Woolf? EVERYBODY!"

Albee employed Davis' persona—that is, harsh, acerbic, diabolic, bitchy, sexy, a bit vulgar, and when she wanted to be, hilarious.

Years later, director Mike Nichols was asked, "What would you have changed if you had it to do over again?"

He responded, "I would have cast **James Mason** as George."

"My adoptive parents mocked my aspiration to become a writer, wanting me to become some corporate thug," Albee said. "I had to follow my dream—and that involved escaping from that stultifying, suffocating environment."

Darwin expressed his highest praise for Albee's *The Zoo Story*, written in 1958, and also for his *The Sandbox*, released the following year. One of its protagonists had been inspired by Albee's grandmother, a crotchety but amusing old lady who had brightened his dreary life as a boy.

But what intrigued Darwin the most at the time was Albee's upcoming work, *Who's Afraid of Virginia Woolf?* (1962), which had originally been titled *Who's Afraid of the Big Bad Wolf?*

Even today, it remains Albee's best-known and most iconic play. Darwin clearly remembered attending its first-ever premiere (October 13, 1962) at Manhattan's Billy Rose Theatre.

Despite the high praise heaped upon this cathartic domestic drama, Albee came under heavy fire for it. He told Darwin, "If they hurt me, I'll hurt them. I value friendship such as yours, but don't cross me. Otherwise, you'll have a tiger by the tail. I am not hysterically involved in politics or social justice. I view myself as a clinical observer of this cesspool we call life."

Over dinner one night with Herlihy and Darwin at the San Remo, Albee announced that he'd sold *Virginia Wolff* to Warner Brothers for half a million dollars plus ten percent of the gross, a business arrangement whose sweetness was almost unheard of at the time.

"Warner's assured me that it will co-star Bette Davis and James Mason, and I've already discussed it with Miss Davis. She's wetting her panties to do it, and Mason would be ideal as her henpecked husband."

Albee revealed that during his creation of the play's female lead *[the haranguing, shrewish, evil-minded character of Martha]*, he'd constantly kept Davis in mind. "I even used Davis' famous line, 'What a dump!' from the film that ended her career at Warner Brothers, *Beyond the Forest* (1949)."

According to Albee, "I saw Martha as acerbic, bitchy, vulgar, a harridan who eviscerated her husband, yet still somewhat sexy in a decaying sort of way. In her opening lines, she mentions 'The Poker Night.' Actually, I inserted that just to tantalize Tennessee Williams. That was his original title for what was eventually released as *A Streetcar Named Desire*."

Three weeks later, when Darwin and Herlihy rendezvoused again with the playwright, Albee told them something startling before the press found out: "I'm heartbroken. Richard Burton and Elizabeth Taylor have been miscast and inserted into my baby! Bette Davis is furious. She's been screaming at me, 'This is not the first time Warners has betrayed me.'"

"I think Elizabeth is far too beautiful to play a harridan," Albee said. "She said she's committed to the project, and then she told me that her friends all think she's lost her mind. 'The more they tell me not to do it, the more I want to play Martha,' she told me."

[Albee went on that evening to relay that he had unsuccessfully tried to convince Katharine Hepburn and Henry Fonda to sign on as the dramatic leads on Broadway. "Would you believe it?" he said. "Hepburn rejected it, telling

"ON GOLDEN POND"

Albee also fantasized that **Henry Fonda** and **Katharine Hepburn** might be cast as Martha and George. They're pictured above in *On Golden Pond* (1981), many years after the more brutal *Virginia Woolf* had "ripped the skin off" America's illusions about academic gentility.

Way back in 1942, Fonda had already demonstrated his skill at portraying tormented academics in his role of a beleaguered professor in *The Male Animal*. As such, he seemed an obvious choice for George in *Virginia Woolf*.

Why Hepburn? She had previously played a prosperous *bourgeoise* in Albee's Pulitzer Prize-winning play, *A Delicate Balance* (the 1973 screen version). But she later said, much to Albee's distress, "I never knew what it was about."

me, 'I'm not a good enough actress to play Martha.' Then Fonda told me he'd never read the script, and that if he had, he'd have gone for it. It had been his stupid agent who had rejected it, saying, 'a husband with no balls is not for my client.'"

"Then, still trying to cast the Broadway version, I went to Richard Burton, who rejected it as a stage play, although Elizabeth eventually persuaded him to do the movie. He said he had reservations about playing such an 'American character.'"

"Then, before I left his suite," Albee said, "he asked me one thing."

"And what might that have been?" Herlihy asked.

"Burton asked me if I'd like to suck his cock. But I took a raincheck."]

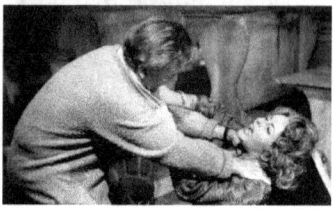

Domestic & Academic Hell: **Richard Burton** and a shrewish **Elizabeth Taylor** getting expressive in their film version of Edward Albee's *Who's Afraid of Virginia Woolf?*

Some of their fans claimed they were acting out a virtual reality version of their own dysfunctional marriage.

***

Since its debut as a major American play, many drama critics have suggested that *Who's Afraid of Virginia Woolf?* should have been cast entirely with gay men. Some of them went on to say that Albee had actually conceived his play as a commentary on the jealousy and bitchery of same-sex unions, but that later, at the last minute, he changed the genders of his players, thereby "cleaning up the casting for a more generalized audience."

Albee himself, as it happened, denied all that, and never supported redefining his most famous play as an homosexual venue.

Yet despite his position, it eventually came to pass that a theatrical producer proposed casting—get this—Henry Fonda, Richard Burton, Warren Beatty, and Jon Voight as the protagonists of what would have been "a counter-culture, *über* and *avant-garde* revival" of Albee's wrenching play.

According to Albee, "I rejected the proposal, even though it probably would have led to theater audiences lined up around the block buying tickets."

***

No one seemed more surprised than Albee at the Academy Awards presentation when Elizabeth Taylor won her second Oscar for her performance in *Who's Afraid of Virginia Wolff?* as Martha. [*She'd won the first for her performance as a prostitute in* BUtterfield 8 *(1960). As Martha, she beat out each of the two Redgrave sisters—Vanessa as the lead in* Morgan, *and Lynn as the lead in* Georgy Girl].

And whereas Burton had been nominated as Best Actor for his performance that year in Albee's play, he lost the prize to Paul Scofield for his role in *A Man for All Seasons*.

***

With the passage of years, Albee would receive three separate Pulitzer Prizes for drama: *A Delicate Balance* in 1967; *Seascape* in 1975; and *Three Tall Women* in 1994.

Who's Afraid of Virginia Wolff? might have won one too, had it not been for disputes among members of the jury, some of whom interpreted the play as vulgar. But later, as it happened, the more liberal Tony Award Committee awarded Albee their coveted prize for it instead.

Elizabeth Taylor wins an Oscar for her portrayal of the tormented harridan, Martha in *Who's Afraid of Virginia Woolf?*

America's perception of academia would never be the same.

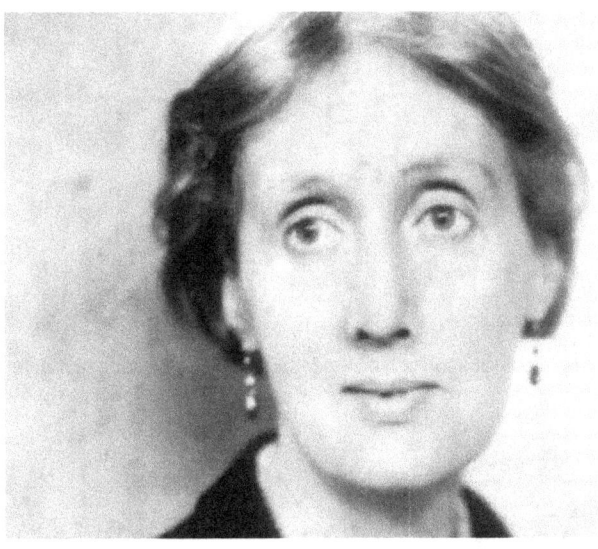

Who the Hell Was Virginia Woolf?
AND WHY, WITHIN ACADEMIC CIRCLES, WAS SHE SO SCARY?

Born (her words) into "a very communicative, literate, letter writing, visiting, articulate, late nineteenth century world," **Adeline Virginia Woolf** (1882-1941) was a modernist English writer.

In the 1970s, during the heyday of Edward Albee, her influence on feminist criticism became one of the most fashionable and widely discussed subjects in the Women's Movement and in Academia.

It's been suggested that Albee's character of Professor George Mason might have lost his job if he'd trivialized, or misstated, Woolf's influence in a classroom. Thus, the terror elicited by the legacy of Virginia Woolf.

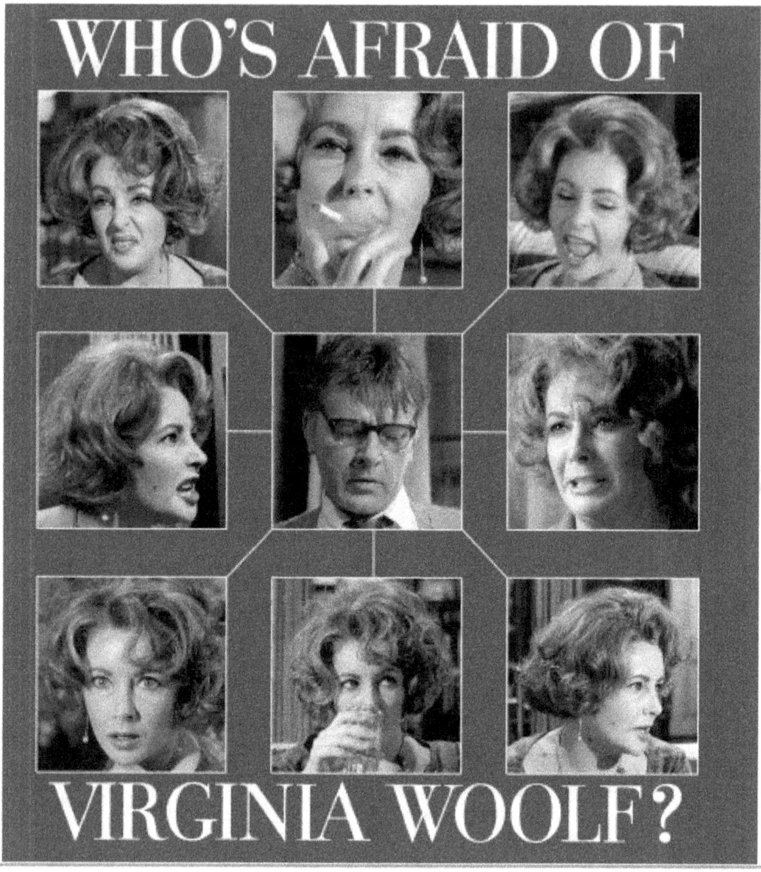

WHO'S AFRAID OF VIRGINIA WOOLF?

Fans of **La Liz** reveled in her personification of a bitter, drunken, perhaps insane harridan.

A young director, Dov Fahrer, who knew Albee quite well, told the press that the playwright had written *Who's Afraid of Virginia Woolf?* as a tense drama between two homosexual couples. "Albee's idea was to have the play performed by four men, and when that approach didn't sell, he changed the characters to two straight couples."

Albee adamantly denied it.

Until he was blocked by Albee, Fahrer wanted to bring the play to Broadway with an all-star cast comprised of (left to right) **Henry Fonda, Warren Beatty, Richard Burton,** and **Jon Voight**

Chapter Sixteen

GRACE KELLY

Beauty, Good Manners, Lucky Breaks, & The Triumph of Myth Over Reality

The marriage of **Grace Kelly** to **Prince Rainier** of Monaco on April 19, 1956 was hailed as "The Wedding of the Century." Invitations to the ceremony and the receptions that followed were as precious as diamonds.

In London, however, Queen Elizabeth cabled her regrets, telling her associates, "Too many movie stars will be there. As far as I'm concerned, Miss Kelly is just a minor Hollywood starlet, marrying a very minor prince."

Although other crowned heads were invited, only one showed up, the Aga Khan. His son, Prince Aly, had previously sustained a torrid affair with Grace.

It was just as well that the English monarch did not attend. It quickly devolved into a media circus.

The Queen was not alone in negative comments. Bing Crosby, Grace's former co-star and "exiled" lover, said: "Why would Grace settle for being the Princess of a minor principality when she could have become the princess of the world if she'd stayed in Hollywood and continued her career?"

The Denver Post grumbled that Rainier was "beneath her station." The communist *Daily Worker* regretted that Grace had chosen a husband "who can't lay bricks." The *Chicago Tribune* asserted that, "Grace Kelly is too well bred to marry the silent partner in a gambling parlor."

Another of her lovers, Frank Sinatra, also added a barb: "A hooker in Monaco told me that, unlike *moi*, the Prince is lousy in bed."

In the left-hand photo, Grace lived up to the the grace in her name when she accepted the 1954 Best Actress Oscar for her co-starring role in *The Country Girl* with Sinatra and Crosby.

The otherwise gala Oscar ceremony that year was darkened by charges of "robbery," as Judy Garland fans denounced the Academy's choice, claiming that the Oscar actually belonged to Judy for the greatest performance of her life: *A Star Is Born*.

In 1961, Darwin flew to Paris for the French premiere of *The Zoo Story*, a one-act play by Edward Albee. Their mutual friend, James Leo Herlihy, had been cast as its male lead, and its timing coincided with the on-site research Darwin was gathering for the coverage of Paris in *The Frommer Guides*.

The Zoo Story was a heavy drama, critics defining it as "an exploration of isolation, loneliness, miscommunication, social disparity, and dehumanization in a materialistic world."

Herlihy had arranged for Darwin to sit in the theater's front row, where two seats to his immediate left remained unoccupied. Suddenly, timed to coincide with the beginning of the play, Princess Grace of Monaco made a dazzling entrance before moving to occupy one of those empty seats. She was accompanied by a very handsome man in his early twenties. For a moment, Darwin assumed it was her security guard, but was later informed by Herlihy that he was her lover.

Seated next to him, Grace turned to Darwin, acknowledging him with a smile just as the lights dimmed and the curtain went up.

When the play was over, Grace and her young escort made a brief appearance at the cast party. There, from a discrete distance, Darwin confessed to Herlihy that he'd always harbored a slight grudge against Grace because of her Oscar win for *The Country Girl* in 1954.

"Grace, of course, was brilliant as the deglamorized wife of a weak-willed, alcoholic actor as portrayed by Bing Crosby," he said. "But my vote went to Judy Garland for her role in *A Star is Born*. Garland delivered one of the greatest screen performances in the history of film. But now that Grace is here, all is forgiven. Please introduce me."

For years before he met her, Darwin had followed the life and loves of Grace Kelly. He continued to follow her after her marriage to Prince Rainier of Monaco. Based on his duties as senior co-author of both *Frommer's France* and *Frommer's Provence & The French Riviera*, he made annual visits (he sometimes referred to them as "pilgrimages") to

Grace, pictured above with him in *The Country Girl*, made two pictures with William Holden. That was followed by *The Bridge at Toko-Ri* (1955).

As revealed by Donald Sec, a close friend of Holden, "Grace follows her usual pattern of seducing her married leading man. Her affair with Bill was common gossip in Hollywood. At thirty-six, my buddy is still very handsome, with a charming smile and the aura of a very confident male animal. Of course, he drinks heavily, but no one is perfect."

Confidential reported, "Night after night, the Cadillac of Bill Holden is seen parked in front of Grace Kelly's apartment house. On the set of *The Country Girl*, Crosby and Holden are feuding over which of them is entitled to the comforts of Grace."

Monaco.

According to Danforth Prince, "Darwin always planned to write a biography of Grace Kelly, and over the years, he gathered reports and bulletins about virtually everything anyone had ever said, written, or observed about her life and status as one of the entertainment industry's 'ultimate blonde goddesses.'"

[Darwin, in fact, as eventually published in some of the celebrity biographies he wrote, had researched and described the Philadelphia-born diva's once-secret trysts with, among others, John F. Kennedy, Paul Newman, Marlon Brando, and Rock Hudson.]

It had been Grace who was first offered the role of Maggie the Cat for the movie version (1958) of Tennessee Williams' *Cat on a Hot Tin Roof*. She had also been considered as the female lead opposite Rock Hudson in the epic saga of Texas, *Giant* (1956). *[That coveted role was awarded instead to Elizabeth Taylor.]*

What follows by Darwin Porter is one of the most tantalizing overviews ever filed by any journalist about Grace, Her Serene Highness, the Princess of Monaco. It covers part of the heady, exhilarated, adulation-filled period of her life when she was a widely desired and spectacularly sought-after Hollywood movie star.

HER SERENE HIGHNESS
STEAMY SECRETS OF "THE ICE PRINCESS"

"Grace Kelly was a conniving woman. She almost ruined my best friend Mal's [Mrs. Ray Milland's] marriage. She fucked everything in sight. She was worse than any woman I'd ever known."
— Skip Hathaway, wife of Henry Hathaway,
Grace Kelly's director in *Fourteen Hours* (1951).

"She was a real, white-gloved lady, who only became a whore when the bedroom door was locked."
— Alfred Hitchcock

According to those who knew her well, **Her Most Serene Highness, the Princess of Monaco** in private did not behave like the ice-cold blonde goddess she played on screen.

A former lover, Don Richardson, claimed, "She screwed everybody she came into contact with who was able to do anything good for her. She screwed agents, producers, directors. And there was really no need for it. She was on her way."

Director Henry Hathaway's wife once said, "Grace wore those white gloves, looking all prissy and proper, but she was no saint. Just ask Bing Crosby, Cary Grant, William Holden, Prince Aly Khan, David Niven, Spencer Tracy, Ray Milland, Jimmy Stewart, and many others."

"What was going on off screen competed with what was going on screen," claimed director John Ford. He'd been assigned to remake *Red Dust* (1932) into a new adventure film called *Mogambo* (1953), featuring Clark Gable, Ava Gardner, and Grace Kelly. Ironically, Gable was cast into the same role [*that of the crusty hero, Vic Marswell*], that he'd originally played in *Red Dust*. His co-star in that film had been Jean Harlow, interpreting a role originally intended for Greta Garbo.

Grace was looking forward to a sojourn in Africa—"I've read so much about it." She even studied Swahili and expressed delight that she'd get to see the wilds of Uganda, Tanganyika, and Kenya during the shoot. She was also interested in having an affair with Clark Gable, fully aware that her co-star, Ava Gardner, had already beaten her to him.

Clark Gable was cast in *Mogambo* (1953), which was shot in Africa with his leading ladies, **Ava Gardner** (left) and **Grace Kelly** (right). Even though she denied it, Ava had had an affair with him when they co-starred in *The Hucksters* (1947).

When Ava saw Grace falling for Gable, she warned her: "Don't! He's had every woman at MGM in the 1930s, and he's still on a conquest. But when he's through with a woman, he tosses her aside and moves on to his next victim."

Grace responded, "You've thrown down the gauntlet. I'm going to go after the lug."

The team behind *Mogambo* had originally conceived it as a vehicle for Stewart Granger (who wrote disparagingly about Gable in his memoirs); Deborah Kerr was envisioned for the role that eventually went to Grace Kelly; and Lana Turner was the inspiration for the part that was ultimately assigned to her closest friend, Ava.

Grace had been acquainted with Ava's husband, Frank Sinatra, before he even arrived in Africa. She claimed she'd met him when she was a teenager but provided no details of that encounter.

When she wasn't sleeping with Gable, Grace hung out with Ava, who told her that her marriage to Frank was near to its end. "I don't think we can make it. He's also broke. He's on his way here, but I had to pay his

On the set of *Mogambo*, Ava Gardner, right in front of Grace Kelly, decided to see for herself if the legend about Watusi men was true.

Up went the breechclout of **a Watusi** for an up-close inspection by Ava's experienced appraisal.

plane fare."

Night after night on location in Africa, Grace overheard Ava and Frank battling and screaming at each other.

Grace later wrote to Cary Grant, "The tent next to mine is co-inhabited by Frank and Ava. After three hours of physical and verbal violence, there is sudden silence. Then their bed starts to creak for the next hour or so."

Sam Zimbalist, who began his career at sixteen as a film cutter, was the producer of *Mogambo*, having previously produced both *King Solomon's Mines* (1950) and *Quo Vadis* (1951).

During the filming of *Ben-Hur* (1959), Zimbalist told Gore Vidal, one of the movie's script writers, an anecdote about what happened during the making of *Mogambo*.

For location shots, Ford had hired many Watusis, who wore breechclouts. One afternoon in the hot African sun, both Grace and Ava were walking beside a row of these elegant men. "Do you think their cocks are as big as people claim?" Ava asked Grace.

"How in the hell do you think I would know that?" Grace said, flabbergasted at Ava's remark.

"I think it's about time we both took a look at some black dick." Impulsively Ava reached for the breechclout of one of the Watusis and lifted it. A large cock was exposed in the sunshine. The Watusi just smiled at this Western woman as his penis began to harden.

"Let's get out of here," Grace urged Ava.

As she departed, Ava yelled out, "Frank's bigger than that."

Instead of being horrified at Ava's lasciviousness, Grace was attracted to her earthy Tarheel appeal. Ava was profane, outspoken, and outrageous. More lady-like, Grace pretended to be horrified, yet was drawn to Ava's sense of ribald humor. Nothing seemed to daunt her, and if she felt like saying something, she did so with absolute freedom.

Cast as a prim, frigid wife in *Mogambo*, Grace delivered a better performance than she did in the 1952 *High Noon*, where she was in love with Gary Cooper both on and off the screen.

Coop claimed, "She looked like a cold dish until a man gets her pants down, and then she ex-

In 1954, **Grace Kelly** attended the premiere of *Rear Window*. She was flanked by its director, **Alfred Hitchcock** (left) and her lover, fashion designer **Oleg Cassini** (right).

The Paris-born son of Russian aristocrats, Cassini later admitted, "I fell in love with Grace after seeing her in *Mogambo*. Competition was stiff at that time as she was deeply involved with that French actor, Jean-Pierre Aumont. I decided to woo her, and launched the campaign of my life."

"Gene Tierney, my former wife, told me I was a far better lover than John F. Kennedy, but not as good as Prince Aly Khan."

plodes."

Her friend, author Gore Vidal, claimed, "Grace almost always lays her leading man."

The very handsome William Holden said, "I loved her very, very much. I was married, so our affair remained for the most part secret. But at some point, I came to realize there was no point in pursuing our love affair. I was the one who walked out on her. In contrast, her love affair with Ray Milland, her co-star in *Dial M for Murder* (1954), became a matter of public record. Everyone in Hollywood gossiped about her romantic link with this also-married man."

Different from the misinformation it sometimes spread, Confidential *magazine* got it right: *"After one look at Grace, Ray Milland went into a tailspin that reverberated from Perino's to Ciro's. The whole town soon hee-hawed over the news that suave Milland, who had a wife and family at home, was ga-ga over Grace. He pursued her ardently and Hollywood cackled."*

Grace received good reviews for her work in *Mogambo*. Her performance was eventually nominated for an Oscar as Best Supporting Actress. She lost the award to Donna Reed, cast as a prostitute on the eve of the Japanese attack on Pearl Harbor in *From Here to Eternity*. Ironically, Frank was nominated for Best Supporting Actor in that film. Unlike Grace, he walked home with an Oscar.

With Ava absent from his life, Frank became despondent after his return to Hollywood. There, he learned that Grace had ended her romance with fashion designer Oleg Cassini, who had wanted to marry her. Frank decided to call her for a date, as he'd been wanting to seduce her ever since Africa. He would have were it not for Ava and Clark Gable, who monopolized her off-screen time.

Grace told Frank. "I'd love to go out with you. Ava told me you pack a powerful punch." Even though Ava had, indeed, "promoted" Frank that way, in saying it like that, Grace shocked herself. Perhaps some of Ava's boldness had rubbed off on her.

As part of his first date with her, Frank took Grace back to his hotel suite, where he spent the rest of the weekend with her. Ava heard about the off-the-record weekend and, with no semblance of jealousy, called Grace to gossip. "How was he?" Ava asked. "Did I exaggerate?"

"Not at all," Grace said. "It was everything you said and more. What surprised me was how gentle and sensitive he was to a woman's need. I didn't figure that for Frank."

"I'm getting tired of going to bed with guys who have had every woman in Hollywood," Ava said. "I've decided I want to break in a virgin male."

In spite of her demure demeanor, Grace had an impish sense of humor. She was fully aware of how provocative Ava had been with Frank, and she devised a scheme that would surpass the best of Ava's outrages. At the end of a very expensive meal at Chasen's, Frank was generously settling the tab.

"I'll pay the tip," Grace announced. Then, to Frank's shock, she unzipped the waiter's black trousers and inserted two one-hundred dollar bills into the region around his crotch before zipping him up.

Red faced, the handsome, well-built waiter retreated. Without losing her cool, Grace turned to Frank. "Don't worry, darling, you've got twice as much as he has."

After their inaugural fling, Grace and Frank resumed their secret romance when they were cast together in the *High Society*, a 1956 musical remake of the 1940 film *Philadelphia Story* that had starred Katharine Hepburn, James Stewart, and Cary Grant. Alongside Celeste Holm, Frank was cast as one of the two reporters from *Spy* magazine sent to cover society nuptials. Grace assumed the leading female role of the fanciful and very rich bride, Tracy Lord. During its filming, Frank referred to the beautiful, quixotic Grace as "a cross between Aimee Semple McPherson and Queen Elizabeth."

It was the **Wedding of the Century.** At least that's how much of the world press interpreted it. Uncharitably, one critic wrote, "Grace Kelly is marrying the prince of an amusement park."

There was one complication, most of it occurring off camera. In their battle for the affections of Grace, Frank was pitted against Bing Crosby, who'd been assigned Grant's role of C.K. Dexter-Haven. Crosby wanted Grace for himself and didn't welcome competition from Frank.

High Society's script called for Grace to make her singing debut in a duet with Crosby called "True Love," a song written by Cole Porter. Unknown to Crosby, Grace rehearsed the number at length with Frank. She told him, "I wish I could duet with you. You sing so much better than Bing."

Grace Kelly, as the wife of the ruler of Monaco, welcomes **Aristotle Onassis** and the opera star, **Maria Callas**, his mistress, to Grace's kingdom.

That was "music" to Frank's jealous, love-starved ears.

To the surprise of virtually everyone involved, "True Love" went platinum. Years later in Monaco, the sounds of "True Love" could frequently be heard echoing through the halls of the Grimaldi family's palace. During one of his visits to Monte Carlo, Frank told Grace, "I taught you well. You went platinum before me."

In September of 1955, a year before Grace and Frank made *High Society*, Grace's eager Monegasque suitor, Prince Rainier, arrived in Los Angeles and installed himself in a luxurious villa in Bel Air. For the next six weeks, Grace discreetly lived with her future husband, sneaking off on occasion to see Frank. "When she wants to play-act at being a princess, she's with Rainier," Sinatra told Ava, "But when she wants a good fuck, she comes to the man who knows how to do it."

Frank chose not to attend the high-profile marriage (April 19, 1956) of Grace to Prince Rainier. It wasn't because he was jealous of the prince, but because, as he was in London being fitted for white tie and tails in preparation for the event, he read about the sensational appearance of Ava in Monaco.

He decided that if he arrived in the wake of his bitter divorce from her, it would upstage Grace's wedding. He called her and explained, "I'm not coming, because this is your day."

She understood.

Even after her marriage to Rainier, Grace continued her romantic interest in Frank, though they saw each other only occasionally. Years later, in 1978, she invited him to her daughter Caroline's wedding to playboy Philippe Junot, who was seventeen years her senior.

[At that event, Frank sang the grim and unfunny "My Way," with lyrics expressed by a dying man facing the final curtain. "The song seemed an odd selection for my wedding," Caroline later said. "Couldn't he have sung 'High Hopes' instead?"]

Frank resumed his affair with Grace when he sang at the French premiere of *Kings Go Forth* (1958), a romance/action film in which he co-starred as a U.S. soldier during World War II alongside Tony Curtis and Natalie Wood. *[Frank had an affair with her.]* At some point Frank and Grace managed to slip away to a private villa owned by David Niven, who also had had an affair with Grace. During the remainder of their lives, Frank's sexual links with Grace resumed whenever they came together. On June 9, 1962, Frank showed up in Monaco again, appearing at the Sporting Club. He also made appearances in Grace's boudoir whenever the prince was away.

For one of his many farewell performances, this one at the Los Angeles Music Center on June 13, 1971, Frank delivered one of his best shows. In the audience sat Princess Grace. The once romantic couple got together for a drink. Reportedly, Frank made a pass at her and asked her, "Can you do it again for old time's sake?" She demurely held him off. "Let's just be dear old friends who cherish a wonderful memory."

He agreed.

During the early 1970s, Frank showed up frequently in Monaco, occupying the most glamorous suite on the eighth floor of the Hotel de Paris. He was seen everywhere from the Monaco Beach Club to the tennis courts of the local Country Club. Business was said to boom in Monaco whenever he was in town.

In 1978, at the age of 21, **Caroline of Monaco** married **Philippe Junot,** in a dynastic continuance very different from what prevailed during the wedding of her parents. It was the first of Caroline's three marriages.

Since 1999 she has remained married to Ernst August, Prince of Hanover (born 1954), the heir to the defunct throne of the former Kingdom of Hanover and the male heir of George III of the United Kingdom.

Through her father, Caroline is linked to the Ducs de Polignac, one of the most illustrious families of France's *ancien régime*.

Barbara Marx, the ex-wife of Zeppo Marx, was the fourth and final wife of Frank Sinatra, the marriage lasting until his death, perhaps because she was "the most understanding" of his many wives.

According to Barbara, "Frank seduced some of the most famous women on the planet, from Nancy Reagan to Marilyn Monroe, but I let my lusty little Italian go for it. From the beginning, I didn't expect him to be faithful, I was much more interested in being Mrs. Frank Sinatra, a title I cherished. I was willing to pay the price to hold onto him."

Two of the most memorable moments in *High Society* are depicted above. On the left, **Frank Sinatra** sings "You're Sensational" to **Grace Kelly**.

On the right, **Bing Crosby** and Grace record what became a hit song, "True Love," which temporarily convinced Grace she should have been a singer rather than an actress. But that conceit soon vanished when both Bing and Frank convinced her not to pursue a singing career.

While Bing's wife, Dixie, was at home battling cancer, Bing and Grace used Alan Ladd's residence for their sexual trysts.

Many years after **Grace Kelly's marriage to Prince Rainier,** Frank Sinatra and Peter Lawford visited her at her palace.

They found a confused Grace filled with regret. She missed Hollywood and felt she had made a big mistake, giving up a glorious career. "I was a big fish in a big town, but now I'm a big fish in a small town."

Later that evening, whereas Peter went back to the Café de Paris "looking for love," Frank found it in Grace's bedchamber. Their affair resumed.

Frank Sinatra made a famous quote about **Grace Kelly**, his co-star in *High Society*. "She is the squarest person I know."

That was his public assessment. In private, he told his cronies, "What I said about Grace was true only before you get her in bed. Once bedded, she's one hot tamale, a crazed nymphomaniac. She'd do it with the pool boy if his bikini was revealing enough.

When their co-star in *High Society*, Bing Crosby, was cast with Grace in *The Country Girl (1954)*, he fell madly in love with her and proposed marriage.

Rejected by Grace, Bing carried a torch for her for years.

GRACE KELLY: The Triumph of Myth Over Reality

"If anything, Princess Grace was discreet," said a former assistant manager of the Hotel de Paris. "I assisted Sinatra on numerous occasions. Sometimes he stayed with us for a month or so."

On April 19, 1981 Frank invited Grace and Rainier to a celebration of their silver wedding anniversary at his home in Palm Springs. There Grace met a glamorous blonde, ex-showgirl Barbara Marx, who had become Frank's fourth and final wife.

Later in the evening, Grace quipped half-jokingly into his ear. "You only married her because she looks like a dime store version of me."

After years of mellowing and self-adjusting, **His and Her Serene Highnesses** released this "official portrait" of one of the most-watched couples in the Western Hemisphere.

Grace's friends, Cary Grant and Gregory Peck, joined in the festivities. Privately Grace met Frank and told him the truth. "Where has love gone?" she asked him. "The Prince and I are merely keeping up appearances. We have so many differences these days, and we fight a lot. Both of us have lovers on the side. I miss America so. I miss you. Why didn't you marry me and take me away before I got locked into this Princess role?"

Although Sinatra may have been merely portraying a gallant gentlemen, he told her, "Not running away and marrying you has been the biggest regret of my life."

In March of 1982, in Grace's "home town" of Philadelphia, Frank saw Grace for the last time. He and Barbara Marx attended "The Tribute to Grace Kelly" at the Annenberg Center for the Performing Arts. Stewart Granger and James Stewart were also among the honored guests.

As part of her goodbye to Frank, Grace met with him privately. "I'm going to buy a condo very soon in Manhattan, and I want you to become one of my most frequent visitors. If you wish, I'll give you the key. Another place to hang your hat."

"Consider me your number one guest," he promised her.

***

In a car, after it crashed through a barricade on a winding *corniche* on the French Riviera, Grace met her tragic death on September 14, 1982.

Grief stricken, Frank told Cary Grant, "Everyone said Grace lived a fairytale life. A prince. A palace. Her story usually ends by people saying, 'they lived happily ever after.' What has not been written is what came after they lived happily ever after."

QUESTION: WHAT CELEBRITY COURTIERS WERE ROMANTICALLY LINKED TO THE OSCAR-WINNING "ICE QUEEN" WHO BECAME "HER SERENE HIGHNESS?"

ANSWER: EACH OF THE MEN NOTED BELOW. AT THE TIME, ALL OF THEM WERE HOUSEHOULD NAMES.

| John F. Kennedy | Robert Evans | Clark Gable | Cary Grant |

| Prince Aly Khan | William Holden | Bing Crosby | Ray Milland | David Niven |

| The Shah of Iran | Oleg Cassini | Jean-Pierre Aumont | Gary Cooper |

GRACE KELLY: The Triumph of Myth Over Reality

THE ICE BLONDE (GRACE KELLY) VS. THE TARHEEL BEAUTY
AVA GARDNER

AVA GARDNER: She was The Naked Maja. The Barefoot Contessa. Lady Brett. The rise of a beautiful North Carolina farm girl—barefoot and with a thick Southern accent—to the pinnacle of Hollywood is the stuff of legend. She became Mrs. Mickey Rooney, Mrs. Artie Shaw, Mrs. Frank Sinatra. She loved booze, bullfighters, and bitches of the night. Her close friends ranged from Ernest Hemingway to Adlai Stevenson. Her own life, however, was more dramatic than any role she portrayed on the screen.

Ava Gardner was called "the world's greatest beauty." But in the golden age of movie-making, the tabloids, which documented her steamy private life, had a lot more to say than that.

Studio packaged, Ava was one of the last of the great Hollywood sex goddesses. But studio chief Louis B. Mayer went ballistic trying to keep her personal scandals from destroying her career.

"Unless he was a gay blade," said an MGM studio publicist, "every red-blooded male who ever saw an Ava Gardner movie wanted to take her to bed."

On the eve of their first wedding anniversary, Ava Gardner announced to her husband, Frank Sinatra, that she was heading to Africa to film *Mogambo* directed by John Ford. Frank virtually had no money at this point and was forced to consent to let her go. After many bitter fights, she made arrangements to leave California for Kenya, with transfers in New York, London, and ultimately Nairobi.

Since nothing was breaking for him in America, Frank decided to join her as a silent member of John Ford's "safari" of 150 whites and 350 natives. An 1,800-yard airstrip had been hacked out of the jungles to receive small planes from Nairobi, carrying food, drink, letters, film equipment, and medical supplies.

At the airport, a reporter asked, "Frankie, is John Ford gonna find you a role in *Mogambo*?"

"Yeah," Frank shot back. "I'm gonna go native in black face—maybe with my cock hanging out!"

Then Ava, who was drunk before she even boarded the plane, chimed in: "Frank will be doing his thing in some clubs in Africa, using Tarzan as his opening act."

Celebrating their first anniversary on a plane en route to Nairobi, Ava drank what she called "piss-warm champagne" and accepted a diamond-studded ring from Frank. She would later receive the bill for it.

"I've been married to him for a year," she told the captain. "My marriages to Artie Shaw and that Mickey Rooney runt didn't last that long. I'm the restless type. Show me a man in tight pants, and I'm off to the races."

In Africa, on the second day of the shoot, Ava discovered that Ford had a gay streak in him. She accidentally walked in on the director when he was deep-throating one of the handsome "white hunters" hired for *Mogambo*.

During filming in Africa, Frank had nothing to do all day except wait for Ava, who seemed dismissive, treating him more like her secretary than her husband. He kept reading and re-reading the novel, *From Here to Eternity*, as his agents worked to get him the tragic role of Maggio in the novel's upcoming film adaptation.

Grace Kelly (*left*) and **Ava Gardner** (*right*) co-starred with Clark Gable in *Mogambo* (1953).

Frank traveled to Africa with Ava, but was very sensitive about how he'd be regarded, especially by Clark Gable. "Here I am, a fucking has-been, carrying booze to my working spouse, the biggest movie star in Hollywood."

In Africa, Frank attacked photographers and spent most of his time in the steamy jungle enraged and lashing out, often at Ava.

The situation on the set didn't get much better when Frank, one drunken night, confronted *Mogambo's* director, John Ford. "Is it true you used to suck off John Wayne back in the good old days? I always wondered how a no talent guy like The Duke broke into show business."

Ford, the most closeted of Hollywood homosexuals, ignored him.

Ford may have found himself a white hunter, but Ava also became fascinated by Frank ("Bunny") Allen, another strapping white hunter who arranged movie safaris. But with Frank hanging around, she didn't dare risk chasing after Bunny.

On days when heavy rains forced her to stay alone in her tent with Frank, they fought bitterly, Ava making accusations about Marilyn Monroe and him.

Only a week after his arrival in Kenya, word reached Sinatra that Columbia had granted him a screen test for the role of Maggio in *From Here to Eternity* (1953).

Hastily kissing Ava goodbye, and on a ticket she'd paid for, he returned to Hollywood.

After his departure, in the stifling jungle heat, Ava discovered she was pregnant.

During Frank's absence, Ava flew to London and aborted their child, although she had previously claimed that her greatest joy in life would involve becoming the mother of Frank's child. But when Grace Kelly asked her about this, Ava said, "A lady has the privilege of changing her mind."

In defending her decision to have an abortion, Ava said, "MGM had all sorts of penalty clauses about their stars having babies. Frank and I couldn't even take care of ourselves. How were we going to look after a kid?"

Ava later claimed she'd had a miscarriage. Cameraman Robert Surtees disputed that. "Ava hated Frank so intensely at this point she was horrified at the thought of giving birth to 'Little Frankie Junior,' as she put it. My wife accompanied her to London. It was a God damn abortion. She told my wife, 'I hated Frankie so much, I wanted the baby to go unborn.'"

Although his Hollywood screen test for the role of Maggio in *From Here to Eternity* had gone well, Frank flew back to Africa, at Ava's expense, uncertain that he'd get the role. He arrived just in time for Christmas, bringing Ava a mink coat and a diamond ring he'd purchased with money from one of his gangster friends, perhaps Lucky Luciano. This would be Frank's last major attempt to win Ava back.

While on location in Kenya, Frank learned of the abortion of his baby and of Ava's affair with Bunny Allen. "All I remember about Christmas of 1953 was Frank denouncing Ava as a whore and a baby killer," Grace said.

Harry Cohn, with a lot of persuasion from Ava, finally agreed to give Frank the role of Maggio, for which he'd be paid only $10,000. Ava told

MOGAMBO

When **Clark Gable** arrived in Africa to film *Mogambo* in 1953, he was accompanied by two of the most beautiful women in the world: **Grace Kelly** and **Ava Gardner**. "I always had trouble deciding whether I liked chocolate or vanilla better," Gable told director John Ford.

He of course was referring to Grace's blonde hair and Ava's dark curls. Mogambo translates from Swahili as "passion," and no other word could better describe the off-screen sex going on during the making of this film.

Ava's all-time favorite movie was *Red Dust* in which a young Gable had starred opposite Jean Harlow as "Honey Bear," a slut in the bush. Now Ava was replacing her idol, Harlow, in Gable's arms.

"As you know," Ava told Grace, "Clark doesn't have all that much to penetrate with, but Frankie's weapon sure knows how to reach virgin territory."

Gable and Grace, "I practically had to agree to fuck Cohn to get Frank that God damn role."

After a brief, troubled Christmas together with Ava, Frank flew back once again on that long trip to Hollywood to accept the role of Maggio. Much of *From Here to Eternity* would be shot on location in Hawaii.

An Oscar for Best Supporting Actor for his role in that film lay in his future. The part would mark a comeback for him.

On the set of *Mogambo*, both Frank and Ava had been witnesses to Gable's affair with Grace.

Ava later said that she wanted Grace to sample Gable as a lover, claiming that she'd already been sexually intimate with him in 1947 during the filming of *The Hucksters*. "I felt it was Grace's turn," Ava was quoted as saying.

When she had first met Ava beside the Kagera River in Central Africa, Grace had been shocked by her heavy drinking, her "potty mouth," and her uninhibited behavior.

But during the long weeks of shooting, Grace gradually warmed to Ava, and in time they became "friends for life."

At the completion of the film, Ava invited Grace to stop over with her for a few days for a Roman holiday, and Grace accepted. According to the testimony of Guido Volta, a chauffeur in Rome in the 1950s who hauled around everyone from Elizabeth Taylor to Frank Sinatra, Ava took the future princess of Monaco on a tour of the city's brothels. At first Grace declined, but Ava could be persuasive.

With Guido as their guide, the two women set off for visits to establishments that included (according to their English translations), "The World of Earthly Pleasures,"

"Our director, John Ford, wanted him, but I got him first," or so proclaimed Ava Gardner during the filming of *Mogambo* in Kenya. She was referring to the great white hunter, **Frank Maurice ("Bunny") Allen,** depicted above.

A British-born professional safari guide in Africa, he escorted everybody from Prince Charles to Mick Jagger through some aspect of their shooting expeditions in Africa.

Bunny fell bigtime for Ava Gardner during the location filming, and he also came on strong to Grace Kelly. He was also the lover of Isak Dinesen, author of the novel *Out of Africa*.

Before the filming of *Mogambo*, he scouted the Congo River for locations for *The African Queen*, but claimed, "I never had an affair with Katharine Hepburn or Humphrey Bogart, although Robert Morley came on to me."

"One Hundred and One Desires Fulfilled," "No Pleasure Too Great or Too Small," "Memories Are Made of This," and "The Garden of Delights." At the various Roman bordellos, Ava bought drinks for all the hookers, introducing them to Grace and urging them to tell "only their best stories."

At the final bordello, according to Guido, "Miss Kelly became fascinated by a strikingly handsome young man, Antonio Guarnieri, who at the time was about 23 years old, and who worked as a waiter in the joint. Just before dawn, I drove Ava, Miss Kelly, and Antonio back to the women's suites at the Hotel Excelsior on the Via Veneto. Ava sat up front with me, while Miss Kelly and Antonio got acquainted in back. At the hotel, the future princess of Monaco invited Antonio up to her suite for a nightcap. That must have been one long drink. It lasted for three days and nights and ended only when I came back to drive Miss Kelly to the airport. At the airport, Antonio and Miss Kelly engaged in the world's longest good-bye kiss. When I drove Antonio back to Rome, he cried all the way."

After telling Grace good-bye, Ava flew back to London for more film work. To her horror, she discovered that she was pregnant once again. She didn't want to go to the same hospital for another abortion—"they asked too many God damn questions"—so she checked into a small nursing home near Wimbledon where abortions were quietly performed. She later told friends, "Of course I could have hired Frank's mother, Dolly Sinatra. She knows her way around an abortion table."

In her memoirs, Ava wrote, "Clearly someone told Frank about what I was doing, because as long as I live I'll never forget waking up after the operation and seeing him sitting next to the bed with tears in his eyes. But I still think I was right."

One of Ava's most famous films, *The Barefoot Contessa* (1954), was actually based on the life of another screen sex goddess, Rita Hayworth.

When the film's director, **Joseph Mankiewicz** *(with Ava in photo, above),* still beaming from his success with *All About Eve* (1950), called Ava in Rome, she invited him up to her suite. He was startled to find her lying naked on the sofa, sipping champagne.

"I can play more than barefoot," she said, wiggling her naked toes at him before raising her legs in the air. "Hop on, big guy."

After the second abortion, Frank told friends, "I should have beaten her fucking brains out for aborting my kid, but I loved her too much." Later he changed his position, telling Sammy Davis Jr., "I don't think that second kid was mine."

Already in Hollywood, "Frank had found his *cojones* once again," Ava said. "He was no longer as dependent on me as before. His record sales were picking up; he was in a hit movie, and he often preferred nights with his gangland friends instead of me. But I wasn't sitting around the living room knitting at night."

She told Lana, "I've resumed my wild, wild ways—and to hell with Frank."

When she wasn't with one of her male lovers, she cruised Santa Monica Boulevard at night, often picking up as many as three or four prostitutes and bringing them home with her. Sometimes she didn't want sex with them, but just wanted them to talk to her, smoking, drinking, and sharing their experiences with her.

She did have sex with any number of these hookers. According to reports, she paid them well and treated them kindly. Many of Ava's pickups often preferred women to men anyway, and were only too happy to disappear into the night with what the press called "The World's Most Beautiful Animal."

One night, Ava rented herself out as a hooker.

The director, Joseph Mankiewicz, wanted to cast Marlon Brando and Ava Gardner together as romantic leads in *The Barefoot Contessa* after Elizabeth Taylor turned it down. Brando also turned down the role, the part eventually going to Humphrey Bogart. Taking the director into his confidence, Brando revealed that Ava liked to socialize and hang out at bordellos. She became particularly interested in one that specialized in offering "movie stars" to its male clients, and to a few female clients as well.

The madam of the bordello claimed that "if you can't fuck the real thing, we offer you the mock." Clients got a look-alike, and were allowed to spend time with their screen favorite—"Joan Crawford," "Marilyn Monroe," "Elizabeth Taylor," "Jane Russell," "Judy Garland," and even "Margaret O'Brien" for those who liked them really young.

Brando told Mankiewicz that Ava wanted to be taken to the bordello to meet the madam. "That's not all," Brando said. "With the permission of the madam, Ava wanted to exchange places that coming Saturday night with her stand-in."

"That's wild!" Mankiewicz said. "It's incredible. May I be the first customer to hire the real Ava for the night?"

Brando pondered the request for a minute. "If you showed up as Ava's first client, I would just shit my pants. I don't know what Ava would shit."

In *High Society*, **Grace Kelly** shares a tender moment with **Frank Sinatra**. In her personal life, she shared many tender moments with him. Frank was wise to the changing whims of Grace. "If Grace couldn't be with her *beau du jour*, she loved the man she was with."

"Our affair had hardly ended, and there was Grace seen cozying up to Sinatra at Chasen's," said designer Oleg Cassini.

Between affairs, she didn't let any moss grow on her. Neither did Sinatra. He claimed to be in mourning over his breakup with Ava Gardner. But going in a split second from Ava to Grace wasn't bad. According to Cassini, "In Hollywood, she was the actress on everybody's lips. She was the *numero uno* in Tinseltown. Every producer wanted her for a movie role, and every stud wanted to bed up."

"I once thought she was mine, but I gave up and faced reality," Cassini said. "Grace would have many lovers before and during her reign as princess of Monaco."

Brando escorted Ava to the bordello that Saturday night and made the arrangement for Ava with the madam. She was in a bedroom awaiting her first customer when Mankiewicz arrived downstairs to be introduced to the madam. She personally escorted him to Ava's bedroom, while Brando wandered off "to do my duty with 'Betty Grable.'"

The story was spread around Hollywood, and many men queried Mankiewicz about his evening in Ava's whorehouse bedroom, "The lady—and she is a lady—deserves her privacy," Mankiewicz replied.

The next day, Frank learned about what had happened. Instead of phoning Mankiewicz, an angry Frank called Brando. "Listen, creep, and listen good. I know all about you and Ava. Stay away from her! Don't ever come within twenty feet of her even at a party. You got that? First offense, broken legs. Second offense, cracked skull. If you live through all that, cement shoes. One more false step and you've had it."

The love of his life: **Frank Sinatra** and **Ava Gardner** at the races.

According to Ava, "My troubles with Frank were never in bed. We were always great in bed. Our troubles began when I was on my way to the bidet."

Then he slammed down the phone.

One night, Ava agreed to meet Frank for dinner at Chasen's in Beverly Hills. After dinner, he wanted her to come back with him to his apartment, but she refused.

"I have a date," she told him.

"A date at this late hour?" he protested.

"Come on, Frankie, you're the master of the date at two o'clock in the morning."

She ordered a final drink and turned to confront him on the booth where they were sitting.

"I've decided to leave you forever. After that time in the hospital in London, I don't want to have children any more. I told Papa Hemingway only the other day that I wanted to lead a hedonistic life. I don't want to be tied down to you or to any husband—and definitely no children. The dream is over. I'm going to lead the gay life in Madrid."

"I still love you, and I guess I always will," he said. "If you ever change your mind, call me. I'll come running back to you. All you have to do is say the word."

"You're a darling man, Frank," Ava said. "But not for me. You'll find others. All my future lovers will come in quickly through the front door and out the back."

As an afterthought, she added, "Incidentally, unlike you who'll go on to other wives, I'll never marry again."

Aging Ava

Years of sexual dissipation and heavy boozing caused Ava to lose her legendary beauty. Her housekeeper reported that she'd often stare at her face in the mirror and say to her image, "Too many bullfighters, baby. Too many dicks. Too many George C. Scotts. Too many Artie Shaws. Too many Roberts." (No doubt, among others, she was referring to Robert Walker, Robert Mitchum, Robert Taylor, and Robert Evans.)

At night, she'd watch reruns of her old movies. After re-screening such films as *The Snows of Kilimanjaro* (1952), she'd call one of her former co-stars to reminisce. In that instance, it was Gregory Peck:

"Greg, baby, could it have been true? Was I really the most beautiful woman on the face of the earth, and you its most beautiful man?"

Gallantly, Peck answered: "That's true in your case, Ava, my dear, but I had serious competition back then. After all, Jerry Lewis and Broderick Crawford were two good-looking studs."

Frank Sinatra defined January 25, 1990, the "saddest day of my life." He'd just put down the phone after a call from London. His beloved Ava had died of pneumonia at the age of sixty-seven.

Shortly before her death, Ava told a reporter, "I drank too much, partied too much in the Fifties. It's all caught up with me. I didn't age well, honey child. And all I had to sell was my looks. I was never that great an actress. Now, I'm what's called 'a faded beauty.'"

A friend reported on her last comment about Barbara Marx Sinatra. "She may think she's the Queen today. But baby, I sat on that fucking throne when she was just a Las Vegas showgal."

When Frank heard that Ava was sick, he sent her $50,000. Potty-mouthed Ava, in her usual sarcastic way, said, "Is that all there is? I never said that to him when his dick went in me."

Fifty friends showed up at her funeral on a stormy day at the Sunset Memorial Park in North Carolina. The Rev. Francis C. Bradshaw began the oration: "Ava Gardner was no saint...."

Her last phone call had been to her co-star Stewart Granger at three o'clock in the morning. "It's Ava, darling. I was just watching the two of us in *Bhowani Junction* (1956). Weren't we beautiful?"

> WHEN I'M OLD AND GRAY, I WANT TO HAVE A HOUSE BY THE SEA & PAINT, WITH A LOT OF WONDERFUL CHUMS, GOOD MUSIC & BOOZE AROUND, AND A DAMN GOOD KITCHEN TO COOK IN.
> AVA GARDNER

BRANDO'S GRACE

How Stanley Kowalski & a Future Princess Took Home Their Oscar Gold

& Celebrated Their Wins Together in Bed

Marlon Brando, at the time the hottest and most sought-after screen actor in the world (and the celebrity world's most unremorseful bad boy), is depicted above (left) as the brutish Stanley Kowalski in Tennessee Williams *A Streetcar Named Desire* (1951).

In the upper right-hand photo, he's shown with **Eva Marie Saint** (the role Grace Kelly had unwisely rejected) in yet another film for which Brando would win an Oscar, *On the Waterfront* (1954). Eva Marie Saint, for her performance in it, won Best Supporting Actress.

In Los Angeles, it was the night of March 30, 1955 at the Pantages Theater. Seemingly half the world would be listening to the Academy Award presentations, where Marlon had been nominated as best actor of the year for his performance in *On the Waterfront*. In fact, the picture had been nominated for eight Oscars, elevating it up into the category of *Gone With the Wind*. Even composer Leonard Bernstein had been nominated for an Oscar for its music score.

In addition to having three actors nominated for one picture—Lee J. Cobb, Rod Steiger, and Karl Malden—Eva Marie Saint was up for best supporting actress, ironically competing with Katy Jurado, Marlon's girlfriend, for her performance in *Broken Lance* (1954). Other nominees that night included the picture itself, Elia Kazan for best director, Budd Schulberg for best screenplay, and Boris Kaufman for best cinematography.

Ironically, Grace Kelly had been offered the lead female role in *On The Waterfront*, but had rejected it. Marlon later admitted that he was "in great conflict" about attending the ceremonies. Even at this early date in his career, he didn't believe in the granting of awards for acting. He recalled that on the night of the ceremony itself, as he was being driven to the presentation, he was still pondering whether he should put on formal wear.

Marlon was not the only one concerned that night about what he should wear. Backstage at the theater, Sam Spiegel was in a semi-hysterical state pacing up and down. Earlier in the day, he'd called Kazan. "I feel like a whore with flu in a World War II cathouse in Honolulu, with two hundred sailors waiting for their turn at me. What if the fucker turns up in a ripped T-shirt and dirty jeans?"

Right before the beginning of the ceremonies, Marlon emerged from his dressing room looking immaculate in black tie and tux. "You've got class, boy," Spiegel told him.

"If only I could say the same for you," Marlon responded in an insult to his producer.

Spiegel remained "the nervous nelly," as the ceremony began, still pacing up and down. To anyone who'd listen, he asked, "What if Brando tells the audience to shove it?"

Backstage, Marlon encountered Bob Hope. "This is such a terrible competition," he said to a somewhat flabbergasted Hope. "There's such a hysterical feeling to win. It makes actors lose sight of the real objective. I feel like I'm being shipped off to Devil's Island to get my ears chopped off."

"Crosby did that to me years ago," Bob Hope quipped before walking away. Later he'd stage a mock fight on stage with Marlon, pretending to try to grab the Oscar from his hands.

Marlon was once again pitted against that sentimental favorite, Humphrey Bogart, to whom he'd lost back in 1951 for *The African Queen*. Marlon had vied for the gold that year for his iconic role as Stanley Kowalski in Tennessee Williams' *A Streetcar Named Desire*, in which he'd starred opposite Vivien Leigh, who did win her second Oscar that night.

This time Bogie was nominated for *The Caine Mutiny (1954)*. Marlon's other competition was Bing Crosby, another sentimental favorite. The "boys in Vegas" were betting on Crosby, who had starred in *The Country Girl (1954)*. Ironically, the author of that screenplay was Clifford Odets, Marlon's former lover and still a friend.

In another touch of irony, Marlon was competing that year against James Mason for *A Star Is Born*, a role Marlon turned down although it would have given him a chance to play opposite Judy Garland whom he admired. Marlon didn't expect much competition from Dan O'Herlihy in *Adventures of Robinson Crusoe*. Marlon was pissed at director Luis Buñuel for having made the film in the first place. Marlon had always wanted to play Robinson Crusoe himself.

Spiegel thought things were going his way when Eva Marie was announced as an early winner. She'd arrived pregnant at the theater. Earlier in the evening, Marlon had jokingly told reporters that he—not her husband—was the father. Accepting the award, the actress gasped, "I think I may have the baby right here." A few titters could be heard across the room. The next morning some puritanical members of the press reproached Eva Marie for her statement. Louella Parsons found the remark "tasteless," and Hedda Hopper thought "it cheapened the ceremony."

Finally, Marlon's big moment came, as Bette Davis walked across the stage in the very same way she'd done in *Beyond the Forest* (1949), which had ended her long career at Warner Brothers. She was wearing a skull cap to cover her bald head, which had been shaven for her role in *The Virgin Queen* (eventually released in 1955).

When gossip maven Louella Parsons saw this picture of **Marlon Brando** kissing **Grace Kelly** after their joint Oscar triumphs, she delivered a zinger:

"As far as I am concerned, he can drop dead. He has the manners of a chimpanzee, and a swelled head the size of a Navy blimp."

Taking the white envelope from Price & Waterhouse, she opened it. Reading it, she let out a whoop and then exclaimed in a cracked voice: "MARLON BRANDO!"

On stage, Marlon's speech was short. "Thank you very much." Holding up the Oscar, he noted, "It's much heavier than I imagined. I had something to say and I can't remember what I was going to say for the life of me. I don't think that ever in my life have so many people been so directly responsible for my being so very, very glad. It's a wonderful moment, and a rare one, and I am certainly indebted. Thank you."

In front of the audience of his peers, Marlon appeared young and awkward, but sincere—"not the arrogant prick he'd been portrayed in the press," said Elia Kazan.

Backstage Marlon was kissing everybody in sight, beginning with Bette Davis whom he hadn't seen since the night she came backstage to "mother him" when he was appearing in *A Streetcar Named Desire* (1951).

Then he walked over to congratulate Grace Kelly, reminding her that if he'd accepted the role he would have co-starred with her in *High Noon* (1952). "Too bad you didn't," she said flirtatiously. "We would have had a good time."

"So it's true what they say about you and your leading men?" he said with a mocking tease to his voice.

"That's for you to find out for yourself, Mr. Brando," she said. At some point in the evening he slipped her the phone number where he'd be later that night.

"You were great!" he told Grace when reporters surrounded them. "Personally I thought Crosby and Garland would beat us out."

One member of the press shouted at Grace, "Kiss him!"

"I think *he* should kiss *me*," she demurely responded.

Marlon happily obliged, kissing her again and again until the photographers were satisfied.

Privately he told her that he should never have made *On the Waterfront*. "I hold the film in contempt. I was awful in it." He held up his Oscar. "Look at how Hollywood rewards mediocrity!"

Some members of the press had been disappointed. Hoping for hot copy, reporters had wanted Marlon to behave outrageously. Instead he told them, "I'm sick to death of having reporters stand around staring at me."

Louella Parsons came up to Marlon to congratulate him. He almost kissed her before realizing it was his archenemy who had written all that unflattering copy about him when he'd first arrived in Hollywood. He shook her hand instead, then whispered that he was going to give her an exclusive "for old time's sake."

Then, as his "exclusive," he said, "The other night I was fucking Katy Jurado up on the roof of a house in Laurel Canyon. As you know, she was one of the nominees tonight. Now Katy is a Latina woman who likes to give voice to her passion. As we were deep into the dirty deed, she started screaming, 'Fuck me! Fuck me! Fuck me, Marlon Brando!' As I plunged all of my twelve inches into her, she shouted at the top of her voice: 'MARLON BRANDO MARLON BRANDO! I'M CUMMING!' I clapped my hand over her mouth and hissed at her, 'For fuck's sake,' I told her, 'don't use my God damn name.' Now print that!" Then he turned and walked away from her.

"I left Louella with her mouth open like she was catching flies," he later said.

Just before Grace was left the theater, she approached Marlon once again. This time she gave him a kiss on the lips, explaining that she was rushing off to Romanoff's to celebrate with Bing Crosby. At the time she was having an affair with her co-star in *The Country Girl*. "I feel embarrassed," she said. "After all, I got my Oscar but you took his."

Marlon went to the home of Jay Kanter, his agent, who had assembled an array of well-wishers, each wanting to congratulate Marlon. The French champagne flowed, Marlon preferring to take his bubbly in a souvenir mug from the city of Los Angeles instead of in one of Kanter's crystal goblets.

Pulling off his dinner jacket and loosening his tie, he plopped down on Kanter's sofa. Before him on the coffee table he placed his newly won Oscar. In front of the other guests, he addressed his Oscar. "I hope you're

"It's true that I've made friendships with my leading ladies," said Gary Cooper who was cast opposite **Grace Kelly** (left) and **Katy Jurado** (right) in the classic western, *High Noon* (1952).

Cooper (right) did indeed get extra friendly with both **Grace** and Katy during *High Noon's* filming

"They were each so totally different on screen, each of them intense, understated, demure, and restrained. Yet each became a wildcat at night."

gay," he told the statuette.

A guest asked,"Why do you want him to be gay?"

"Because I'm going to win a companion for him, and they don't make female Oscars," Marlon said.

Many observers of the Hollywood scene made predictions that night about Marlon's future. At post-ceremony parties all over the city, insiders predicted that Marlon's "wild years are over."

"He's become part of the Hollywood establishment," pronounced Sam Spiegel, who apparently never became a member himself.

"The Oscar has pacified Marlon," Hedda Hopper told the gathering at one party. "Now he's a major star. Take it from Hedda, Brando will start acting like a star."

How wrong she was.

Back at Kanter's gathering, a call came in at one-thirty that morning for Marlon. Getting up from the sofa, he seemed to know who was on the other

In a rare photo, press baron **William Randolph Hearst** is pictured with **Bette Davis** (center) and **Louella Parsons** at a costume party at San Simeon.

On the night that Marlon walked off with a Best Actor Oscar for *On the Waterfront*, he gave Bette a kiss, but extended only a limp handshake to Parsons.

Parsons told Brando, "I didn't vote for you. I voted for Bogie in *The African Queen*."

end of the line.

After taking the call, Marlon confronted Kanter in the hallway. "Make my excuses, would you? I've got to bug out. A rendezvous with a fellow Oscar winner."

His agent demanded to know where he was going at this hour.

"I've got a date with a blonde," Marlon said. "And there are still those people who spread the rumor that I don't like blondes."

On the set of High Society *(1956),* **Frank Sinatra** *and* **Grace Kelly** *seemed to be living it up, drinking champagne on screen and making love off screen.*

* * *

The paths of Grace Kelly and Marlon had almost crossed several times in previous years. Looking like a highly polished product of a finishing school, Grace had only just departed from the offices of agent Edith Van Cleve in 1951 before Marlon arrived. His agent told him that she'd just signed "a girl I flipped over after talking to her for only fifteen minutes. Her name is Grace Kelly. I think she's going to become a big Hollywood star. She's not only serenely beautiful but talented!" Edith was instrumental in getting Grace cast in a small role in Henry Hathaway's drama, *Fourteen Hours*, released by 20th Century Fox in 1951.

Working at a theater in Colorado during the summer of 1951, Grace fell in love with Gene Lyons, a good-looking Irish actor with a "brooding charisma" that many critics likened to Marlon's.

In New York, Edith kept Marlon posted on Grace's fast-emerging career. She often said she'd like to have both Grace and Marlon cast in the same film together.

"When I heard that Grace had fallen for Lyons, I was a bit dismissive," Edith said. "Another would-be Method actor, I thought. I told Grace this." Edith even told Marlon about Grace's affair with Lyons, since Lyons was often compared to Marlon.

"Oh, no, not another Brando clone," he said.

"I mentioned this very point to Grace," Edith said. "And guess what she told me? Grace said she'd 'rather have the real thing.'"

Marlon smiled smugly. "Glad to know that," he said. "I'll have to put Grace Kelly on my ever-growing list of stars and starlets to seduce."

Marlon's MCA agent in Hollywood, Jay Kanter, had also been an early promoter of Grace. In fact, Kanter was the agent who brought Grace to the attention of Stanley Kramer and Fred Zinnemann during the casting of *High Noon*.

It had been Edith's dream to see her two favorite clients, Grace Kelly and Marlon, cast in *High Noon*. Both Zinnemann and Kramer, who had produced *The Men* with Marlon, found Grace "very straitlaced and very virginal." She got the part, along with Marlon's girlfriend, Katy Jurado, playing the third lead. The film, of course, would bring Gary Cooper his second Oscar. To win it, he had to beat out the closest runner-up, Marlon for his role in *Viva Zapata!*

The affair between Grace and Marlon might have happened months before it actually did. In addition to such rejects as Joanne Woodward and Elizabeth Montgomery, Kazan had briefly considered casting Grace Kelly in the Eva Marie Saint role in *Waterfront*. "But I finally decided that was ridiculous," Kazan confessed. "Who would have believed Grace Kelly as the girl who grew up in the wilds of the Hoboken waterfront?"

Grace Kelly at her loveliest, the girl thousands of American women desperately tried to emulate.

In her dainty white gloves, Grace's rivaled the poise of Jacqueline Kennedy. But Grace's image was deceiving.

Before their respective Oscar winnings brought them together, Marlon was well aware of Grace's reputation for seducing the A-list stars of Hollywood, of which he was now an exclusive member.

"Despite her lady-like poise, and her somewhat aloof air, Grace had the mentality of a streetwalker," Edith later said. Author Gore Vidal once called her "an easy lay — she was notorious for that."

Only five years older than Grace, Marlon was a bit young by her standards. She was known for her preference for older leading men. During her Hollywood career, the average age of her leading men was forty-six.

When Grace met Marlon, she was already deep into her affair with crooner Bing Crosby, her co-star in *The Country Girl*. He was twenty-six years older than she was. Actually their affair had begun a year and a half before they'd made a film together.

Their affair was often conducted at the home of actor Alan Ladd, a close friend of the singer. Before heading for bed, he often turned out the lights in the living room, leaving the pair on his sofa. "Just lock the door when you guys leave," Ladd would often tell Bing and Grace.

Edith remains the main source of information about the affair between Marlon and Grace. But she regretted that Marlon provided only scant details, "although he used to keep me regally entertained with a lot more information about his affairs with famous actresses, especially those he seduced when appearing on the stage in *Streetcar*. I once told Marlon that listening to his tales of seduction was tantamount to my getting off. So he used to call and say, 'I've got another conquest to report to you. This one is going to make you cream your bloomers.'"

Apparently, during Marlon's first hour with Grace, he had to listen to her complaints about Bing Crosby. Although she'd just won the Oscar for *The Country Girl*, he claimed that Bing had almost denied her the role, since he had approval of his leading lady. "He thought I was too beautiful," Grace told Marlon. "Not drab enough."

"Bing Crosby has a point there," Marlon said.

Unknown to Marlon at the time, Bing had fallen deeply in love with Grace and wanted her to marry him since the death of his wife, Dixie Lee, had left him a widower. "But I'm not in love with him," Grace had told her friends. She also told the same friends that Bing was refusing to take no for an answer.

From left to right, the stars of *The Country Girl:* **Grace Kelly, Bing Crosby**, and **William Holden**.

Crosby recalled, "I seduced many of my leading ladies. When I met Grace, I dumped Jane Wyman, Reagan's ex and my co-star in *Just for You* (1952).

What happened in Grace's suite around three o'clock that morning is still not known in exact details, but Bing arrived for a showdown with Grace. Instead of that, he found a nude Marlon in her bed.

"That must have been doubly difficult for Bing," Edith said. "Earlier in the evening he'd been denied the Oscar by Marlon, his last chance. Now he finds the same young nude stud in Grace's bed. Reportedly, there were fisticuffs. What chance did an aging, drunken singer have against a well-built young actor who was also a boxer? Marlon was a bit vague, but I gathered that he knocked out the voice behind *White Christmas*."

From what Edith gathered, Grace called both the house doctor and the hotel manager. A drunken Bing was removed to another suite as Grace and Marlon resumed their affair.

Edith speculated—and it was pure conjecture on her part—that Grace knew that Bing was going to drop in on her after he'd made the round of Hollywood parties where well-wishers tried to console him for his loss of the Oscar to Marlon.

"Frankly, I think Grace wanted to dump Bing and just used Marlon to help her do just that," Edith said. "Since he wouldn't listen to her refusals of marriage, and since he kept begging her to marry him, the drama queen in Grace came up with a way to make her point. What better way to tell a man that you're not going to marry him than to dramatize it with a nude Marlon Brando in your bed with a full erection raring to go."

After Oscar night, Bing Crosby joined Frank Sinatra in developing a life-long hatred for Marlon.

Today, Grace Kelly's fame resides in more places than show-biz. Depicted above is the postage stamp issued in her honor after her marriage to Rainier of Monaco.

The lower photo evokes memories of everyone in Monaco of the role she played there during her reign as the principality's most celebrated spokesperson.

IN MEMORIAM, REST IN PEACE
GRACE KELLY

Bricklayer's Daughter, Movie Star, International Icon,
and a Princess of Monaco
(1929-1982)

Chapter Seventeen

THE BIZARRE STORY OF THE POLITICAL LOYALTIES AND CENSORSHIP PROBLEMS WHIRLING AROUND THE MOST BEAUTIFUL WOMAN IN THE WORLD
HEDY LAMARR

Two views of the actress the world knew as **Hedy Lamarr**, left photo, as seventeen-year-old **Hedwig Kiesler**, nude after simulating an orgasm onscreen in Gustav Machaty's avant-garde film, *Ecstasy* (1933).

Right photo, near the end of her career, with **Victor Mature**, playing Samson, who wishes he hadn't snubbed her in her portrayal of the bloodthisty courtesan Delilah in Cecil B. De-Mille's romantic Biblical drama, *Samson and Delilah* (1949).

Toward the end of her career, around the time she met Darwin Porter (they shared the same literary agent) she was self-absorbed and oblivious to the shock waves her peppery dialogue seemed to catalyze among judgmental listeners.

She visited **Magnolia House** for parties hosted by Darwin, who sometimes escorted her to parties and social events in Manhattan.

As the years went by, and from all reports, Howard Hughes, the aviator and producer, didn't bring many women to orgasm. Starlets, call girls, and Las Vegas chorines reported the same sad story. But in 1939 Hughes met "the queen of orgasms," as she was called—based on the plot of her first movie—in Hollywood.

267

In one of her first films, Gustav Machaty's *Extase*, filmed in 1932, Hedy was billed as Hedy Kiesler. (Just before the launch of her film career in Hollywood, she was renamed by Louis B. Mayer as Hedy Lamarr in honor of Barbara LaMarr, one of Hughes' early girlfriends, and an actress who seems to have elicited genuine sorrow from Mayer at the time of her early death.) Released in America as *Ecstasy*, the movie had made Hedy a notorious figure in cinema. Hughes had screened it ten times and had been fascinated by the scene that depicted her swimming, then running through the woods in the nude. The director had also asked the actress to play a scene in the film in which she simulated orgasm. In real life, Hedy didn't have to fake such passion. It was genuine.

Hughes was savvy enough to know that Hedy had little talent as an actress. But she was one of the world's true beauties. "Even if she can't act," he told Noah Dietrich, his chief aide. "I can always look at her."

On a visit to the set of *Lady of the Tropics* (1939), being filmed at Metro-Goldwyn-Mayer, Hughes encountered Hedy after she'd just finished playing a love scene with his sometimes boyfriend, Robert Taylor. They shook hands and looked into each other's eyes before the actress retreated to her dressing room.

Later, when they were alone, Taylor revealed to Hughes that he was going to marry Barbara Stanwyck sometime in the very near future. He wanted to know if Hughes had any objections to his wedding the bisexual star. Hughes urged marriage onto the beautiful young man, claiming it would end speculation in Hollywood about Robert's homosexuality. Even though Hughes had rejected the possibility of a "lavender marriage" with Katharine Hepburn, he thought it would be right for his friend. "Stanwyck will throw the bloodhounds off your trail," he told Robert. "Fan magazines will be writing about the great Taylor/Stanwyck romance and

Photo depicts billionaire industrialist and film producer **Howard Hughes** at table with then-starlet **Ginger Rogers.**

Middle and lower photos: **Lamarr** as a "half-caste' temple dancer with **Robert Taylor** in *Lady of the Tropics* (1939). She seduced him on screen, but failed to lure him off screen.

quit concentrating on what you might really be up to. Besides, it'll take the heat off me."

Before leaving the set that day, Hughes knocked on Hedy's door and handed her his private phone number at Muirfield. "Give me a call some night," he suggested to her.

"Mr. Hughes, in Austria, where I come from, it is the gentleman who calls the lady."

"You're in America now," he warned her, "and we have different customs here, especially if we reside in Hollywood." He tipped his fedora to her and walked away.

Later, before its release, he had a copy of *Lady of the Tropics* sent to his home at Muirfield where he screened it in private. He later told Ben Hecht, writer of its screenplay, "Beautiful fuckable Taylor. Beautiful fuckable Lamarr. Beautiful costumes. Exotic story. Lousy picture. But just watching those two on screen will give you something to jerk off to."

In 1966 in New York, Darwin's literary/theatrical agent Jay Garon, director of the Garon/Brooks Agency, hosted a party for Hedy, celebrating the release of her ghostwritten tell-all autobiography, *Ecstasy and Me*. At the party, she spoke candidly about her aborted affair with Howard. But, first, she showed Darwin the results of a recent "elbow lift." After she introduced him to her latest boyfriend—"he's in porno, darling"—she launched into gossip about Hughes, goaded on with an extra dry gin martini.

"I made a man out of Howard Hughes," she said, startling her attentive audience. "I met him on the set of *Lady of the Tropics* in which I was appearing with one of his boyfriends. I forget his name."

"Robert Taylor," Garon butted in.

"Yes, that one. Remember how Greta Garbo devoured him in *Camille*?"

She leaned back on the sofa and asked her porno star to take off her high heels and massage her feet. "At first I was angry when Howard asked me to call him instead of him calling me. But he

Hedy Lamarr with Clark Gable in *Comrade X* (1940)

with **John Garfield** in *Tortilla Flat* **(1942)**

and with **William Powell** in *The Heavenly Body* (1944).

Many gossip witnesses attest to Hedy's romantic and/or sexual affairs with each of the actors depicted on this page.

Other affairs included long or short-term liaisons with Errol Flynn, Charlie Chaplin, James Stewart, Victor Mature, John F. Kennedy, Jean-Pierre Aumont, George Montgomery, Charles Boyer, Burgess Meredith, David Niven, Otto Preminger, George Sanders, Walter Wanger, Rudy Vallee, and Jock Whitney.

was handsome, a little bit sexy, and very, very rich. I finally broke down and made the call. I don't know why. At the time I could have had any other man in Hollywood. All the big stars. Gable. Tracy, James Stewart—they were calling me." She looked with contempt at the young man massaging her shapely feet. "In those days I didn't have to pay for it."

When she reached Hughes by phone that long-ago night at Muirfield, he invited her to come over right away. "I had pictured him inviting me to The Cocoanut Grove and arriving in a big, fat limousine, with sprays of orchids. Nothing like that happened. I put on a simple dirndl I'd purchased in Vienna and drove over to see him. In that garb, I looked like a fourteen-year-old. I'd heard that Howard liked them young. At his home, his housekeeper showed me into his living room. The devil didn't even bother to get up. He was wearing a ratty old bathrobe and some shoddy bedroom slippers. Later that night, I found out he didn't even have on a pair of pajamas under that robe. What a very casual way to receive a lady, I thought."

"He just sat there looking at me," she said. "Didn't even offer me a cocktail. I sat across from him, and we chatted about my life in Austria, my career at MGM. At some point the conversation got personal. I told him that Louis B. Mayer had exposed himself to me in his office and had asked me to perform oral sex on him."

She related that Hughes had given her some career advice. "He told me that a big war was coming, and that Hollywood would soon be churning out one war movie after another. He said that I should tell the studio to cast me only as beautiful Nazi spies. He thought I'd gain international fame if I stuck to playing Nazi spies. Later, I would play spies. But that night I thought that Howard was assuming I might have Nazi leanings, because my country was now controlled by Hitler. I informed him that I was a loyal American."

She did admit that at a party she and her husband, munitions king Fritz Mandl, had hosted back in Austria before the war, Adolf Hitler had kissed her hand. "Obviously he didn't know I was a Jewess."

"Howard seemed eager to learn about my background as Lady Mandl,"

Upper photo: **Fritz Mandl**, munitions supplier for the Third Reich and (middle photo) **Hedwig Kiesler Mandl,** aka **Lady Mandl,** aka **Hedy Lamarr,** in January of 1937, shortly after their wedding, and

(lower photo) **Schloss Schwarzenau,** their Renaissance-era home, later the site of filming for *The Sound of Music* (1965).

she claimed. "I told him that I had two bodyguards and twenty servants in those days. Fritz gave me everything. All the jewelry in the world, beautiful gowns, eight cars. But he kept me a virtual prisoner and had me guarded day and night. He loved power and beautiful women. It was said that whenever he wanted to drum up some business for his munitions sales, he'd merely start a war somewhere."

"Considering that Howard was practically ready for bed when he greeted me, I just assumed at one point he'd make a pass at me," she said. "It was growing later and later. He made no move to seduce me. Finally, he asked me rather bluntly, 'Would you like to make ten thousand dollars in cash?'"

"I was insulted," she said. "I informed him that a prominent member of the Krupp family in Germany had once offered to give me half a million dollars in diamonds, emeralds, and rubies for 'one night of ecstasy' with me. I refused him."

"Sensing that he'd insulted me, Howard apologized," she claimed. "He said I had misunderstood him. For the ten thousand dollars, he wanted me to pose nude for him. From that photograph, he was going to instruct his engineers—if that's what they were—to make a life-sized replica of me in rubber. Realistic down to the last detail. He even wanted my vagina molded from life so that my dummy would have an exact duplicate of my sexual organs. I was horrified at the suggestion."

Hedy's last and final film was **The Female Animal** (1958), in which she was typecast as a glamourous but fading screen actress. Jane Powell played her emotionally disturbed daughter. They both compete for the love of George Nader.

"I found George an exciting male," Hedy said. "Rock Hudson arrived on the set to retrieve him after work. He was even more exciting. But, alas, they had eyes only for each other."

"He said that the reason for the dummy was that he didn't feel worthy of taking the real me," she claimed. 'You're too much of a goddess,' he told me."

At that point in her recitation, Hedy's porn-stud boyfriend mocked Howard's comment. "I'll have to use that line on some chick some night. It's a great seduction technique."

Hedy scolded him for being "a naughty boy," then continued. "I got up from the sofa and stood before Howard. 'You're worthy,' I told him."

"I kneeled down on the carpet and opened his bathrobe," she said. "I told him 'why bother with some stupid rubber dummy when he could have the real thing?' I performed oral sex. He took me into his library, and we made love all night. Don't believe all those stories that jealous women spread about Howard being impotent. He was very virile with me."

"Howard bedded me that night, and I think it was more thrilling for him than it was for me," she claimed, "even though I experienced multiple orgasms. He seemed to view this as the greatest accomplishment of his career. I think he considered himself lucky if he gave a woman one orgasm. What he didn't know was that I experienced frequent orgasms when having sex with most men. With some men, I had uncountable orgasms."

Hedy was perhaps the only movie star memoirist who ever wrote publicly about her tendency for multiple orgasms.

Despised autocrats (**Mussolini,** *left*, and **Hitler,** *right*) shared a mutual fascination with erotic clips of Hedwig (Hedy) Kiesler (Lamarr).

Her husband, munitions king Fritz Mandl, supplied weapons to the two war-mongering dictators.

On another note, she added, "Men have told me that they can get an orgasm just by looking at me on the screen. I know for a fact that men attended my movies and masturbated under their jackets."

After the night of the orgasms, Hedy claimed that Howard "fell madly in love with me and sent me flowers every day, but our affair lasted for just a few short weeks."

"What went wrong?" she was asked.

"He wanted to marry me and make a prisoner of me," she said. "I wasn't ready for that. I had been married to Fritz when I became Lady Mandl in Austria, and he kept me under guard all the time, not wanting another man to look at me. I couldn't go through an experience like that ever again."

She was asked what the jealous Mandl thought of her nudity on the screen in *Ecstasy*. "He tried to purchase all the prints, but never succeeded because of bootleg copies. Benito Mussolini refused to sell Fritz his copy, and I know for a fact that Hitler watched the film several times."

"There was no way I could escape from Fritz and plunge into a marriage with yet another man who wanted to imprison me," she said. "Of course, Howard was

Algiers (1938) teamed **Hedy** with the French heartthrob **Charles Boyer**, cast as Pepe Le Moko, who is wanted by the French police.

In the Casbah, "the melting pot of the world," he encounters Hedy's "Gaby," who was described as "Impeccably attired in a black evening gown with pearls, her lipstick glistening on full sensual lips, her eyebrows arched, skin white as marble."

very rich, like Fritz, and I tend to like very rich men. But on my own, I made thirty million dollars. Regrettably, I wasted it all and made many bad decisions. I stupidly turned down the starring role in Casablanca, fearing it might be too similar to my role in Algiers. That Swedish peasant, Ingrid Bergman, got it instead. I also turned down Gaslight which the bitch also took. I finally told Howard I didn't need him. Later in life, I would need him, but by then it was too late."

She claimed that she repeatedly warned him not to fall in love with her, as so many other unfortunate men had done. She cited the case of Ritter Franz von Hochstatten, who came from one of Germany's most distinguished families. "I wouldn't give up my career to marry him, and he hung himself. I didn't want that to happen to Howard, but I feared he'd do something drastic when I turned him down."

"Had I married Howard," she said, "he would never have had any need for another woman. When you have the world's most beautiful woman in your bed, there is no need for any other."

Any girl can be glamorous. All you have to do is stand still and look stupid - Hedy Lamarr

Portrait of **Frau Mandl** (Hedy) as an Austro-German socialite during the Nazi takeover of Germany in the 1930s, a LONG way from Hollywood.

Before the end of that long-ago party in 1966, the agent, Jay Garon, Hedy's porno boyfriend, and Darwin each assured Hedy that she was the most spectacular creature since God created Eve—and that she ranked up there with Helen of Troy. Even Agnès Sorel in the Middle Ages did not equal her beauty.

"Why else would Cecil B. DeMille cast me as Delilah?" she asked. "The temptress of the ages."

"Because you knew how to deliver a mean haircut," Garon quipped.

***

[Hedy was driven to Magnolia House on Staten Island on two separate occasions, Darwin also escorted her to social events in New York and visited her in later years in Florida. She told him fascinating stories about her life,

At last, her remarkable, almost unbelievable story is the subject of a movie, *Bombshell: The Hedy Lamarr Story*.

Her story began in Vienna in 1914 when she was born on the eve of World War I, whose aftermath included the collapse of the Austro-Hungarian Empire. She had always wanted to be an actress, and by 1933, she appeared in Gustav Machaty's notorious film, *Ecstasy*, in which she was seen running nude in the woods. In that controversial, avant-garde film, she was also depicted in the throes of orgasm. (Machaty achieved the desired effect by sticking a pin into her).

She abandoned her career when she married Fritz Mandl, an Austrian arms merchant selling munitions to fuel the Nazi war machine. Ironically, both the sadistic Mandl and Hedy were Jewish.

During that loveless marriage, she entertained, and was entertained by, the elite hierarchies of the Fascist world. She found Hitler "an arrogant, dangerous *poseur*," and Mussolini "a pompous ass."

On a hunt for new talent in Europe, Louis B. Mayer discovered the divorced actress and signed her to an MGM contract, hoping to replace Greta Garbo, who would soon retire.

She became an overnight sensation upon the release of *Algiers* (1938), starring Charles Boyer. Luminous, she was forever after associated with praise for her porcelain skin, her large, marbly eyes, her lilting Viennese accent, her Mona Lisa smile, and her aura of mystery. Throughout the course of the 1940s (the heyday of her film career), she seemed more like a celluloid mannequin than a natural woman.

Some of the era's most famous movie stars seduced her, including Errol Flynn, Charlie Chaplin, James Stewart, Robert Taylor, Stewart Granger, Victor Mature, William Powell, and John Garfield.

Along the way, she picked up five more husbands and had an affair with a young naval hero, who had recently returned from the war in the Pacific. "John F. Kennedy was charming, handsome, charismatic, and a real heartbreaker," she told Darwin.

As the years wore on, Hedy tried, unsuccessfully, to rescue her fading beauty with cosmetic surgeries.

Often dazed and confused, she became involved in two shoplifting incidents. The first was in June of 1961 at the May Company Department Store in Los Angeles, where she walked out with gold slippers and various sundries. At the time, her purse contained $14,000 of undeposited checks.

Yes, as Louis B. Mayer choreographed it, everyone DID want to see more and more and more of Hedy. Who was the inspiration for the name Mayer gave the Austro-German exile reportedly fleeing from the (much contested) allegations of abuse in her well-connected marriage to the Nazi arms dealer Fritz Mandl?

She was silent screen star **Barbara LaMarr** (*center photo above*), whom gossips said had infatuated Mayer since his adolescence, and who did, indeed, bear some similarities to the exotic European import (**Hedwig Kiesler Mandl**) that Mayer was promoting so relentlessly at the time.

Gustav Machaty (1901-1963), the ultra avant-garde Czech film director who stuck a pin into Hedwig Kiesler.

It was a jab that (to viewers at least) evoked an orgasm, as displayed in Hedy's early, and most scandalous film, *Ecstasy* (1933)

The second shoplifting incident transpired in August of 1991 in Casselberry, Florida. Once again, she walked out with unpaid merchandise—in this case, $21.48 worth of laxative tablets and eyedrops. Eventually, both charges were dropped.

"She was a dear, tormented soul, obsessively sharing memories of a fabled life," Darwin said.

She died on January 19, 2000, age 85, in Altamonte Springs, Florida. Her son, Anthony Loder, flew with her ashes to Austria and tossed them into the winds rustling through the Vienna Woods. She left a $3.5 million estate.

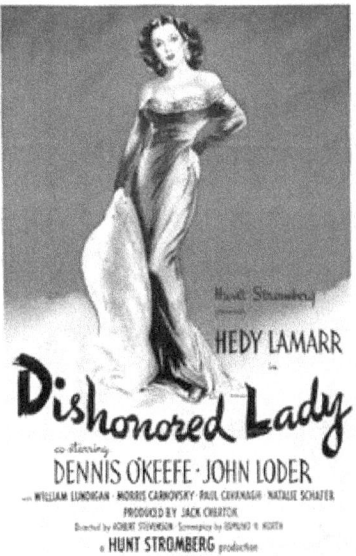

Swathed in furs, **Hedy Lamarr** arrives at a formal affair with **Sir John Loder**, the British actor and her third husband. They had co-starred in *Dishonored Lady* (1947).

He was out of work, but she demanded he pay room and board at their Beverly Hills home. For months he was ordered out of her bedroom, but unexpectedly summoned back for only one night. After a certain time had passed, she came into their living room and announced, "I am pregnant, and I want a divorce."

The "forbidden movie" arrives in America

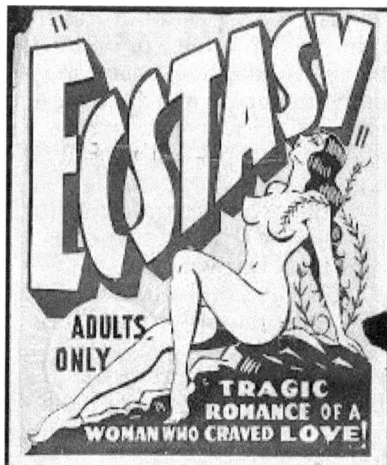

Poor Hedy.... Despite her inbred glamour and Central European gloss, she never managed to escape the whiff of softcore porn that had launched her career as an actress.

Her salty language, earthy references, and what even her friends described as a relentless streak of narcissism didn't help.

But the notoriety cut both ways. Whereas the images at the top of this page replicate the erotic thrill she catalyzed to late-night moviegoers at porn theaters in Times Square, the lower images show the effects that millions of dollars of Hollywood press, makeup, and PR contributed to the creation known throughout World War II and the decade that followed as **THE MOST BEAUTIFUL WOMAN IN THE WORLD.**

Hedy as Tondelaya in *White Cargo*

They called her "GIVE IT HELL HEDY!!"

Perhaps it was her German accent, or at least during the debut of her career, her frequent errors in grammar. But something about Hedy Lamarr lent itself to camp. It was a quality that some drag queens tried—with varying degrees of success— to emulate.

In this tribute to Hedy Lamarr's sometimes over-the-top allegiance to whatever was pop cultish at the moment, HEEEEERE'S HEDY.

Hedy, *(left)* dolled up with Judy Garland (center) and Lana Turner (right) in *Ziegfeld Girl*

Hedy (second from left) with her co-stars in *Boom Town* (left to right) Spencer Tracy, Claudette Colbert, & Clark Gable

Hedy, bad and beautiful, as a bloodthirsty courtesan in *Samson & Delilah*

  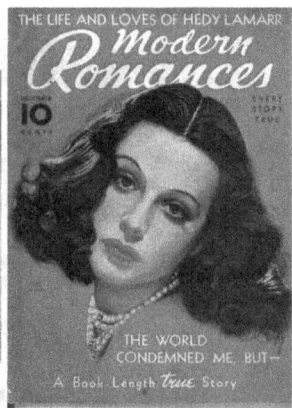

In a whirlwind that was ironic by anyone's standards, the mysterious European import, reincarnated as **Hedy Lamarr**, appeared as a cover girl in a daunting array of newspapers, including (*left*) the June 1, 1942 cover of LIFE during some of the bloodiest victories of the Nazi regime, in the midst of which she had been a prominent hostess.

One can only imagine what Hitler and his cronies said about it from their fortresses in Berlin.

Her detractors (including many of the people Darwin Porter introduced her to) defined Hedwig Kiesler Mandl Markey Loder Stauffer Lee Boies (aka **Hedy Lamarr**) as self-enchanted. But, as Darwin editorialized, "Anyone who looked like Hedy, a survivor of six marriages and a life story that's almost beyond imagination, can be forgiven a personal quirk or two."

In the final years of her life, in a style replicated by Marlene Dietrich, the worldly and very sophisicated Lamarr lived in seclusion, communicating—even with her close friends and children—only by telephone. A grotesque shadow of her former beauty, she often stayed on the phone for up to seven hours a day, almost never leaving the confines of her Florida home.

HEDY LAMARR
1914-2000
REST IN PEACE

Chapter Eighteen

JACK DEMPSEY
THE WORLD'S HEAVYWEIGHT BOXING CHAMPION

AND HIS WIDELY PUBLICIZED DALLIANCE WITH THE SEX VAMP

MAE WEST
"IT AIN'T NO SIN"

Between World Wars One and Two, the World's Heavyweight Boxing Champ **Jack Dempsey** ignited the imagination of the American public, prompting some of the greatest writers and artists of that era to depict his exploits in newspaper articles, in history books, and on canvas.

Depicted above is *George Bellows' iconic 1924 painting, Jack Dempsey and (Luis Angel) Firpo.* It elevated Dempsey into a revered symbol of the American definition of fortitude, perseverance, and grit.

Dempsey himself—a two-time visitor to Magnolia House during his later years—emerged as the winner and hero of both the painting and the fight.

He also won the seductive affections of America's then-reigning sex goddess, **Mae West**, depicted in the right-hand corner, above.

279

"I was a pretty good fighter. But it was the writers who made me great."

—Jack Dempsey

According to Darwin, "It never occurred to me that I would one day meet Jack Dempsey, the former Heavyweight Boxing Champion (1919-1926) of the world. He entered my world late in his own life, and we became friends. He rarely discussed boxing with me."

"He knew I was a Hollywood writer, and he liked sharing a dream that never came true. Instead of a star in the ring, he wanted to be a star on the screen like John Wayne and Gary Cooper."

Darwin's meeting came about through an unlikely source. To get a fine arts insurance policy covering Magnolia House and its contents, he had to hire an appraiser. He was led to an art and antiques specialist who was credited as "the best in the business." He was also warned that the candidate "is an effeminate flamer."

Stanley Cranston pranced into his life and spent most of his first day at Magnolia House going about his work. Darwin agreed to drive him back to Manhattan, where Cranston had scheduled a dinner with a client and his wife.

A Hollywood poll in the 1920s cited boxer **Jack Dempsey** as "the sexiest man in the world." Fan mail from "love-sick" females poured in from across the country, sometimes including graphic details about what they wanted Dempsey to do to them.

He had been told that he could bring a guest to the dinner, and consequently, Darwin was included in the gathering. To his amazement, it included Jack Dempsey and his fourth wife, the former Deanna Piatelli.

"I liked Jack, a kind and generous man," Darwin said. "He was not the super macho thug I had in mind, that of a boxer who rose to fame clobbering other boxers in the ring."

"Not only that, but I found we had a mutual interest in Hollywood. It seemed that Jack had never really wanted to be a boxer, but a movie star like John Wayne and Gary Cooper, a leading man to the sex goddess, Mae West."

"Before I had my second dinner with Jack, I read up on his career," Darwin confessed.

Subsequent generations might be unaware of this, but at one time in the Roaring Twenties, during his reign as the heavyweight boxing champion of the world, Jack Dempsey was the most famous man on the planet.

Born in 1895 to an impoverished family in Colorado, he was of Irish, Cherokee, and Jewish ancestry. As a boy, he attended the Mormon Church.

Restless and wanting to be on his own, he ran away at the age of sixteen and survived riding the rails and sleeping in hobo camps. As he told Darwin, "I think I learned to use my fists by beating the hell out of those boy molesters I came across."

As he grew older and was in need of money, he would barge into a seedy tavern and issue a challenge. "I can't sing. I can't dance. But I can lick any SOB in here. Wanna take me on?"

He always found a challenger, and betting was high. As the victor, he made off with his share. By the time he hit Salt Lake City, he was billing himself as "Kid Blackie."

"One night in this mining town, a group of guys—I think all of them were homosexuals—offered a $500 purse if I'd enter the ring with their local stud. I'd get the money if I won, but only if I'd box without my trunks. Same for the kid. I won."

During World War I, he worked in a shipyard and kept up with his boxing bouts. He was nonetheless defined as a "slacker" for not enlisting in the U.S. Army. *[He had tried to enlist, but was classified as 4-F.]*

On the night of July 4, 1919, Dempsey came into world prominence by defeating heavyweight champ Jess Willard in Toledo,

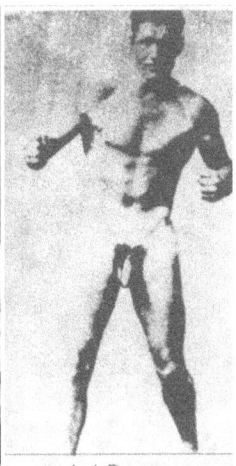

Jack Dempsey

Jack Dempsey, pictured here with an aide, circa 1919, recalled, "Before my notorious fight against champ Jess Willard, I didn't realize my inner fury. I was soon to commit the worst carnage in modern boxing history. I beat his blood-soaked body until he was spitting out teeth from his broken jaw."

Mae West summoned her photographer to snap a picture of her lover, **Jack Dempsey**, in the nude. She told him it was only for her private enjoyment to hang in her luxurious bathroom. The photographer retained the negative, and prints of it were distributed underground across the nation.

The Champ (Jack Dempsey) & the Vamp (Mae West)

Ohio. Nicknamed "the Pottawatmie Giant," Willard stood 6'7" and weighed 245 pounds, in contrast to Dempsey, who stood 6'1" and weighed 187. He KO'd Willard seven times, leaving him with broken ribs, broken teeth, a broken jaw, and deep fractures to the bones and muscles of his face.

After winning the title, Dempsey toured America, performing at circuses and staging exhibitions. He also got to work in boxing scenes in low-budget silent films.

One of the most highly touted of his matches was his fight against the French World War I hero, Georges Carpentier. George Bernard Shaw had hailed him as "The Greatest Boxer in the World."

The Dempsey/Carpentier fight took place on July 2, 1921 in Jersey City, the first million-dollar gate in boxing history.

Before 91,000 fans in the auditorium, and broadcast to a radio audience of millions, it was "The Fight of the Century." Carpentier broke his left thumb in the first round but soldiered on to lose.

***

Dempsey first met Mae West when he attended her stage play (*The Music World of 1921*) in Manhattan. As he claimed, "I laughed louder than anybody else in the audience, and thought Mae West was one hot number. She even called me onstage to referee a mock

One summer evening in 1919 in the searing heat of Toledo, Ohio, **Jack Dempsey** dethroned **Jess Willard**, the heavyweight champion of the world.

It was something akin to manslaughter. Ringside reporter Damon Runyon described it best: "A bleeding, helpless hulk, Willard, the Kansas giant, was mangled by Dempsey, the young mountain lion of the Sangre de Cristo Hills of Colorado. Blood was dripping from head to toe, his eyes nearly blinded, his limbs shook like custard. Contusions, cuts, abrasions—the hearing in one ear gone, ribs busted—what a sight."

boxing match. At the end, she whispered to me to come to her dressing room after the curtain fell. It was the beginning of a torrid affair."

"I didn't leave her hotel suite until Monday morning," he said. "Mae brought in a photographer friend of hers to photograph me in the nude. It seemed that she had a thing for boxers, both black and white. She said that you couldn't say a lot about them until they removed their boxing trunks."

He was at her apartment when the reviews of her show arrived.

Variety wrote that in her act "she left nothing undone. In her skin-tight clothes, she cooched and wiggled and took falls and vamped. She was pretty snappy."

The New York World likened her shimmy to a woman "trying to get out of a straight jacket without the

In her films, **Mae West** was most often pictured in floor-length gowns. But in her heyday, she didn't mind posing for cheesecake.

"In the 1940s," she said, "Betty Grable's legs were voted the most beautiful in the world. But in my heyday, my gams would beat out hers in any contest."

Years after Jack Dempsey exited from her life, Mae West continued her public fascination with prizefighters, athletes, and bodybuilders. Left photo above shows **Rocky Graziano** (Heavyweight Boxing Champ from 1952-1956) mock-sparring with a visibly aged **Mae** for a publicity shot just prior to one of his fights.

Right-hand photo above shows Mae in yet another publicity shot with a body-building extra, **Ric Drasin**, during the filming of her ultra-campy final film, *Sextette* (1978). Although it was a commercial failure, fans and sociologists alike found it fascinating as an insight into her die-hard sense of narcissim.

The Champ (Jack Dempsey) & the Vamp (Mae West)

use of her hands."

As Dempsey heard years later, West didn't limit access to her all-white boudoir, with its mirrored ceiling, just to boxers and wrestlers. Coming and going were the likes of Duke Ellington, too.

She also went after movie stars known for their endowments, including Forrest Tucker (he referred to his penis as "The Chief"); George Raft (Mae named his "Black Snake"); Steve Cochran (he celebrated his as "The Schvantz"); Gary Cooper ("The Montana Mule"), David Niven ("The Beer Can"); and Cary Grant ("who doesn't measure up").

"When I rejected a proposition from Jack, he accused me of being a lesbian," **Myrna Loy** claimed.

She also went for gangsters, notably Owney Madden and Bugsy Siegel.

At one point, Dempsey amused West by proposing that the two of them, as a romantic duo, become lovers on the screen.

As the world knows, that didn't happen, the honor going instead to George Raft, Cary Grant or his lover, Randolph Scott, brutish Victor McLaglen, handsome Johnny Mack Brown, gay Edmund Lowe, and even W.C. Fields.

Mae's career ended in *Sextette* (1976), where she co-starred (and sometimes feuded) with Ringo Star, Tony Curtis, Timothy Dalton, George Hamilton, and Dom DeLuise. Even Walter Pidgeon got in on the act.

***

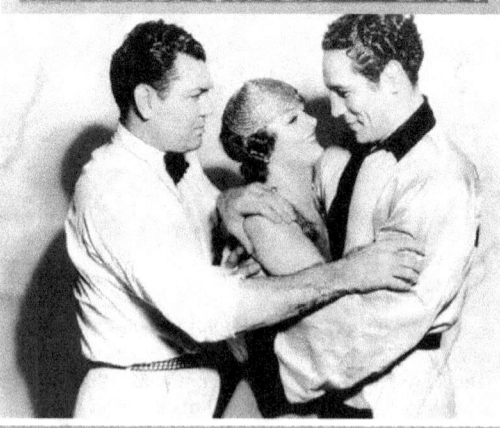

In *The Prizefighter and the Lady*, Myrna Loy is trapped between two bruisers, **Jack Dempsey** (left) and Italian-born **Primo Carnera**, nicknamed "the Ambling Alp" by his legions of fans. .

As was inevitable, Dempsey in time lost his title. This came in September of 1926 when he boxed Gene Tunney, a former U.S. Marine, in Philadelphia. After a grueling ten rounds, Tunney was declared the victor.

As Dempsey explained to his then wife, Estelle Taylor, "I forgot to duck, honey."

Years later, President Ronald Reagan would use Dempsey's exact words when, in the aftermath of an assassination attempt, he told Nancy the same thing.

Movie star handsome: Here's **Jack** after a "cosmeticization" by the Hollywood film industry.

Dempsey still clung to his dream of becoming a Hollywood leading man, and he was elated when director W.S. Van Dyke from MGM called him about appearing in his latest movie, *The Prizefighter and the Lady* (1933).

Darwin learned about what went on behind the scenes during the making of that early talkie from Myrna Loy in Florida. She was touring onstage in Tampa and St. Petersburg with a friend of his in a play called *Relatively Speaking*.

"Van Dyke didn't make it clear to Dempsey," she said, "and he was horribly disappointed when he arrived on the set to find he was not playing the boxer, but himself as the referee in a bout between Max Baer and the then-heavyweight champ, Primo Carnera. Dempsey was humiliated. Not only was Baer a bigtime boxer and in his prime, but he was a rival for the affections of Mae West."

On Broadway, in the era of Damon Runyon, **Jack Dempsey** was a key player, welcoming diners to his hot spot restaurant in the Brill Building between 49th and 50th Streets. Many journalists defined it as "An American institution."

Myrna told Darwin that originally, under the direction of Howard Hawks, *The Prizefighter and the Lady* was to have been a vehicle for Clark Gable and Norma Shearer. After Shearer dropped out, the role went to Jean Harlow, which was convenient, since she was engaged in an affair with Gable at the time.

"We teased each other a lot on the set, playing dirty tricks on each other," Myrna said. "When I heard that Baer was terrified of mice, I released a toy mouse into the ring while the boxing match was being shot. Baer jumped into the arms of Carnera!"

"Max was not only afraid of that little toy, but Van Dyke told me he was nervous as hell during a kissing scene with me. He had seen me in other films onscreen, and thought I was a grand lady—and that made him scared."

"I was cast as Belle Mercer, who had this thing for boxers, evoking Mae West in her private life. When Max kissed me, I could feel him shaking. His smooch was like that of a high school boy on his first date. Imagine this timidity from a giant boxer who had once killed a man in the ring."

Dempsey never became a movie star but morphed into an icon of the 20th Century. Sports writers praised his exceptional punching power and aggressive fighting. By 1950, the Associated Press named him the greatest boxer of the previous fifty years.

In Manhattan on May 31, 1983, at the age of 87, Dempsey suffered a heart attack and died. He was buried in Southampton on Long Island.

The time he spent at Magnolia House was memorialized with the installation of two garden plaques, depicted below, which were installed on one of its terraces, in his memory, shortly after his death.

His widow, Deanna, lived until 2003.

Magnolia House Remembers

Jack Dempsey

Prizefighter, Actor, Restaurateur and Mensch

(1895-1983)
Rest in Peace

"A champion is someone who gets up when he can't."
—Jack Dempsey

MAE WEST
SIZE MATTERED

Born in 1893, The Little Chickadee wasn't so little. Looking her up and down, Adolph Zukor, Paramount honcho, said, "When I look at that dame's tits, I know what lusty means." Costume designer Edith Head said, "I've seen Mae West without a stitch and she's all woman. No hermaphrodite could have bosoms, well, like two large melons."

West loved boxers, black or white, including Jack Dempsey. For years she kept a nude picture of him over her toilet. She also liked wrestlers and especially men with well-built physiques and endowments. That's why she hired Mickey Hargitay (Mr. Universe) and Steve Cochran for her stage act. She wasn't opposed to what she called "The Music Men" either, namely, Duke Ellington and Oscar Hammerstein II. Of the magician, Harry Houdini, she said, "He didn't escape my trap."

She dated George Raft but finally concluded that, "He liked a boy's rosebud more than my bush." Gangsters gave her a special thrill, especially Benjamin "Bugsy" Siegel. "That mobster knew how to shoot in more ways than one."

When she appeared with Cary Grant, she claimed, "I knew he was a homosexual before he did." She failed to seduce another homosexual, Rock Hudson. Later he said, "She was just plain and simply a sweet old lady who told me marvelous stories about her life." She even told him about the day that Marlene Dietrich tried to seduce her. "I go for men, and then only if they're hung like Anthony Quinn."

The Champ (Jack Dempsey) & the Vamp (Mae West)

MAE WEST
Sizing Up Mae's Men:
Muscle Mattered; Color Didn't

Mr. Universe, Hungarian-born actor **Mickey Hargitay**, later, the husband of Jayne Mansfield

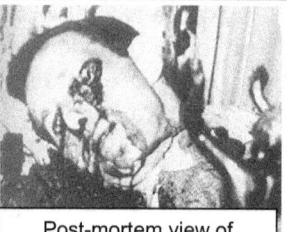

Post-mortem view of mobster **Mickey Cohen**

Mae with Hollywood actor and tough guy **George Raft**

World Heavyweight Boxing Champ (1937-49) **Joe Louis**

Marvelous **Mae**

Composer, pianist, & jazz artist **Duke Ellington**

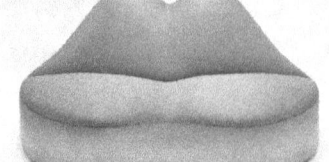

Surrealist artist Salvador Dali's design for a sofa inspired by **Mae West's lips**

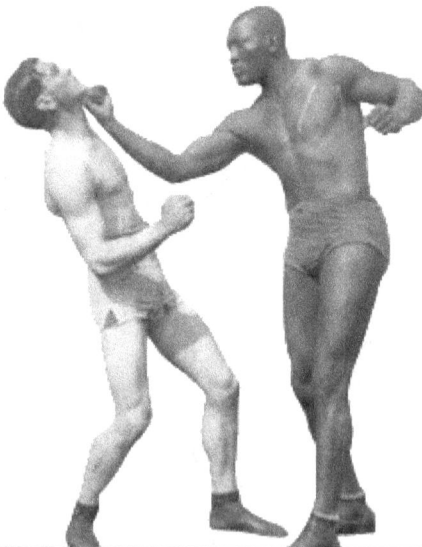

"The Galveston Giant," World Heavyweight Champion **Jack Johnson** (right) vs. Stanley Ketchel (1909).

Chapter Nineteen

How Magnolia House Developed a Close Relationship to the Memory of Those Bombshells from Budapest

THE GABOR SISTERS

and their Formidable Mother

JOLIE

Blood Moon's **Bombshells from Budapest** explored the tangled, glamorous lives of not only their family's matriarch, **Jolie Gabor** (right), but of her combustible daughters—Magda, Zsa Zsa, and Eva.

The Hollywood Book Festival defined it as the **Best Biography of 2013**. It revealed tons of never-before-told secrets of relentlessly charming women born into an era when girls like them were reared to be courtesans like Madame du Barry.

In 2013, Darwin Porter wrote, and Danforth Prince produced, the most insightful, most comprehensive, and most scandal-soaked biography of the Gabor sisters *(Those Glamorous Gabors)* ever published. At least some of the information had been distilled from Darwin's conversations in the kitchen of Magnolia House with Jolie Gabor, the stylish and very outspoken mother of the Gabor sisters. Jolie would sometimes visit her long-time friend, the cabaret chanteuse Greta Keller, then a guest of Darwin and a resident of his house. *[For more about Ms. Keller and her long-*

term residency in Magnolia House, please refer to Chapter 14 of this book.]

Here in the sections that follow are some excerpts from Darwin's biography, *Those Glamorous Gabors*, each replicated in honor of their mother, Jolie, whose insights into cuisine, European history, her world-famous daughters, and affairs of the heart used to keep Greta, Darwin, and other members of their entourages entertained for hours. CHEERS! And in honor of Jolie Gabor, happy reading.

***

Except for fans and aficionados, Jolie Gabor is a forgotten name today. But for much of the latter half of the 20th Century, she and her daughters "The Blondes from Budapest—Great Courtesans of the 20th Century" dominated gossipy headlines throughout America.

Zsa Zsa became the most famous, followed by Eva, who reached her greatest exposure on the hit TV sitcom, *Green Acres* (1965-71). Least famous (but ironically, the richest) of the three was the oldest sister, Magda.

Born in Central Europe at the twilight of the Austro-Hungarian Empire, Magda, Zsa Zsa, and Eva, transferred their glittery dreams and gold-digging ambitions to Hollywood.

They supplemented America's most imperial age with "guts, glamour, and goulash," and reigned as modern equivalents of Helen of Troy, Madame du Barry, and Madame de Pompadour.

More lethal than an army, they conquered kings, dukes, and princes, always with a special passion for millionaires, as they amassed fortunes, broke hearts, and amused sophisticated *voyeurs* on two continents. With their wit, charm, and beauty, thanks to training inspired by the glittering traditions of the Imperial Habsburgs, they became famous for being famous.

Today's Paris Hilton is an offspring of this fabulous clan.

These Magyar temptresses collectively entrapped some 20 husbands and seduced perhaps 500 other men, many plucked directly from the pages of *Who's Who in the World*. They included such towering figures as John F. Kennedy and Conrad Hilton, who made Zsa Zsa his bride, at least for a while.

Add to that list Tyrone Power, Glenn Ford, Frank Sinatra, Kemal Atatürk (Dictator of Turkey), Charles de Gaulle, Richard Burton, Sean Connery, Prince Aly Khan, Franchot Tone, Rafael Trujillo, Jr., Mario Lanza, George Sanders, and the Dominican playboy, Porfirio Rubirosa.

Could it be? Say it isn't so. To the list, one might also add Richard M. Nixon.

Talk show host Merv Griffin once

Eva (left), **Zsa Zsa** (center), and **Magda** (right) gather to celebrate one of Zsa Zsa's birthdays.

One could never be sure which birthday it was. As she aged, Zsa Zsa kept changing the date of her birth. *[Her birth records listed it as February 6, 1917.]*

asked Zsa Zsa how many husbands she'd had: "*Dah-link,* you mean my own or another woman's?"

Many of the book's details about the early days of the Gabors in Budapest were gleaned from interviews with elderly people who knew them before their flight to America. Over a period of at least twenty years, Darwin and his publisher, Blood Moon's CEO, Danforth Prince, visited Budapest yearly to gather interviews and documentation about the Gabors, and to update successive editions of the travel guide they originated and updated at biannual intervals, *Frommer's Hungary.*

Greta, incidentally, had commissioned Darwin to ghost-write her cookbook, *Food for Love,* many of whose recipes originated with the Hussars.

Jolie, too, had written a cookbook, and was coyly angling to enlist Darwin in its redaction, too.

Darwin always looked forward to Jolie's visits because—in addition to turning out fabulous meals in the imperial 19th-century style, she would also relay a gaggle of stories about her fabled past and her sometimes renegade, free-wheeling daughters.

Although it would take a thousand pages to relay the histories whirling around these women, here are some excerpts, each of them culled from *Those Glamorous Gabors*, a widely reviewed title that was voted Best Biography of the Year at the Hollywood Book Festival (2013).

***

It was four o'clock on a dull gray February afternoon in the Hungarian capital of Budapest. The year was 1924. Behind the wheel of her Mercedes, painted a battleship gray, Jolie Gabor was rolling down *Andrassy út*, known as "The Fifth Avenue of Budapest."

In those days, only six ladies of Budapest owned and drove their own cars.

On the seats beside and in back of her sat her beloved daughters—nicknamed "Magdika," age 9; "Zsazsilka," 7; and "Evika," 5.

In the mid-1980s, Porter and Prince were assigned the authorship of what became **that era's pre-eminent travel guide to Austria and Hungary.**

In Budapest, elderly eyewitnesses still remembered the scandals and sensations visited upon their city by **THOSE GLAMOROUS GABORS.**

Jolie trained her daughters in the courtly etiquette of the Austro-Hungarian Empire. Decades later, amid the seismic changes unleashed by World War II, Magda, Zsa Zsa, and Eva adroitly applied them to the postwar entertainment industry of Hollywood.

Depicted above is the interior of Budapest's **Cafe Gerbeaud**, more than a century after the scene described in the pages of this chapter.

Suddenly the sun broke through for the first time that day, adding an extra sparkle to Jolie's diamonds. While getting dressed, she'd told her beautiful daughters, "These are my daytime diamonds. For the evening, I really dazzle. That's when a woman should bring out the king's ransom stones."

She wanted to make a spectacular appearance that afternoon at tea. Both Jolie and her daughters wore scarlet-colored dresses that matched the upholstery of the Mercedes. The clothing had been designed by Jeanne Lanvin, who also designed matching gray coats for each of the Gabors, which duplicated the exact color of the vehicle itself.

The fashion-conscious Jolie preferred the French designer. She was celebrated for her mother-and-daughter outfits and exquisite *robes de style*, as well as for her modern and global approach to fashion. Before heading out, Jolie had also doused her daughters in *Après l'Ondée* by Guerlain (1906). "It's a piece of art created from heliotrope, violet, and iris that gently touches our skin like a scent from heaven."

Goddesses Three, born into the twilight of the Habsburgs, replete with all the niceties and social graces.

Arriving at the Café Gerbeaud, the Gabors, from inside their car, were greeted by a doorman in a puce-colored uniform. Starched, gloved, and beribboned, the daughters emerged first onto the sidewalk.

Franz Lutsky was the manager of the Café Gerbeaud, on *Vörösmarty tér*, which had been founded in 1858 by Swiss confectioner Emile Gerbeaud. It was Jolie's favorite rendezvous. He always reserved the best table for her. Privately he referred to her as "This Magyar mother hen with her three beautiful spring chickens."

Although the café was bustling at that time of day, nearly all of the patrons stopped to take note of the new customers making such a glamorous entrance.

Depicted above on the right are **Vilmos** and **Jolie**, cordial ex-spouses, greeting each other before his death, at a family reunion in Vienna for which Vilmas, still a resident of Hungary, had to receive government approval from the communist regime to attend.

The uninhibited trio on the left are the Gabor sisters (left to right, **Eva, Magda, and Zsa Zsa**) in a *kaffeeklatsch* without display of the ferocious competition that occasionally permeated their notoriously glamorous tribe.

Later, Magda would recall, "Everything that mother did in those days was to teach us a lesson. That day at the café, the lesson involved how to make an entrance. Her forever advice was, 'When you arrive in town, don't keep it a secret.'

The Gabors were about to embark on a life so glamorous Jolie often said in later years, "No one would believe it!"

As designer Donald F. Reuter put it: "The early lives of the Gabors is a fascinating tale that reads like a cross between *Doctor Zhivago* and *Gypsy*, with a generous sprinkling of *Fiddler on the Roof* and *Auntie Mame* thrown in for good measure."

With a grand flourish, the *maître d'hotel* guided Jolie, followed by her "three *vonderful wimmen*" down the long railroad-style layout of the café until they arrived at one of the sitting areas, decorated in a tone of scarlet that matched their dresses. The aging waiter, who had been born in 1854, knew what to bring to table. The aromatic coffee had been dispensed from a *cafetière* whose perimeter was sheathed in hand-painted panels of Herend porcelain—one of only three on Earth, and the confection he brought was the celebrated chocolate-and-marzipan royal torte. "It's positively sinful," Jolie told her daughters. "But a woman born into a man's world must be sinful to advance herself."

***

FAMILY AFFAIRS

Zsa Zsa Gets Indiscreet with Her Stepson, NICKY HILTON

"I was just breaking him in, dah-link, for his future bride, Elizabeth Taylor."

Voyeurs Behind a One-Way Mirror Spy on Zsa Zsa Having Sex with ERROL FLYNN

Shortly after her arrival in the United States, from war-torn Central Europe, on April 10, 1942, Zsa Zsa married the hotel magnate, Conrad Hilton, at the Hotel La Fonda in Santa Fe, New Mexico. Before the wedding, she'd met his three sons, especially one nicknamed Nicky, who had been born in 1926.

"A man's best friend is his mother," or so said young Nicky, when he met his new mother and was most flirtatious with her.

Zsa Zsa told Eva, her matron of honor, "Little boys like Nicky grow up in the most delightful ways. If he takes after his father, 'little' won't be the word to use to describe him."

During the course of most of her marriage to Conrad, Zsa Zsa claimed that "He was always on some business trip to somewhere."

A few months into her marriage, Zsa Zsa began to host her own Hollywood parties at Hilton's Bel Air mansion. Most of A-list movie stars accepted her invitation, unless they had already accepted an invitation to a party next door at the home of Ouida and Basil Rathbone. Ouida had become seriously angry at Zsa Zsa's attempt to upstage her as the most important hostess in Hollywood.

One night, a drunken Errol Flynn showed up on Zsa Zsa's doorstep. He had not been invited but was well-received by the hostess because despite his notoriety, he was one of the leading box office attractions in America.

Earlier, he'd told his pal, actor Bruce Cabot, "I've already fucked one Gabor sister…Why not the other? I hear there's a third one in Hungary, but I'm not going to risk my life to fly to Budapest to plug her. I'll wait until she, too, arrives in Hollywood, as you know she will."

Zsa Zsa later recalled, "Errol was a flirtatious devil. He was about the handsomest man I'd ever seen. It should be against the law for men to look that great."

In a memoir, she had written, "I did not fall prey to Errol Flynn's much vaunted charms. Conrad was out of town, and Errol and I danced together. He whispered to me, 'Darling, come to my house and sleep with me tonight,' his voice pulsating with passion. 'When you wake up in the morning, you will look out my window and see stallions outside—and then you will see what a stallion I am.'"

As it happened, she didn't return to his home with him that night. She waited until the following evening when he invited her to a dinner party at his home on Mulholland Drive.

He liked to pull stunts on female stars, including putting a snake in the dressing room of Olivia de Havilland. For Zsa Zsa, he planned something sexier. As he told actor Bruce Cabot, "I'm hiring Freddie as one of the waiters tonight."

Cabot knew what that meant.

[In Hollywood legend and lore, there were three different Freddies—one in the 1930s, another in the 1940s, and one—whom Joan Collins encountered—in the 1950s. Each of these Freddies had a thick penis that extended for more than a foot. These young men, whose real names have been lost to history, hired themselves out for sex with the stars (they serviced both men and women) or sometimes as party gags.]

Flynn on several occasions had had sex with the 1940s version of Freddie. He'd also devised a gag to use on unsuspecting female guests. He ac-

Zsa Zsa's first husband was Burhan Belge, press director of the Foreign Ministry of Turkey. He took her to Ankara, where she soon became the mistress of **Kemal Atatürk** (left), the dictator revered as "the Father of Modern Turkey."

Of her many husbands, the most famous in America was **Conrad Hilton** (right), the devoutly Catholic founder of the hotel chain.

quired a large salad bowl and arranged for an opening to be drilled into its side.

At the dinner party, at which Zsa Zsa was his guest of honor, he ordered Freddie to produce an erection as a means of "plugging the hole" in the side of the salad bowl. The chef then placed greens in the bowl, and Freddie, outfitted as a waiter, "served the salad" to whomever Flynn had designated.

Zsa Zsa, as she lifted the greens from the bowl onto her plate, screamed when she encountered "a huge, pulsating salami hiding there."

David Niven's biographer, Graham Lord, wrote that "penises were a constant Flynn-Niven preoccupation" when those two actors lived together. Freddie was often a major attraction at their parties. The guests of Flynn and Niven were astonished at Freddie's ability to perform autofellatio."

Three views of the very handsome and very debauched **Errol Flynn**. In the upper right, he's depicted as a prizefighter in *The Perfect Specimen* (1937).

Freddie didn't always serve his penis with salad. One night when Hedy Lamarr was the guest of honor, Freddie's mammoth organ appeared atop a silver tray otherwise spilling over with hors d'oeuvres—quail eggs, caviar, smoked salmon, thin slices of raw beef, and tiny prawns.

A hungry Hedy Lamarr was rather aggressive that night, stabbing at the hors d'oeuvres with a fork. Howling in pain, Freddie dropped the tray and retreated to the bathroom for emergency First Aid.

A few hours later, after that raucous X-rated dinner, Zsa Zsa assumed that the house was emptied of guests, except for Flynn and herself. As he'd done with so many other women before her, the swashbuckling star invited her out onto his terrace to take in the panorama over the sparkling lights of Los Angeles.

"Everything looks so beautiful by moonlight," she said. "All the ugliness is gone."

"You don't need the glow of the moon to enhance your beauty," he assured her, repeating a line he'd used so many times before.

At another party at her Bel Air home, Zsa Zsa told Mickey Rooney about her experience at Flynn's dinner party. After listening to her, he relayed his own story about another Flynn dinner party he attended with Clark Gable, Spencer Tracy, Robert Taylor, and Wallace Beery. "We knocked on the door, and it was opened by a pair of exquisitely beautiful female twins—they were absolutely nude!"

Zsa Zsa would later tell Greta Keller, "Errol from time to time had been charged with rape. But he didn't have to rape me. I was a willing victim. He was just as romantic in life as he was on the screen. Imagine, both Captain Blood and Robin Hood wrapped into six feet, two inches of thrilling manhood."

Her memory of their romantic nights together was ruined three weeks later when at a party, Hedda Hopper informed her that there was a two-way mirror in Errol Flynn's bedroom.

"You must have put on quite a show," the gossip maven said. "Your audience included Bruce Cabot and perhaps his other two drunken buddies, Alan Hale and Guinn (Big Boy) Williams."

"I didn't feel that before, but after that, I felt I had been raped," Zsa Zsa said.

She vowed never to speak to Flynn again.

***

In her memoirs, Zsa Zsa, consistently denied affairs with such men as Howard Hughes or Errol Flynn. Yet in those same memoirs, she willingly made an even more damaging admission, asserting that she fell in love and had a voluntary sexual liaison with Conrad Hilton's son (her stepson), Nicky Hilton.

As she frankly admitted, "I had always loved Nicky Hilton, my stepson; now I began to love Nicky, the man. He was sexy and exciting, but not quite as dazzling as Conrad."

"It was a night of grand passion," she later told Greta Keller. At the time, her unofficial godmother was singing at the Stanhope Hotel in New York, and Nicky and Zsa Zsa attended three of the concerts comprising that engagement. No one, not even Walter Winchell in his syndicated column, noted their joint appearance in the audience. Since Conrad was out of town, people assumed that Nicky was merely functioning as a diligent and attentive stepson and escorting his stepmother to dinners and night clubs. No one seemed to notice that they were holding hands under the table.

"A love affair like ours wasn't so unusual," Zsa Zsa told Greta. *[Ironically, Greta herself, when she was in her eighties, would end up with a lover, Wolfgang Nebmaier, in his twenties.]*

"Actually, Nicky was closer to my age than I was to Conrad's age." Zsa Zsa was only nine years older than her stepson.

"In many ways, I was instrumental in restoring his manhood," she claimed. "All of his life, he'd lived in his father's shadow. Nicky

In the left photo, **Zsa Zsa** and **Nicky Hilton** are all smiles. He was both her stepson and her lover.

On the right, Nicky is seen with his new bride, **Elizabeth Taylor**. He was the first of her many husbands.

liked to drink and to carouse and didn't really apply himself to running the hotels. He wanted to party. Conrad constantly attacked him and belittled him. Instead of building him up and supporting his son, he tore Nicky down."

"During the long years of our affair," she said, "I constantly praised his manhood. He was a stallion. Ever since he was fourteen, both homosexuals and hot-to-trot females had sought him out. He was handsome, rich, and possessed a magnificent weapon that he'd inherited through Conrad's genes. Both of them were Texas bulls."

Nicky photographed badly, but in person, he was extremely handsome, speaking in a soft Texas drawl. He was tall and broad-shouldered and wore tailor-made suits from Savile Row in London. Even as a teenager, he had a reputation as a playboy, his dark brown eyes suggesting mischief and desire.

Even though he looked like he'd just graduated from college, he was a man of the world, having launched affairs with members of both sexes. He was at ease moving within high society, as he'd spent his early teenage years meeting movie stars, industrial tycoons, presidents, senators, and fading members of the European aristocracy.

"Yes, Nicky was bisexual," Zsa Zsa said, "which did not come as a shock to me ever since I'd seen Bill Tilden, that child-molesting tennis pro, going down on him in Charlie Chaplin's dressing room off the tennis courts. Homosexuals restored his sense of manhood by the constant praise heaped onto that weapon of his. Even Tyrone Power, Eva's future all-time lover, 'bottomed' for him. I had never heard that expression before I came to America, but I thought it apt."

"Nicky might have indulged in sex with homosexuals, but I can assure you he was always the man in such situations."

"He had such a commanding presence with women," she said. "It was amazing for one so young. Over the years, there were many reports of his violence toward women, especially from his first wife, Elizabeth Taylor, but during our affair, which lasted for years, he always treated me with great respect, love, and tenderness."

"Perhaps I exaggerate. He could get a bit rough in the bedchamber, but in a way that most women would adore. From reading American romance novels, which sell in the millions, I think women like to be devoured by a strong man who is a skilled swordsman. I can assure you that no woman ever left Nicky Hilton unsatisfied."

As a teenage boy, he'd also been pursued by movie stars with voracious sexual appetites. He jokingly called them "child molesters, but in my case, the child wanted to be molested."

An example of a star who Nicky had seduced (or vice versa) was Joan Crawford, who had once bedded Jackie Cooper when he was sweet sixteen. One night when Nicky checked into the Plaza Hotel, Crawford telephoned his suite and invited him over for cocktails.

He confessed that he accepted Crawford's invitation. "She was ready to go," he told Zsa Zsa. "We did it on the living room floor of her suite. She couldn't wait until we got to her bedroom. It would have been a memorable experience for me, but she had the most awful breath."

Lana Turner had been another of his conquests. "She even made a movie (*Week-End at the Waldorf*; 1945) at Dad's hotel."

The hotel heir didn't really work, although in time, he held two major posts—one as the vice president of the Hilton Corporation, and the other as the manager of the swanky Bel Air Hotel, which he referred to as "my fuck pad."

It was at this hotel that Zsa Zsa would prepare her famous "Dracula Goulash" for Nicky before bedtime in the privacy of his hotel suite.

Debates about fidelity never came up between Nicky and Zsa Zsa. Over the years, when he wasn't with her, he was seen with actresses such as Denise Darcel, Terry Moore (rumored to have married Howard Hughes), or else with socialites like Kay Spreckels and Hope Hampton. Ironically, Conrad, Sr. had previously dated both Spreckels and Hampton.

[In 1955, Spreckels, aged 39, became the fifth and final wife of Clark Gable.]

Zsa Zsa was well aware that Nicky occasionally pursued women who had previously visited his father's boudoir. He was always after that final approval whenever he heard one of them say, "You're a better lover than your father."

"Nicky was a wonderful lover," Zsa Zsa told Greta, "but he was more than that. He was a supportive friend. We could even complain about our other lovers with each other. There was another compelling reason that made my affair with Nicky so exciting. When I married Conrad, he was almost the grandfather type, though still reasonably virile."

"With Nicky, I was getting a younger version of Conrad, which his first wife had gotten, but which I never got to experience because of the difference in our ages."

"As much as they disliked each other, Nicky was definitely his father's son. They were men used to getting their way. Women were theirs to command. Both had forceful personalities, and both were strong and terribly sexy."

"The subject of marriage did come up on occasion," she claimed, "but only when we'd had too much champagne. We decided almost from the beginning that it would be too scandalous for me to divorce Conrad only to marry his son. After all, I didn't want to be dropped from the social register."

Zsa Zsa also told Greta, "When I became Nicky's lover, I honestly felt that I had gone to bed with Conrad for the final time. As soon as I got back to California, I was going to file for a divorce. But like so many other plans I'd plotted and schemed, this one didn't work out."

As seen in her heyday, **Jolie Gabor** asserted, "I was born into *belle-époque* gaiety. Then World War I roared in."

WITH RESPECT AND AFFECTION
THIS CHAPTER HAS BEEN CONFIGURED IN MEMORY OF
JOLIE GABOR AND HER THREE ASTONISHING DAUGHTERS

REST IN PEACE

Chapter Twenty
Postscript from the Edge—Boomer Times' Media Buzz

BOOMER TIMES & MEDIA BUZZ

MAGNOLIA HOUSE PROUDLY ReINTRODUCES
WELLNESS ADVISOR, GERONTOLOGIST, MAGAZINE
PUBLISHER, RADIO GURU, & *GRANDE DAME*

ANITA FINLEY

THE GUIDING LIGHT BEHIND
BOOMER TIMES & SENIOR LIFE MAGAZINE & MEDIA BUZZ

BoomerTimes
& SeniorLife Magazine

A Monthly Magazine
Serving
Active Adults in
South Florida
Since 1990

Baby | Boomers

"You are the salt of the earth. You have borne the pain and joy of motherhood and have earned every beautiful wrinkle and laugh line...so keep smiling and make time for your children and other children. Everyone needs a mother, but especially a grandmother, if you have reached that glorious age. Don't regret it...salivate it."

—Anita Finley, addressing mothers everywhere

WHO IS ANITA FINLEY, AND WHAT ARE PEOPLE SAYING ABOUT BOOMER TIMES?

She was an early admirer of Darwin Porter. She heard about him during the publicity generated by the long-ago publication of his seminal overviews of Bogart (*The Secret Life of Humphrey Bogart*; 2003) and Hepburn (*Katharine the Great*; 2004).

She's also one of the South's leading gerontologists, a modern-day Amazon, and a Renaissance woman seemingly capable of thriving wherever she happens to land. She's a woman of influence, shaping public opinion and spreading wide her message of tolerance and love.

It's as a radio host that Anita commands her largest audience. Darwin regularly appears on her show.

He also writes MEDIA BUZZ, an artfully gossipy monthly column crafted at Magnolia House and distributed through *Boomer Times* as a regular supplement of *The Miami Herald*. For more information about it, and the **Boomer Expo Exhibitions** she choreographs, click on *www.BoomerTimesFL.com*.

Anita Finley is one of the best educated, best informed and most charming of the many guests who have passed through my life and through Magnolia House. She's also a qualified and sought-after public speaker, promoting her personal conviction that it's never too late to learn or to try something new She also organizes and choreographs an annual symposium about wellness and health, the C.U.R.E. Symposiums.

Blood Moon extends recognition and gratitude to Anita, a woman we love. She will always be welcome at Magnolia House.

Danforth Prince, Publisher
Blood Moon Productions, Ltd.

BoomerTimes RADIO

LISTEN TO ANITA EVERY SATURDAY FROM 6-9AM ON
WWNN 95.3 FM, 103.9 FM AND 1470 AM

FROM ANYWHERE IN THE WORLD CLICK ON
HTTPS://BOOMERTIMESFL.COM/BOOMER-TIMES-RADIO/

WHAT IS DARWIN PORTER'S MEDIA BUZZ?

It's newsy, it's gossipy, it's fun, it's produced inside Magnolia House, and it tends to generate headlines. Some reprints of *Media Buzz* appear within the pages that follow.

Headlines inspired by Media Buzz appeared within several major international newspapers AFTER their revelations first appeared in Boomer Times. Here are some pithy examples:

THE XXX-RATED LIFE OF PETER O'TOOLE

*

KIRK DOUGLAS, A CENTURY OF CONQUESTS

*

ME TOO! THE CASTING COUCH, YESTERDAY AND TODAY

*

JAMES DEAN: THE "OTHER" (AFTER MARILYN AND JFK) ICON OF "THE AMERICAN CENTURY"

*

THEN-MARRIED VIVIEN LEIGH BEDDED GUYS—AND GALS!

*

PAUL NEWMAN & STEVE McQUEEN WERE LOVERS

*

JUNE ALLYSON SLEPT WITH TWO PRESIDENTS

*

HOW LIZ TAYLOR BEDDED TINSELTOWN

*

BILL CLINTON TRIED TO SEDUCE JACKIE KENNEDY IN A WRESTLING MATCH IN HER NEW YORK APARTMENT

*

HEDY LAMARR, MOTHER OF THE CELLPHONE

Media Buzz
By Darwin Porter
As it appeared in the August 2019 edition of Boomer Times

Burt Reynolds
The Florida Boy
Who Became King of the Box Office

In the 1970s and '80s, Burt Reynolds represented a new breed of movie star: Charming and relentlessly macho, with footprints in country-western, rural America, he was a good old Southern boy who made hearts throb and audiences laugh. He was Burt Reynolds, a former football hero, and a guy you might have shared some jokes with in a redneck bar. After an impressive but tormented career, rivers of negative publicity, a self-admitted history of bad choices, and a spectacular fall from Hollywood grace, he died in Jupiter, Florida, at the age of 82 in September of 2018.

He lives again in the pages of my latest biography, *Burt Reynolds: Put the Pedal to the Metal*, co-authored with Danforth Prince.

During his heyday, when he reigned as the premier American male sex symbol of the 1970s, he posed nude for a woman's magazine. Even though, by his admission, it ultimately hurt his career, fan mail from horny females poured in from across the nation, with outrageous requests for him to seduce them "any time he was passing through."

For five years, both in terms of earnings and popularity, he was the number one box office star in the world, most visibly in *Smokey and the Bandit* (1977), which became the biggest-grossing car-chase film of all time. As he put it, "I was hotter than a firecracker, a hunk of male flesh who likes nothing better than lying on my bearskin rug, making love to some of the most beautiful women in the world." Perhaps he was referring to his romantic and sexual involvements with the French goddess, Catherine Deneuve, or to America's own female sex symbol, Farrah Fawcett.

He might also have been referring to Dolly Parton, Tammy Wynette, Lucie Arnaz, Kim Basinger, Candice Bergen,

Burt Reynolds was the number one selling male box office attraction in America in the 1970s. This book explains why.

Lauren Hutton, Lorna Luft, Sarah Miles, Angie Dickinson, or Elizabeth Taylor. Long before he became famous, and shortly after some well-received appearances in a TV Western (*Gunsmoke*), he picked up Marilyn Monroe on his way to the Actors Studio in New York City.

Love with another VIP came in the form of that singing sensation, Dinah Shore, known as the "Sweetheart of the G.I.s" who won World War II. Their May-September affair sparked endless chatter: "I appreciate older women," he said in a moment of self-revelation, "ever since a rich 42-year-old woman in Palm Beach made love to me for one whole year."

He entered another much-publicized romance with actress Sally Field, the "second love of my life" and his co-star in *Bandit*. After his death, *The Flying Nun* said, "Burt still lives in my heart," but then expressed relief that, because of his recent death, he'd never read what she'd said about him in her memoir.

Men liked him too: He played poker with Frank Sinatra; shared boozy nights with John Wayne; intercepted a "pass" from closeted Spencer Tracy; talked "penis size" with Mark Wahlberg; went "wench-hunting" with Johnny Carson; and threatened to kill Marlon Brando, to whom his appearance was often compared. He also hung out with Bette Davis ("I always had a thing for her.")

His least happy (some said "most poisonous") marriage—to the blonde bombshell, Loni Anderson—was rife with dramas played out more in the tabloids than in the boudoir. According to Reynolds, "She's vain, she's a rotten mother, she sleeps around, and she spent all my money."

This highly revealing biography—the first comprehensive overview of the "redneck icon" ever published—reveals the joys and sorrows of a movie star who thrived in, but who was then almost buried by the pressures and insecurities of the New Hollywood. A tribute to "truck stop" America and to the courageous spirit of a hometown boy who "made good, bigtime," it's about the accelerated life of a courageous spirit who "Put His Pedal to the Metal" with humor, high jinx, and pizzazz.

He predicted his own death: "Soon, I'll be racing a hotrod in Valhalla in my cowboy hat and a pair of aviators." On his tombstone, he wanted it writ: "He was not the best actor in the world, but he was the best Burt Reynolds in the world."

Burt Reynolds was more sensitive, and more complicated, than most of his fans ever gave him credit for. Here, he emotes with **Salome Jens** in *Angel Baby* (1961), which was filmed in Florida.

Media Buzz
By Darwin Porter
As it appeared in the June 2017 edition of *Boomer Times*

Dina Merrill
The Heiress Who Grew Up at Mar-a-Lago

The world took little notice of Dina Merrill, age 93, who died on May 22, 2017, suffering from dementia. The rebellious heiress, who defied her parents to become an actress, grew up at Mar-a-Lago in Palm Beach, dubbed today "the Southern White House."

Between 1924 and 1927, the 126-room estate—part Mediterranean, part Arabian Nights—was constructed for $8 million by Dina's formidable mother, Marjorie Merriweather Post, owner of General Foods (aka "the Post Toasties heiress) and the wealthiest woman in America.

Born Nedenia Marjorie Hutton, the future Dina Merrill was the daughter of the multi-millionaire E.F. Hutton, Wall Street financier and one of the most influential men in America.

With parents like that, Dina grew up in a world of almost unimaginable luxury. Today, at Mar-a-Lago, Ivanka Trump's children occupy her former bedroom and playroom.

Dina often spent months aboard her father's yacht, the *Sea Cloud*, which was a floating palace, with such fixtures as fireplaces, a wine cellar, and a beauty parlor. She often helped to entertain the Duke and Duchess of Windsor, who were frequent guests.

Even as a girl, Dina showed a sharp eye for business. Her father gave her $50,000 to invest, and before she was 16, she had turned it into a million dollars. She urged her father to buy Birdseye Frozen Foods Company for $1.7 million, but he dismissed it a "a passing fad." When its value rose to $22 million, he listened to his daughter and purchased it.

He strongly opposed her wanting to be an actress, viewing it as a profession for "fallen women." She resisted, him and followed her heart. Hailed in Hollywood as "the new Grace Kelly," she ultimately made 100 films or teleplays.

I first met her in 1959, when I was the bureau chief of *The Miami Herald* in Key West. She had flown to the Florida Keys to film *Operation Petticoat* with

In Key West, as an actress in *Operation Petticoat* (1959), **Dina** discovered that her bisexual co-stars, Cary Grant and Tony Curtis, were having an affair.

Tony Curtis and Cary Grant, who had been married to her cousin, Woolworth heiress Barbara Hutton.

She was the epitome of charm, grace, and style, and was forever making the list of America's Best Dressed Women.

Over the years, I encountered her time and again at various charity events and premieres. Between 1966 and 1986, she was married to the Oscar-winning actor, Cliff Robertson. In the late 1960s and 70s, when he was often away shooting movies, she sometimes asked me to escort her to various charity events. She had become a major-league philanthropist.

The last time I saw her was in the late 1970s when the late, great literary agent, Audrey Wood (famous for having launched the career of Tennessee Williams) asked me to take her to see Dina appearing in an off-Broadway production of Tennessee's *Suddenly, Last Summer*. Katharine Hepburn had starred in the 1959 movie version, winning an Oscar nomination.

Over a late night supper in her lavish Manhattan apartment, Dina shared memories of her girlhood. None was more notable than when she'd flown to Moscow with her mother to be entertained by the Soviet dictator Josef Stalin. Post was buying up many art treasures seized by the Communists after the execution of the royal Romanoff family. He needed hard currency for war supplies.

Many of those treasures can be seen today at Hillwood, her former estate outside Washington, D.C., which is now a museum.

Dina was a liberal Republican, favoring pro-choice and women's health issues. When her mother died in 1973, she willed Mar-a-Lago to the National Park Service, hoping that it would be designated as a winter vacation retreat for U.S. Presidents. Jimmy Carter said, "Not for me."

When the government found it too costly to maintain, they gave it back to Dina and to Post's other two daughters.

They had a hard time getting rid of it, and kept lowering the price until Donald Trump purchased it in 1985 for only $7 million, one of the great real estate bargains of all time.

As the world knows, he turned it into a private club. When he became president, he raised the membership fee from $100,000 to $200,000.

For the most part, Dina remained silent about what happened to Mar-a-Lago. However, she did make one comment, as her mother's estate became a club: "A honeymoon haven for Michael Jackson and Elvis Presley's daughter. A setting for beauty pageants. A private club. Of course, Mother once hired performers from Ringling Brothers and Barnum & Bailey circuses to set up tents on her grounds for a charity event. But it's a different type of circus today."

Dina's formidable mother, **Marjorie Merriweather Post**, became one of the richest women in the world by peddling breakfast cereal to Baby Boomers.

Media Buzz
By Darwin Porter
As it appeared in the October 2019 edition of *Boomer Times*

Hollywood Casting
HITS, MISSES, & AND "WHAT MIGHT HAVE BEEN"

In the most absurd casting idea in the history of Hollywood, the wisecracking comedian, Groucho Marx, pleaded with David O. Selznick, producer of *Gone With the Wind* (1939), to cast him as Rhett Butler.

Selznick may have considered it for two seconds before showing Marx to the door. Instead, he toyed with casting Gary Cooper, Ronald Colman, Errol Flynn, Basil Rathbone, and Fredric March, but the public demanded Clark Gable.

Practically every actress in Hollywood, from Bette Davis to Joan Crawford, even Lana Turner, wanted to play Scarlett O'Hara. At the last minute, a relatively unknown British actress, Vivien Leigh, graced the screen in her Oscar-winning portrayal.

Another great picture from 1939, *The Wizard of Oz*, might have had Shirley Temple cast as Dorothy, but Fox wouldn't release her. Louis B. Mayer reluctantly cast "my little hunchback," Judy Garland, as Dorothy. Deeply insecure, she walked down the yellow brick road into screen immortality.

The entire history of Hollywood would have to be rewritten if the original stars who were cast had actually completed their respective movies. *Casablanca* (1942) is hailed by some critics as the greatest film ever made. What would it have been like with Ronald Reagan and Ann Sheridan in the leading roles? Of course, it would be Humphrey Bogart and Ingrid Bergman remembering, "We'll always have Paris."

Cary Grant rejected Frank Capra's *It's a Wonderful Life* (1946), which means that every Christmas we get to watch James Stewart, fresh out of the U.S. Army, on our TV screens.

Three great actresses, each in their most memorable roles, competed for the Oscar in 1950: Bette Davis, Gloria Swanson, and Judy Holliday. Each of them almost lost their star parts.

Claudette Colbert signed for

 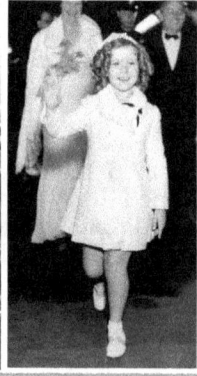

After sitting through the first screening of *The Wizard of Oz*, starring **Judy Garland,** Louis B. Mayer said: "Thank god Zanuck turned me down, and I didn't get 'Little Miss Lollipop' (**Shirley Temple**) for Dorothy. Imagine Temple screwing up 'Over the Rainbow.'"

All About Eve as Margo Channing but couldn't perform after injuring her back. In her place, Bette Davis rushed into the role. Before that, studio chief Darryl F. Zanuck had considered Susan Hayward, Marlene Dietrich, and Katharine Hepburn.

The director of *Sunset Blvd.*, Billy Wilder, offered the role of Norma Desmond to Pola Negri, Mae West, and Mary Pickford before awarding it to Swanson. In it, she gave her greatest screen portrayal as the unhinged silent screen diva, Norma Desmond.

Montgomery Clift was originally tapped to play her gigolo, Joe Gillis, but rejected the role. In his place, the part went to William Holden.

Judy Holliday, for her performance as the daffy blonde in *Born Yesterday* (1950), beat out Swanson and Davis for the Best Actress Oscar. MGM had originally considered Lucille Ball, Barbara Stanwyck, and Rita Hayworth as *Born Yesterday's* female lead.

From Here to Eternity (1953) is hailed in some quarters as one of the best of all World War II dramas. But it might have had Robert Mitchum and Joan Crawford in bathing suits on the beach at Pearl Harbor playing one of the most torrid love scenes ever. Burt Lancaster and Deborah Kerr took the roles. They turned each other on, since they launched an off-screen affair, too.

Grace Kelly won the Best Actress Oscar in 1954 for *The Country Girl*, opposite Bing Crosby. She beat out Judy Garland in her second most memorable role in *A Star is Born*. For a very brief time, Greta Garbo considered making a comeback in *The Country Girl*.

In 1956, four veteran actors— William Holden, Clark Gable, Alan Ladd, and Gary Cooper—competed for the role of Bick Benedict in Edna Ferber's *Giant*. Instead, a relative newcomer, Rock Hudson, won the career-making role. Grace Kelly was to be his leading lady, but when she ran away with the Prince of Monaco, the choice role went to Elizabeth Taylor.

Frank Sinatra was originally tapped to play the lead in *Carousel* (1956), but the role went to Gordon MacCrae. That same year, although Dinah Shore and Marlon Brando were to star in *The King and I*, the lead roles went to Deborah Kerr and Yul Brynner instead.

Billy Wilder's *Some Like It Hot* (1959) is hailed as the greatest of all screen comedies. The original cast had Mitzi Gaynor cast opposite Sinatra and Bob Hope in drag. At the last minute it would be Tony Curtis and Jack Lemmon dressing up like female musicians.

As originally conceived, Joan Collins was set to star in *Cleopatra* (1963). Also up for the role were two examples of almost impossible miscasting: Marilyn Monroe and Audrey

Gary Cooper (right) was the original choice to play Rhett Butler in *Gone With the Wind*, but he rejected it. Later, the public demanded **Clark Gable** (left) as Rhett Butler.

After seeing the final version, Coop said, "What if I had played Rhett and fucked up the epic?"

Hepburn. Of course, it would be Elizabeth Taylor, falling in love with her co-star Richard Burton, who would bring the ill-fated production to the screen.

In 1964, it was assumed that Julie Andrews would co-star in *My Fair Lady* in the wake of her triumph on Broadway. But Audrey Hepburn ended up as Eliza Doolittle instead. She was to have co-starred with Cary Grant, but the male lead went to Rex Harrison.

Doris Day turned down the memorable role of Mrs. Robinson in *The Graduate* (1967), the role eventually awarded to Anne Bancroft, whose character seduced Dustin Hoffman onscreen.

Two great pictures in 1972 might have had very different casts. *The Godfather* became Brando's most memorable role, but Burt Lancaster and Laurence Olivier were among the runners-up.

Henry Fonda and Charlton Heston were once set to co-star in *Deliverance* in the wilds of northeast Georgia. But at the last minute, the parts went to Jon Voight and Burt Reynolds—his most memorable role.

Talk about bizarre casting: Bette Midler, Barbra Streisand, and even Cher were considered to star in the 1976 remake of *King Kong*, the part ultimately won by Jessica Lange.

In modern times, Tom Cruise was set to star as Jack Dawson in that super box office bonanza, the ill-fated *Titanic* (1997). But Leonardo DiCaprio won the role instead.

We could go on and on with enough bizarre casting to fill a book, but at least you get the idea of what might have been.

Indeed, the brilliant and vivacious and immortal
VIVIEN LEIGH
was awarded the female lead in *Gone With the Wind*, but who were some of the other actresses who ferociously competed for the role of **Scarlett O'Hara?**

Tallulah Bankhead

Paulette Goddard

Bette Davis

Joan Crawford

Lana Turner

Katharine Hepburn

Susan Hayward

Lucille Ball

Media Buzz

By Darwin Porter
As it appeared in the September 2019 edition of *Boomer Times*

Celebrity First Ladies

MICHELLE OBAMA VS. MELANIA TRUMP
VS. THE IMPOSSIBLE MODEL ESTABLISHED BY
ELEANOR ROOSEVELT.
"IT'S THE HARDEST UNPAID JOB IN THE WORLD"

Few American First Ladies endured the pain and humiliation that Patricia Nixon, the wife of Richard Nixon, faced in the White House where she lived from 1969 to 1974.

Her husband was forced to resign over the Watergate scandal, and the camera recorded her holding back her tears.

The remarkable differences among First Ladies have been revealed once again in the new book, *Melania and Michelle: First Ladies in a New Era,* by Tammy Vigil. This is a nonpartisan book that pinpoints the wide differences between these two highly placed figures. Vigil claims that the only thing the two have in common is that whatever they do will find some

Talk about diversity among First Ladies: No trio of them could be as different as **Michelle Obama** *(left)*, **Eleanor Roosevelt** *(center)*, and **Melania Trump** *(right)*.

Of course, the two younger ones didn't have to face what Eleanor did. With her husband, Franklin, she had to bring America out of its greatest depression and win the most vicious war in the history of humankind.

group hating and denouncing them.

Michelle had to face false rumors spread to millions of people on the web that, because of her well-muscled arms, she is a man in drag. Another "fake news" item appeared under the head—MICHELLE OBAMA IS TRANSGENDERED.

Take popularity, for example. Michelle is one of the most popular women in America, rating at least a 53% approval, although some polling has put her at 65%. In contrast, Melania lags way behind: Only one in four Americans approve of her.

During her tenure in the White House, Michelle called herself "Mom-in-Chief," referring to how she reared her two daughters under the glare of a spotlight. In contrast, Melania does everything she can to conceal her son, Barron, from the press.

As a skilled lawyer and litigator, Michelle was prepared for the job, battling hostile lawyers in front of judges. In the White House, she was not exactly a co-president, but a skilled negotiator and adviser behind the scenes.

Melania, to much of the world, appears like a "trophy wife," standing by her husband silently and always looking beautiful, exquisitely dressed, and made up, sometimes referred to as the "Mannequin First Lady."

She actually is an intelligent woman who speaks more languages than any other First Lady. She rarely comments on political issues, though she has denounced "bullying." She made one widely printed comment: "I wish he wouldn't tweet so much."

She also had to endure the humiliation of having nude pictures released that she'd posed for in the 1990s, some where she shared a lesbian embrace with another model.

Long before Melania, Jacqueline Kennedy Onassis had to endure even more revealing nudes taken of her secretly on the Greek Island (Skorpios) owned by Aristotle Onassis.

Of course, both Michelle and Melania have made missteps. When Barack Obama won the Democratic primary, his wife said, "For the first time in my life, I am really proud of my country." She was instantly denounced as unpatriotic.

At the GOP convention in 2016, that nominated her husband, Melania gave the shortest speech in First Lady history. Regrettably, one hawk-eyed reporter revealed that part of it was plagiarized from Michelle's 2008 convention speech.

Every American First Lady has faced trials and tribulation, some, of course, far more than others.

Take Dolley Madison, First Lady from 1809 to 1817. During the War of 1812, British troops planned to raid the White House, kidnap her, ship her to London, and parade her naked through the streets as a war trophy.

Alerted that the British were coming, she fled from the White House, taking only Gilbert Stuart's portrait of George Washington and some beautiful red draperies.

After eating the dinner she had planned that night, the British general burned down the White House.

The United States won the battle, and at the victory celebration, Dolley showed up in a stunning scarlet gown made of that drapery material. The scene was repeated years later by Scarlett O'Hara (the draperies she converted into a dress were, in her case, green) in *Gone With the Wind*.

No First Lady was ever as commanding as Eleanor Roosevelt, wife of

FDR, who was First Lady from 1933 to 1945, some of the darkest years in American history. The Roosevelts had to be a beacon of hope during the Great Depression and during World War II, the greatest conflict in world history.

She made her mark, becoming "the ears and eyes" of her crippled husband, as she toured relentlessly, trying to right a wrong wherever she found it. She stood for women's liberation, civil rights, and a host of other liberal causes.

In 1942, the worst year for the Allies, she took a dangerous flight to war-torn London, where she walked the bombed-out streets. She brought tears of joy to Londoners who lined the streets. "She gave us hope when it appeared that all was lost," said a widow who had lost both her husband and her three children in "The Blitz."

Mrs. Roosevelt capped a remarkable career in 1948, three years after leaving the White House. At the United Nations, she ruled Soviet delegates out of order and passed the first-ever Declaration of Human Rights, immortalizing herself and making her the greatest woman of the 20th Century.

Chances are that no one now alive will ever see the likes of Eleanor Roosevelt anytime soon. What they are likely to witness is the first female President of the United States introducing the "First Man."

Media Buzz
Que Será, Será
By Darwin Porter
As it appeared in the May 2019 edition of *Boomer Times*

What If, Back in Hollywood,
Doris Day
Had Married Ronald Reagan & Become First Lady?

As the world knows, that singing sensation, Doris Day, the top female movie star of the 1960s, died recently at the age of 97. What most of her fans don't know is that she came close to becoming First Lady of the United States.

Doris' affair with Ronald Reagan began in 1948 when both of them were under contract at Warner Brothers. His movie career was winding down as hers was blossoming.

Both of them were cast in that feel-good musical, *It's a Great Feeling* (1949). Jane Wyman, who was divorcing Reagan, also was appearing in a cameo. Months before, she'd given birth to their second child, a baby girl who had lived for only a few hours.

Around the time that Wyman delivered her Oscar-winning performance in *Johnny Belinda* (1948), playing a deaf mute who is raped, she'd fallen for her co-star, Lew Ayres. He proposed that she divorce Reagan and marry him, but he changed his mind months later, and left her.

The male lead of *It's a Great Feeling* was Jack Carson, who had been dumped by Doris after a months-long affair. He confessed to Reagan, "She tried to talk me out of drinking two quarts of liquor a day, and I tried to wean her from smoking three packages of Camels a day."

Doris met Reagan one afternoon when both of them arrived, alone, for lunch at the Warners commissary. They shared a table. Reagan later told a jealous Carson, "I thought Doris was a freckle-faced little darling."

Their first date didn't go well. Reagan spent a good part of the evening lamenting his failed marriage to Wyman. Doris discussed her own marital problems with husband #1 (Al Jordan, 1941-43 and #2 (George Weidler, 1946-49).

Their subsequent dates became far more romantic, and they were often seen dancing the night away at their favorite little club on the Sunset Strip with its all-black band.

"We often closed down the club," Doris said. "But I knew Ronnie wanted to do more than dance. He held me so close I could feel his pressing need. When he invited me back to his bachelor pad in the Hollywood Hills, I said, 'Let's go for it.'"

When **Doris Day** was not free to fly to Miami with **Ronald Reagan**, he secretly took another blonde, the budding starlet, Marilyn Monroe, but didn't want to be seen in public with her.

As she later confessed to Ginger Rogers, "Ronnie is a far better lover than my two husbands, with a lot more stamina that either Jack Carson or Tyrone Power."

"I dig Ronnie and think he's really cute," she said. "When I'm in love, I want to make love with that man of mine all the time."

Producer Ross Hunter claimed, "No one knows that under those dirndls Doris wears lurks one of the hottest asses in Tinseltown."

After his first seduction of her, Reagan asked Doris to come and live with him, and she accepted, moving in the next day.

He told his close friend, George Murphy, that he'd fallen in love with her. *[A former song-and-dance man, Murphy became the U.S. senator from California. He was instrumental in urging Reagan to run for governor one day.]*

"Doris would be an ideal first lady, and at your campaign rallies, she could warm up the crowd singing 'Sentimental Journey.'"

Shortly after that, Reagan placed a diamond ring on Doris' finger, and she accepted his proposal. She didn't know at the time that he'd positioned that same ring on the finger of Adele Jergens, the "champagne blonde" of the 1940s and star of *Ladies of the Chorus* (1948) alongside a newcomer, Marilyn Monroe. When Monroe met Reagan, she lured him away from Jergens, who broke off the engagement and returned the diamond.

After his proposal to Doris, Reagan flew to London to make *The Hasty Heart* (1949) with Patricia Neal. Neal had been dumped by Gary Cooper, who had returned to his faithful wife, Rocky. *[Emotionally vulnerable in the wake of her breakup with Cooper, Neal briefly succumbed to Reagan's pre-presidential charms. Word reached Doris of Reagan's intimacies with Neal, but she never confronted him with a direct accusation.]*

Then, by coincidence, both Reagan and Doris were cast together in an upcoming movie, *Storm Warning* (1951), each of them co-starring alongside Ginger Rogers. "Me and Ginger in the same movie?" Doris said. "Our fans will think it's a musical. Actually, it's a tragic story about the KKK, and I'm killed at the end of it."

"During filming, Doris and Ronnie were so very much in love," Ginger said. "I knew they'd have a happy marriage."

The Miami premiere of *Storm Warning* was presented in a movie theater on Flagler Street, and both Doris and Reagan were corralled into attending. But Doris came down with the flu and couldn't accompany him from Hollywood. So instead of Doris, Reagan invited Marilyn Monroe. (He had been dating her on and off.) She accepted, hoping for publicity with a splashy appearance with him at the premiere.

But to her chagrin, Reagan secretly stashed her at the Helen Mar Hotel (he stayed at more expensive lodgings at another hotel) and wouldn't let her attend the premiere. She became so angry at him that she flew back to Los Angeles and ended their affair.

Back in Hollywood, Doris made plans for their wedding. Reagan had also been secretly dating then-starlet Nancy Davis. She was on the road to thirty and still unmarried. Her heart had been broken when her lover, Clark Gable, refused to marry her.

She wanted a husband and none of her previous lovers had agreed to walk down the aisle. They had included Spencer Tracy, Peter Lawford, Robert Walker, Yul Brynner, and Frank Sinatra.

Ronald Reagan and **Nancy Davis** (upper photo) became screen lovers in *Hellcats of the Navy*, released in 1957 by Columbia.

In the lower photo, Ronald and Nancy stand before their wedding cake in 1952.

As Reagan confessed to one of his best friends, William Holden, "Unlike my feelings for Doris, when I met Nancy, no bells rang, no fireworks exploded."

One night, Nancy told him she was pregnant with his child and that he had to marry her. Very reluctantly, he agreed. They were married before the birth of their daughter, Patti, whom they claimed had been born prematurely.

"Ronnie broke my heart when he told me about Nancy," Doris said. "I was madly in love with him, and I think we would have had a great marriage. But he had a cheating heart."

It was around that time that Marty Melcher entered Doris' life. She was on the rebound from Reagan, and she married him (1951-68). It ended disastrously. He squandered the $20 million she'd saved during the course of her career, and after his death, he left her with $500,000 in debt.

In 1952 *[the same year that Reagan married Nancy in a real-life ceremony]*, he also married Doris as part of the plot of a movie. Set in the depths of the Depression, it was *The Winning Team* (1952), a baseball flick.

Sometimes, during reflections on her life, Doris summed up her philosophy of life with this refrain: *QUE SERÁ, SERÁ.*

> **GENTLE READERS: DID YOU KNOW?**
>
> That Darwin Porter always wanted to write the political equivalent (**Washington Babylon**) of his scandal-soaked anthologies about Hollywood?
>
> And Did You Know? That Darwin, at presstime for this book, is BURSTING with book ideas he's eager to develop into best-sellers?
>
> SO, because life is short and time is fleeting, here's a very brief selection from fifty years of research he's conducted into the **IMPOSSIBLY LURID SCANDALS** that have, over the decades, enveloped Washington, D.C. beginning with the founding of the Republic.

Special Feature: EIGHT SCANDALOUS PRESIDENTS or FIRST LADIES

"Queers," a "Raving Lunatic," "A Fellatio Queen," & an Overdressed Belle Showing off her Big Tits.

***

#1. Martha & George Washington

Martha Washington, called "The Mother of Our Country," was First Lady from 1789 to 1797, a period of service she likened to being "a state prisoner." She'd married poor boy George Washington in 1759.

Before that, she was wed to Daniel Parke Custis, who was actually her godfather and twenty-one years her senior. He died in 1757, leaving her with two children, 17,000 acres of land, and 300 slaves. She became one of the richest women in the colonies.

It was said that George married her for her money, because he was really in love with his married neighbor, Sally Fairfax.

In many ways, it was an absentee marriage. During the eight years of the Revolutionary War, George made only two trips to Mount Vernon and on each of them, stayed for only two days.

Some historians have defined Washington as "a ladies' man," but there may have been another, secret, side to him.

An idealized portrait of **George and Martha Washington**, as conceived by engraver Benjamin Hall in 1867.

Washington's Rose, the object of his affection: **Sally Fairfax.** Alas, she was a married woman.

Le Marquis de Lafayette. "A kiss from ear to ear for 'my sweetheart.'"

Author Michael Bronski wrote: "It was in 1778 that Washington began a romantic, if not sexual, affair with Jean de Lafayette. In his letters he referred to the French general as "the man I love," and in his letters to Washington, Lafayette called him "my sweetheart."

Another historian wrote, "When Washington met Lafayette on the battlefield at Yorktown, the younger Frenchman kissed him from ear to ear with as much ardor as ever an absent lover kisses his mistress on his return."

When they had to part, Lafayette asked for a locket of Washington's hair "to carry with me always."

#2. Dolley Madison

Dolley Madison was married to President James Madison and served as First Lady from 1809 to 1817. She may have been as close as America came during the 19th Century of having an empress. And long before the emergence of Jacqueline Kennedy and Melania Trump, she was the first fashion icon in the White House.

The term "First Lady" was introduced by her, and she's been hailed as the *suma inter pares (first among equals)* of presidential spouses.

One of her admirers was Aaron Burr, who may have taken her virginity. It was he who introduced her to Madison, who married her in 1794.

Dolley Madison, "as remembered" in 1873 by engraver Evert Duyckinick.

"Little Jemmy," as she called her husband, became Secretary of State in 1801. Because President Thomas Jefferson and Vice-President Burr were widowers, Dolley became the *de facto* hostess of the White House.

In all of American history, she was the most prepared to be First Lady.

After the British chased her from the White House, she returned and moved into a private home with Jemmy. Overnight, she became the toast of Washington, giving parties even though the capital had been ravished.

She was the best-dressed woman outside London and Paris, wearing elegant gowns of silk and satin. She had an ample bosom and shocked Washington society by her plunging *décolletage*. She also introduced the wearing of turbans from which two-foot feathers spouted. She was also addicted to snuff.

A Daguerrotype image of late-in-life **Dolley Madison.**

At the end of her life, she was a pauper, begging for money and trying to hawk her tell-all memoirs. Her drunken, gambling son, John Payne Todd, squandered her money. Like Martha Washington, Dolley had been married before, having wed John Todd, Jr., in 1790.

Since her death in 1849, her fame and legacy have grown, and she is now ranked as one of the most celebrated First Ladies in American history.

#3. Mary Todd Lincoln

Mary Todd Lincoln was First Lady from 1861 to 1865 and married to Abraham Lincoln. Her most famous sound bite was, "What world of anguish this is—and how I have been made to suffer."

By 1839, she moved to Springfield, Illinois, where she met a lanky lawyer, Abe Lincoln, a young man who had no money and lacked social graces.

Unknown to her at the time, he was living with Joshua Fry Speed for four years, sleeping with him in a small bed and becoming his lover.

Lincoln's biographer, Carl Sandberg, phrased it poetically and delicately: "Providence had given these two men streaks of lavender, spots soft as May violets."

Unlike her husband, **Mary Todd Lincoln** wanted to "rain down fire and brimstone" on the defeated South.

Mary's relationship with Abe was turbulent, filled with arguments and jealous rages, but she prevailed and married him in 1842. Even as a girl growing up, she told her parents, "One day, I want to be wed to the President of the United States."

She urged Abe to go into politics, and he was elected to the U.S.Congress in 1846. She became one of his most ardent supporters, almost nightly urging him on.

In 1860, the newly formed Republican Party nominated him as their presidential candidate, and her dream was coming true. Of course, as the world knows, his election blew up into a Civil War and, ultimately, his assassination.

Wedding portrait (Nov. 4, 1842, in Springfield, IL) of **Abraham Lincoln and Mary Todd.**

When her favorite son, Willie, died in 1862, she tried to communicate with her dead son by holding séances at the White House. Then, months before her husband's death, she warned Lincoln that she'd had a premonition of his assassination.

Her final years were tragic as she sold Lincoln's possessions to raise money for herself and her two remaining sons. One disaster followed another, as her youngest son, Tad, died in 1871.

Four years later, an Illinois court judge pronounced her insane. Her oldest son, Robert, testified that she was crazy.

After Lincoln's death, his biographers began to reveal aspects of his secret life.

In 1831, Abe, then 22, became involved with 19-year-old Billy Greene. The younger man later claimed, "The moment I laid eyes on Abe, I noted that his thighs were as perfect as a human being could

Joshua Fry Speed at the age of around 50. The most intimate relationship of Lincoln's life was with a slave owner in his early twenties.

be. We shared a bed so small that if one of us turned over, the other would have to do likewise." He would recall his time with Abe as "the most glorious period of my life."

When Abe was 28, he moved to Springfield, Illinois, where on his first day in town, he med Joshua Fry Speed, 23. The young man invited him to share his bed, and Lincoln did just that for four ears.

As reported, Joshua became the love of Lincoln's life. And he was heartbroken, almost suicidal, when Joshua moved back to Kentucky where he was a slave owner.

Lincoln's law partner, William Herndon, wrote that "Speed, more than onyone dead or living, was devoted to Abe. No two men have ever been more intimate. They shared everything together—and not just a small bed."

As President of the United States, Abe Lincoln became involved with Captain David Derickson of the 150th Pennsylvania Volunteers, knicknamed "The Bucktail Brigade." Lincoln was 53 at the time, and the captain 44.

The President was outside Washington reviewing troops when he first met the captain. He asked him to ride back to Washington with him, and, according to reports, the captain never left his side for the next four months. They became so close that the President even let him sit in on Cabinet meetings, discussing how the Civil War was going. The two men often inspected troops together.

Captain David Derickson was Lincoln's constant companion during the day and his bed partner at night.

When Derickson was called back to his post, the President countermanded the order, telling General Grant, "The Captain and I are getting quite thick."

Later, Virginia Woodbury, wife of the Assistant Secretary of the Navy, interpreted the relationship as "scandalous. The Bucktail soldier is devoted to the President and even sleeps with him."

Thomas Chamberlin, Derickson's commanding officer, wrote: "The Captain has advanced so far in the President's confidence that he spends every night in bed with him at Lincoln's summer retreat from Washington. He even makes use of Lincoln's nightshirt."

It was in their bedroom at his summer retreat that Lincoln began to write the Emancipation Proclamation.

#4. Ida Saxton McKinley

Ida Saxton McKinley was the wife of President William McKinley and First Lady from 1897 to 1901, the year her husband was assassinated.

Ida Saxton McKinley made a glamourous entrance at the Inaugural Ball, dressed in a white satin gown, and immediately passed out.

Most of the time during her tenure at the White House, she remained in bed because of various ailments. She used the time effectively, crocheting 3,500 pairs of slippers.

#5. Grace Coolidge

Grace Coolidge, wife of Calvin Coolidge, lived in the White House from 1923 to 1929. She first spotted her future husband aboard a steamship when she peered into his bathroom through a porthole. He was naked, standing in front of a mirror. "Then and there, I decided he would be my husband," she later claimed.

#6. Bess Truman

Were it not for Bess Truman, the White House as it appears today would not be standing. After Roosevelt's death in 1945, Harry Truman and his wife, Bess, moved into the White House. On their first night, their bed almost fell through the rotting floor. She learned that there were plans to raze the entire building and to construct an all-new copy. She objected, asserting that the White House was a historic monument and should be preserved. She and Harry moved out as work began.

Dour and unrelentingly frumpy: **Bess Truman,** with her husband, **Harry S Truman**, at his inauguration.

#7. Jacqueline Bouvier Kennedy

Jackie Kennedy served as First Lady from 1961 until her husband's assassination in Dallas in November of 1963. During her tenure at the White House, she became the most famous woman in the world. Known for her beauty, charm, and grace, she "reigned" in stark contrast to the style of Mamie Eisenhower, married to the two-term President and former General Dwight Eisenhower.

During Jacqueline's time there, she had to rear two children and deal with her philandering husband. In his day, JFK would seduce such stellar women—as well as dozens of

Jacqueline Kennedy married two of the world's most famous men, President John F. Kennedy and the Greek shipping tycoon, Aristotle Onassis.

She said, "I don't think there are any men who are faithful to their wives. Men are such a combination of good and evil."

lesser-known ones—as Joan Crawford, Hedy Lamarr, Lana Turner, Marlene Dietrich, Judy Garland, and Marilyn Monroe.

One night, Jacqueline told the gossipy author Truman Capote, "The man I really wanted to marry was William Holden."

#8. Nancy Davis Reagan

The former MGM starlette, Nancy Davis, was married to President Ronald Reagan , and they ruled over the White House from 1981 to 1989. Ironically, as Reagan became one of the most popular Presidents, she became one of the most unpopular First Ladies.

During her days as a starlet at MGM, Davis became known as "The Fellatio Queen of Hollywood." She sustained several high profile affairs, including romances with, among others, Yul Brynner, Broadway star Alfred Drake, Peter Lawford, Robert Walker, Frank Sinatra, and Spencer Tracy.

Her first choice of a husband was Clark Gable, but he spurned her offer.

Many books have been written about **Ronald Reagan**, mostly about his presidency in the 1980s; a few have been written about **Nancy**, including her own memoir; and very few about his first wife, the Oscar-winning actress, **Jane Wyman**, who was a bigger star than either Reagan or Nancy.

Love Triangle is the only book that explores their stardom and love lives in Hollywood and the compromises they confronted during their climb up the Hollywood ladder.

In his heyday, the future president was known as a "Hollywood horndog," with notable conquests.

Scribes & Messengers
(Authors' Bios)

DARWIN PORTER

As an intense nine-year-old, **Darwin Porter** began meeting movie stars, TV personalities, politicians, and singers through his vivacious and attractive mother, Hazel, an eccentric but charismatic Southern girl who had lost her husband in World War II. Migrating from the Depression-ravaged valleys of western North Carolina to Miami Beach during its most ebullient heyday, Hazel became a stylist, wardrobe mistress, and personal assistant to the vaudeville *comedienne* **Sophie Tucker**, the bawdy and irrepressible "Last of the Red Hot Mamas."

Virtually every show-biz celebrity who visited Miami Beach paid a call on "Miss Sophie," and Darwin, as a pre-teen loosely and indulgently supervised by his mother, was regularly dazzled by the likes of **Judy Garland, Dinah Shore,** and **Frank Sinatra.**

It was at Miss Sophie's that he met his first political figure, who was actually an actor at the time. Between marriages, **Ronald Reagan** came to call on Ms. Sophie, who was his favorite singer. He was accompanied by a young blonde starlet, **Marilyn Monroe**.

At the University of Miami, Darwin edited the school newspaper. He first met and interviewed **Eleanor Roosevelt** at the Fontainebleau Hotel on Miami Beach and invited her to spend a day at the university. She accepted, much to his delight.

After graduation, he became the Bureau Chief of *The Miami Herald* in Key West, Florida, where he got to take early morning walks with the former U.S. president **Harry S Truman**, discussing his presidency and the events that had shaped it.

Through Truman, Darwin was introduced and later joined the staff of **Senator George Smathers** of Florida. His best friend was a young senator, **John F. Kennedy.** Through "Gorgeous George," as Smathers was known in the Senate, Darwin got to meet Jack and Jacqueline in Palm Beach. He later wrote two books about them—*The Kennedys, All the Gossip Unfit to Print*, and one of his all-time bestsellers, *Jacqueline Kennedy Onassis—A Life Beyond Her Wildest Dreams*.

For about a decade in New York, Darwin worked in television journalism and advertising with his long-time partner, the journalist, art director, and arts-industry socialite **Stanley Mills Haggart.**

Stanley (as an art director) and Darwin (as a writer and assistant), worked as freelance agents in television. Jointly, they helped produce TV commercials that included testimonials from **Joan Crawford** (then feverishly promoting Pepsi-Cola); **Ronald Reagan** (General Electric); and **Debbie Reynolds** (Singer sewing machines). Other personalities appearing and delivering televised sales pitches included **Louis Armstrong, Lena Horne,** and **Arlene Dahl,** each of them hawking a commercial product.

Beginning in the early 1960s, Darwin joined forces with the then-fledgling **Arthur Frommer** organization, playing a key role in researching and writing more than 50 titles and defining the style and values that later emerged as the world's leading travel guidebooks, *The Frommer Guides,* with particular emphasis on Europe, New England, and the Caribbean. Between the creation and updating of hundreds of editions of detailed travel guides to England, France, Italy, Spain, Portugal, Austria, Hungary, Germany, Switzerland, the Caribbean, and California, he continued to interview and discuss the triumphs, feuds, and frustrations of celebrities, many by then reclusive, whom he either sought out or encountered randomly as part of his extensive travels. **Ava Gardner, Debbie Reynolds,** and **Lana Turner** were particularly insightful.

He also penned more than thirty-five uncensored, unvarnished, and unauthorized biographies on subjects that included **Burt Reynolds, Kirk Douglas, Playboy's Hugh Hefner, Debbie Reynolds and Carrie Fisher, Bill and Hillary Clinton, Ronald Reagan and Nancy Davis, Jane Wyman, Jacqueline Kennedy, Jack Kennedy, Lana Turner, Peter O'Toole, James Dean, Marlon Brando, Merv Griffin, Katharine Hepburn, Howard Hughes, Humphrey Bogart, Michael Jackson, Paul Newman, Steve McQueen, Marilyn Monroe, Elizabeth Taylor, Rock Hudson, Frank Sinatra, Vivien Leigh, Laurence Olivier, the notorious porn star Linda Lovelace, Zsa Zsa Gabor and her sisters, Tennessee Williams, Gore Vidal,** and **Truman Capote.**

As a departure from his usual repertoire, Darwin also wrote the controversial *J. Edgar Hoover & Clyde Tolson: Investigating the Sexual Secrets of America's Most Famous Men and Women,* a book about celebrity, voyeurism, political and sexual repression, and blackmail within the highest circles of the U.S. government.

Porter's biographies, over the years, have won thirty first prize or "runner-up to first prize" awards at literary festivals in cities or states which include New England, New York, Los Angeles, Hollywood, San Francisco, Florida, California, and Paris.

Darwin can be heard at regular intervals as a radio and television commentator, reviewing the ironies of celebrities, pop culture, politics, and scandal.

A resident of New York City, Darwin is currently at work on biographies of **July Garland and Liza Minnelli;** the temperamental and philanthropic Queen of Off-Broadway, **Lucille Lortel;** comedians **Lucille Ball and Desi Arnaz**; and the avant-garde playwright some critics define as the greatest (female) lover in the history of Silent-Era Hollywood, **Mercedes De Acosta.**

DANFORTH PRINCE

In 2004, **Danforth Prince** established Blood Moon Productions, a publishing venture devoted to salvaging and compiling the oral histories of America's entertainment industry.

Prince launched his career in journalism in the 1970s at the Paris Bureau of *The New York Times*. In the early '80s, he joined Darwin Porter ito help develop the first editions of many of the titles within *The Frommer Guides*. Together, they articulated the travel scenes of more than 50 nations, most of them within Europe and the Caribbean. Authoritative, comprehensive, and best-selling, they became "travel bibles" for millions of readers.

Prince, in collaboration with Porter, is also the co-author of some award-winning celebrity biographies, each configured as a title within **Blood Moon's Babylon series.** These have included *Hollywood Babylon— It's Back!; Hollywood Babylon Strikes Again; The Kennedys: All the Gossip Unfit to Print; Frank Sinatra, The Boudoir Singer, Elizabeth Taylor: There Is Nothing Like a Dame; Pink Triangle: The Feuds and Private Lives of Tennessee Williams, Gore Vidal, Truman Capote, and Members of their Entourages*; and *Jacqueline Kennedy Onassis: A Life Beyond Her Wildest Dreams*. More recent efforts include *Lana Turner, Hearts and Diamonds Take All; Peter O'Toole—Hellraiser, Sexual Outlaw, Irish Rebel; Bill & Hillary—So This Is That Thing Called Love; James Dean, Tomorrow Never Comes; Rock Hudson Erotic Fire; Carrie Fisher and Debbie Reynolds, Princess Leia & Unsinkable Tammy in Hell, Playboy's Hugh Hefner, Empire of Skin; Kirk Douglas: More Is Never Enough;* and *Burt Reynolds, Put the Pedal to the Metal*.

For years, both Porter and Prince had became fascinated by the career of the real estate mogul and reality TV star, **Donald Trump**, then changing the skyline of Manhattan.

They began collecting data on Trump, squirreling it away in boxes, with the intention of one day writing his biography of this charismatic celebrity. In 2016, on the eve of that year's Presidential elections, they co-authored *Donald Trump, The Man Who Would Be King*, an exposé of the decades of pre-presidential scandals associated with **the controversial president** during the rambunctious decades when no one ever thought he'd actually get elected. It later won three literary awards at book festivals in New York, California, and Florida.

Prince is also the co-author of four books on film criticism, three of which won honors at regional bookfests in Los Angeles and San Francisco.

A graduate of Hamilton College and a native of Easton and Bethlehem, Pennsylvania, he is the president and founder of the Georgia Literary Association (1996), and of the Porter and Prince Corporation (1983) which has produced dozens of titles for Simon & Schuster, Prentice Hall, and John Wiley & Sons. In 2011, he was named "Publisher of the Year" by a consortium of literary critics and marketers spearheaded by the J.M. Northern Media Group.

He has electronically documented some of the controversies associated with his stewardship of Blood Moon in at least 50 documentaries, book trailers, public speeches, and TV or radio interviews. Most of these are available on **YouTube.com** and **Facebook** *(keyword: "Danforth Prince")*; on **Twitter** *(#BloodyandLunar)*; or by clicking on **BloodMoonProductions.com**.

Prince is also an innkeeper, running a historic bed & breakfast in New York City, **Magnolia House (www.MagnoliaHouseSaintGeorge.com)**. Affiliated with AirBnb, and increasingly sought out by filmmakers as an evocative locale for moviemaking, it lies in St. George, at the northern tip of Staten Island, a district that's historically associated with Henry James, Theodore Dreiser, the Vanderbilts, and key moments in America's colonial history.

Set in a terraced garden, it's been visited by literary and show-biz stars who have included Tennessee Williams, Gloria Swanson, Jolie Gabor, Ruth Warrick, Greta Keller, Lucille Lortel, and many of the luminaries of Broadway. It lies within a ten-minute walk to the ferries sailing at 20- to 30-minute intervals to Lower Manhattan.

Publicized as "a reasonably priced celebrity-centric bed & breakfast with links to the book trades," and the beneficiary of rave ("superhost") reviews from hundreds of previous clients, **Magnolia House** is loaded with furniture and memorabilia that Prince collected from around the world during his decades as a travel journalist for the Frommer Guides.

Long ago and far away:
Darwin Porter (right) and Danforth Prince

*YES, it's a monument to celebrity irony and legend.
It's also NYC's most fascinating Bed & Breakfast.*

*Come with your friends for the night and stay for breakfast because
IT'S SHOW BIZ, DAHLING...*

Magnolia House

As stated by its manager, **Danforth Prince**, "Magnolia House results from my 30-year role as co-author of many titles, and many editions, of *The Frommer Guides*, each of which included evaluations of the bed and breakfast inns of Europe. Whereas I'm still lodged on the upper floors of this building, most of it now operates as a "Superhosted" AirBnb with links to the early days of the Frommer Guides, 'the Golden Age of Travel,' and Blood Moon's associations with Broadway, Hollywood, and the Entertainment Industry. Say hello and, if it works for you, stay with as many as seven or eight of your friends for a celebrity sleepover at Magnolia House!"

As described within the pages of this book, edgy media associations have always been part of the Magnolia House experience. Previous guests have included **Tennessee Williams** (*"Magnolia House reminds me of Blanche DuBois' lost plantation, Bellereve!"*); Golden Age film personality **Joan Blondell** (a close friend of celebrity biographer and co-owner, **Darwin Porter**); **Greta Keller** (the very famous rival of Marlene Dietrich) **Lucille Lortel** (the philanthropic but very temperamental Queen of Off-Broadway); **Jolie Gabor** (mother of the three "Bombshells from Budapest," **Zsa Zsa, Eva, and Magda**); and a host of other stars, *starlettes, demimondaines* and hellraisers of all descriptions and persuasions.

For photographs, testimonials from previous guests, and more information, click on

www.AirBnb/h/Magnolia-House   or on
www.MagnoliaHouseSaintGeorge.com.

Magnolia House is the historic landmark in NYC where Blood Moon researches, writes, & publishes its award-winning entertainment about how America interprets its celebrities.

Now, There's a GUIDEBOOK to accompany your visit to one of NYC's Most Intriguing Landmarks:

Published in 2018, this is Volume One of Blood Moon's MAGNOLIA HOUSE series. It specifically addresses its history and how a gig with **THE FROMMER GUIDES** evolved into a celebrity adventure directly linked to show-biz.

As stated by Danforth Prince, "It's been a helluva ride, 'lo these many years, churning out travel guides and the traumatic, sometimes tragic, life stories of the notorious and merely famous celebrities we've written about. Magnolia House with its affordable overnight accommodations presents us with the opportunity of meeting some of the fans of the subjects we've 'exposed' in print."

WHAT IS MAGNOLIA HOUSE? In the immediate aftermath of the Civil War, its owners gave it a name that evoked their native Virginia. Dating from the 1830s, it's a *Grande Dame* with a knack for nourishing high-functioning eccentrics. Many of them have lived or been entertained here since New York's State Senator Howard Bayne, a transplanted Southerner, moved in with his wife, the daughter of the Surgeon General of the Confederate States of America, in the aftermath of that bloodiest of wars on North American soil, the War between the American States. Since then, many dozens of celebrities—some of them notorious—have whispered their secrets and rehearsed their ambitions within its walls.

This is the story of how this "Wise Victorian Lady"—in its role as the editorial headquarters for many of THE FROMMER GUIDES and later for BLOOD MOON PRODUCTIONS—adapted to America's radically changing tastes, times, circumstances, and values.

STATEN ISLAND'S HISTORIC MAGNOLIA HOUSE
CELEBRITY & THE IRONIES OF FAME:

A MEMOIR ABOUT TRAVEL GUIDES, TABLOID EXPOSÉS,
& THE LANDMARK WHERE THEY WERE PRODUCED.

Softcover, 6" x 9", with 230 pages, at least a hundred photos, and scads of gossip about who did what to whom during the course of 50 years as headquarters for the world's preeminent travel journalists. Available everywhere online through Amazon.com, BarnesandNoble.com, or as a free giveaway to overnight guests. ISBN 978-1-936003-65-5.

Judy Garland & Liza Minnelli
Too Many Damn Rainbows

Judy and Liza were the greatest, most colorful, and most tragic mother-daughter saga in show biz history. They live, laugh, and weep again in the tear-soaked pages of this remarkable biography. Darwin Porter and Danforth Prince have compiled a compelling "post-modern" spin.

According to Liza, "My mother—hailed as the world's greatest entertainer—lived eighty lives during her short time with us."

Their memorable stories unfold through eyewitness accounts of the typhoons that engulfed them. They swing across glittery landscapes of euphoria and glory, detailing the betrayals and treachery which the duo encountered almost daily. There were depressions "as deep as the Mariana Trench," suicide attempts, and obsessive identifications on deep psychological levels with roles that include Judy's Vicky Lester in *A Star is Born* (1954) and Liza's Sally Bowles in *Cabaret* (1972).

Lesser known are the jealous actress-to-actress rivalries. Fueled by klieg lights and rivers of negative publicity, they sprouted like malevolent mushrooms on steroids.

As Judy faded into the 1960s, Liza roaringly emerged as a star in her own right. "I did it my way," Liza said. She survived the whirlwinds of her mother's drug addiction with a yen for choosing all the wrong men in patterns that weirdly evoked those of Judy herself.

For millions of fans, Judy will forever remain the cheerful adolescent (Dorothy) skipping along a yellow brick road toward the other side of the rainbow. Liza followed her down that hallucinogenic path, searching for the childhood, the security, and the love that eluded her.

Judy Garland, an icon whose memory is permanently etched into the American psyche, continues to thrive as a cult goddess. Revered by thousands of die-hard fans, she's the most poignant example of both the manic and depressive (some say "schizophrenic") sides of the Hollywood myth. A recent film portrayal by Renée Zellweger helped promote and perpetuate her image.

Deep in her 70s, Liza is still with us, too, nursing memories of her former acclaim and her first visit as a little girl to her parents at MGM, the "Dream Factory," during the Golden Age of Hollywood.

Judy Garland & Liza Minnelli: Too Many Damn Rainbows
Darwin Porter & Danforth Prince
Softcover, 6" x 9", with hundreds of photos.   ISBN 9781936003693
Available Everywhere April 2020

THE SEDUCTIVE EXPLOITS OF
MERCEDES DE ACOSTA
HOLLYWOOD'S GREATEST LOVER

BLOOD MOON: Unearthing the Secrets of the Grand Divas of the Early Film Industry—It's a Tough Job, but Somebody's Got to Do It!

This, Volume Three of Blood Moon's Magnolia House series, focuses on the Silent Screen and the "Story Behind the Stories" of some of the women who evolved into the stage and screen's most admired goddesses.

Here are firsthand accounts derived from Mercedes de Acosta, a frequent visitor to Magnolia House and famous for her affairs with bisexual members of the upper echelons of Broadway and Hollywood. It's a red-faced glimpse of what happened AFTER the vamps and sirens of the early 20th Century walked down the red carpet of show-biz fame and—in rare instances—fortune.

The Seductive Exploits of Mercedes de Acosta, Hollywood's Greatest Lover

Darwin Porter & Danforth Prince
Softcover, 6" x 9", with hundreds of photos.   ISBN 978-1-936003-75-4
Available Everywhere May 2020

LOVE TRIANGLE:
RONALD REAGAN
JANE WYMAN, & NANCY DAVIS

HOW MUCH DO YOU REALLY KNOW ABOUT THE REAGANS?

THIS BOOKS TELLS EVERYTHING ABOUT THE SHOW-BIZ SCANDALS THEY DESPERATELY WANTED TO FORGET.

Unique in the history of publishing, this scandalous triple biography focuses on the Hollywood indiscretions of former U.S. president Ronald Reagan and his two wives. A proud and Presidential addition to Blood Moon's Babylon series, it digs deep into what these three young and attractive movie stars were doing decades before two of them took over the Free World.

As reviewed by Diane Donovan, Senior Reviewer at the California Bookwatch section of the Midwest Book Review: "Love Triangle: Ronald Reagan, Jane Wyman & Nancy Davis may find its way onto many a Republican Reagan fan's reading shelf; but those who expect another Reagan celebration will be surprised: this is lurid Hollywood exposé writing at its best, and outlines the truths surrounding one of the most provocative industry scandals in the world.

"There are already so many biographies of the Reagans on the market that one might expect similar mile-markers from this: be prepared for shock and awe; because Love Triangle doesn't take your ordinary approach to biography and describes a love triangle that eventually bumped a major Hollywood movie star from the possibility of being First Lady and replaced her with a lesser-known Grade B actress (Nancy Davis).

"From politics and betrayal to romance, infidelity, and sordid affairs, Love Triangle is a steamy, eye-opening story that blows the lid off of the Reagan illusion to raise eyebrows on both sides of the big screen.

"Black and white photos liberally pepper an account of the careers of all three and the lasting shock of their stormy relationships in a delightful pursuit especially recommended for any who relish Hollywood gossip."

In 2015, LOVE TRIANGLE, Blood Moon Productions' overview of the early dramas associated with Ronald Reagan's scandal-soaked career in Hollywood, was designated by the Awards Committee of the HOLLYWOOD BOOK FESTIVAL as Runner-Up to Best Biography of the Year.

LOVE TRIANGLE: Ronald Reagan, Jane Wyman, & Nancy Davis
Darwin Porter & Danforth Prince
Softcover, 6" x 9", with hundreds of photos.   ISBN 978-1-936003-41-9

THIS BOOK ILLUSTRATES WHY *GENTLEMEN PREFER BLONDES*, AND WHY MARILYN MONROE WAS TOO DANGEROUS TO BE ALLOWED TO GO ON LIVING.

Less than an hour after the discovery of Marilyn Monroe's corpse in Brentwood, a flood of theories, tainted evidence, and conflicting testimonies began pouring out into the public landscape.

Filled with rage, hysteria, and depression, "and fed up with Jack's lies, Bobby's lies," Marilyn sought revenge and mass vindication. Her revelations at an imminent press conference could have toppled political dynasties and destroyed criminal empires. Marilyn had to be stopped…

Into this steamy cauldron of deceit, Marilyn herself emerges as a most unreliable witness during the weeks leading up to her murder. Her own deceptions, vanities, and self-delusion poured toxic accelerants on an already raging fire.

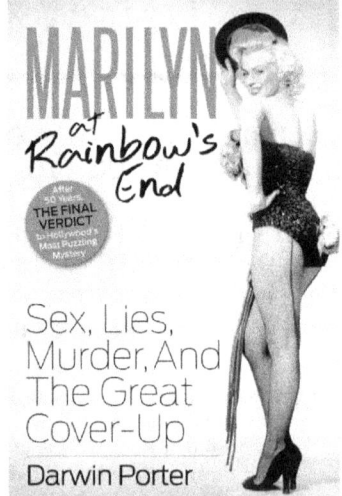

"This is the best book about Marilyn Monroe ever published."
—**David Hartnell**, Recipient, in 2011, of New Zealand's Order of Merit (MNZM) for services to the entertainment industry, as defined by Her Majesty, Queen Elizabeth II.

Winner of literary awards from the New York, Hollywood, and San Francisco Book Festivals

MARILYN AT RAINBOW'S END
SEX, LIES, MURDER, AND THE GREAT COVER-UP, BY DARWIN PORTER
ISBN 978-1-936003-29-7
Temporarily sold out of hard copies, but available for E-Readers

"Darwin Porter is fearless, honest and a great read. He minces no words. If the truth makes you wince and honesty offends your sensibility, stay away. It's been said that he deals in muck because he can't libel the dead. Well, it's about time someone started telling the truth about the dead and being honest about just what happened to get us in the mess in which we're in. If libel is lying, then Porter is so completely innocent as to deserve an award. In all of his works he speaks only to the truth, and although he is a hard teacher and task master, he's one we ignore at our peril. To quote Gore Vidal, power is not a toy we give to someone for being good. If we all don't begin to investigate where power and money really are in the here and now, we deserve what we get. Yes, Porter names names. The reader will come away from the book knowing just who killed Monroe. Porter rather brilliantly points to a number of motives, but leaves it to the reader to surmise exactly what happened at the rainbow's end, just why Marilyn was killed. And, of course, why we should be careful of getting exactly what we want. It's a very long tumble from the top."

—ALAN PETRUCELLI, Examiner.com, May 13, 2012

CARRIE FISHER & DEBBIE REYNOLDS
PRINCESS LEIA & UNSINKABLE TAMMY IN HELL

It's history's first comprehensive, unauthorized overview of the greatest mother-daughter act in showbiz history, Debbie Reynolds ("hard as nails and with more balls than any five guys I've ever known") and her talented, often traumatized daughter, Carrie Fisher ("one of the smartest, hippest chicks in Hollywood"). Evolving for decades under the unrelenting glare of public scrutiny, each became a world-class symbol of the social and cinematic tastes that prevailed during their heydays as celebrity icons in Hollywood.

It's a scandalous saga of the ferociously loyal relationship of the "boop-boop-a-doop" girl with her intergalactic STAR WARS daughter, and their iron-willed, "true grit" battles to out-race changing tastes in Hollywood.

Loaded with revelations about "who was doing what to whom" during the final gasps of Golden Age Hollywood, it's an All-American story about the price of glamour, career-related pain, family anguish, romantic betrayals, lingering guilt, and the volcanic shifts that affected a scrappy, mother-daughter team—and everyone else who ever loved the movies.

"Feeling misunderstood by the younger (female) members of your gene pool? This is the Hollywood exposé every grandmother should give to her granddaughter, a roadmap like Debbie Reynolds might have offered to Billie Lourd."
—Marnie O'Toole

"Hold onto your hats, the "bad boys" of Blood Moon Productions are back. This time, they have an exhaustively researched and highly readable account of the greatest mother-daughter act in the history of show business: Debbie Reynolds and Carrie (Princess Leia) Fisher. If celebrity gossip and inside dirt is your secret desire, check it out. This is a fabulous book that we heartily recommend. It will not disappoint. We rate it worthy of four stars."
—MAJ Glenn MacDonald, U.S. Army Reserve (Retired), © MilitaryCorruption.com

"How is a 1950s-era movie star, (TAMMY) supposed to cope with her postmodern, substance-abusing daughter (PRINCESS LEIA), the rebellious, high-octane byproduct of Rock 'n Roll, Free Love, and postwar Hollywood's most scandal-soaked marriage? Read about it here, in Blood Moon's unauthorized double exposé about how Hollywood's toughest (and savviest) mother-daughter team maneuvered their way through shifting definitions of fame, reconciliation, and fortune."
—Donna McSorley

Another compelling title from Blood Moon's Babylon Series
Winner of the coveted "Best Biography" Award from the 2018 New York Book Festival

CARRIE FISHER & DEBBIE REYNOLDS,
UNSINKABLE TAMMY & PRINCESS LEIA IN HELL
Darwin Porter & Danforth Prince

630 pages Softcover with photos. Now online and in bookstores everywhere
ISBN 978-1-936003-57-0

This is What Happens When A Demented Billionaire Hits Hollywood

HOWARD HUGHES
HELL'S ANGEL
BY DARWIN PORTER

From his reckless pursuit of love as a rich teenager to his final days as a demented fossil, Howard Hughes tasted the best and worst of the century he occupied. Along the way, he changed the worlds of aviation and entertainment forever.

This biography reveals inside details about his destructive and usually scandalous associations with other Hollywood players.

"The Aviator flew both ways. Porter's biography presents new allegations about Hughes' shady dealings with some of the biggest names of the 20th century"
—New York Daily News

"Darwin Porter's access to film industry insiders and other Hughes confidants supplied him with the resources he needed to create a portrait of Hughes that both corroborates what other Hughes biographies have divulged, and go them one better."
—Foreword Magazine

"Thanks to this bio of Howard Hughes, we'll never be able to look at the old pinups in quite the same way again."
—The Times (London)

Winner of a respected literary award from the Los Angeles Book Festival, this book gives an insider's perspective about what money can buy —and what it can't.

814 pages, with photos. **Available everywhere now, online and in bookstores.**

ISBN 978-1-936003-13-6

LANA TURNER

The Sweater Girl, Celluloid Venus, Sex Nymph to the G.I.s who won World War II, and Hollywood's OTHER Most Notorious Blonde

Beautiful and Bad, Her Full Story Has Never Been Told. UNTIL NOW!

Lana Turner was the most scandalous, most copied, and most gossiped-about actress in Hollywood. When her abusive Mafia lover was murdered in her house, every newspaper in the Free World described the murky dramas with something approaching hysteria.

Blood Moon's salacious but empathetic new biography exposes the public and private dramas of the girl who changed the American definition of what it REALLY means to be a blonde.

Here's how CALIFORNIA BOOKWATCH and THE MIDWEST BOOK REVIEW described the mega-celebrity as revealed in this book:

"Lana Turner: Hearts and Diamonds Take All belongs on the shelves of any collection strong in movie star biographies in general and Hollywood evolution in particular, and represents no lightweight production, appearing on the 20th anniversary of Lana Turner's death to provide a weighty survey packed with new information about her life.

"One would think that just about everything to be known about The Sweater Girl would have already appeared in print, but it should be noted that Lana Turner: Hearts and Diamonds Take All offers many new revelations not just about Turner, but about the movie industry in the aftermath of World War II.

"From Lana's introduction of a new brand of covert sexuality in women's movies to her scandalous romances among the stars, her extreme promiscuity, her search for love, and her notorious flings - even her involvement in murder - are all probed in a revealing account of glamour and movie industry relationships that bring Turner and her times to life.

"Some of the greatest scandals in Hollywood history are intricately detailed on these pages, making this much more than another survey of her life and times, and a 'must have' pick for any collection strong in Hollywood history in general, gossip and scandals and the real stories behind them, and Lana Turner's tumultuous career, in particular."

Lana Turner, Hearts & Diamonds Take All
Winner of the coveted "Best Biography" Award from the San Francisco Book Festival
By Darwin Porter and Danforth Prince
Softcover, 622 pages, with photos. ISBN 978-1-936003-53-2
Available everywhere, online and in stores.

SCARLETT O'HARA,
Desperately in Love with Heathcliff,
Together on the Road to Hell

Damn You, Scarlett O'Hara
The Private Lives of **Vivien Leigh** and **Laurence Olivier**

Here, for the first time, is a biography that raises the curtain on the secret lives of Lord Laurence Olivier, often cited as the finest actor in the history of England, and Vivien Leigh, who immortalized herself with her Oscar-winning portrayals of Scarlett O'Hara in Gone With the Wind, and as Blanche DuBois in Tennessee Williams' A Streetcar Named Desire.

Dashing and "impossibly handsome," Laurence Olivier was pursued by the most dazzling luminaries, male and female, of the movie and theater worlds.

by **Darwin Porter** and **Roy Moseley**

Lord Olivier's beautiful and brilliant but emotionally disturbed wife (Viv to her lovers) led a tumultuous off-the-record life whose paramours ranged from the A-list celebrities to men she selected randomly off the street. But none of the brilliant roles depicted by Lord and Lady Olivier, on stage or on screen, ever matched the power and drama of personal dramas which wavered between Wagnerian opera and Greek tragedy. Damn You, Scarlett O'Hara is the definitive and most revelatory portrait ever published of the most talented and tormented actor and actress of the 20th century.

Darwin Porter is the principal author of this seminal work.

"The folks over at TMZ would have had a field day tracking Laurence Olivier and Vivien Leigh with flip cameras in hand. Damn You, Scarlett O'Hara can be a dazzling read, the prose unmannered and instantly digestible. The authors' ability to pile scandal atop scandal, seduction after seduction, can be impossible to resist."

—THE WASHINGTON TIMES

DAMN YOU, SCARLETT O'HARA
THE PRIVATE LIFES OF LAURENCE OLIVIER AND VIVIEN LEIGH

Darwin Porter and Roy Moseley

Winner of four distinguished literary awards, this is the best biography of Vivien Leigh and Laurence Olivier ever published, with hundreds of insights into the London Theatre, the role of the Oliviers in the politics of World War II, and the passion, fury, and frustration of their lives together as actors in the West End, on Broadway, and in Hollywood.

ISBN 978-1-936003-15-0   Hardcover, 708 pages, with about a hundred photos.

DONALD TRUMP
IS THE MAN WHO WOULD BE KING

This is the most famous book about our incendiary President you've probably never heard of.

Winner of three respected literary awards, and released three months before the Presidential elections of 2016, it's an entertainingly packaged, artfully salacious bombshell, a scathingly historic overview of America during its 2016 election cycle, a portrait unlike anything ever published on CANDIDATE DONALD and the climate in which he thrived and massacred his political rivals.

Its volcanic, much-suppressed release during the heat and venom of the 2016 Presidential campaign has already been heralded by the Midwestern Book Review, California Book Watch, the Seattle Gay News, the staunchly right-wing WILS-AM radio, and also by the editors at the most popular Seniors' magazine in Florida, BOOMER TIMES, which designated it as their September choice for BOOK OF THE MONTH.

TRUMPOCALYPSE: *"Donald Trump: The Man Who Would Be King* is recommended reading for all sides, no matter what political stance is being adopted: Republican, Democrat, or other.

"One of its driving forces is its ability to synthesize an unbelievable amount of information into a format and presentation which blends lively irony with outrageous observations, entertaining even as it presents eye-opening information in a format accessible to all.

"Politics dovetail with American obsessions and fascinations with trends, figureheads, drama, and sizzling news stories, but blend well with the observations of sociologists, psychologists, politicians, and others in a wide range of fields who lend their expertise and insights to create a much broader review of the Trump phenomena than a more casual book could provide.

"The result is a 'must read' for any American interested in issues of race, freedom, equality, and justice—and for any non-American who wonders just what is going on behind the scenes in this country's latest election debacle."

Diane Donovan, Senior Editor,
California Bookwatch

DONALD TRUMP, THE MAN WHO WOULD BE KING
WINNER OF "BEST BIOGRAPHY" AWARDS FROM BOOK FESTIVALS IN
NEW YORK, CALIFORNIA, AND FLORIDA
by Darwin Porter and Danforth Prince
Softcover, with 822 pages and hundreds of photos. ISBN 978-1-936003-51-8.

Available now from Amazon.com, Barnes&Noble.com,
and other internet purveyors, worldwide.

LINDA LOVELACE
INSIDE LINDA LOVELACE'S DEEP THROAT
Degradation, Porno Chic, and the Rise of Feminism

The most comprehensive biography ever written of an adult entertainment star, her tormented relationship with Hollywood's underbelly, and how she changed forever the world's perceptions about censorship, sexual behavior patterns, and pornography.

Darwin Porter, author of more than thirty critically acclaimed celebrity exposés of behind-the-scenes intrigue in the entertainment industry, was deeply involved in the Linda Lovelace saga as it unfolded in the 70s, interviewing many of the players, and raising money for the legal defense of the film's co-star, Harry Reems.

In this book, emphasizing her role as an unlikely celebrity interacting with other celebrities, he brings inside information and a never-before-published revelation to almost every page.

"This book drew me in..How could it not?" Coco Papy, Bookslut.

The Beach Book Festival's Grand Prize Winner for
"Best Summer Reading of 2013"

Runner-Up to "Best Biography of 2013" The Los Angeles Book Festival

---

Another hot and insightful commentary about major and sometimes violently controversial conflicts of the American Century, from Blood Moon Productions.

Inside Linda Lovelace's Deep Throat, by Darwin Porter
Softcover, 640 pages, 6"x9" with photos.
ISBN 978-1-936003-33-4

HOW THE FBI AND ITS G-MEN INVESTIGATED HOLLYWOOD

Darwin Porter's saga of power and corruption has a revelation on every page—cross dressing, gay parties, sexual indiscretions, hustlers for sale, alliances with the Mafia, and criminal activity by the nation's chief law enforcer.

It's all here, with chilling details about the abuse of power on the dark side of the American saga. But mostly it's the decades-long love story of America's two most powerful men who could tell presidents "how to skip rope." (Hoover's words.)

Winner of 2012 literary awards from the **Los Angeles** and the **Hollywood Book Festivals**

"EVERYONE'S DREDGING UP J. EDGAR HOOVER. Leonardo DiCaprio just immortalized him, and now comes Darwin Porter's paperback, *J. Edgar Hoover & Clyde Tolson: Investigating the Sexual Secrets of America's Most Famous Men and Women.*

It shovels Hoover's darkest secrets dragged kicking and screaming from the closet. It's filth on every VIP who's safely dead and some who are still above ground."

—Cindy Adams, The New York Post

"This book is important, because it destroys what's left of Hoover's reputation. Did you know he had intel on the bombing of Pearl Harbor, but he sat on it, making him more or less responsible for thousands of deaths? Or that he had almost nothing to do with the arrests or killings of any of the 1930s gangsters that he took credit for catching?

"A lot of people are angry with its author, Darwin Porter. They say that his outing of celebrities is just cheap gossip about dead people who can't defend themselves. I suppose it's because Porter is destroying carefully constructed myths that are comforting to most people. As gay men, we benefit the most from Porter's work, because we know that except for AIDS, the closet was the most terrible thing about the 20th century. If the closet never existed, neither would Hoover. The fact that he got away with such duplicity under eight presidents makes you think that every one of them was a complete fool for tolerating it."

—Paul Bellini, FAB Magazine (Toronto)

J. EDGAR HOOVER AND CLYDE TOLSON
Investigating the Sexual Secrets of America's Most Famous Men and Women
Darwin Porter
Softcover, 564 pages, with photos   ISBN 978-1-936003-25-9.   Also available for E-Readers

PINK TRIANGLE

The Feuds and Private Lives of TENNESSEE WILLIAMS, GORE VIDAL, TRUMAN CAPOTE, & Famous Members of their Entourages

Darwin Porter & Danforth Prince

This book, the only one of its kind, reveals the backlot intrigues associated with the literary and script-writing enfants terribles of America's entertainment community during the mid-20th century.

It exposes their bitchfests, their slugfests, and their relationships with the glitterati—Marilyn Monroe, Brando, the Oliviers, the Paleys, U.S. Presidents, a gaggle of other movie stars, millionaires, and international débauchés.

This is for anyone who's interested in the formerly concealed scandals of Hollywood and Broadway, and the values and pretentions of both the literary community and the entertainment industry.

"A banquet... If PINK TRIANGLE had not been written for us, we would have had to research and type it all up for ourselves...Pink Triangle is nearly seven hundred pages of the most entertaining histrionics ever sliced, spiced, heated, and serviced up to the reading public. Everything that Blood Moon has done before pales in comparison.
Given the fact that the subjects of the book themselves were nearly delusional on the subject of themselves (to say nothing of each other) it is hard to find fault. Add to this the intertwined jungle that was the relationship among Williams, Capote, and Vidal, of the times they vied for things they loved most—especially attention—and the times they enthralled each other and the world, [Pink Triangle is] the perfect antidote to the Polar Vortex."
—Vinton McCabe in the NY JOURNAL OF BOOKS

"Full disclosure: I have been a friend and follower of Blood Moon Productions' tomes for years, and always marveled at the amount of information in their books—it's staggering. The index alone to Pink Triangle runs to 21 pages—and the scale of names in it runs like a Who's Who of American social, cultural and political life through much of the 20th century."
—Perry Brass in THE HUFFINGTON POST

"We Brits are not spared the Porter/Prince silken lash either. PINK TRIANGLE's research is, quite frankly, breathtaking. PINK TRIANGLE will fascinate you for many weeks to come. Once you have made the initial titillating dip, the day will seem dull without it."
—Jeffery Tayor in THE SUNDAY EXPRESS (UK)

PINK TRIANGLE—The Feuds and Private Lives of Tennessee Williams, Gore Vidal, Truman Capote, and Famous Members of their Entourages
Darwin Porter & Danforth Prince
Softcover, 700 pages, with photos   ISBN 978-1-936003-37-2   Also Available for E-Readers

THOSE GLAMOROUS GABORS
BOMBSHELLS FROM BUDAPEST

Zsa Zsa, Eva, and Magda Gabor transferred their glittery dreams and gold-digging ambitions from the twilight of the Austro-Hungarian Empire to Hollywood. There, more effectively than any army, these Bombshells from Budapest broke hearts, amassed fortunes, lovers, and A-list husbands, and amused millions of voyeurs through the medium of television, movies, and the social registers. In this astonishing "triple-play" biography, designated "Best Biography of the Year" by the Hollywood Book Festival, Blood Moon lifts the "mink-and-diamond" curtain on this amazing trio of blood-related sisters, whose complicated intrigues have never been fully explored before.

"You will never be Ga-bored...this book gives new meaning to the term compelling. Be warned, Those Glamorous Gabors is both an epic and a pip. Not since Gone With the Wind have so many characters on the printed page been forced to run for their lives for one reason or another. And Scarlett making a dress out of the curtains is nothing compared to what a Gabor will do when she needs to scrap together an outfit for a movie premiere or late-night outing.

"For those not up to speed, Jolie Tilleman came from a family of jewelers and therefore came by her love for the shiny stones honestly, perhaps genetically. She married Vilmos Gabor somewhere around World War 1 (exact dates, especially birth dates, are always somewhat vague in order to establish plausible deniability later on) and they were soon blessed with three daughters: Magda, the oldest, whose hair, sadly, was naturally brown, although it would turn quite red in America; Zsa Zsa (born 'Sari') a natural blond who at a very young age exhibited the desire for fame with none of the talents usually associated with achievement, excepting beauty and a natural wit; and Eva, the youngest and blondest of the girls, who after seeing Grace Moore perform at the National Theater, decided that she wanted to be an actress and that she would one day move to Hollywood to become a star.

"Given that the Gabor family at that time lived in Budapest, Hungary, at the period of time between the World Wars, that Hollywood dream seemed a distant one indeed. The story—the riches to rags to riches to rags to riches again myth of survival against all odds as the four women, because of their Jewish heritage, flee Europe with only the minks on their backs and what jewels they could smuggle along with them in their decolletage, only to have to battle afresh for their places in the vicious Hollywood pecking order—gives new meaning to the term 'compelling.' The reader, as if he were witnessing a particularly gore-drenched traffic accident, is incapable of looking away."

—New York Review of Books

Those Glamorous Gabors, Bombshells from Budapest, by Darwin Porter & Danforth Prince
Softcover, 730 pages, with hundreds of photos   ISBN 978-1-936003-35-8

ROCK HUDSON
EROTIC FIRE

In the dying days of Hollywood's Golden Age, Rock Hudson was the most celebrated phallic symbol and lust object in America.

This book describes his rise and fall, and the Entertainment Industry that created him.

Rock Hudson charmed every casting director in Hollywood (and movie-goers throughout America) as the mega-star they most wanted to share PILLOW TALK with. This book describes his rise and fall, and how he handled himself as a closeted but promiscuous bisexual during an age when EVERYBODY tried to throw him onto a casting couch.

Based on dozens of face-to-face interviews with the actor's friends, co-conspirators, and enemies, and researched over a period of a half century, this biography reveals the shame, agonies, and irony of Rock Hudson's complete, never-before-told story.

In 2017, the year of its release, it was designated as winner ("BEST BIOGRAPHY") at two of the Golden State's most prestigious literary competitions, the Northern California and the Southern California Book Festivals.

Rock Hudson Erotic Fire

Darwin Porter & Danforth Prince
Another Outrageous Title in Blood Moon's Babylon Series

It was also favorably reviewed by the Midwestern Book Review, California Book Watch, KNEWS RADIO, the New York Journal of Books, and the editors at the most popular Seniors' magazine in Florida, BOOMER TIMES.

ROCK HUDSON EROTIC FIRE
By Darwin Porter & Danforth Prince
Softcover, 624 pages, with dozens of photos, 6" x 9"
ISBN 978-1-936003-55-6

Available everywhere now, online and in bookstores.

HOLLYWOOD BABYLON

It's Back! (Volume One) and
Strikes Again! (Volume Two)

Profoundly outrageous, here are Blood Moon's double-header spins on exhibitionism, sexuality, and sin as filtered through 85 years of Hollywood indiscretion

Winner of the Los Angeles Book Festival's Best Nonfiction Title of 2010, and the New England Book Festival's Best Anthology for 2010.

"If you love smutty celebrity dirt as much as I do, then have I got some books for you!"
The Hollywood Offender

"These books will set the graves of Hollywood's cemeteries spinning."
Daily Express

"Monumentally exhaustive...The ultimate guilty pleasure"
Shelf Awareness

Hollywood Babylon It's Back!
& Hollywood Babylon Strikes Again!

Darwin Porter and Danforth Prince
Hardcover, each 380 outrageous pages, each with hundreds of photos

[Whereas Volume One is temporarily sold out, and available only as an e-book, Volume Two, also available as an e-book, still has hard copies in stock]

ISBN 978-1-9748118-8-8 and ISBN 978-1-936003-12-9

CONFUSED ABOUT HOW TO INTERPRET THEIR RAUCOUS PAST? THIS UNCENSORED TALE ABOUT A LOVE AFFAIR THAT CHANGED THE COURSE OF POLITICS AND THE PLANET IS OF COMPELLING INTEREST TO ANYONE INVOLVED IN THE POLITICAL SLUGFESTS AND INCENDIARY WARS OF THE CLINTONS.

BILL & HILLARY
SO THIS IS THAT THING CALLED LOVE

"This is both a biographical coverage of the Clintons and a political exposé; a detailed, weighty exploration that traces the couple's social and political evolution, from how each entered the political arena to their White House years under Bill Clinton's presidency.

"Containing gossip, scandal, and biographical sketches, it delves deeply into the news and politics of its times, presenting enough historical background to fully explore the underlying controversies affecting the Clinton family and their choices.

"Sidebars of information and black and white photos liberally peppered throughout the account offer visual reinforcement to the exploration, lending it the feel and tone of both a gossip column and political piece - something that probes not just Clinton interactions but the D.C. political milieu as a whole.

"The result may appear weighty, sporting over five hundred pages, but is an absorbing, top recommendation for readers of both biographical and political pieces who will thoroughly enjoy this spirited, lively, and thought-provoking analysis."
— THE MIDWEST BOOK REVIEW

***

Shortly after its release in December of 2015, this book received a literary award (Runner-up to Best Biography of the Year) from the New England Book Festival. As stated by a spokesperson for the Awards, "The New England Book Festival is an annual competition honoring excellence in books, with particular focus on projects that deserve closer attention from the academic community. Congratulations to Blood Moon and its authors, especially Darwin Porter, for his highly entertaining analysis of Clinton's double-barreled presidential regime, and the sometimes hysterical over-reaction of their enemies."

Available Everywhere, in Bookstores and Online
BILL & HILLARY—SO THIS IS THAT THING CALLED LOVE
Softcover, with photos. ISBN 978-1-936003-47-1

JACQUELINE KENNEDY ONASSIS

A LIFE BEYOND HER WILDEST DREAMS

After floods of analysis and commentary in tabloid and mainstream newspapers worldwide, this has emerged as the world's most comprehensive testimonial to the flimsier side of Camelot, the most comprehensive compendium of gossip ever published about America's unofficial, uncrowned queen, Jacqueline Kennedy Onassis. Its publication coincided with the 20-year anniversary of the death of one of the most famous, revered, and talked-about women who ever lived.

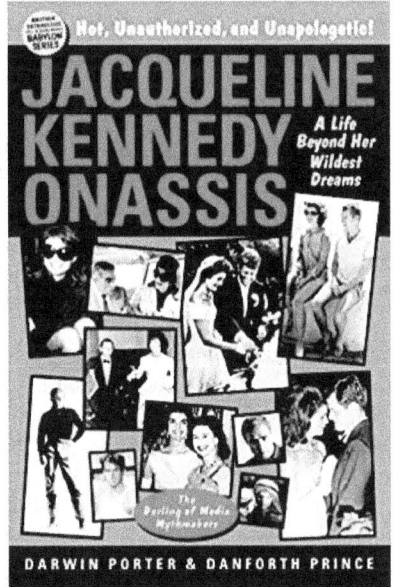

During her tumultuous life, Mrs. Onassis zealously guarded her privacy and her secrets. But in the wake of her death, more and more revelations have emerged about her frustrations, her rage, her passions, her towering strengths, and her delicate fragility, which she hid from the glare of the world behind oversized sunglasses. Within this posthumous biography, a three-dimensional woman emerges through the compilation of some 1,000 eyewitness testimonials from men and women who knew her over a period of decades.

An overview of the life of Mrs. Onassis is a natural fit for Blood Moon, a publishing enterprise that's increasingly known, worldwide, as one of the most provocative and scandalous in the history of publishing.

"References to this American icon appear with almost rhythmic regularity to anyone researching the cultural landscape of America during the last half of The American Century," said Danforth Prince. "Based on what we'd uncovered about Jackie during the research of many of our earlier titles, we're positioning ourselves as a more or less solitary outpost of irreverence within a landscape that's otherwise flooded with fawning, over-reverential testimonials. Therein lies this book's appeal—albeit with a constant respect and affection for a woman we admired and adored."

Based on decades of research by writers who define themselves as "voraciously attentive Kennedyphiles," it supplements the half-dozen other titles within Blood Moon's Babylon series.

JACQUELINE KENNEDY ONASSIS—
A LIFE BEYOND HER WILDEST DREAMS
Darwin Porter and Danforth Prince
Biography/Entertainment   6" x 9"   700 pages with hundreds of photos
ISBN 978-1-936003-39-6   Also available for E-readers.

PETER O'TOOLE

Hellraiser, Sexual Outlaw, Irish Rebel

At the time of its publication early in 2015, this book was widely publicized in the *Daily Mail,* the *New York Daily News,* the *New York Post,* the *Midwest Book Review, The Express (London), The Globe,* the *National Enquirer,* and in equivalent publications worldwide

One of the world's most admired (and brilliant) actors, Peter O'Toole wined and wenched his way through a labyrinth of sexual and interpersonal betrayals, sometimes with disastrous results. Away from the stage and screen, where such films as *Becket* and *Lawrence of Arabia,* made film history, his life was filled with drunken, debauched nights and edgy sexual experimentations, most of which were never openly examined in the press. A hellraiser, he shared wild times with his "best blokes" Richard Burton and Richard Harris. Peter Finch, also his close friend, once invited him to join him in sharing the pleasures of his mistress, Vivien Leigh.

"My father, a bookie, moved us to the Mick community of Leeds," O'Toole once told a reporter. "We were very poor, but I was born an Irishman, which accounts for my gift of gab, my unruly behavior, my passionate devotion to women and the bottle, and my loathing of any authority figure."

Author Robert Sellers described O'Toole's boyhood neighborhood. "Three of his playmates went on to be hanged for murder; one strangled a girl in a lovers' quarrel; one killed a man during a robbery; another cut up a warden in South Africa with a pair of shears. It was a heavy bunch."

Peter O'Toole's hell-raising life story has never been told, until now. Hot and uncensored, from a writing team which, even prior to O'Toole's death in 2013, had been collecting under-the-radar info about him for years, this book has everything you ever wanted to know about how THE LION navigated his way through the boudoirs of the Entertainment Industry IN WINTER, Spring, Summer, and a dissipated Autumn as well.

Blood Moon has ripped away the imperial robe, scepter, and crown usually associated with this quixotic problem child of the British Midlands. Provocatively uncensored, this illusion-shattering overview of Peter O'Toole's hellraising (or at least very naughty) and demented life is unique in the history of publishing.

PETER O'TOOLE
Hellraiser, Sexual Outlaw, Irish Rebel
Darwin Porter & Danforth Prince
Softcover, with photos. ISBN 978-1-936003-45-7

HUMPHREY BOGART
THE MAKING OF A LEGEND

DARWIN PORTER

A "CRADLE-TO-GRAVE" HARDCOVER ABOUT THE RISE TO FAME OF AN OBSCURE, UNLIKELY, AND FREQUENTLY UNEMPLOYED BROADWAY ACTOR

WITH STARTLING NEW INFORMATION ABOUT BOGART, THE MOVIES, &
GOLDEN AGE HOLLYWOOD

Whereas Humphrey Bogart is always at the top of any list of the Entertainment Industry's most famous actors, very little is known about how he clawed his way from Broadway to Hollywood during Prohibition and the Jazz Age.

This pioneering biography begins with Bogart's origins as the child of wealthy (morphine-addicted) parents in New York City, then examines the love affairs, scandals, failures, and breakthroughs that launched him as an American icon.

It includes details about behind-the-scenes dramas associated with three mysterious marriages, and films such as The Petrified Forest, The Maltese Falcon, High Sierra, and Casablanca. Read all about the debut and formative years of the actor who influenced many generations of filmgoers, laying Bogie's life bare in a style you've come to expect from Darwin Porter. Exposed with all their juicy details is what Bogie never told his fourth wife, Lauren Bacall, herself a screen legend.

Drawn from original interviews with friends and foes who knew a lot about what lay beneath his trenchcoat, this exposé covers Bogart's remarkable life as it helped define movie-making, Hollywood's portrayal of macho, and America's evolving concept of Entertainment itself.

This revelatory book is based on dusty unpublished memoirs, letters, diaries, and often personal interviews from the women—and the men—who adored him.

There are also shocking allegations from colleagues, former friends, and jilted lovers who wanted the screen icon to burn in hell.

All this and more, much more, in Darwin Porter's exposé of Bogie's startling secret life.

542 PAGES, WITH HUNDREDS OF PHOTOS   ISBN 978-1-936003-14-3

PAUL NEWMAN

THE MAN BEHIND THE BABY BLUES
HIS SECRET LIFE EXPOSED

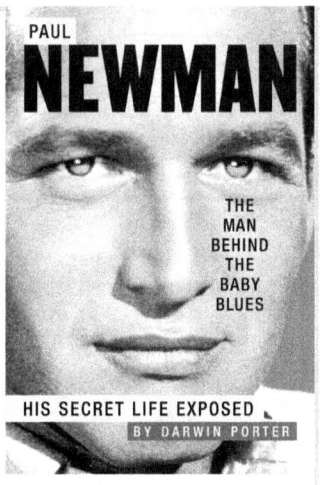

Drawn from firsthand interviews with insiders who knew Paul Newman intimately, and compiled over a period of nearly a half-century, this is the world's most honest and most revelatory biography about Hollywood's pre-eminent male sex symbol.

This is a respectful but candid cornucopia of once-concealed information about the sexual and emotional adventures of an affable, impossibly good-looking workaday actor, a former sailor from Shaker Heights, Ohio, who parlayed his ambisexual charm and extraordinary good looks into one of the most successful careers in Hollywood.

Whereas the situations it exposes were widely known within Hollywood's inner circles, they've never before been revealed to the general public.

But now, the full story has been published—the giddy heights and agonizing crashes of a great American star, with revelations and insights never before published in any other biography.

"Paul Newman had just as many on-location affairs as the rest of us, and he was just as bisexual as I was. But whereas I was always getting caught with my pants down, he managed to do it in the dark with not a paparazzo in sight. He might have bedded Marilyn Monroe or Elizabeth Taylor the night before, but he always managed to show up for breakfast with Joanne Woodward, with those baby blues, looking as innocent as a Botticelli angel. He never fooled me. It takes an alleycat to know another one. Did I ever tell you what really happened between Newman and me? If that doesn't grab you, what about what went on between James Dean and Newman? Let me tell you about this co-called model husband if you want to look behind those famous peepers."

—Marlon Brando

Paul Newman, The Man Behind the Baby Blues,
His Secret Life Exposed, by Darwin Porter
Recipient of an Honorable Mention from the New England Book Festival
Hardcover, 520 pages, with dozens of photos.
ISBN 978-0-9786465-1-6   Available everywhere, online and in bookstores.

JAMES DEAN

Tomorrow Never Comes

Honoring the 60th Anniversary of His Violent and Early Death

America's most enduring and legendary symbol of young, enraged rebellion, James Dean continues into the 21st Century to capture the imagination of the world.

After one of his many flirtations with Death, which caught up with him when he was a celebrity-soaked 24-year-old, he said, "If a man can live after he dies, then maybe he's a great man." Today, bars from Nigeria to Patagonia are named in honor of this international, spectacularly self-destructive movie star icon.

Migrating from the dusty backroads of Indiana to center stage in the most formidable boudoirs of Hollywood, his saga is electrifying.

A strikingly handsome heart-throb, Dean is a study in contrasts: Tough but tender, brutal but remarkably sensitive; he was a reckless hellraiser badass who could revert to a little boy in bed.

A rampant bisexual, he claimed that he didn't want to go through life "with one hand tied behind my back." He demonstrated that during bedroom trysts with Marilyn Monroe, Rock Hudson, Elizabeth Taylor, Paul Newman, Natalie Wood, Shelley Winters, Marlon Brando, Steve McQueen, Ursula Andress, Montgomery Clift, Pier Angeli, Tennessee Williams, Susan Strasberg, Tallulah Bankhead, and FBI director J. Edgar Hoover.

Woolworth heiress Barbara Hutton, one of the richest and most dissipated women of her era, wanted to make him her toy boy.

Tomorrow Never Comes is the most penetrating look at James Dean to have emerged from the wreckage of his Porsche Spyder in 1955.

Before setting out on his last ride, he said, "I feel life too intensely to bear living it."

Tomorrow Never Comes presents a damaged but beautiful soul.

JAMES DEAN—TOMORROW NEVER COMES
Darwin Porter & Danforth Prince
Softcover, with photos. ISBN 978-1-936003-49-5

Blood Moon's Respectful Farewell
to a Great American Movie Star

KIRK DOUGLAS
MORE IS NEVER ENOUGH

Oozing Masculinity, a Young Horndog Sets Out to Conquer Hollywood and to Bed Its Leading Ladies.

Of the many male stars of Golden Age Hollywood, Kirk Douglas became the final survivor, the last icon of a fabled, optimistic era that the world will never see again. When he celebrated his birthday in 2016, a headline read: LEGENDARY HOLLYWOOD HORNDOG TURNS 100.

He was both a charismatic actor and a man of uncommon force and vigor. His restless and volcanic spirit is reflected both in his films and through his many sexual conquests.

Douglas was the son of Russian-Jewish immigrants, his father a collector and seller of rags. After service in the Navy during World War II, he hit Hollywood, oozing masculinity and charm. Conquering Tinseltown and bedding its leading ladies, he became the personification of the American dream, moving from obscurity and (literally) rags to riches and major-league fame.

The *Who's Who* cast of characters roaring through his life included not only a daunting list of Hollywood goddesses, but the town's most colossal male talents and egos, too. They included his kindred hellraiser and best buddy Burt Lancaster, John Wayne, Henry Fonda, Billy Wilder, Laurence Olivier, Rock Hudson, and a future U.S. President, Ronald Reagan, when winning the highest office in the land was virtually unthinkable.

Over the decades, he immortalized himself in film after film, delivering, like a Trojan, one memorable performance after another. He was at home in *film noir*, as a western gunslinger, as an adventurer (in both ancient and modern sagas), as a juggler, as Tennessee Williams' "gentleman caller," as a Greek super-hero from Homer's *Odyssey*, and as roguish sailor in the Jules Verne yarn, exploring the mysteries of the ocean's depths.

En route to his status as a myth and legend, his performances reflected both his personal pain and the brutalization of the characters he played, too. In *Champion* (1949), he was beaten to a fatal bloody pulp. As the sleazy, heartless reporter in *Ace in the Hole* (1951), he was stabbed with a knife in his gut. As Van Gogh in *Lust for Life* (1956), he writhed in emotional agony and unrequited love before slicing off his ear with a razor. His World War I movie, *Paths of Glory* (1957) grows more profound over the years. He lost an eye in *The Vikings* (1958), and, as the Thracian slave leading a revolt against Roman legions in *Spartacus* (1960), he was crucified.

All of this is brought out, with photos, in this remarkable testimonial to the last hero of Hollywood's cinematic and swashbuckling Golden Age, an inspiring testimonial to the values and core beliefs of an America that's Gone With the Wind, yet lovingly remembered as a time when it, in many ways, was truly great.

KIRK DOUGLAS: MORE IS NEVER ENOUGH
Darwin Porter & Danforth Prince; ISBN 978-1-936003-61-7; 550 pages with photos.
Available everywhere now

AVAILABLE NOW FROM BLOOD MOON:
THE COMPREHENSIVE, UNAUTHORIZED EXPOSÉ EVERY PLAYBOY AND EVERY PLAYMATE WILL WANT TO READ

Hugh Hefner, the most iconic Playboy in human history, was a visionary, an empire-builder, and a pajama-clad pipe-smoker with a pre-coital grin.

In 1953, he published his first edition of *Playboy* with money borrowed from his puritanical, Nebraska-born mother. Marilyn Monroe appeared on the cover, with her nude calendar inside.

Rebelling against his strict upbringing, he lost his virginity at the age of 22.

His magazine, punctuated with nudes and studded with articles by major literary figures, reached its zenith at eight million readers. As a "tasteful pornographer," Hef became a cultural warrior, fighting government censorship all the way to the U.S. Supreme Court. As the years and his notoriety progressed, he became an advocate of abortion, LGBT equality, and the legalization of pot. Eventually, he engaged in "pubic wars" with Bob Guccione, the flamboyant founder of Penthouse, which cut into Hef's sales.

Lauded by millions of avid readers, he was denounced as "the father of sex addiction," "a huckster," "a lecherous low-brow feeder of our vices," "a misogynist," and, near the end of his life, "a symbol of priapic senility."

During his heyday, some of the biggest male stars in Hollywood, including Warren Beatty, Sammy Davis, Jr., Mick Jagger, and Jack Nicholson, came to frolic behind Hef's guarded walls, stripping nude in the hot tub grotto before sampling the rotating beds upstairs. Even a future U.S. president came to call. "Donald Trump had an appreciation of Bunny tail," Hef said.

Hefner's last Viagra-fueled marriage was to a beautiful blonde, Crystal Harris, 60 years his junior. "There's nothing wrong in a man marrying a girl who could be his great-granddaughter," he was famously quoted as saying.

This ground-breaking biography, the latest in Blood Moon's string of outrageously unvarnished myth-busters, was the first published since Hefner's death at the age of 91 in 2017. It's a provocative saga, rich in tantalizing, often shocking detail. Not recommended for the sanctimonious or the faint of heart, and loaded with ironic, little-known details about the trendsetter's epic challenges, it 's available everywhere NOW.

PLAYBOY'S HUGH HEFNER
EMPIRE OF SKIN
by Darwin Porter and Danforth Prince
978-1-936003-59-4